LAW AND
MENTAL HEALTH

Pergamon Titles of Related Interest

Nietzel/Dillehay PSYCHOLOGICAL CONSULTATION IN THE COURTROOM
Weisstub LAW AND PSYCHIATRY I
Weisstub LAW AND PSYCHIATRY II
Weisstub LAW AND PSYCHIATRY IN THE CANADIAN CONTEXT:
Cases, Notes and
Materials

Related Journals*

INTERNATIONAL JOURNAL OF LAW AND PSYCHIATRY
JOURNAL OF CRIMINAL JUSTICE

*Free specimen copies available upon request.

LAW AND
MENTAL HEALTH

International Perspectives
Volume 1

Edited by

David N. Weisstub

Institut Philippe Pinel, Université de Montréal
Osgoode Hall Law School, Toronto

PERGAMON PRESS
New York • Oxford • Toronto • Sydney • Paris • Frankfurt

Pergamon Press Offices:

U.S.A.   Pergamon Press Inc., Maxwell House, Fairview Park,
                        Elmsford, New York 10523, U.S.A.

U.K.   Pergamon Press Ltd., Headington Hill Hall,
                        Oxford OX3 0BW, England

CANADA   Pergamon Press Canada Ltd., Suite 104, 150 Consumers Road,
                        Willowdale, Ontario M2J 1P9, Canada

AUSTRALIA   Pergamon Press (Aust.) Pty. Ltd., P.O. Box 544,
                        Potts Point, NSW 2011, Australia

FRANCE   Pergamon Press SARL, 24 rue des Ecoles,
                        75240 Paris, Cedex 05, France

FEDERAL REPUBLIC   Pergamon Press GmbH, Hammerweg 6,
OF GERMANY   D-6242 Kronberg-Taunus, Federal Republic of Germany

Copyright © 1984 Pergamon Press Inc.

Library of Congress Cataloging in Publication Data

Main entry under title:

Law and mental health.

    Bibliography: p.
    Includes index.
    1. Mental health laws. I. Weisstub, David N.,
1944-   . [DNLM: 1. Mental health—Legislation.
2. Forensic psychiatry. WM 33.1 L416]
  K3608.L38   1984   344'.044   84-2926
  ISBN 0-08-031602-6   342.444

$V.1$

$49,397$

Printed in the United States of America

Contents

v

Preface

Law and Mental Health is a relatively young field which has burgeoned in the past two decades into an area of special prominence in law reform and interdisciplinary legal studies. The association of the mental health professions with law has expanded knowledge of many pressing issues of our day such as the nature of human responsibility; the bond that is established between the patient and his doctor; our treatment of deviant elements within our population, like sexual offenders; and determining the parameters of citizens' roles as jurors. The field has not been restricted to the insights and research derived from the analytical or clinical models of law and medicine, but has benefited from the many participants who perform vital tasks in the mental health process and in the manifold research efforts devised to assess its efficacy.

The division of labour in the area of Law and Mental Health covers a wide terrain which operates on various levels of abstraction stretching from clinical and empirical methodologies to more legalistic and philosophical modalities. Some of the important work has focussed on giving us a critical knowledge in places where abstractions have failed to explain certain patterns of behaviour and the social and individual treatments that we might deem appropriate to them. In other parts of the mental health system, it has been through the reflections based on legal doctrines or philosophical assumptions that we have managed to escape the quandaries into which practises or theories had fallen.

The freshness of the field has proven that no categories are sacrosanct and that even the question of categorization of disease should always be open for discussion. In this manner, Law and Mental Health has been an area of law which has served as a model for testing, from many points of view, our notions about the way knowledge evolves. There is almost no place in the corpus of Law and Mental Health where we cannot benefit from a probing of our scope of reference and from the insights to be gained through a comparative analysis of diverse cultures and distinctive legal codes or procedures.

This series of volumes was conceived to meet an increasingly wide demand to consolidate the diffuse body of knowledge which has come under the penumbra of Law and Mental Health. The plan of this series is to incorporate novel insights into chapters which will enable us to take stock of what we know and, moreover, of what we do not know pertaining to the vital issues in mental health law. Perhaps the most cogent reason for attending to these scholarly needs is that this information is essential if we are to be able to respond effectively to controversies about the social responsibilities urgently pressed upon us.

Under the auspices of the *International Journal of Law and Psychiatry*, ten international congresses have already been held in North America and abroad. These have pointed out how necessary it is to establish a network of colleagues for mutual exchange of ideas among the range of critics and decision-makers who need to appreciate both similarities and dissimilarities in the way problems are analyzed and solved in jurisdictions other than their own.

This comparative process has been the mainstay of the *International Journal of Law and Psychiatry*, published by Pergamon Press for almost a decade. The existence of the Journal has itself substantially contributed to the demand for comprehensive texts which would pull together the disparate strands into a manageable format. These volumes will be published in yearly sequence by Pergamon Press and will, hopefully, succeed in informing serious scholars and practitioners about the growth of law reform, the development of research, the organization of knowledge, and the evolution of philosophical concepts or frameworks around which the mental health system is being built.

It is no accident that the first volume is princi-pally dedicated to American jurisprudence and theories. This is a proper reflection of a geographi-cal fact about which there should be little dispute. Through the experience of having developed the active subspecialties of forensic psychiatry and psychology and a specialized mental health bar, the United States has been a forerunner and, in-deed, has functioned as a testing ground in the field. This in no way denies or diminishes the significance of a tradition of scientific and meta-physical inquiry established outside the United States some centuries ago in Continental Europe. Nevertheless, no one can fail to recognize the magnitude of case law and empirical data which have been part of the American experience since the second world war. It is thus useful to summa-rize much of this intellectual and procedural background in order to control an almost un-wieldly state of knowledge and, at the same time, to assess the valuable benefits we might derive from looking more closely at the ways other juris-dictions have dealt with social conflicts arising from mental disorder.

The first volume, therefore, is situated squarely in the midst of current debates which are literally part of yesterday's news. In the past few years, the issues of social responsibility pertaining to mental illness have tested the conscience and will of the public and its elected decision-makers. The quar-rels about what should be blatantly defined as a matter of social and legal decision-making, as op-posed to medical definition, have begun to plague us in the life of the courts and in the process of law reform. Throughout the industrial nations, the number of commissions and task forces which have to meet urgent deadlines involving the re-structuring of social principles of a basic sort is almost startling. The issues go to the heart of social liberal democratic values, such as the right of self-determination and the limits of our toler-ance for socially destructive acts.

The authors who have been chosen for these difficult tasks have all been recognized for their unique attributes. George Dix, an eminent authority on American criminal law, has pro-vided us with a veritable handbook on the range of options arising from the much-discussed Hinck-ley case. This should prove very helpful to policy planners in criminal law who need a realistic assessment of the debates and legislative reforms that have been cropping up in the United States over the last couple of years. This is timely because serious criminal law reforms are pres-ently under consideration in such countries as Japan, Canada, Australia and Sweden, to name only a few. The question of responsibility for criminal acts is the most crucial theme that mental health professionals face in their work and it is, therefore, an enlightening complement to be able to place alongside George Dix's essay, Sey-mour Halleck's in-depth appraisal about the in-teraction between law and psychiatry on the question of responsibility. This essay has far-reaching consequences for the operation and con-ceptualization of the mental health system. As one of America's foremost authorities in forensic psychiatry, Professor Halleck has offered us here a document in which he has certainly struggled to give credibility to the practices of clinical psy-chiatry in the face of all the distortions and up-heavals that have followed the recent insanity law disputes.

The essay by Vernon Quinsey is a very orderly and systematic treatment of a multifaceted sector of scientific research. He has managed to give an extremely helpful checklist to anyone interested in the current status of research findings with respect to sexually aggressive males in their relations with women. The literature on pedophilia was not cov-ered by Dr. Quinsey, who left it for another proj-ect which, happily, is currently underway; it emerged that the literature demanded a compre-hensive evaluation in its own right. The chapter written by Vernon Quinsey directs us finally to the research that is badly needed to fill in the blanks in our scientific armoury, and fulfills an ideal that we associated with the project from the outset: to help focus attention on meaningful priorities for research.

Needless to say, the addition of the chapters by the now-renowned co-authors, Appelbaum and Gutheil, has done much to enhance the quality of our first effort. We find in Dr. Appelbaum's re-view on informed consent a model, such as only he is capable of producing, around which to con-trol the voluminous outpourings which have dom-inated the academic literature on the consent topic over the past decade. Because he is a scholar who has based himself in a clinical environment the better to justify his theoretical hypotheses on the real needs and wants of both practitioners and patients, his retrospective here should well stand the test of time. We can profitably return to the literature on consent with his chapter to guide us through its many intricacies.

The chapter of his collaborator, Thomas G. Gutheil, on forensic assessment shows the value of a blueprint when approaching the manifold tasks that face the mental health practitioners. One of the problems that we see revealed time and time again in the courtroom and in daily practices is the inability of practitioners and, for that matter, legal specialists, to distinguish the particularized roles and responsibilities that make up the mental health system and its interrelationship with legal criteria and procedures. What emerges from Dr. Gutheil's study is that some empirical information is needed to illuminate the lacunae between theory and practice and, most specifically, from the perspective of patients. The call for studies in law and action which came from the earliest thinkers in sociological jurisprudence at the beginning of the 20th century, who asked us to figure out the level of legal understanding on the part of all players in the drama of legal interactions, has special relevancy and sensitivity in the area of Law and Mental health. For here perhaps more than anywhere else in the legal system, it is critical for us to know what everyone in the system is thinking and feeling. As the most pertinent players in the drama, patients often have so much of their emotions and liberties invested in the outcome. It is the gift of Dr. Gutheil that he has managed to write simply and clearly in a way that will have utility for practice.

Finally, the volume is strengthened by an exhaustive account of a highly technical domain of psychological expertise, the validity and reliability of jury selection techniques. In law practice, this is often the subject of stiff confrontation. It is a breakthrough in scholarship to have on hand from Professor Bruce Dennis Sales, the editor of *The American Journal of Law and Human Behavior*, and also author and editor of many works in the specialty of forensic psychology, a combined effort with his research associates, Hafemeister and Suggs, which is a state-of-the-art account of the literature. One might expect that this chapter will be a staple of reference for future scholarship on these issues. What can be seen through a perusal of the texts is that the authors have integrated practical experience with scientific skills of assessment and critique into a complex fabric which nevertheless allows us to see this broad territory clearly. They have distilled and analyzed an extremely diverse body of knowledge and, in their multidisciplinary gifts have a similarity of purpose: to inform us, in their role as experts, of the existing state of knowledge, with regard to theory and practice, in six of the major subjects of Law and Mental Health.

It is the purpose of subsequent volumes to survey the research in other linguistic traditions— Spanish, French, German, Italian, Dutch, and Scandinavian—as well as legislative and judicial trends, for example, in the Commonwealth countries. Some major topics in the field scheduled for upcoming volumes are malpractice, terrorism, the courtroom privileges of mental health experts, de-institutionalization, psycho-biological research in criminality, guardianship, and competency. Certain areas, such as assessment and diagnosis from the point of view of the science of psychology, will be expanded to complement existing chapters. We intend that this series will also cover elusive categories like the psychopathic or criminal personality and that it will explore philosophically and historically relevant matters such as law and the unconscious, and the history of the asylum.

It is an intrinsic feature of the project that the chapters are more descriptive than analytical, but, at the same time, the authors have given us pertinent assessments of their appointed fields of expertise. This has been more appropriate in some cases than others, particularly in situations where a lifetime effort to enlighten such fundamental concepts as responsibility requires in itself some statement of intellectual commitment.

Given the character of the field, the chapters vary to some degree both in their nature and intention, but each exposes a specially crafted approach to what the issues themselves demand. It is, nonetheless, up to the readership and the specialist, who must see the utility in the product, to judge. The able editorial committee of this project, to whom I am deeply grateful, tried to be sensitive to those factors, but ultimately of course, I must personally bear the responsibility for any shortcomings that remain.

Any large enterprise such as this requires a generous institutional sponsorship and we are thus grateful to the Institut Philippe Pinel de Montréal and to its directeur général, Dr. Lionel Béliveau, for their kind support in this undertaking. I am, too, especially thankful for the active participation of the professional community of the Institut Philippe Pinel in the determination of the priorities for the project and its overall evolutionary design. As is always the case in any long-term intellectual endeavour, there are a number of persons who have carefully worked to coordinate the fine tuning of the process. And here I wish to record my indebtedness to Dr. Eli Bernard Wiesstub, of the Department of Psychiatry at Stanford University, Nicole Fernbach, Jill Lazar Matus, and Fred Ernst.

David N. Weisstub

Préface

Le droit de la santé mentale est une branche relativement jeune du droit qui a connu un grand essor au cours des vingt dernières années. Ce secteur est devenu particulièrement important dans le contexte de la réforme du droit et pour les études juridiques interdisciplinaires. Ce phénomène provient du fait que l'ensemble des professions de la santé mentale a été à l'avant-garde des problèmes les plus brûlants, notamment la nature de la responsabilité, la relation entre le patient et son médecin, le mode de traitement des déviants dans notre population (par exemple, les délinquants sexuels) ainsi que la détermination des conditions d'exercice des fonctions de jurés par les citoyens. Le droit de la santé mentale n'est pas limité aux points de vue et à la recherche tirés des modèles analytiques ou cliniques du droit et de la médecine, car il bénéficie des interventions de nombreux participants dont la tâche revêt une importance cruciale dans le processus de la santé mentale, compte tenu des innombrables efforts qui sont déployés pour évaluer son efficacité.

La "division du travail" dans le domaine du droit de la santé mentale s'opère sur un vaste champ, à différents niveaux d'abstraction s'étendant des secteurs cliniques et empiriques jusqu'à des considérations plus juridiques et philosophiques. Une partie des travaux essentiels ont été consacrés à l'élaboration d'une connaissance critique, là où les abstractions n'avaient pas pu expliquer certains modèles de comportement, ainsi que les traitements sociaux et individuels qui semblent appropriés dans ces cas-là. Dans d'autres secteurs de la santé mentale, c'est la réflexion fondée sur les doctrines juridiques ou philosophiques qui nous a sortis des écueils où la théorie et la pratique nous avaient entraînés.

La nouveauté du domaine fait qu'aucune de ses catégories n'est figée et que même la question de la classification des maladies demeure ouverte. De cette façon, le droit de la santé mentale a servi de modèle pour la vérification de nos concepts sur la façon dont la connaissance évolue du point de vue de la professionalisation, sur l'idéologie et sur l'engagement par rapport aux valeurs sociales et philosophique. Il n'existe pratiquement aucun secteur en droit de la santé mentale où nous ne puissions bénéficier d'une remise en cause de notre cadre de référence, ou de réflexions pouvant être inspirées par une analyse comparative des différents cultures et des codes ou procédures juridiques distincts.

La présente série de volumes a été conçue pour répondre à une demande soudaine qui s'est manifestée dans plusieurs points du globe pour que soit cristallisé cet ensemble diffus de connaissances connues sous le nom de "droit de la santé mentale". Cette série vise à incorporer les nouvelles découvertes qui ont été faites dans des volumes grâce auxquels nous pourrons faire le point sur ce que nous savons et, aussi, sur ce que nous ignorons, dans les aspects les plus importants du droit de la santé mentale. Le nécessité de cette démarche de recherche intellectuelle tient sans doute, avant tout, au fait que les données que nous obtiendrions permettraient de répondre de façon efficace aux controverses sociales que nous connaissons quotidiennement.

Jusqu'à présent, dix congrès ont été tenus sous l'égide de l'International Journal of Law and Psychiatry, tant en Amérique du Nord qu'à l'étranger. Ces congrès nous ont permis de voir combien il était d'une importance cruciale que soit établi un réseau de relations professionnelles et d'échanges mutuels d'idées entre les critiques efficaces et les décisionistes. Ces groupes doivent être conscients à la fois des ressemblances et des différences qui existent dans les modes d'analyse des problèmes et de leur résolution à travers le monde.

Ce processus comparatif a toujours été le point d'appui de l'International Journal, publié par Pergamon Press, depuis une dizaine d'années. L'existence du Journal a contribué de façon substantielle à favoriser l'élaboration de textes complets et généraux permettant de mettre de l'ordre dans un ensemble de connaissances autrement disparate. Ces volumes seront publiés tous les ans par Pergamon Press, et nous espérons qu'ils attireront l'attention de professeurs émérites et de praticiens sur l'évolution actuelle dans les différents pays en matière de réforme du droit, de développement de la recherche, d'organisation des connaissances et sur le plan de l'évolution des concepts philosophiques ou des modèles de référence autour desquels s'articulent les fondements du droit de la santé mentale, au fur et à mesure de leur élaboration.

Il n'est pas fortuit que le premier volume soit principalement consacré à la jurisprudence américaine et aux théories mises en oeuvre dans ce pays. Il s'agit là d'une juste réflexion sur un fait géographique qui ne doit pas faire l'objet de contestation, à savoir que les États-Unis ont été des précurseurs et, en fait, même des expérimentateurs, dans ce domaine grâce à la poussée qu'ils ont faite en créant deux sous-spécialités, la psychiatrie et la psychologie légale, et aussi une catégorie d'avocats spécialisée dans les questions de psychiatrie légale. Cela dit, il ne faudrait en aucune façon réduire l'importance de la longue tradition qui avait été établie à l'extérieur des États-Unis par les chercheurs en science et en métaphysique, plusiers siècles auparavant, sur le continent européen. Cependant, il est impossible de ne pas reconnaître l'incomparable floraison de jurisprudence et de données empiriques qui s'est produite aux États-Unis depuis la Deuxiéme guerre mondiale. Il convient donc de résumer la plupart de ces connaissances tant au niveau théorique qu'au niveau procédural si l'on veut maîtriser le quantité impressionnante de connaissances existantes et, en même temps, évaluer l'utilité que pourrait avoir un examen plus approfondi des méthodes utilisées dans les différents ressorts judiciaires pour régler les conflits sociaux causés par des maladies mentales.

Le premier volume s'inscrit, par conséquent, tout à fait au coeur des controverses qui font littéralement partie de notre vie quotidienne. Au cours des dernières années, les questions de responsabilité sociale relevant de la maladie mentale ont constitué un test de la conscience et de la volonté du public, en général, et de ses représentants élus, en particulier. Les débats sur la question de savoir ce qui devrait être clairement défini comme des matières à caractère social ou juridique, par opposition à toute définition médicale, ont commencé à envahir les instances judiciaires

et les organes de réforme du droit. On est impressionné par le nombre de commissions et de groupes de travail qui doivent se hâter de procéder, dans des délais très courts, à la restructuration des principes sociaux fondamentaux, et ce, dans tous les pays industrialisés. Ces problèmes mettent directement en cause les valeurs sociales de la démocratie libérale, notamment le droit à l'autodétermination et les limites de notre tolérance envers les actes qui portent atteinte à la société.

Les auteurs qui ont été choisis pour ces tâches difficiles ont tous été reconnus pour leurs grandes qualités individuelles qui leur ont permis de se distinguer dans leurs domaines de connaissances respectifs.

George Dix, pénaliste éminent en droit américain, nous a présenté ici un véritable manuel sur la gamme d'options qui ont résulté de l'affaire Hinckley, laquelle a fait l'objet de nombreuses controverses. Son article devrait être d'une grande utilité pour les planificateurs en matière de droit pénal qui désirent avoir une évaluation réaliste des questions et des réformes législatives dont le nombre a été considérable aux États-Unis, ces deux dernières années. Une telle démarche arrive à un moment propice car des réformes importantes du droit pénal sont envisagées, à l'heure actuelle, dans des pays comme le Japon, le Canada, l'Australie et la Suède, pour n'en nommer que quelques-uns. La question de la responsabilité des actes criminels constitue le point crucial auquel les spécialistes de la santé mentale semblent se heurter dans leur travail et, par conséquent, il convient parfaitement de placer à côté de l'article de George Dix, l'étude approfondie qu'a faite Seymour Halleck sur l'interaction entre le droit et la psychiatrie en matière de responsabilité. Son article aura des répercussions importantes au niveau du fonctionnement et de la conception du régime de la santé mentale. En sa qualité de grand spécialiste américain de la psychiatrie légale, le professeur Halleck nous a offert ici un document où il a véritablement tenté d'affirmer la crédibilité de la pratique en psychiatrie clinique, face à tous les mouvements de critique et de contestation qui ont entouré les débats récents sur le régime juridique de l'aliénation mentale.

L'article de Vernon Quinsey constitue une analyse très structurée et systématique d'un secteur de la recherche scientifique qui est très compartimenté. L'auteur a fait une récapitulation précieuse pour tour ceux qui souhaitent connaître l'état actuel des découvertes scientifiques, sur l'agressivité masculine dans les relations sexuelles avec les femmes. La question de la pédophilie a été laissée de côté par Vernon Quinsey, vu qu'elle fait l'objet d'un de ses projets de recherche actuellement en cours (ce dont nous nous réjouissons); il s'est, en effet, rendu compte que cet aspect exigeait d'être traité à part et de façon tout à fait exhaustive. Le chapitre qu'a produit Vernon Quinsey nous entraîne finalement dans la recherche qui s'impose pour combler les lacunes de notre arsenal scientifique et accomplir, de ce fait, un idéal qui était le nôtre dès le début de ce projet, à savoir attirer l'attention des spécialistes sur des priorités de recherche valables.

Il n'est point besoin de souligner que la contribution des co-auteurs maintenant célèbres que sont les professeurs Appelbaum et Gutheil a aussi beaucoup amélioré la qualité de notre premier volume. En effet, sans doute comme seul le professeur Appelbaum pouvait la faire, l'étude du consentement éclairé que nous vous présentons ici constitue un modèle qui permet d'organiser les nombreux ouvrages et articles auxquels il fait référence dans ce domaine et qui ont fait autorité dans le monde universitaire au cours des dix dernières années. Il a su établir sa réputation de savant grâce à son travail au niveau clinique, qui a lui permis de justifier ses hypothèses théoriques d'après les besoins et les désirs réels à la fois des praticiens et des patients et, par conséquent, sa rétrospective ici devrait avoir une portée à long terme. Grâce à son article, nous pourrons maintenant nous reporter à l'ensemble des publications sur le consentement, munis d'un instrument précieux qui nous guidera à travers les dédales du sujet.

Le chapitre de son collaborateur, Thomas G. Gutheil, en matière d'évaluation en psychiatrie légale vient encore confirmer la valeur d'une démarche systématique lors de l'étude des multiples tâches que doivent assumer les praticiens de la santé mentale. L'une des difficultés qui surgit sans arrêt devant les tribunaux et dans la pratique quotidienne tient au fait que les praticiens ne peuvent pas, ni d'ailleurs les spécialistes du droit, faire de distinctions entre les rôles et les responsabilités particulières qui constituent le régime de la santé mentale et ses rapports avec les critères et les procédures juridiques. L'étude de Thomas Gutheil fait ressortir le besoin de données empiriques pour réparer, encore une fois, le décalage qui existe entre la théorie et la pratique et, tout particulièrement, du point de vue des patients.

Déjà les penseurs et les sociologues, au début du vingtième siècle, avaient insisté sur la nécessité d'étudier ces questions pour mettre en évidence le niveau de compréhension qu'avaient les intervenants dans les interactions avec le droit, et ce besoin de recherche théorique revêt une importance particulière dans le domaine du droit de la santé mentale. En effet, peut-être ici plus que n'importe où ailleurs en droit, il est essentiel que nous connaissions les sentiments et réactions de tous ceux qui participent. Comme ils en sont les acteurs les plus importants, les patients ont souvent un enjeu émotif considérable dans le drame judiciare qui va, en fin de compte, déterminer leur liberté. Grâce à son grand talent, Thomas Gutheil a réussi à traiter ce sujet d'une façon simple et claire qui le rend accessible à tous et lui donne un très grand intérêt pratique.

Enfin, la qualité du volume est encore rehaussée par un compte rendu exhaustif sur un domaine d'une grande technicité en psychologie, à savoir la validité et la fiabilité des techniques de sélection des jurés. Dans la pratique juridique, cette question fait souvent l'objet de grands débats, et la contribution du professeur Bruce Dennis Sales constitue un grand pas en avant dans la recherche. Bruce Sales est le rédacteur de l'American Journal of Law and Human Behavior, et il est aussi l'auteur et le rédacteur de nombreux articles dans le domaine spécialisé qu'est la psychologie légale. L'article est le fruit d'une recherche collective entre Sales et ses collaborateurs Hafemeister et Suggs; il s'agit d'un bilan sur l'état de la question. Ce chapitre servira sans doute d'élément de référence dans toute recherche ultérieure sur ces questions.

Nous pouvons voir, grâce à un examen rapide des textes ici présentés, que les auteurs ont intégré leur expérience pratique et leurs compétences scientifiques en matière d'évaluation et de critique dans une oeuvre qui nous permet d'appréhender le caractère complexe de ce vaste domaine qu'est le droit de la santé mentale. Ils se sont livrés à une analyse fouillée d'un champ de connaissances extrêmement diversifié mais, avec leurs talents multidisciplinaires, ils avaient cependant une intention commune, à savoir de nous informer, en leur qualité d'experts, sur l'état actuel des connaissances, eu égard à la théorie et à la pratique, dans six des principaux secteurs du droit de la santé mentale. Cela ne veut pas dire que nous nous arrêterons là car nous allons ensuite découvrir comment d'autres systèmes juridiques et d'autres traditions linguistiques ont pu traiter de ces différents sujets.

Nous avons l'intention, dans les prochains volumes, de pousser la recherche vers d'autres horizons, notamment les cultures espagnole, française, allemande, italienne, hollandaise et scandinave, ainsi que dans les tendances législatives et judiciaires qui se manifestent, par exemple, dans les pays du Commonwealth. Qui plus est, parmi les principaux sujets du domaine qui doivent être traités dans les volumes à venir, il y aura la responsabilité des médecins, le terrorisme, les privilèges des experts de santé mentale en cour, le courant de désinstitutionalisation, la recherche psychobiologique en criminalité, la tutelle et la compétence, pour n'en citer que quelques-uns. Certains secteurs seront complétés par des rajouts aux chapitres déjà publiés, notamment sur l'évaluation et les diagnostics du point de vue de la psychologie. De plus, nous souhaitons que cette série de volumes couvre des catégories aussi diffuses que la personnalité du psychopathe ou du criminel, et qu'elle explore des questions philosophiques ou historiques comme le rôle de l'inconscient dans le droit et l'histoire des asiles.

De par la nature du projet, les chapitres revêtent plus un caractère descriptif qu'analytique, mais les auteurs fournissent cependant des évaluations pertinentes sur leur domaine de spécialisation respectif. Cette démarche s'est avérée plus adaptée dans certains cas que dans d'autres, surtout lorsque la clarification de concepts aussi fondamentaux que la responsabilité, par exemple, aurait exiger de l'auteur une déclaration d'engagement intellectuel.

Etant donné l'essence du droit de la santé mentale, les chapitres diffèrent dans une certaine mesure à la fois dans leur nature et dans leur intention, mais ils ont chacun une approche particulièrement soignée et adaptée aux questions à traiter. Ce sera cependant aux lecteurs et aux spécialistes d'évaluer en dernier ressort la qualité de ces contributions. L'honorable comité de rédaction de ce projet, auquel j'exprime toute ma reconnaissance, a été sensible à tous ces facteurs, mais je dois, en dernier lieu, porter la responsabilité des lacunes qui demeurent éventuellement.

Tout projet de l'envergure de celui-ci ne peut être mis sur pied sans le financement généreux d'une institution, et nous tenons à exprimer toute notre gratitude envers l'Institut Philippe Pinel de Montréal et son directeur général, le docteur Lionel Béliveau, pour avoir soutenu ce projet dont l'ampleur était considérable. Je tiens aussi à remercier toute la communauté professionnelle de l'Institut Philippe Pinel pour son active participation dans la détermination des priorités du projet et dans sa conception générale. Comme toujours dans les entreprises intellectuelles, plusieurs personnes ont travaillé avec acharnement à la coordination, et je remercie donc le docteur Eli Bernard Weisstub du département de Psychiatrie de l'Université Stanford, Nicole Fernbach, Fred Ernst, Jill Lazar Matus, et enfin ma collaboratrice de toujours, Lola Rosamund Weisstub.

David N. Weisstub

LAW AND MENTAL HEALTH

1.
Criminal Responsibility and Mental Impairment in American Criminal Law: Response to the Hinckley Acquittal in Historical Perspective

George E. Dix

ABSTRACT. *Reactions to the insanity acquittal of John Hinckley on charges arising from Hinckley's attempt to assassinate President Reagan are examined against the background of American criminal responsibility law. Traditionally, this body of law emphasized the availability of the defense of insanity. The major issue has been whether the defense should be available upon proof that an offender was impaired but only in such a manner as affected the offender's capacity to control his conduct. By the time of the Hinckley acquittal, a majority of American jurisdictions had expanded the insanity defense so as to permit acquittal upon impairments of either a cognitive or volitional nature.*

In addition, some American jurisdictions permit a criminal defendant to rely upon evidence of psychological abnormality to establish that the defendant did not act with the mens rea *required by the offense charged and therefore cannot be convicted. Recently, other vehicles have been developed to accommodate defendants' claims of impairment. Some jurisdictions permit offenders impaired at the time of their conduct but not entitled to acquittal to be found "guilty but mentally ill." Impairment is sometimes made a specific mitigating consideration in sentencing.*

The Hinckley acquittal stimulated substantial discussion of responsibility issues. Generally, this discussion consisted of further consideration of issues previously identified. Much pre-Hinckley discussion focused upon the logical ramifications of the philosophical foundations of criminal liability for responsibility law. The Hinckley acquittal, however, focused attention upon the practical realities of various responsibility doctrines as they are administered. Some conceptually appropriate positions may be so difficult to administer or so subject to abuse in practice that they are ultimately undesirable.

Little long-run enthusiasm was generated after the Hinckley acquittal for abandoning any insanity defense and relegating defendants to use of evidence of impairment to show lack of mens rea. *A number of jurisdictions, however, did adopt a "guilty but mentally ill" option and procedures that facilitated post-acquittal detention of offenders in mental health facilities.*

But the major result of the Hinckley acquittal is a trend towards abandonment of volitional impairment as a basis for a defense of insanity. This trend is based upon the perception that present clinical skills do not permit the accurate identification of those offenders who in fact were so impaired in this fashion as to make their conviction inappropriate. Whether this trend will have a significant effect is unclear. It may well be that such a narrowing of the criterion will not affect the admissibility of evidence in or the outcome of such cases.

1

SOMMAIRE. Dans cette étude, les réactions â l'acquittement pour cause d'aliénation mentale de John Hinckley, auteur d'une tentative d'assassinat sur la personne du président Reagan, sont placées dans le contexte du droit américain de la responsabilité criminelle. C'est un domaine du droit où le recours possible à la défense d'aliénation mentale a toujours eu beaucoup d'importance. Il s'agissait surtout de savoir si l'on pouvait se prévaloir de cette défense sur la preuve de l'affaiblissement des facultés du délinquant, mais seulement dans la mesure où cet état l'empêchait de se maîtriser. Au moment de l'acquittement de Hinckley, une jurisprudence majoritaire aux Etats-Unis avait étendu la défense d'aliénation mentale de façon à permettre l'acquittement pour déficience d'ordre cognitif ou volitif.

De plus, quelques tribunaux américains permettent au défendeur criminel de se prévaloir de la preuve d'anormalité psychologique pour établir qu'il n'avait pas l'intention coupable exigée par l'infraction et que, par conséquent, il ne peut pas être condamné. Récemment, d'autres moyens ont été trouvés pour accueillir les défenses fondées sur l'affaiblissement des facultés. Certaines juridictions acceptent que le défendeur dont les facultés étaient affaiblies au moment de son acte, mais qui n'a pas droit à l'acquittement, soit jugé "coupable, mais aliéné". L'état d'affaiblissement constitue parfois une circonstance atténuante dans la sentence.

L'acquittement de Hinckley a donné lieu à une discussion très vive des problèmes de responsabilité. En général, le débat était un prolongement des discussions sur les problèmes déjà soulevés avant cette affaire. En effet, le débat antérieur portait avant tout sur les ramifications logiques du droit de la responsabilité dans les fondements philosophiques de la responsabilité criminelle. L'acquittement de Hinckley a cependant attiré l'attention sur les réalités pratiques des différentes doctrines de la responsabilité, selon leur mode d'application. Certaines positions, pourtant justifiées sur le plan conceptuel, peuvent s'avérer d'application si difficile ou si susceptibles d'abus dans la pratique qu'elles en deviennent finalement peu souhaitables.

L'acquittement de Hinckley a seulement causé un faible mouvement en faveur de l'abandon de la défense d'aliénation mentale qui réduirait les défendeurs à invoquer l'affaiblissement de leurs facultés pour prouver leur absence d'intention coupable. Toutefois, un certain nombre de juridictions ont opté pour le verdict de culpabilité, mais avec déclaration d'aliénation, et pour des procédures propres à faciliter la détention des délinquants dans des établissements de soins psychiatriques, après leur acquittement.

Mais l'acquittement de Hinckley a eu comme principal effet de créer un mouvement vers l'abandon, à titre de défense, de l'affaiblissement comme fondement de la défense d'aliénation mentale. Cette tendance est fondée sur l'idée que les moyens cliniques actuels ne permettent pas de déceler, avec exactitude, qui sont les délinquants dont les facultés étaient si affaiblies que cela rendait la condamnation vide de sens. Reste à savoir si cette tendance aura un effet important. Il se peut très bien que cette réduction du critère n'aura pas d'incidence sur la preuve ni sur l'issue jurisprudentielle des causes.

Introduction

Few legal events in recent times have given rise to as much public reaction as the June 1982 decision by a Washington D.C. jury that presidential assailant John Hinckley was "not guilty by reason of insanity" of various charges arising out of the assassination effort. This public reaction stimulated substantial legislative concern with criminal responsibility law. It is reasonably certain that the legislative concern will result in changes in the legal procedures and standards for evaluating American defendants' claims that they lack full, or any, responsibility for their criminal conduct.

This paper undertakes to examine those post-*Hinckley* changes that already occurred against the background of American criminal responsibility law. Such an evaluation of the significance of the *Hinckley* acquittal must ask, first, whether it resulted in any significant contribution to the long-standing and complex controversy as to how defendants' psychological impairments are most appropriately accommodated in processing those accused of crime. Second, it is obviously necessary to inquire whether the changes made as the result of *Hinckley* will have important long-run effects upon American responsibility law. Finally, consideration must be given to whether any such important changes as may have resulted are reasonably based or, as might be feared, are instead the product of impulsive response to an offensive incident.

This chapter addresses these concerns in several steps. First, an extensive inquiry is made into pre-*Hinckley* responsibility law, the issues that have been raised in this area, and those trends that can be identified as having developed before the *Hinckley* acquittal. As the chapter progresses, the *Hinckley* acquittal itself and reactions to it are examined. This examination suggests that the most important long-term effect of the *Hinckley* acquittal is likely to be the abandonment of the traditional trend in American responsibility law towards development of a completely exculpating defense of impaired volition. The merits of this abandonment of a volitional impairment defense are addressed specifically in the third section of the chapter, and some conclusions are offered in the final section.

Pre-*Hinckley* responsibility law showed an early and continued emphasis upon the insanity defense as the major vehicle for accommodating defendants' claims of impairment. While attention tended to be devoted primarily to the criterion for resolving claims of insanity, a variety of subsidiary procedural issues were recognized as of substantial importance in obtaining satisfactory administration of any criterion. Dissatisfaction with the all-or-nothing nature of the decision required by the insanity defense doctrine as well as conceptual overlap between insanity and *mens rea* requirements of substantive criminal law also gave rise to a confusing body of law—often referred to as "diminished capacity"—that sometimes rendered evidence of psychological impairment admissible on whether or not the defendant was shown to have acted with the requisite *mens rea* as an alternative to use of such evidence to support a claim of insanity.

Similar desires to provide for consideration of impairment not sufficient in nature or seriousness to justify exoneration, as well as other concerns, more recently have led to efforts to provide a structured method for consideration of impairment in the sentencing of defendants found sufficiently responsible for conviction. This is evident in schemes for determining whether life imprisonment or the death penalty should be imposed upon conviction for capital offenses and in some structured procedures for noncapital sentencing.

Accommodation of such impairment was also, in part, the perceived advantage of providing trial juries with the alternative of finding a defendant neither guilty nor not guilty by reason of insanity but instead, "guilty but mentally ill."

Throughout these developments there is a consistent concern that appropriate, but not excessive, significance be given to defendants' impaired volition. To some extent, the defense of insanity was expanded to permit complete exculpation in some cases on the basis of such impairment. But the development of the diminished capacity doctrine and the provisions for accommodating impairment in sentencing, or a determination that an accused is guilty but mentally ill, were designed, in part at least, to permit consideration of volitional impairment. Under local insanity doctrine, volitional impairment was not relevant to the complete defense or was not of sufficient seriousness to justify complete exculpation.

Also running through this development is continual ambivalence as to whether consideration of impairments ought to be entrusted to the trial jury or to the presiding judge. Insanity and diminished capacity, of course, assumed that defendants were entitled to have the issue determined by trial juries. Many—although not all—of the provisions for consideration of impairment in sentencing would provide for the issue to be entrusted instead to the presiding judge.

The *Hinckley* acquittal, as will be developed in the second section of this chapter, did not result in the development of new alternatives or even in new arguments or considerations bearing upon the choices provided by those alternatives developed in the long pre-*Hinckley* history of American responsibility law. It did, however, focus concern upon the desirability of entertaining defendants' claims of volitional impairment, at least as they are offered to obtain complete exoneration from criminal liability. Insofar as such claims are to be entertained in criminal litigation, *Hinckley* has stimulated increased concern about the wisdom of entrusting juries with responsibility for evaluating those claims.

Much of the debate in American responsibility law has been abstract, in the sense that it has revolved around largely philosophical concerns. There has been periodic concern expressed, however, that greater attention needs to be given to the realities of the day-to-day system, in which criteria or procedures that appear appropriate

conceptually may in fact permit, or even encourage, abuse. It is at least arguable that the
most significant immediate effect of the *Hinckley*
acquittal was to give increased legitimacy to these
"practicality" concerns and therefore to change
somewhat the flavor of discussion concerning
criminal responsibility policy and law.

Pre-*Hinckley* "Responsibility" Law

The extent to which the *Hinckley* acquittal stimulated new proposals or added to the substance of
the debates concerning appropriate choices
among traditional alternatives can be evaluated
only against the background set by pre-*Hinckley*
American responsibility law. Development of this
background is the task of the present section.

The major legal vehicle for accommodating
criminal defendants' claims of psychological abnormality and their potential criminal liability
has been the traditional "defense" of "insanity,"
mental disorder, or nonresponsibility. These terms
will be used interchangeably here. Some courts
and legislatures have recognized, as a largely independent consideration, the relevance of a defendant's impairment to the issue of whether or
not the defendant harbored the state of mind or
mens rea required by the crime charged. The
position that evidence of impairment may be used
to show lack of *mens rea*—the "diminished capacity" doctrine—had been offered, before the
Hinckley acquittal, as an appropriate alternative
to an insanity defense embodying the traditional
criteria. Even before the *Hinckley* acquittal, substantial consideration was given to a third possibility—a finding or verdict that a defendant,
although not entitled to acquittal, was "guilty but
mentally ill." Recent developments in criminal
sentencing in general and capital sentencing in
particular have resulted in somewhat more structured provision being made for addressing psychological impairment in the sentencing process.

The *Hinckley* acquittal gave rise to renewed
interest in many of the traditional responsibility
law issues. The impact of this interest, then, can
be evaluated only if the issues are developed and
the major arguments made in support of the various positions are identified.

Criminal responsibility, like many other aspects
of American criminal law and procedure, has to
some extent been the subject of a trend towards
"constitutionalization." As compared to other
areas, responsibility law has undergone relatively

little such constitutionalization. Nevertheless, it is
necessary to consider the extent to which constitutional, as well as express statutory or case law,
requirements may demand that certain characteristics of defendants' psychological conditions be
given exculpating effect.

The Basis for Responsibility Law

The basic question posed by responsibility law is
why criminal law ought to take into account in
any fashion evidence that persons who have
engaged in antisocial conduct were, at the time of
that conduct, psychologically impaired. This
might be justified in utilitarian terms. Reference
to the functions that criminal conviction and punishment can reasonably be expected to serve, as a
general matter, may suggest that subjecting impaired persons to conviction will not serve those
functions (Goldstein, 1967, pp. 11–20). But this is
seldom a simple inquiry. The impaired, for example, may not be subject to deterrence. Therefore,
to penalize them may not serve the reasonable
hope that as a general rule the enforced threat of
criminal liability deters future offenses. On the
other hand, provision for impaired offenders may
cause unimpaired offenders to anticipate that
they can escape liability by feigning impairment
and thus dilute the deterrent value of the law as it
applies to those who might be deterred.

Similarly, responsibility law channels impaired
persons from the criminal justice system into a
system of enforced treatment perhaps better
suited to their needs. Thus, it may further the
reformative objectives of criminal liability. But
this can obviously be accomplished in other ways,
such as provision for post-conviction sentencing
to treatment in such programs, or transfer of im-
prisoned inmates from correctional to mental
health facilities.

Although all of these arguments have been
made in support of provisions for accommodating
defendants' abnormalities, the primary conceptual support for such provisions lies instead in the
assumption that culpability or blameworthiness is
a necessary prerequisite to criminal liability and
that certain impaired persons, despite proof that
they have engaged in dangerous conduct, lack
that prerequisite (Hermann, 1983). This assumption, in turn, is based upon the view that implicit
in criminal conviction is condemnation for the
offender's blameworthy behavior. Persons who
engage in dangerous conduct in the absence of

such blameworthiness may be restrained and subjected to reformative efforts, but not by means of a process which also condemns them.

To some extent, this relates to retribution as a function of criminal liability. Conviction may serve the appropriate function of expressing society's condemnation of an offender. If, however, the person's conduct does not justify such condemnation, the retributive function of imposing criminal liability will not be served. More broadly, however, this reasoning relates to all functions of criminal liability. There has been continual acceptance of the proposition that whatever societal functions might be served by convicting certain offenders impaired at the time of their conduct, so pursuing these functions is "unjust" if accomplished at the cost of erroneously assigning moral blameworthiness to the offender in the process.

But impairment alone, whether it is psychological or physical, has universally been rejected in American law as sufficiently indicative of nonblameworthiness to justify accommodation. The need to avoid unjustified expansion of our accommodation of impairment, then, has resulted in a perception that the accommodation must make clear to those charged with the accommodation— usually trial juries—that only certain kinds of impairment justify deviation from the normal standards used to determine whether accused persons should be found criminally guilty. The need to develop methods of accommodation that accomplish this has proven to be a difficult one to meet.

The Insanity Defense: Criteria

The major vehicle, of course, for accommodating claims of nonresponsibility has been the "defense" of "insanity." Especially in recently enacted statutory provisions, insanity phraseology is sometimes abandoned in favor of such labels as "defense of mental disorder." Realistically or not, much of the traditional debate over this issue has revolved around the substantive criteria for resolving claims that defendants are entitled to complete exculpation from liability under this type of provision.

SIGNIFICANCE OF THE CRITERIA

Conceptually, of course, the criterion for resolving insanity claims is of major importance. Whether the practical importance of the matter equals its conceptual prominence is, however, another matter.

Much of American criminal law and procedure was developed for application in contested jury trials, although by far the majority of cases are processed without hearings before a jury. Nevertheless, in a jury case the insanity criterion controls, of course, the substance of the instruction to the jury. This, in turn, purports to determine how the jury resolves the claim of insanity. Much of American insanity law revolves around disputes as to how to so instruct the jury. Despite this, instructions in insanity cases are sometimes ambiguous on critical matters; one leading text comments that insanity instructions "may be rambling, imprecise, or even downright misleading" (LaFave & Scott, 1972; p. 316). How damaging or otherwise important this state of affairs is to litigation remains uncertain. Some reason exists to believe that juries may not follow instructions with the care that lawyers debate over them, and therefore inadequate instructions may be of little ultimate significance.

Apart from its effect on jury instructions, the insanity criterion also constituted the standard to be used by the court in resolving those contested cases in which jury trials are waived. It also serves as the standard for determining, in jury trials, whether the prosecution has made a sufficient case to warrant submission to the jury or, in the alternative, whether a directed verdict in favor of the defense is appropriate. If a trial jury rejects a claim of insanity, the criterion also determines whether post-verdict relief should be granted by the trial judge or appellate tribunals.

There is also a widespread perception that the insanity criterion affects the flow of information to the trial jury. In theory, this might be so. A trial judge is, of course, entitled to exclude defensive evidence that is not material to the law governing the case. If a case is being tried under a restrictive formulation of the insanity defense, expert testimony (and other evidence) might be subject to objection on the ground that it fails to logically demonstrate nonresponsibility within the limited criterion to be applied. Whether this in fact occurs is problematic. Where a serious crime has been charged, trial judges may be sufficiently concerned with the risk of excluding evidence that is in fact material that they will, as a practical matter, refuse to scrutinize offered evidence of this sort. The applicable criterion, then, may in fact have little effect upon a defendant's ability to get expert testimony and other information before the trier of fact. Goldstein (1967, pp. 53–57), in his classic examination of the insanity defense, concluded that traditional narrow insanity criteria did not inhibit the flow of expert testimony on matters related to defendants' responsibility. On the other hand, the reported cases make clear that defense evidence has, at least sometimes, been excluded on these grounds (*Carnes* v. *State*, 1925).

The criterion may also affect the manner in which evidence is produced and, to some extent, the way in which questioning and discussion occur. If the criterion being applied is a limited one, witnesses should be asked to testify in those terms and argument and discussion should be phrased in the limited terms of the standard. Again, however, this may not be day-to-day reality. Trial judges may permit questioning, discussion, and argument with only a minor nod to a restrictive applicable standard. Even if expert witnesses are, at some point during testimony, asked to express opinions framed in terms suggested by the limited standards theoretically applicable, this may in no way affect the ability of counsel for either side to elicit background or supporting detail and information.

But, in addition to any such procedural significance as the insanity criterion may have, it seems clear that the criterion also serves an important and independent symbolic purpose (Gussfield, 1968). Adoption of a limited criterion in a legislative enactment or a definitive judicial opinion constitutes a public affirmation of certain views. Such affirmations are often of tremendous importance. This is so, apart from any demonstrated actual effect which adoption of the view may have. It seems certain that much of the dispute concerning insanity criteria can be best explained in terms of efforts to achieve these sorts of symbolic advantages, although the debate almost always occurs in terms of anticipated specific effects of various alternatives.

THE "RIGHT-WRONG" TEST

During the nineteenth century, American courts quite eagerly embraced the English view solidified in 1843 by the House of Lords in the *M'Naghten* case. Under this view, only a defendant who, because of his impairment at the time of the offense, had lost the ability to distinguish right from wrong in regard to the act, or to know the nature and quality of that act is entitled to exculpation (Wharton & Stille, 1905). Platt and Diamond (1966, pp. 1250–51) have demonstrated, however, that American courts generally had accepted the right-wrong standard before 1843. The standard has been frequently embodied in statutes (Arizona Laws, 1977).

As Goldstein (1967, p. 49) has pointed out, much controversy involving the right-wrong test has concerned the meaning of "know" in these formulations. The test obviously becomes a much broader one if "know" or its equivalent is defined as requiring more than minimal conscious awareness. Sometimes the intention to broadly define the term is expressed. The New York statute, for example, provides that the defense requires only that the accused lack "substantial capacity to know or appreciate" the nature and "consequences" of the conduct or its wrongfulness (New York Laws, 1965). It is clear that by providing for the alternative of incapacity to *appreciate*, the drafters intended to expand the criterion beyond what was or might be intended by the use of "know."

A number of statutory versions of the right-wrong test somewhat obscure the issue by avoiding the use of "know" or equivalent phraseology. The Georgia statute, for example, illustrates a pattern in which the issue is posed as whether the accused had "the mental capacity to distinguish between right and wrong" (Georgia Laws, 1968). But the same question is clearly present. Whether "distinguishing" between right and wrong involves more than developing minimal intellectual awareness raises virtually the same problems as the definition of "know" under more traditional statutory frameworks.

The practical significance of this controversy is uncertain. Jury instructions virtually never define the word "know" or its equivalent in precise terms. Only an unusually perceptive jury, then, may find in the instructions given it any implication of the important policy decision that the phraseology of the instructions reflects. Whether juries sensitized to the law's intention regarding the definition of "know" or its equivalent are inclined or able to give effect to this intention is subject to legitimate doubt.

VOLITIONAL IMPAIRMENT

Before the English law of insanity was rigidified in *M'Naghten*, American case law developed some basis for rendering the defense available where the defendant's impairment had not affected his cognitive abilities but had prevented him from exercising normal control over his behavior. Weihofen (1954, p. 85) found evidence in 1834 and 1843 decisions that trial judges had so instructed juries as to make the defendant's inability to forbear the offense a defense to liability.

The seeds planted in these early American authorities grew into the so-called "irresistible impulse" test. Under this criterion, a criminal defendant was entitled to acquittal upon a finding that a mental disorder had caused him to experience an irresistible and uncontrollable impulse to commit the offense, even if he remained able to understand the nature of the offense and its wrongfulness. The phraseology of the criterion suggested that the impairment required must have been one that manifested itself suddenly. Thus it was subject to the criticism that it failed to accommodate impairments that destroyed volition but developed slowly and perhaps insidiously. On the other hand, in administration no such requirement appears to have been imposed. (Goldstein, 1967, p. 71).

Those American jurisdictions that adopted the irresistible impulse criterion added it to the right-wrong test, so that a defendant became entitled to acquittal upon a showing that he met either the right-wrong or the irresistible impulse test. Weihofen, writing in 1954, found no basis for concluding that either position had become a "trend." Continuing disagreement, he concluded, had resulted in a century of diversity among American jurisdictions. (p. 101).

But the impairment of volition criterion experienced a significant push from the American Law Institute's Model Penal Code project. In 1955, the Institute's Council submitted to the membership Tentative Draft No. 4 of the developing code. The comments (American Law Institute, 1955, p. 156) observed that defining the criteria for exculpating certain defendants on the basis of mental abnormality was exceeded by no other problem in intrinsic difficulty. Nevertheless, the Council proposed a provision (Section 4.01) that would exculpate a defendant upon showing that, as a result of mental disease or defect, he either "lack[ed] substantial capacity to appreciate the criminality of his conduct or to conform his conduct to the requirements of law." This was approved by the Institute in 1961 and was incorporated into the final draft of the Model Penal Code, promulgated in 1962. The American Law Institute's endorsement of a volitional criterion obviously provided significant support for

that criterion. In 1975, for example, the House of Delegates of the American Bar Association approved the principle of the insanity criterion set forth in the Institute's Code (American Bar Association, 1975).

During the numerous post-1962 legislative revisions of states' substantive criminal codes, the Model Penal Code proposal was widely adopted. Sometimes modifications were made. Missouri, for example, rejected the Code's requirement of only "substantial impairment" and instead required a showing that the defendant was "incapable of conforming his conduct to the requirements of law" or, in the case of cognitive impairment, that the defendant "did not know or appreciate" the wrongfulness of his conduct (Missouri Laws, 1977).

The Model Penal Code proposal also found support in judicial reconsiderations of the matter. Perhaps the trend towards acceptance of the formulation can be regarded as having culminated in *People* v. *Drew* (1978). The California Supreme Court had repeatedly and strongly adhered to the right-wrong test, a position that arguably stimulated the jurisdiction's convoluted diminished capacity law to be discussed later. In *Drew*, however, the court reconsidered and, as a result, adopted the Model Penal Code's formulation.

By 1982, an American Bar Association committee report indicated that all federal circuits and at least 29 states defined insanity so as to provide for acquittal on the basis of volitional impairment. (American Bar Association Standing Committee, 1983). By the time of the *Hinckley* acquittal, the American Law Institute's formulation of a two-pronged test had clearly become the most frequently followed model.

Whether formal adoption of a specific volitional impairment defense in fact constituted a meaningful change in the law, however, was subject to dispute. Volitional impairment may be put into issue by the traditional right-wrong tests. If "know" or "distinguish" involve more than mere minimal intellectual awareness, they might be defined as to require some or all aspects of the ability to control one's conduct. Juries may be specifically instructed that inability to control one's conduct is irrelevant to liability; this, of course, precludes such a construction of the test. More commonly, however, juries are simply given no interpretation of the critical term. (Goldstein, 1967, p. 50). This leaves the members free to construe the term as they wish, considering—

among other factors—the testimony of experts presented at trial and the arguments of counsel for both sides.

Expansion of the defense to encompass volitional incapacity—assuming that it constitutes a meaningful change—has been supported primarily in terms of the purpose of the defense, that is, the need to exculpate those defendants whose conduct did not demonstrate moral or ethical culpability and for whom the moral condemnation inherent in criminal conviction is therefore inappropriate. Inability to avoid engaging in conduct perceived as criminal, wrong, or both, it was argued, as effectively shows the absence of blameworthiness as does an inability to develop a cognitive understanding of one's conduct. Moreover, the types of impairment were assumed to be somewhat independent. The alternative criteria were expressly based on the factual assumption "that even though cognition still obtains, mental disorder may provide a total incapacity for self-control." (American Law Institute, 1955, p. 157). In *Drew*, the California Supreme Court explained its adoption of the Model Penal Code criteria by reasoning that "current psychiatric opinion . . . holds that mental illness often leaves the individual's intellectual understanding relatively unimpaired, but so affects his emotions or reason that he is unable to prevent himself from committing the act."

Practical difficulties of implementation were regarded as either of minor incremental importance or as surmountable. The Alabama Supreme Court, in *Parsons v. State* (1887), explained:

> It is no satisfactory objection to say that the rule [permitting reliance upon volitional impairment] is of difficult application. The rule in *McNaghten's Case* . . . is equally obnoxious to a like criticism. . . . We think we can safely rely in this matter upon the intelligence of our juries, guided by the testimony of men who have practically made a study of the disease of insanity.

"DISORDER" REQUIRED

American responsibility criteria seldom made any significant effort to identify or limit the types of disorders sufficient to give rise to the defense of nonresponsibility. Traditionally, juries were generally given only "negative" definitions, that is, instructions as to what were not sufficient disorders:

> [Whatever mental condition did exist,] it must exist because of disease of the mind . . . Mere immorality or lasciviousness impelling one to commit an act not due to a disease of the mind, would not be a defense (*Korsak* v. *State*, 1941).

> Excitement or frenzy arising from passion or anger, hatred or revenge, no matter how furious, if not the result of a diseased mind, would not constitute legal insanity, and the jury should not confuse excitement, anger or wrath or acts done under the influence of either or both [sic], for the purpose of revenge, with actual insanity, such as is recognized by law. (*State* v. *Kaufman*, 1932).

In short, the almost universal approach was to make little effort to limit the defense of nonresponsibility by imposing a threshold requirement of any particular syndromes or clinical diagnoses. Rather, limitation of the defense was sought almost exclusively by imposing limiting requirements upon the results that were required for exculpation.

CONSTITUTIONAL RAMIFICATIONS

Given the tendency towards constitutionalization of so much of American criminal procedure, it is somewhat surprising to find so few serious questions being raised concerning the constitutional acceptability of many limited insanity criteria. There are some indications, however, that the existence of the defense itself may be constitutionally mandated.

Several state decisions from early in the 1900s are often cited as holding that state constitutional considerations preclude abolition of the defense of insanity. But their authority is not clear. In *Sinclair* v. *State* (1931) the Mississippi Supreme Court held that a 1928 statute precluding a "defense" of insanity in murder prosecutions violated the state constitutional requirement of due process. This was despite the provision for the jury to find that the defendant was "insane at the time of the crime" and, upon this finding, for the trial judge to certify that the defendant should not be confined in a penitentiary. Such a certification permitted but did not require the governor to transfer the convicted murderer to a hospital as long as hospital mental health care was needed. Criminal liability must as a matter of due process, the court reasoned, include intent and animus. Giving defendants no way to avoid conviction by showing "insanity" violated this fundamental requirement.

In *State* v. *Strasberg* (1910), the Washington legislation at issue clearly barred the trial jury from hearing evidence offered to establish a defense under the "right-wrong" criterion. But the trial judge was authorized to hear evidence of impairment and to "commit" the defendant to a mental hospital in lieu of sentence. Six members of the Washington Supreme Court expressed the view that legislation abolishing the insanity defense would violate the state's constitutional requirement of due process. At least five of them, however, construed the statute before the court as only taking the issue of insanity from the jury and making it an issue for resolution by the judge. As so interpreted, they concluded, the statute violated the jury trial component of the due process mandate. The Louisiana Supreme Court expressly held in *State* v. *Lange* (1929) that defendants' state consitutional right to jury trial precluded the state legislature from removing insanity as a jury issue and providing for its resolution by a jury commission composed of three state institution heads.

Perhaps the most that can be said on the basis of these early decisions is that serious state constitutional problems would be created either by total abolition of any defense of mental impairment or by removing from the trial juries the right to resolve any claim to such a defense. These decisions do not address the content of any limitation that the state constitutions may impose upon the substantive content of the criterion for resolving claims of nonresponsibility. There are, however, somewhat mixed signals from the United States Supreme Court concerning the extent to which the content of the insanity criterion may raise a viable federal constitutional issue.

In *Leland* v. *Oregon* (1952), the defendant contended that his federal constitutional right to due process was violated by trial and conviction in state court for murder under the " 'right and wrong' test of legal insanity in preference to the 'irresistible impulse' test." The Court, however, rejected the argument:

The progress of science has not reached a point where its learning would compel us to require the states to eliminate the right and wrong test from their criminal law. More-

over, choice of a test of legal insanity involves not only scientific knowledge but questions of basic policy as to the extent to which that knowledge should determine criminal responsibility. This whole problem has evoked wide disagreement among those who have studied it. (p. 801)

In light of this, the Court concluded, due process did not mandate trial under an insanity criterion broader than the right-wrong test.

But somewhat different signals were sent out in *Powell* v. *Texas* (1968). Powell was convicted of public intoxication over his claim, supported by expert testimony produced at trial, that his consumption of intoxicating beverages was the product of chronic alcoholism. The psychiatrist testifying for the defense acknowledged that Powell, when sober, knew the difference between right and wrong and that taking his "first" drink was a voluntary act. He further expressed the opinion, however, that once Powell took a drink he lost control over his subsequent actions. Perhaps because of the state's adoption of the right-wrong test, Powell chose not to advance his claim in terms of insanity. Instead, he urged that he had established that the conduct amounting to the offense was "involuntary" and that to penalize such conduct would violate the prohibition against cruel and unusual punishment contained in the Eighth Amendment to the federal Constitution.

Four members of the Court took the position that the Eighth Amendment barred criminal conviction of a person for anything—whether conduct or "being" in a "condition"—which is symptomatic of a disease with which the person is afflicted, if the disease renders the person powerless to avoid that conduct or condition. Four other members of the Court read the Constitutional provision invoked as imposing no such limitation on the criminal law. Instead, they concluded, the prohibition is one against criminalization of a "status." Since Powell had not been convicted of "being" a chronic alcoholic but rather of engaging in the behavior of being drunk in public, he was without the protection of the provision. Justice White, the ninth member of the Court, agreed that the Eighth Amendment prohibited criminal conviction for conduct which was the product of an "irresistible urge." But Powell's evidence, he concluded, failed to show with sufficient persuasiveness that the conduct for which he was being punished—being in public while intoxicated—was so related to his chronic alcoholism as to deprive him of the ability to avoid it.

A majority of the members of the Court in *Powell*, then, accepted that, under certain circumstances at least, the Eighth Amendment to the United States Constitution bars the conviction of a person for behavior which, as the result of abnormality, the person is unable to avoid. Despite this tantalizing hint, however, there have been no further suggestions that the court might be prepared to consider constitutionalizing some or all of the law relating to the criminal responsibility of the psychologically impaired.

"ABUSE" AND ERROR IN INSANITY CASES

Claims of "abuse" of the insanity defense or its equivalent have accompanied its development throughout American history. The 1928 Mississippi legislation rendering insanity unavailable as a defense in murder prosecutions was based, in part at least, upon a perception that the defense was "manufactured in many instances." (*Sinclair* v. *State*, 1931, p. 592, Smith, C.J., dissenting). Support offered for such claims, however, has been primarily impressionistic and anecdotal. This is undoubtedly in part because of the difficulty of defining "abuse." It might, of course, mean results inconsistent with the substance of the applicable legal standard. But the legal standards are so flexible that the "correct" outcome of cases is often difficult to determine. Or it might mean results inconsistent with the underlying purposes of the defense. In any case, even if abuse is defined, the difficulties of determining whether the outcomes of particular cases were "wrong" and the defense was therefore abused in those cases presents almost insurmountable methodological problems. There have, however, been at least two efforts to inquire carefully into the existence and extent of inaccurate application of insanity criteria.

Roby (1978) summarized an unpublished study of 350 persons acquitted on insanity grounds in Michigan trials before September, 1974. The study purported to evaluate abuse and was based upon examinations of the acquittees following their post-acquittal referral to the Center for Forensic Psychiatry. Thirty percent, he reported, had no mental disorder more "serious" than a personality disorder. Fifty percent evidenced some level of more serious disorder but no causal relationship between the disorder and the criminal conduct. The obvious conclusion that only 20% of those acquitted were "legitimately" found to be both disordered and exculpable, Roby declared, constituted "documented abuse" of the insanity defense (p. 375).

In 1978, the New York Department of Mental Hygiene, at the request of New York Governor Hugh Carey, prepared a report on the administration of the insanity defense in that jurisdiction (New York Department of Mental Hygiene, 1978). This included a study of persons acquitted on insanity grounds in the past. The report concluded that insanity acquittees included a number of sub-groups of persons neither "medically psychotic nor legally insane." Specifically, the study noted sub-groups composed of mothers shown to have killed their children and police officers who killed in response to "personal problems." These acquittals, the report concluded, must be explained on grounds other than a logical application of criminal responsibility criteria (p. 71). In a sense, then, the report offered evidence of "abuse" of the defense in practice.

Whether these reports are entitled to much weight is problematic. It is uncertain whether either study used accurate criteria for determining either disorder, causality, or both. Inquiry may also not have adequately addressed the subjects' conditions at the time of the conduct. Effective mental health intervention following the offense may have resulted in remission of symptoms that would otherwise have provided some support for the legal disposition (Criss & Racine, 1980).

SUMMARY

By the time of the *Hinckley* trial, then, the longstanding concern with integrating volitional impairment into responsibility evaluations had resulted in a clear trend towards acceptance of the American Law Institute's formulation of the defense. Under this formulation, substantial loss of volitional capacity constitutes an alternative to cognitive incapacity as a basis for the complete defense. Despite continuing concern with "abuse" of the defense, uncertainty as to how particular cases "should" be resolved under particular formulations of the criteria made evaluation of claims of abuse difficult. There was little serious suggestion, however, that opening the defense to claims of volitional incapacity presented an exceptionally dangerous opportunity for abuse.

Psychological Incapacity and Mens Rea

The evidentiary and conceptual relationship, if any, of criminal defendants' psychological abnormality to the state of mind requirements of various offenses has been a longstanding problem for American criminal law. By the time of the *Hinckley* trial, a number of jurisdictions permitted defendants—under what was often called a "diminished capacity" doctrine—to pursue claims that their abnormality prevented them from having the *mens rea* required by the definition of the crime charged. This doctrine was sometimes viewed as mandated by the logical significance of the substantive criminal law's demand that defendants be shown to have acted with certain states of mind for criminal liability to be appropriate. It was also regarded by some as attractive, however, because it served to circumvent limits which narrow insanity criteria imposed upon the accommodation of defendants' impairment and their criminal liability. In addition, it was perceived as providing for an accommodation that avoided the all-or-nothing decision required by the insanity defense.

Use of impairment to "disprove" the presence of required *mens rea* was also available as an alternative to a defense of insanity or nonresponsibility as a major or sole method of integrating abnormality and responsibility. Careful examination of the diminished capacity doctrine, however, may help explain why proposals to use it as the sole method of accommodating impairment and responsibility were unfavorably received. In part, this may have been because of continuing confusion as to the conceptual relationship between insanity and diminished capacity. In addition, however, diminished capacity presented sufficient problems, as a means of serving its ancillary functions, to reduce its attractiveness as the sole vehicle for integrating impairment and responsibility.

CONCEPTUAL RELATIONSHIP
BETWEEN *MENS REA* AND INSANITY

Early discussions of insanity often assumed that the entire insanity "defense" was merely a vehicle for organizing a defendant's ability to contest the existence of the state of mind required for the crime charged. Since there is universal agreement that the prosecution has the burden of proof on mental state as well as other elements of liability,

this might be more accurately stated as a vehicle for challenging the adequacy of the prosecution's proof of *mens rea*, specifically by producing affirmative evidence of psychological abnormality suggesting the absence of the required mental state.

This position is, however, an oversimplification. Under some constructions of the "right-wrong" test, it is arguable that the insanity "defense" does no more than specifically provide for a defendant to show he lacked the state of mind required by the crime charged. Insofar as state of mind requires awareness of the nature of conduct and the pendency of results, one who was rendered unable to know the "nature" of his actions arguably lacked the conscious understanding required for liability. Furthermore, one whose factual misunderstanding was such that, under the circumstances as he supposed them to be, his actions would be legally permissible, had arguably lost the capacity to know the wrongfulness—that is, the criminality—of his conduct.

But if the insanity defense provides defendants with broader options, it clearly goes beyond mere "disproof" of *mens rea*, at least as that is currently defined. Some have disagreed; Mueller (1961, pp. 115–16), for example, asserted that "*mens rea* is a unity of cognition and volition." But as the concept of state of mind has developed in American substantive criminal law during the last 20 years, it is limited to a defendant's conscious apprehension of factual matters. To the extent that insanity permits a defendant to establish volitional impairment, it puts into issue a matter not addressed by state of mind requirements. Further, *mens rea* ordinarily does not require awareness of legal requirements or that one's conduct violate those requirements. If the insanity defense permits a defendant to show that, by reason of impairment, he was unable to develop an adequate cognitive understanding of the social, ethical, or moral implications of his conduct, this also goes beyond matters logically related to *mens rea* requirements.

Conceptually, the insanity defense has become a vehicle for putting into issue in criminal litigation matters that are otherwise simply placed beyond the scope of dispute. In the absence of an insanity issue, the prosecution has the burden of proving all elements of the crime, including any mental elements. But there is no need for the proof to address the defendant's ability to control his conduct, that is, to act upon his conscious perceptions, or to evaluate the moral or ethical implications of his conduct. If—but only if—the insanity defense is raised do these matters become the subject of dispute. In the absence of indicators of abnormality, they are simply "presumed" in a conclusive sense.

DEVELOPMENT OF "DIMINISHED
CAPACITY" AS A SEPARATE "DEFENSE"

By the early 20th century, some American courts had accepted the argument that a defendant's psychological abnormality could, apart from its significance on the insanity issue, also—or alternatively—form the basis for a challenge to the adequacy of proof of *mens rea*. This appears to have originated in prosecutions for first-degree premeditated murder, in which evidence of the accused's impairment was offered to contest the state's proof that the accused engaged in the requisite premeditation before killing. Integrating this use of evidence of psychological impairment with the defense of insanity has given rise to considerable doctrinal and procedural difficulty.

A defendant charged with premeditated murder who is not shown to have premeditated will almost always be shown to have nevertheless killed in a fashion constituting a lesser included homicide offense. Apparently because such use of psychological abnormality was intended to secure conviction but only for an offense less than that charged, it was sometimes referred to as "partial" responsibility. Its effect, under this approach, was to establish lack of "responsibility" for the more serious offense but not to preclude conviction for a lesser included offense.

Logically, of course, there is no reason why evidence of psychological abnormality need be limited to challenging proof of premeditation or, for that matter, only states of mind required by those crimes with lesser included offenses. If, however, the doctrine permitted a defendant to challenge the adequacy of proof that he had the states of mind required by any of the offenses under which he could be convicted, the doctrine then became difficult to distinguish from the insanity defense.

In large part to preserve a distinction between the two doctrines, those courts that permitted evidence of abnormality to be used to challenge state of mind held or indicated that this use would be permitted only when the state of mind challenged was a "specific intent." This approach had the benefit of limiting use of impairment to those situations where the defendant could be convicted of a lesser included offense. Thus the doctrine

would not completely exculpate the defendant and could be distinguished from the insanity defense which, of course, would have this effect. It also, however, suffered the disadvantage of incorporating all of the considerable uncertainties regarding the definition of "specific intent."

The doctrine has frequently been labeled "diminished capacity," although the rationale for this is not clear. Expert testimony under the doctrine is often to the effect that the defendant, because of his impairment, lacked the capacity to formulate or harbor the mental state at issue. It would follow, whether or not the witness specifically articulates this, that since the defendant lacked the capacity to have the state of mind involved, he did not in fact have that state of mind at the time of the conduct. But there seems to be no reason why this is the only format in which testimony can be produced. A mental health professional may, for example, be unwilling to make a blanket statement that the defendant was incapable of formulating a particular mental state. He may, however, offer the opinion that in the particular circumstances at issue the defendant did not in fact form the required mental state. Whether the expert's inability to testify in terms that involve an intermediate conclusion that the subject lacked the "capacity" to form the mental state at issue will render his testimony inadmissible is uncertain but most unlikely.

Those courts that have accepted the doctrine have often explained its acceptance in terms of simple logical relevancy—if evidence is logically related to proof of an element of the offense charged, it should be admitted. But it is widely perceived that the doctrine is attractive because it tends to mitigate the apparent harshness of a limited insanity defense. While evidence of volitional and other impairments not meeting the stringent insanity standard cannot be used to exculpate, they can—under this doctrine—reduce the severity of the offense for which the defendant can be convicted. The California Supreme Court acknowledged this in *People* v. *Henderson* (1963).

Courts rejecting the doctrine, on the other hand, have generally explained in conclusory terms that the insanity defense is and should be the sole vehicle for accommodating evidence of impairment and criminal liability. This, of course, is ultimately a major modification of *mens rea* doctrine. In effect, the *mens rea* requirement becomes limited to unimpaired defendants. The definition of the offense charged functionally requires certain mental states, unless the defendant is mentally impaired. In those situations, it is suf-ficient—perhaps—that the defendant would have had the state of mind required for the offense charged except for his impairment. Perhaps under-standably, courts have been unwilling to openly acknowledge that such a major modification of *mens rea* law is a logically necessary result of their rejection of the diminished capacity approach.

Rejection of the doctrine can be explained in other terms. Arguably, in practice it is widely abused, with defendants using it to put before juries extensive but confusing testimony that seldom logically tends to show absence of *mens rea*. In some cases, the doctrine permits logically relevant issues to be raised concerning state of mind. But it is so subject to abuse that, on bal-ance, it is appropriate to exclude all such evidence to avoid the extensive abuse and confusion that would otherwise result.

THE MODEL PENAL CODE AND STATUTORY FORMULATIONS

The final draft of the Model Penal Code contin-ued the conceptual confusion in this area. After promulgating its provision for "mental disease or defect excluding responsibility," the Code then offered as an apparently independent provision:

> Evidence that the defendant suffered from a mental disease or defect shall be admissible whenever it is relevant to prove that the defendant did or did not have a state of mind which is an element of the offense. (Ameri-can Law Institute, 1962, Section 4.02[1])

The commentary recognized a sharp division of authority on the matter. Nevertheless, it defended the position taken only in a conclusory manner, characterizing it as a logical consequence of the Code's requirements of states of mind for criminal liability (Commentary to Section 4.01[1], p. 193). In the commentary, at least, there is no indication that the drafters saw any potential conflict or over-lap between the provision at issue and the defense of insanity. Nor is there any suggestion that the drafters were sensitive to any reasons why evidence of impairment should not be given its apparently logically relevant significance.

The language of Section 4.02[1] would appear to sweep away the limitations placed on the doc-trine by some of the decisions. The Code's culpa-bility provisions, of course, were designed to supplant concepts such as "specific intent." Conse-quently, no limitation of the rule to so-called spe-cific intent offenses could have been intended. But neither the language used nor the context suggests any other limitation, such as to those states of mind for which purpose is required. The only requirement for evidence admissibility appears to be logical relevancy. No need exists, therefore, for the testimony to involve a preliminary conclusion of *incapacity* to form the state of mind at issue.

The Model Penal Code approach has been adopted in a number of American jurisdictions. Provision is therefore made both for a nonrespon-sibility "defense" and for consideration of impair-ment as bearing upon whether the defendant acted with the requisite intent, where the evi-dence of impairment logically tends to suggest that the defendant lacked that intent.

DIMINISHED "RESPONSIBILITY": THE CALIFORNIA EXPERIMENT

Among the advantages that its proponents have found in the use of impairment evidence on *mens rea* is the possibility of ameliorating what is re-garded as the inflexible "all or nothing" choice required by the traditional insanity defense. If a defendant's impairment can be used to reduce the seriousness of the offense for which he is liable, the end result may be to give recognition to what some regard as the frequently encountered situa-tion where impairment reduces but does not eliminate culpability.

One difficulty encountered in pursuing this po-tential advantage is that the doctrine ties responsi-bility to existing substantive criminal law *mens rea* requirements. Even if particular conduct is covered by a number of different offenses dif-ferentiated primarily by the offender's mental state at the time of the criminal conduct (such as criminal homicide), those mental states may not be tailored to distinguishing among offenders based upon their psychological impairments and the effect of these impairments upon their culpa-bility. State of mind requirements are ordinarily formulated for purposes of application to normal persons. That they might also serve well the very different function of grading abnormal offenders would be, at best, fortuitous. (Dix, 1971).

The problem is especially great regarding voli-tional impairments. If volitional impairments are irrelevant to a jurisdiction's insanity defense or if a particular defendant's impairment was insuf-ficient to exculpate under that defense, might the impaired volition nevertheless under diminished capacity justify a reduction in the severity of the offense for which the defendant may be convicted? If mental states address only the actor's conscious state of mind and not volition, of course, state of mind requirements hold little promise as a vehicle for reducing liability because of impaired volition.

The California Supreme Court enthusiastically embraced diminished capacity in part as a means of mitigating the effect of its continued adherence to the right-wrong criterion for the defense of insanity. It also, however, quite clearly sought to utilize the doctrine as a means of providing graded responsibility in one limited area, criminal homicide. When this effort floundered on the nature of the *mens rea* requirements for the various California homicide offenses, the court responded by undertaking to redevelop the definition of those offenses so as to more effectively provide for graded responsibility in view of offenders' impairments, including impairments of volitional capacity. It is possible, then, to regard the California cases as a test of the law's ability to use diminished capacity as a means of providing for gradations of liability based upon degrees of impairment.

In *People* v. *Wolff* (1964) the California Supreme Court held that first-degree premeditated murder required that the defendant "maturely and meaningfully reflect upon the gravity of" the contemplated killing, and that this be done with adequate realization of the "enormity" of the nature of the act. If a defendant's psychological impairment caused his reflection or realization to materially fall below this requirement, he had not engaged in the process which the first-degree murder statute required. What sort of effect an impairment must have to preclude liability for first-degree murder was not made clear. The court's language suggests a conclusory standard—was the effect "relevant to appraising the quantum of [the defendant's] moral turpitude and depravity?"

Under California law, a killing not first-degree murder might be either second-degree murder or manslaughter. In *People* v. *Conley* (1966) the California court addressed the requirement of malice aforethought for second-degree murder, which distinguishes murder from manslaughter. Malice, the court held, requires "an awareness of the obligation to act within the general body of laws regulating society," and this can be absent because of a defendant's psychological impairment. If awareness of this obligation is absent, the killing is, at most, manslaughter.

Both *Wolff* and *Conley* dealt with requirements that might not be met in a particular case because of impairment of the defendant's cognitive capacities. In *People* v. *Poddar* (1974), however, the California tribunal held that malice aforethought also required that the defendant be able to act within the law. If, because of his impairment, he was unable to act in accordance with what he perceived was his duty to act within the laws regulating society, he would be guilty of only manslaughter. *Poddar* reflected the court's effort to grade defendants' liability for homicide by reference in part to any psychological impairment—including volitional impairment—they may have experienced at the time of the death-causing conduct.

Whether these major judicial embellishments of statutory definitions accomplished their purpose is problematic. A defendant whose abnormality caused him to not adequately reflect upon the significance of a contemplated killing or to realize the enormity of the evil involved would have his liability "reduced" from first-degree to second-degree murder. This would, among other results, preclude application of the death penalty. A defendant whose abnormality rendered him unaware of his duty to act within the law or unable to act in accordance with that duty, on the other hand, would have his liability further "reduced" to manslaughter. All of these situations were distinguishable from the defendants whose impairments rendered them totally nonresponsible under the right-wrong test. Further, since the California court at the time of *Poddar* continued to reject lack of control as a "defense," it may have been that the loss of capacity to control one's conduct under *Poddar*, which would "reduce" responsibility, was distinguishable from the volitional impairment that in other jurisdictions would preclude liability, because this continued to be "irrelevant" under California law. The lines that this scheme suggests may be impossible to draw in practice. Or, if they can be drawn, they may not adequately reflect culpability appropriately reduced (but not destroyed) because of psychological impairment.

Whatever the merits, the California scheme has been dramatically rejected by that state's legislature. In 1981, the California homicide statutes were amended so as to specifically provide:

To prove [a first degree murder] was "deliberate and premeditated," it shall not be necessary to prove the defendant maturely and meaningfully reflected upon the gravity of his or her act. (California Laws, 1981, codified as California Penal Code, Section 189)

Further, the provision defining second degree murder was amended to include:

An awareness of the obligation to act within the general body of laws regulating society is not included within the definition of malice. (California Laws, 1981, codified as California Penal Code Sec. 188)

The following year this provision was further amended to provide that "acting despite such awareness" is similarly not included within the definition of malice. In addition, the legislation provided that on the trial of a defendant's guilt or innocence:

Evidence that the accused lacked the capacity or ability to control his conduct for any reason shall not be admissible on the issue of whether the accused actually had any mental state with respect to the commission of any crime. (California Laws, 1982, codified as California Penal Code Sec. 21[b])

Whatever clarity these statutory amendments might have provided, however, was arguably offset by other aspects of the 1981 legislation. After declaring that "as a matter of public policy there shall be no defense of diminished capacity, diminished responsibility, or irresistible impulse in a criminal action," the legislation added the following sections:

Evidence of mental disease, mental defect, or mental disorder shall not be admitted to negate the capacity to form any mental state, including, but not limited to, purpose, intent, knowledge, or malice aforethought, with which the accused committed the act. Evidence of mental disease, mental defect, or mental disorder is admissible on the issue as to whether the criminal defendant actually formed any such mental state.

In the guilt phase of a criminal action, any expert testifying about a defendant's mental illness, mental disorder, or mental

defect shall not testify as to whether the defendant had or did not have the required mental states . . . for the crimes charged. The question as to whether the defendant had or did not have the required mental states shall be decided by the trier of fact. (California Laws, 1981, codified as California Penal Code Sections 28, 29)

The first appears to prohibit evidence tending to show the lack of *capacity* to form an intent but not evidence tending to show that the defendant did not *in fact* form that state of mind. The second would seem to bar a defense witness from expressing an opinion phrased in terms of whether or not the defendant did in fact form a given state of mind. Perhaps the bottom line is that a defendant is entitled to produce evidence and argue that because of his impairment he did not in fact harbor the state of mind required by the crime charged. Evidence may not, however, tend to show *incapacity* to form the state of mind and expert witnesses may not express an opinion on the question of whether the defendant in fact failed to develop the awareness required.

Evaluation of the California experiment is difficult. It strongly suggests, however, that even in regard to homicide offenses traditional substantive criminal law renders modern statutory frameworks awkward vehicles for grading liability according to defendants' psychological impairments. This difficulty is substantially increased if volitional impairment is to be integrated into the grading process. Whether the efforts to modify the substantive law of homicide to better accomplish this goal were practical is uncertain. Their unqualified rejection by the state's legislature, however, makes clear that they were immensely unpopular.

CONSTITUTIONAL CONSIDERATIONS

The constitutional issues presented by various substantive criminal law positions on psychological abnormality and state of mind requirements are more complex than the constitutional status of the basic insanity defense issues. Greater difficulty exists in conceptualizing the issues, and this may account for the inadequacies of the judicial discussions. The major question can be posed as follows: May a state, consistent with federal constitutional requirements, adopt requirements of various mental states for criminal liability but also bar defendants from utilizing certain evidence related to psychological impairment in litigating whether those mental states have been proven? Such a position may deprive a defendant of a fair opportunity to contest proof of guilt, as required by due process of law. Since other defendants may introduce other evidence to challenge the prosecution's proof of intent, the bar may operate to deprive some defendants of equal protection of state law. Finally, the bar's operative effect may constitute a deprivation of a defendant's Sixth Amendment right to produce evidence in his own defense at trial.

The United States Supreme Court confronted certain claims related to diminished capacity in *Fisher* v. *United States* (1946). At his trial for first-degree premeditated murder, Fisher produced expert testimony concerning his impairments— psychopathic aggressive tendencies, low emotional responses, and borderline mental deficiency. But the trial judge refused to instruct the jury that in determining the defendant's capacity for, and fact of, premeditation and deliberation, it should consider, among other things, his psychological abnormalities; this was consistent with the judicial decisions of the local courts of the District of Columbia, in which the case arose. No constitutional issue was raised by the defendant or perceived by the Court. "In view of the status of the defense of partial responsibility . . . ," the Court commented, "no contention is or could be made of the denial of due process" (p. 466). Turning to the "substantive" question of whether it should change the rule prohibiting consideration of the defense evidence on premeditation, the Court clearly did not perceive the issue as merely one of whether "logically relevant" evidence should be considered. Instead, it again characterized the defense argument as one for adoption of a concept of "partial responsibility," a "fundamental" and "radical" change from common law notions of criminal responsibility. Such changes in substantive criminal law, where experience has not shown the existing position to be fallacious or unwise, are for the legislature or the local courts, rather than the Supreme Court.

Fisher did not require the Court to address the constitutional necessity of what is essentially the Model Penal Code position. There are some lower court indications that as so defined the issue might go in defendants' favor. In *Hughes* v. *Matthews* (1978), for example, the Seventh Circuit held that Wisconsin's refusal to regard psychiatric expert testimony as relevant to state of mind deprived

the state defendant of his federal right to present a defense. More recently, in *Hendershott* v. *People* (1982) the Colorado Supreme Court considered constitutional challenges to its statute under which evidence of impaired mental condition could be used only to contest the existence of "specific intents." At his trial for recklessly causing bodily injury to another, the defendant was precluded from presenting expert testimony to the effect that because of adult minimal brain dysfunction he lacked the recklessness required by the offense charged because no "specific intent" was at issue. Exclusion of such "reliable and relevant mental impairment" evidence to negate the culpability element, the court reasoned, violated Hendershott's right to due process of law (p. 394).

Perhaps the most important defense of the contrary position is that of the Wisconsin Supreme Court in *Steele* v. *State* (1980). Despite its position that expert testimony is to remain admissible on criminal responsibility, the court rejected the analysis of *Hughes* v. *Matthews*, and concluded that there were important interests that justified rejecting such evidence when offered on state of mind. Most importantly, the court reasoned that the two issues were different and expert testimony on intent was less reliable than that bearing on responsibility. Therefore, the state's interest in excluding evidence unlikely to contribute to a fair and accurate resolution of the issues justified exclusion of expert mental health professional testimony offered on the state of mind issue.

Explaining, the court reasoned that criminal responsibility or insanity is "essentially a moral issue." It requires only "a gross evaluation that a person's conduct and mental state is so beyond the limits of accepted norms that to hold him criminally responsible would be unjust"; no "fine tuning" is required. On this issue, expert testimony is sufficiently reliable to warrant admission. But determining whether a defendant had, at a previous time, the ability to form various states of mind "requires a fine tuning of an entirely different nature." On this issue, expert testimony is insufficiently scientifically sound. Given the risks of such evidence and the difficulty of effective cross-examination, exclusion of such evidence is justified.

NEGATION OF *MENS REA* AS THE SOLE IMPAIRMENT DEFENSE

As might be expected, some have urged that the effect of mental impairment in criminal liability be limited to the significance given to it under the so-called diminished capacity doctrine, that is, that impairment be relevant to criminal liability only if it shows the absence of the *mens rea* required by the crime charged. In 1915, for example, a special committee of the American Institute of Criminal Law and Criminology proposed that the insanity defense be formulated specifically as barring conviction only when the defendant, by reason of mental disease, did not have "the particular state of mind" required by the crime at issue. (Keedy, 1917, p. 536). Professor Keedy suggested that this formulation would return insanity law to its original and logical position. Insanity had become divorced from state of mind requirements, he urged, only because of unfortunate efforts to formulate and apply "medical" tests for determining responsibility (p. 735). The proposal appears to have attracted little judicial or legislative attention, however.

The most serious efforts to embody this approach in responsibility law occurred in connection with efforts to codify and reform federal substantive criminal law during the 1970s.

Professor David Robinson's consultant's report (Robinson, 1970) to the National Commission on Reform of the Federal Criminal Laws urged adoption of this approach. The Commission, however, rejected this in favor of the Model Penal Code's formulation (National Commission on Reform of the Federal Criminal Laws, 1971 p. 40). The Nixon Administration's counterproposal to the Commission's report—what is often referred to as "Senate Bill 1"—proposed enactment of Professor Robinson's suggestion. President Nixon characterized this as "the most significant feature" of his proposed revisions (Dershowitz, 1973, p. 435). Neither proposal, however, was accepted by Congress, which simply did not act on the matter of criminal responsibility.

In 1978, another proposal was made at the state level. In that year, the New York Department of Mental Hygiene report urged adoption of a version of the *mens rea* approach in that jurisdiction. Under the proposed approach, evidence of a defendant's impaired mental condition at the time of the offense would be admissible only if the offense charged was one requiring either intent or knowledge and, when so admitted, would be no more than evidence bearing upon whether the accused acted with either intent or knowledge. (New York State Department of Mental Hygiene, 1978, pp. 8–9).

This approach, the report reasoned, would accommodate the need to give impairment some mitigating significance. By seldom permitting complete exoneration of all criminal liability, however, it would leave those persons found to have engaged in dangerous conduct within the criminal justice system. This would avoid the disruption which the committee found resulted from the diversion of certain offenders. All but three defendants acquitted on insanity grounds during the preceding 10 years, the study found, would be candidates for conviction on a reduced charge under the proposal.

Montana is the only American jurisdiction that, before *Hinckley*, adopted the *mens rea* approach as the sole means of exculpating impaired defendants. In that jurisdiction, 1967 legislation embodied the Model Penal Code criteria for nonresponsibility and for diminished capacity (Montana Laws, 1967). In 1977, the legislature repealed the provision for a defense of mental impairment. This left only a statutory provision authorizing consideration of mental impairment in determining whether *mens rea* was proven. (Montana Laws, 1977, codified as Montana Revised Codes Annotated, Sec. 46-14-102).

Opposition to exclusive reliance upon disproof of *mens rea* has been based largely upon the proposition that this would fail to provide a means of exculpating many offenders who, because of their impairment, are not blameworthy and thus do not warrant the moral condemnation inherent in conviction. Evaluation, of course, is difficult because of the uncertainty as to the meaning of even those formulations of the defense that have received widespread acceptance in American jurisdictions. Insofar as it is perceived that the defense should provide for nonresponsibility because of volitional impairment, of course, this alternative fails to so provide. Thus it is subject to the same objections leveled against the traditional right-wrong insanity criteria.

If it is agreed that only cognitive impairments should give rise to exculpation, however, the issue becomes more difficult. The offender whose disorder caused him to fundamentally misperceive the situation may be entitled to acquittal under both alternatives. Most commonly mentioned in discussion is the person who causes the death of another by strangling the victim under the disorder-induced misperception that the object in his hands is a lemon. But such situations are seldom if ever confronted in criminal litigation.

If an offender believes, because of disorder-induced delusions or hallucinations, that facts exist which render his conduct legally justifiable, the situation is different. One may kill, for example, under the delusion that one's victim is engaged in a deadly assault. Those facts, if accurate, would probably entitle one to kill in self-defense. Under the right-wrong test, a defendant who kills in response to a disorder-induced belief in such facts is probably entitled to acquittal. Under the *mens rea* approach, however, he would not be. Self-defense is not part of the *mens rea* requirements of criminal homicide but is, rather, part of that body of law addressing defenses. Again, however, defendants who can establish that their impairment gave rise to such beliefs may be seldom encountered in practice.

Beyond these situations, the difference in the approaches becomes clouded. Whether a defendant who, because of his impairment, experiences a perception that his conduct is somehow generally justified is entitled to acquittal under the right-wrong test is unclear. Almost certainly no acquittal is required in those jurisdictions phrasing the criterion in terms of a loss of ability to "know" or "understand" the "criminality"—as contrasted with "wrongfulness"—of one's actions. Under a logical application of the *mens rea* approach, however, acquittal would be clearly inappropriate.

SUMMARY

Dissatisfaction with the all-or-nothing choice posed by the insanity defense, the criteria for applying that defense (which were viewed as narrow—including some that excluded volitional impairment), and a perception of logical necessity, combined to encourage acceptance of the doctrine of "diminished capacity." A substantial number of American jurisdictions rejected it, however. To some extent, such rejections were based on the ground that recognition of the doctrine would be inconsistent with the defense of insanity. Even where it was accepted, it appears to have proven an inappropriate vehicle for accommodating claims of volitional impairment not permitted under the jurisdiction's insanity criterion. The California Supreme Court's confusing effort to overcome these difficulties has recently been rejected by that state's legislature.

Several serious proposals were made before *Hinckley* to use the evidentiary significance of impairment on *mens rea* as the sole vehicle for accommodating impairment and criminal liability. But only one jurisdiction embraced this approach. The complexities and uncertainties of the

meaning of the diminished responsibility approach in application undoubtedly gave rise to much of the unwillingness to place sole reliance upon it to perform what was almost universally agreed to be a necessary and important task. Suggestions in the case law that the doctrine might permit impairment to be used only where the crime charged was one requiring proof of a "specific" intent carried an especially disturbing hint that exclusive reliance upon the *mens rea* approach might deny defendants charged with "non-specific intent" offenses any means of presenting their impairment as a basis for exculpation.

"Partial Responsibility": An Untried Alternative

The interest in diminished capacity has been based in significant part upon a perception that American responsibility law might appropriately provide for reducing the seriousness of the crime for which a defendant may be convicted where the defendant was psychologically impaired at the time he acted although not so impaired as to warrant exculpation. Despite this apparent interest in providing for partial or reduced responsibility, however, there has been little or no interest in directly pursuing this objective by adoption of a general provision for "partial responsibility."

Given the disputes in American law concerning nonresponsibility, such a provision would seem to have substantial merit. To the extent that there are persuasive reasons for denying defendants an opportunity for exculpation on the basis of volitional impairment, for example, it may be an acceptable compromise to extend them the opportunity to achieve a reduction in the seriousness of the offense on this basis. In other situations, impairment not sufficiently "serious" to justify exculpation for other reasons might reasonably be regarded as indicating reduced blameworthiness sufficiently enough to demand recognition. Partial responsibility, of course, would eliminate the perhaps unfortunate need to choose between "full" responsibility and no responsibility created by defendants' assertion of insanity as a defense.

Traditionally, the lack of interest in this possibility might be explained in part by the absence of a comprehensive statutory framework governing criminal liability. The absence of such a framework may make incorporation of a general provision for graded responsibility quite difficult. But in recent years many American jurisdictions have developed relatively coherent codes that place all offenses in one of a limited number of categories distinguished by the applicable penalties. Such codes would readily permit the incorporation of a further provision mandating that an offense should be reduced to the next lower category upon a finding by the trier of fact that the defendant, although not insane at the time of the crime, was sufficiently impaired to reduce his responsibility. Even under the more traditional schemes, this same result could be accomplished by providing that upon such a determination, the penalty is limited to, for example, two-thirds of that generally provided for upon conviction of the offense. (Dix & Sharlot, 1973, pp. 1318–19). These possibilities, however, appear to have attracted virtually no serious legislative consideration.

The reasons for this are not at all clear. Perhaps, however, the matter of gradation of liability is too subtle a matter to effectively compete for legislative attention, given other demands upon lawmaking bodies. The potential value of a scheme that would reduce but not eliminate culpability may appear to some courts when the tribunals are faced directly with cases in which such a scheme would make an important difference. But in the abstract, the merits of such a proposal are overshadowed by issues such as the proper formulation of the insanity defense criteria.

Sentencing and "Diminished" Responsibility

Critics of American procedures for inquiring into defendants' responsibility have often suggested that a more rational approach to the matter would consist of regarding any psychological impairments, including those bearing upon defendants' volitional impairments, as relevant to— and perhaps only as relevant to—disposition or sentencing. The procedural context during sentencing is generally less rigid, so barriers to full development of information might be reduced. Since there is often great discretion in sentencing, the accommodation between impairment and penalty would not require the all-or-nothing choice posed by assertion of an insanity defense. And since sentencing is often a responsibility of the trial judge rather than the jury, the accommodation would be made by a person who might be expected to be more receptive to matters that lay jurors might find too complex to assimilate.

In the large number of situations in which sentencing authorities have long had discretion in regard to sentence, evidence of such impairment has been regarded as relevant to sentence. But this has had little impact upon formal law for several reasons. First, the sentencing alternatives available to American sentencing authorities seldom included nonpenal commitments to treatment facilities. Trial judges probably have authority to make receipt of treatment a condition of probation. Since dispositions involving institutionalization in treatment institutions were seldom available, however, there was relatively little incentive for defendants to vigorously assert reduced responsibility during sentencing.

More importantly, American sentencing procedure has traditionally been largely unstructured. Criteria for invoking various alternatives and for determining the severity of chosen alternatives have seldom been formalized or articulated. Proponents of mental health professional involvement in sentencing, of course, have regarded this lack of structure as an advantage. Mental health input at this stage, unlike that at the guilt-innocence stage, need not be elicited in terms of a legal standard with which mental health professionals may have discomfort. But the absence of specific structural provision for addressing reduced responsibility in sentencing has probably led defense lawyers to overlook the potential value of such evidence. To the extent that it has been used, moreover, its utilization has been a low visibility process and for that reason has attracted little attention.

Several recent developments have changed this somewhat. One is the federal constitutional demand for structure in capital sentencing. Another is the trend towards "presumptive" sentencing and the resulting structure in noncapital sentencing. Both make provision for consideration of impairments of responsibility insufficient to constitute defenses, and thus might be regarded as providing for partial nonresponsibility in the sentencing context.

CAPITAL SENTENCING

Under traditional statutory schemes, the penalty of death was available only upon conviction of specifically designated offenses; first-degree murder, under schemes that distinguished two degrees of the offense, was the major example. But the procedure for addressing the penalty issue was almost entirely unstructured.

In *Furman* v. *Georgia* (1972), the United States

Supreme Court held that imposition of the death penalty under this traditional framework violated the prohibition against cruel and unusual punishment in the Eighth Amendment to the United States Constitution. *Gregg* v. *Georgia* (1976) and its companion cases made reasonably clear that the Court would demand that capital punishment schemes permit sentencing authorities—whether they be judges or juries—to exercise discretion in choosing life or death but also that this discretion be directed and limited. It is still not entirely clear precisely what this mandate requires. But two subsequent decisions, *Lockett* v. *Ohio* (1978) and *Enmund* v. *Florida* (1982), strongly suggest that capital sentencing schemes must permit sentencing authorities to consider, in mitigation of penalty, potentially extenuating aspects of the offense for which the penalty is being imposed and the offender who has been convicted of it.

Among the most common methods of complying with what appears to be the federal constitutional requirement have been sentencing statutes that set out lists of potentially aggravating and mitigating considerations. Following conviction of a capital offense, a sentencing hearing is held at which both the prosecution and the defense are entitled to introduce evidence. Either side, of course, may offer evidence supporting the penalty which it urges and in rebuttal of evidence offered by the other side. The sentencing authority is sometimes required to specifically determine what aggravating and mitigating circumstances have been established. In any case, these are to be considered in making the life-or-death decision. Under some schemes, a penalty of death is permissible only if the sentencing authority determines that at least one aggravating circumstance exists and that the mitigating considerations, if any, do not outweigh the aggravating circumstances found.

None of the Supreme Court decisions to date have specifically addressed application of these general considerations to situations in which a defendant's case for mitigation rests in significant part upon a claim of psychological abnormality. It does seem reasonably clear, however, that such abnormality is a potentially mitigating consideration which the Eighth Amendment demands be given consideration. A number of capital sentencing schemes implement this constitutional mandate by specifically identifying what might usefully be regarded as a form of "partial irresponsibility" that must be considered in making the capital sentencing decision.

The Florida capital sentencing scheme is illustrative. Following conviction of a capital felony, a sentencing hearing is held; this is before a jury unless the jury is waived. If a jury hearing is held, the jury renders an advisory opinion as to the appropriate penalty, based upon whether any mitigating circumstances determined to exist outweigh any aggravating circumstances found. After any such advisory opinion is rendered, the trial judge must then determine sentence pursuant to the same criterion. If death is imposed, the decision must be supported by written findings of fact concerning aggravating and mitigating circumstances. Among the mitigating circumstances identified by the statute is that:

(f) The capacity of the defendant to appreciate the criminality of his conduct or to conform his conduct to the requirements of law was substantially impaired. (Florida Laws, 1972)

In regard to nonresponsibility as a defense to liability, Florida adheres to the "right-wrong" test. As a matter of doctrine, then, impairment of a capital defendant's volitional capacity is irrelevant before conviction. During the sentencing proceeding, however, this becomes an issue upon which both jury and judge may be required to pass and upon which written findings of fact, supported by the record, will be required if a penalty of death is imposed.

The hearing in *State* v. *Greenawalt* (1981), under the Arizona capital sentencing procedure, illustrates the sort of partial responsibility case that these statutes permit and arguably encourage. Greenawalt was convicted of four murders committed in the course of a prison escape. He was accompanied by one Gary Tison, a fellow inmate. At the sentencing hearing, a defense psychiatrist testified that in his opinion Greenawalt had a borderline organized personality structure. As a result, he episodically experienced breaks with reality "comparable to those that are found in the full blown psychotic illnesses." Because of his lack of self-identity, the witness continued, Greenawalt became submissive when placed around an authoritative figure such as Tison. As a result of his severe dependence on Tison and resulting relinquishment of autonomy, Greenawalt experienced a severe disability of judgment and ability to perceive reality. A state psychiatric witness, however, testified that he found no signs of psychotic behavior or extreme dependence in

Greenawalt and thus disagreed with the diagnosis made by the defense witness. The conflict in the testimony was resolved in the state's favor and this was upheld on appeal. But the result of the statutory scheme was clearly to make "partial nonresponsibility" a major issue in the sentencing hearing.

"STRUCTURED"
NONCAPITAL SENTENCING

Some recent changes in American sentencing structures reflect a disenchantment with the traditional assumption that unstructured flexibility in sentencing is inherently desirable. One side effect of the resulting trend towards increasing the amount of structure in noncapital sentencing is the potential creation of another form of "partial nonresponsibility" somewhat analagous to that created by some American capital sentencing schemes.

Among the noncapital sentencing structures that have gained in popularity during the recent reforms is so-called "presumptive" sentencing. Under this approach, a statute establishes a fixed term of imprisonment that is to be "presumed" appropriate. But a higher or lower term—again most likely specified in the statute—may be imposed if the prosecution or the defense establishes the existence of certain aggravating or mitigating circumstances. Establishment of these, in effect, rebuts the "presumption" that the general term is appropriate. Impairment of a defendant's responsibility, although insufficient to constitute a defense against liability, is often among the mitigating considerations that can be offered in support of an argument for a sentence below the presumptive one.

The Arizona sentencing scheme (Arizona Laws, 1977) is illustrative. Specific sentences are set out for offenses in different classes. But the sentencing judge is authorized to increase the sentence by up to 25% or reduce the sentence by up to 50% on the basis of aggravating and mitigating circumstances set out in the statute. Specific findings must be made on these circumstances and "reasons in support of such findings" must be set out in the record. Among the mitigating circumstances is the following:

2. The defendant's capacity to appreciate the wrongfulness of his conduct or to conform his conduct to the requirements of the law was significantly impaired, but not so impaired as to constitute a defense to prosecution. (Arizona Laws, 1977, codified as Arizona Revised Statutes Sec. 13-702[E][2])

Evidence of impaired responsibility would almost certainly also be relevant under more general provisions in other sentencing schemes. Under the Illinois statute, for example, among the factors in mitigation is:

(4) that there were substantial grounds tending to excuse or justify the defendant's criminal conduct, though failing to establish an excuse. (Illinois Laws, 1977)

SUMMARY: THE NEW
"DIMINISHED" RESPONSIBILITY

Those opposed to extensive provision for consideration of defendants' impairment in determining guilt or innocence have often agreed that such impairment might properly be considered in determining penalty following conviction. As some American jurisdictions have given more structure to the process for determining penalty, it is not surprising to find express provision being made for consideration of psychological impairment not of the seriousness or type sufficient to exonerate under the jurisdictions' insanity provisions.

Many of these provisions reflect continuing concern with volitional impairment, even if meritorious objections are found to considering it as a basis for complete exoneration. To the extent that sentencing is a function performed by the presiding judge rather than the jury, the provisions may reflect in part a concern that risks of abuse of such evidence can be reduced by making its consideration a matter for judges rather than jurors.

Given that evidence of a convicted defendant's psychological abnormality could traditionally be considered in choosing among penalties where discretion existed, what if anything is the long-run significance of the developments discussed above? At least two possibilities appear.

First, specific statutory provision for reduced or partial responsibility is likely to focus attention upon reduced responsibility in practice. This, in turn, is likely to increase the number of efforts to establish it. Accurately or not, defense lawyers will probably construe such statutory provisions as indicating that matters specifically enumerated are of special importance, even if those provisions merely codify what was permissible under earlier case law. Moreover, defense lawyers are likely to tailor their efforts in light of the statutory provisions. Efforts will be made, then, to have mitigating evidence directed to the statutory criteria. Defense evidence in mitigation is likely to be increasingly presented in terms of the statutory standard, that is, in terms of impairments affecting volition and understanding.

Second, the statutes and their emphasis upon findings is likely to increase appellate judicial discussions of issues of partial nonresponsibility. Under traditional law, the almost completely unstructured discretion trial judges (and juries) enjoyed in sentencing made appellate discussion of most sentencing subissues unnecessary. But the new structures are likely to give rise to viable appellate issues concerning such matters as the meaning of various terms in the criteria and the sufficiency of evidence to establish partial nonresponsibility as a mitigating consideration.

Verdict of "Guilty but Mentally Ill"

Another approach to accommodating criminal defendants' impairments that developed before the *Hinckley* acquittal is widely regarded as being based upon 1975 Michigan legislation providing for a new verdict of "guilty but mentally ill" (Michigan Laws, 1975). While the Michigan legislation undoubtedly has been the focus of recent discussion, earlier legislative efforts embodied much the same approach. The legislation (Mississippi Laws, 1928) at issue in *Sinclair* v. *State* (1931), for example, permitted the jury to find the defendant guilty but mentally ill and provided that this might have some effect upon the defendant's later correctional treatment.

The Michigan legislation was apparently an effort to reduce the number of what were perceived to be improper insanity acquittals without creating those problems presented by outright abolition of the insanity defense. Public and legislative sensitivity to insanity acquittals in the state had been raised by the results of a 1974 decision of the Michigan Supreme Court, *People* v. *Mcquillan*. In *Mcquillan*, the state's provision for automatic commitment of defendants found not guilty by reason of insanity was struck down as violative of equal protection demands. In the resulting process of reevaluating defendants committed under the invalidated procedure, a large number of these persons were administratively released because of doubt as to whether they could be shown to meet the legal standard for civil commitment. Two committed violent offenses soon after their

return to the community, stimulating demands for reform (Smith & Hall, 1982, pp. 82–83).

Under the Michigan scheme, a trial judge presiding over a jury trial in which the defense of insanity has been raised must, "where warranted by the evidence," instruct the jury on two alternatives to conviction or acquittal of the defendant. One, of course, is a verdict of not guilty by reason of insanity. The other is a verdict of guilty but mentally ill. The jury is to be further instructed that a verdict of guilty but mentally ill is to be returned only if it finds, beyond a reasonable doubt, that the defendant is guilty of the offense charged and that the defendant was mentally ill but not legally insane at the time of the commission of that offense. Mental illness, as used in this criterion, is defined as:

> a substantial disorder of thought or mood which significantly impairs judgment, behavior, capacity to recognize reality, or ability to cope with the ordinary demands of life.

A defendant who is found guilty but mentally ill is apparently not to be "convicted." He is, however, subject to any sentence which might be imposed upon conviction for the offense. If the defendant is committed to the Department of Corrections, "he shall undergo further evaluation and be given such treatment as is psychiatrically indicated for his mental illness or retardation." Should he be paroled, any treatment so recommended by the facility in which he was treated during incarceration is to be made a condition of parole. Failure to continue treatment is a basis for parole revocation.

When the Michigan scheme was proposed, opponents urged that it constituted a back-door abolition of the insanity defense. Juries would sometimes wish to have their verdict reflect the defendant's lack of culpability; in addition, however, jurors would be concerned with possible release following a verdict of not guilty by reason of insanity. In such situations, it was argued, juries would compromise on the guilty but mentally ill verdict. Even meritorious insanity claims would be rejected in favor of the more attractive verdict of guilty but mentally ill. The opportunity to "compromise" would be fraud upon the jury, it was further suggested, because contrary to the implied suggestion the compromise of guilty but not mentally ill would not in fact assure treatment following disposition.

These fears may have been unjustified. A recent study of the implementation of the Michigan scheme found that the scheme has not in fact reduced acquittals on insanity grounds (Smith & Hall, 1982, pp. 100–101). The study also concluded that defendants found guilty but mentally ill are not likely to receive more or better mental health care than defendants convicted and simply sentenced (pp. 104–105). It did suggest, however, that the legislative "promise" of treatment for a significant number of persons committed to correctional programs might stimulate a general improvement in the availability of mental health care to those in the correctional system (p. 106).

The danger of improper jury compromises is, of course, increased if juries cannot be adequately informed concerning objective criteria for choosing properly between verdicts of not guilty by reason of insanity and guilty but mentally ill. Whether the definitions of insanity and guilty but mentally ill permit juries to be adequately informed is somewhat problematic. Perhaps the definitions simply do not lend themselves to lay juror understanding. The Indiana Supreme Court, however, upheld that state's guilty but mentally ill scheme (which is similar to the Michigan provision described above) against a number of constitutional attacks, including the argument that the definitions are so vague as to create an unacceptable risk of arbitrary application. (*Taylor* v. *State*, 1982).

The United States Attorney General's Task Force on Violent Crime, in its *Final Report*, supported further use of the Michigan scheme (United States Department of Justice, 1981). Insanity acquittals, the report suggested, are sometimes irrational ones returned by juries that simply wish to express compassion concerning an accused's mental problems and have no method other than an insanity acquittal to do so (p. 54). Authorizing juries to return a verdict of guilty but mentally ill would reduce such improper acquittals on insanity grounds, the report reasoned, because it would give juries a more rational means of expressing the view that the defendant is impaired and should be treated while confined. Thus it recommended that the Attorney General support or propose legislation authorizing such a verdict in federal criminal cases.

Criss and Racine (1980) provide some basis for believing that the guilty but mentally ill verdict functions as intended. Following up on Roby (1978), discussed above, they concluded that after enactment of the guilty but mentally ill alternative in Michigan the percentage of insanity acquittees found to have no serious disorder decreased from 43.8% in 1974 to 12.1% in 1979. Insofar as Roby documented abuse of the insanity defense, Criss and Racine arguably documented reduction of that abuse after juries were given the option of finding impaired but responsible defendants guilty but mentally ill. Smith and Hall (1982), on the other hand, concluded that most defendants found guilty but mentally ill under the Michigan statute would, if that alternative had not been available, have simply been found guilty rather than not guilty by reason of insanity.

The Insanity Defense: Procedural Aspects

As with many doctrines of substantive criminal law, various procedural matters related to the implementation of the doctrines concerning criminal responsibility may be as important—or perhaps more important—than the substance of the doctrines themselves. Several procedural aspects of criminal responsibility gave rise to special pre-*Hinckley* concern.

BURDEN OF PROOF

Weihofen (pp. 212–13), writing in 1954, found that those American jurisdictions which had addressed the issue were about evenly split on the allocation of the burden of proof concerning insanity or its equivalent. In *Davis* v. *United States* (1895), the United States Supreme Court held that as a matter of substantive federal criminal law, the burden of proving responsibility is on the prosecution. As a result, a defendant is entitled to acquittal if the trier of fact entertains a reasonable doubt as to whether or not he was responsible. But in *Leland* v. *Oregon* (1952), the Court held that a state rule requiring a defendant to prove insanity by proof beyond a reasonable doubt did not deny a state defendant his federal constitutional right to due process of law.

In the intervening years, however, the Supreme Court has held that the due process clause of the Fourteenth Amendment protects the accused in a state criminal proceeding against conviction "except upon proof beyond a reasonable doubt of every fact necessary to constitute proof of the crime with which he is charged" (*In re Winship*, 1970). This imposes some limits upon the states' ability to shift to the defendant the burden of proof on various issues, but the nature of these limits is unclear (*Mullaney* v. *Wilbur*, 1975; *Patterson* v. *New York*, 1977).

The defense of insanity or nonresponsibility may be conceptualized as putting into issue the accuracy of basic assumptions concerning persons subject to the law—such as the presence of ability to control one's conduct—that are not ordinarily subject to dispute. Insofar as this is the case, a claim of nonresponsibility does not address the adequacy of proof of any element of the offense. Thus, under the apparent rationale of *Mullaney* and *Patterson*, it is a matter which federal constitutional standards do not require the prosecution to prove. But as was discussed earlier, at least some formulations of the defense can also be conceptualized as merely a formalization of a defendant's ability to challenge the proof of state of mind by offering evidence suggesting that he did not harbor the requisite state of mind. If the defense is so conceptualized, placement of the burden of proof on the defendant becomes much more difficult to justify in constitutional terms.

Perhaps, however, the burden of proof matter can be addressed as follows: Generally, the prosecution must and will have the burden of proving all elements, including ones related to the defendant's state of mind, beyond a reasonable doubt. When, however, the adequacy of the prosecution's case is challenged only by evidence relying upon purported psychological abnormality, special considerations come into play. The evidence and testimony are especially likely to be confusing and of minimal scientific reliability. If juries confronted with such evidence are told that they must acquit if this evidence raises a reasonable doubt, there may be an unacceptably high risk of unjustified acquittals due to what are actually "unreasonable" doubts generated simply by confusion. This risk justifies a limited rule which instructs juries as follows: When there is evidence satisfactory to prove that the defendant had the state of mind required by the crime charged and only evidence based on psychological abnormality suggests otherwise, the evidence based on psychological abnormality should control only if it preponderates over the other evidence.

There is some reason to believe that niceties such as nuances in the allocation of burdens among various issues may be of little practical importance in criminal litigation. Especially where interjection of an emotionally charged claim of nonresponsibility occurs during trial of a serious criminal charge, it may well be that jurors are so pervasively affected by other influences that the formal assignment of the burden of proof is of no significance. When the Supreme Court addressed the federal constitutional requirements relating to the burden of proof in civil commitment proceedings, it commented that "candor suggests" that efforts to determine what lay jurors will understand by instructions on burden of proof may be an academic exercise and that how standards of proof affect jury decisionmaking may be "unknowable" (*Addington* v. *Texas*, 1979).

DISPOSITION OF DEFENDANTS FOUND NONRESPONSIBLE

At common law, a defendant found to have been nonresponsible because of mental impairment was entitled to an unconditional acquittal. English legislation adopted in 1800, however, provided that an acquittal on insanity grounds was to be so designated in the jury verdict and a defendant so acquitted was to be committed until the Crown chose to release him. American jurisdictions adopted similar procedures during the 19th century (Weihofen, 1954, p. 362). These provisions differed widely ("Commitment Following an Insanity Acquittal," 1981, p. 605). Some mandated indefinite commitment upon the return of the acquittal. Some permitted but did not require such automatic commitments, while others required inquiry into the defendant's condition at the time of the acquittal and permitted commitment only upon a determination that he was then insane (pp. 366–67). The commitments, however, were generally indefinite. Release was possible in some jurisdictions at the discretion of hospital authorities but in others only upon authorization of the committing court (p. 376).

It is in regard to these provisions that judicial enforcement of federal constitutional requirements has had its most pervasive effect upon American criminal responsibility law. The United States Supreme Court had not, before the *Hinckley* acquittal, addressed commitments following responsibility acquittals. But in *Jackson* v. *Indiana* (1972), the Court found substantial limitations in equal protection and due process on the procedure for commitment of defendants found incompetent to stand trial. Most importantly, the Court held that, in the context before it, these federal constitutional doctrines prohibited subjecting the incompetent defendant to commitment under a more lenient commitment standard and a more stringent release standard than were applicable to impaired persons committed on a "civil" basis. *Jackson* has been widely read as requiring, in the context of other "criminal" commitments, substantial similarity between the criteria and procedure used for those commitments and the provisions for civil commitments.

This has coincided with several trends affecting civil commitment. These trends are undoubtedly the product of both perceived constitutional limitations on the civil commitment process and professional preference for noninstitutional treatment of impaired persons. Criteria for civil commitment have tended to narrow, often requiring that a proposed patient be shown to pose a substantial threat of serious physical harm to himself or others. The duration of civil commitments tends to be limited; open-ended or indefinite commitments are now greatly limited in availability.

The *Jackson* prohibition against at least some greater restrictiveness in criminal commitment criteria and procedures as compared with civil commitment, when combined with the developing restrictions on the availability of civil commitment, cast doubt upon the constitutionality of many schemes for processing defendants acquitted on responsibility grounds. Some case law suggested that acquitted defendants could be detained only pursuant to the same criteria administered by the same procedures as was used for compelled treatment of impaired persons not involved in the criminal process (*Behman* v. *Edwards*, 1982; *Ingber*, 1982).

Following the *Hinckley* acquittal, the United States Supreme Court addresssed these matters. This is discussed in a later section of this chapter.

JURY INSTRUCTIONS ON
POST-ACQUITTAL PROCEDURE

There is wide agreement that juries in criminal cases should determine the sufficiency of the evidence to prove a defendant's guilt without reference to the consequences of finding the defendant guilty. As a general rule, determination of the appropriate disposition is the role of the sentencing judge. The jury's determination of guilt or innocence should be made without regard to the sentence that may or will be imposed. Generally, therefore, juries are not told the sentences that may be imposed if the defendant is found guilty. A major issue, however, is whether interjection of the insanity defense justifies an exception to this general rule barring jury consideration of the dispositional consequences of its findings.

The traditional position among American jurisdictions is that no exception is justified and consequently, juries should not be instructed concerning the procedural results of a determination that the defendant is not guilty by reason of insanity. A substantial number of American jurisdictions, perhaps still a majority, continue to adhere to that position (*Curry* v. *State*, 1981; *State* v. *Williams*, 1982; *Strickland* v. *State*, 1981).

A substantial number of jurisdictions, however, recognize an exception to the general rule under which a jury is told the basic procedural consequences of a verdict of not guilty by reason of insanity. The "leading" cases are probably those decided by the District of Columbia Circuit Court of Appeals. This court required such instructions in *Taylor* v. *United States* (1954), and reaffirmed in *Lyles* v. *United States* (1957). A significant number of states have adopted what is sometimes called the "*Lyles* rule" providing for such instructions (*People* v. *Thompson*, 1979, overruling *Ingles* v. *People*, 1931; *State* v. *Nuckolls*, 1980, overruling *State* v. *Graimm*, 1973).

The rationale for an exception is what is perceived to be the exceptional risk that failure to inform the jury of the consequences of an acquittal will result in the jurors assuming that an acquittal will result in outright release. This, in turn, is regarded as likely to distort the jurors' evaluation of the evidence bearing upon nonresponsibility, given their likely desire to avoid having a dangerous and impaired person turned loose in the community (*Lyles* v. *United States*, 1957).

Some opposition to recognition of an exception is based upon the desirability of the traditional position that evaluations of evidence sufficiency should be made abstractly and without regard for the procedural consequences of the resulting determination. In addition, however, concern has been expressed that so instructing the jury might distort its decisionmaking in another and potentially even less desirable manner. Assured that acquittal on insanity grounds would result in detention, the jury may therefore return such a verdict to maximize implementation of its desire to assure detention of the defendant (*State* v. *Garrett*, 1965). This potential is especially unfortunate if the instructions create in the mind of the jury a perception that the post-acquittal procedure is more likely to result in long-term detention than in fact it is.

Another objection to *Lyles* instructions is that they cannot be complete. No instruction can "give a jury complete and accurate information about all the possible future decisions with respect to a person found to be not guilty by reason of insanity" (*Curry* v. *State*, 1981). Thus the instruction may not prevent the jury speculation that is its target. Or—and perhaps worse—it may give the jury a misleading impression concerning what will in fact occur if it returns a verdict of not guilty by reason of insanity. Perhaps, however, an instruction can inform the jury of the basic framework for processing an acquitted defendant and also make clear that what decisions will be made concerning any particular defendant simply cannot be anticipated. Whether jurors can usefully assimilate this information and still avoid being improperly influenced by speculation concerning the decisions that would be made concerning the particular defendant on trial is not clear.

SUMMARY: PRE-*HINCKLEY* STATUS OF AMERICAN RESPONSIBILITY LAW

The *Hinckley* acquittal occurred at a time when American responsibility law appeared to have largely settled the major structural issues and was developing primarily in several peripheral areas. Despite suggestions that existing *mens rea* doctrine might adequately permit consideration of defendants' impairment, American jurisdictions almost uniformly rejected this approach in favor of a separate defensive doctrine—insanity or its equivalent—as the major vehicle for accommodating such impairments. Unsatisfactory experience with the initial "productivity" rule in the District of Columbia confirmed the traditional position that a somewhat detailed criterion for resolving claims of nonresponsibility was necessary to guide trial juries. While some jurisdictions still adhered to a "right-wrong" criterion for resolving insanity issues, the clear trend was towards formulations similar to that proposed by the American Law Institute.

The major issue in the development of insanity criteria has been the extent to which, if at all, defendants' volitional impairment should be regarded as sufficient for exculpation. The prevailing pre-*Hinckley* trend was one of acceptance of such impairment as an adequate basis for exculpation if the impairment was shown to have resulted in a substantial incapacity to conform to recognized and cognitively understood legal requirements. Faced with the choice among the *mens rea* approach, the right-wrong insanity approach, and the broader formulation of the insanity

approach that accommodated volitional impairment, American jurisdictions had overwhelmingly rejected the first and, as between the second and third, tended to favor the latter.

But the more recent development of American responsibility law reflected an effort to expand accommodation of abnormality. This reflected discomfort with the insanity defense's need to choose between complete exoneration and conviction as charged. Thus there was a significant trend towards development of other means of accommodating claims of abnormality not sufficient to justify exculpation.

Abnormality might be used, then, to challenge the adequacy of proof of *mens rea*, at least that *mens rea* required by the most serious offense for which conviction might be had. It might also be used in an effort to persuade the sentencing authority to show leniency, and such use was specifically authorized in capital and other more structured provisions for the exercise of sentencing discretion. In a few jurisdictions, trial juries were authorized to find a defendant guilty but mentally ill, thus giving some formal effect to a conclusion that the offender was impaired but that exculpation was not appropriate. To some extent, these provisions shifted the responsibility for considering evidence of impairment from lay jurors to the judges, in reflection of concern that as provision was made for consideration of more subtle matters, juries became less appropriate decisionmakers. But in general, juries continued to be given responsibility for administering those doctrines that made provision for defendants' impairments.

The decrease in dispute concerning the traditional issue—the insanity criterion—was also accompanied by increased concern regarding various procedural issues related to the administration of that standard. Concern with jurors' ability to objectively evaluate evidence, for example, was reflected in the controversy as to whether those jurors should be told the procedural consequences of an acquittal on responsibility grounds.

Responsibility law issues throughout the development in this area tended to be addressed quite abstractly. Major consideration was given to the logical dictates of the major philosophical assumptions of criminal liability theory, specifically that conviction is appropriate where, but only where, moral culpability has been demonstrated. Throughout the development there runs a thread of concern with "practicality," and specifically with the possibility that in actual administration the positions suggested by philosophical concerns may be abused or prove otherwise disruptive. The recent emphasis upon procedural matters, for example, arguably reflects the view that what is done with exculpated defendants and how much jurors are told about this may be, as a practical matter, more important than what jurors are told about the criterion for resolving claims of nonresponsibility. But, in general, relatively little attention appears to have been given these practical concerns in the several decades preceding the *Hinckley* acquittal.

The *Hinckley* Acquittal and Its Aftermath

The law that John Hinckley sought to invoke in the District of Columbia courtroom and the procedures that he sought to use in this effort, then, represented the product of long-standing concern, experimentation, and development regarding criminal responsibility issues. This section examines the *Hinckley* trial, its aftermath, and those changes in responsibility law and discussion that have resulted or are likely to result from these events.

When considered in light of the background of American criminal responsibility law, the post-*Hinckley* furor must be regarded as having given rise to no new proposals regarding the appropriate relationship between defendants' impairment and criminal liability. Moreover, insofar as the furor stimulated further consideration of previously developed alternatives, it cannot be said to have added new arguments or considerations.

At most, the *Hinckley* acquittal has resulted in a focus of emphasis upon several considerations that have been a part of the ongoing criminal responsibility debate. One is the danger of jury confusion and resulting misapplication of the defense when a defendant's argument is based upon a claim of volitional impairment. Another is the risk of placing an unrealistic burden on the prosecution if the defendant is not given the burden of proof on a claim of nonresponsibility. A third is the need for adequate assurance that nonculpable but nevertheless dangerous defendants acquitted on responsibility grounds are processed in a manner that adequately protects society from them.

All of these considerations bear upon what might be regarded as the "practical realities" of the administration of responsibility law, as contrasted with the demands of the philosophical foundations of criminal liability. Perhaps the major immediate impact of the *Hinckley* acquittal has been widespread acceptance that such realities must be given greater weight even when they seem to contradict the demands of more abstract, philosophical concerns.

This section will first address the *Hinckley* litigation itself. Attention will then be turned to a number of matters prominent in post-acquittal discussions.

The Hinckley *Case*

John Hinckley unquestionably fired the gunshots that, on March 30, 1981, wounded President Reagan and three others outside of the Hilton Hotel in Washington, D.C. Similarly, there is little doubt that at the time he fired those shots, Hinckley entertained the conscious desire to wound and probably to kill at least the President. Moreover, there is virtually no disagreement that Hinckley's conscious motive for the assaults was a desire to develop a personal relationship with actress Jodie Foster. Hinckley's extended trial was devoted almost entirely to inquiring whether his actions, intention, and motives were sufficiently related to underlying psychological pathology to require his acquittal on insanity grounds.

Although much of the earlier testimony offered by both sides was designed to lay the groundwork for, or to refute, Hinckley's claim of nonresponsibility, most attention focused upon the experts who testified directly on the insanity issue. Five experts—four psychiatrists and a psychologist—were called by the defense. The Government rested after calling two psychiatrists to testify in rebuttal. In final argument, the Government acknowledged that even its witnesses had agreed that Hinckley had some mental abnormalities. It characterized these, however, as the mental equivalent of "a sniffle and head cold" and argued that they had little, if any, relationship to Hinckley's actions.

The trial judge instructed the jury under the Model Penal Code formulation of the insanity test. Further, the jury was told that the Government had the obligation to prove sanity beyond a reasonable doubt. Under *Lyles*, the jury was informed that an acquittal on insanity grounds would result in further proceedings regarding the defendant. Nevertheless, the *New York Times* reporter covering the trial described the courtroom audience as "stunned" when the verdicts of not guilty by reason of insanity were announced. The defense lawyers, he reported, appeared thunderstruck by their success.

Public reaction was swift and unfavorable. Although expressing reservations, a United States Senate Subcommittee invited at least some of the jurors to testify within days of the acquittal. Five appeared. There was widespread agreement that the result of the Hinckley trial was in some way improper, although the trial judge and jury were perceived as simply having applied existing "law." But law that required or permitted this trial to end in a verdict other than that of guilty, it was widely claimed, was seriously in need of revision.

To some extent, it is clear that the offense widely taken was to the symbolic significance of the verdict rather than to its practical importance. Hinckley, of course, was not released but instead was committed to a highly secure mental health facility. To some extent, public reaction reflected an erroneous perception that the verdict somehow embodied a conclusion that the Government had not proved Hinckley's commission of the assaultive conduct charged. But primarily it reflected offense at the failure of the trial to attach to Hinckley the formal—and largely symbolic—label of "guilty."

Scrutiny of various possible revisions was immediately begun and, in some instances, reform measures were soon adopted. Several aspects of this scrutiny are of special significance. In December of 1982, the Board of Trustees of the American Psychiatric Association gave final approval to a position statement developed by a "work group" (American Psychiatric Association, 1982). Three months later, in February of 1983, the House of Delegates of the American Bar Association approved three recommendations concerning the defense of nonresponsibility that constituted a significant change in the Association's previous position in that area (American Bar Association, 1983). The United States Department of Justice continued to urge modification of the law. When, however, the Reagan Administration proposed its Comprehensive Crime Control Act of 1983 (President of the United States, 1983), the administration's proposals differed significantly from the Department's earlier position. A National Commission on the Insanity Defense was established by the National Mental Health Association; the commission issued a report in March of 1983 (National Commission on the Insanity Defense, 1983).

Several of the areas of special concern in the scrutiny conducted by these entities as well as that occurring in other forums require specific consideration.

"Abandonment" of the Insanity Defense: The Mens Rea *Alternative*

As might be expected, the *Hinckley* acquittal brought cries that the accommodation of defendants' impairment and their criminal responsibility should be minimized. This might best be accomplished, it was urged by some, by abandoning a separate defense of insanity or nonresponsibility and considering evidence of impairment only as bearing upon whether a criminal accused in fact entertained the *mens rea* required by the crime charged. United States Attorney General William French Smith initially articulated the Justice Department's continued support of the proposition that psychological abnormality be limited to "disproof" of *mens rea*. The Department regarded constitutional considerations as requiring that some provision be made for accommodating defendants' claims of impairment, but it concluded that the *mens rea* approach would limit that accommodation as much as was constitutionally permissible (Smith, 1982).

The American Bar Association, however, characterized this position as an abolitionist approach and as "an unfortunate and unwarranted overreaction to the *Hinckley* verdict." Similarly, the National Commission on the Insanity Defense argued against this "virtual elimination of the insanity defense" (National Commission on the Insanity Defense, 1983, p. 30). The American Psychiatric Association's statement did not address the matter directly but its opposition to the abolition of the insanity defense (American Psychiatric Association, 1982, pp. 8–9) appears to be an implicit rejection of the approach.

Just as the *"mens rea* only" approach generated little pre-*Hinckley* support, it seldom found its way into post-*Hinckley* legislation. It was, however, embodied in Idaho law by a 1982 revision of that state's responsibility laws (Idaho Laws, 1982); this took place before the *Hinckley* acquittal but was quite likely influenced by concern generated by Hinckley's already publicized claim to exculpation. The resulting legislation provided that: "Mental condition shall not be a defense to any charge of criminal conduct." It continued, however, with the caveat that: "Nothing herein is intended to prevent the admission of expert evidence on the issues of *mens rea* or any state of mind which is an element of the offense, subject to the rules of evidence" (Idaho Laws, 1982, codified as Idaho Statutes Annotated, Section 18-207).

The Idaho legislation, however, attempted to balance this with structured provisions for considering psychological impairment in sentencing. "Evidence of mental condition shall be received, if offered," it provided, "at the time of sentencing." Further, if the defendant's mental condition is a significant factor in determining the sentence to be imposed, the trial court was directed to consider such factors as:

- The extent to which the defendant is mentally ill;
- The degree of illness or defect and level of functional impairment;
- The prognosis for improvement or rehabilitation;
- The availability of treatment and level of care required;
- Any risk of danger which the defendant may create for the public, if at large, or the absence of such risk;
- The capacity of the defendant to appreciate the wrongfulness of his conduct or to conform his conduct to the requirements of the law at the time of the offense changed. (Idaho Laws, 1982, codified as Idaho Statutes Annotated, Section 19-2523)

The "*mens rea* only" approach of the Idaho legislation to accommodating impairment and the determination of guilt is, then, almost unique. Its reliance upon further accommodation of impairment in sentencing, however, is consistent with the pre-*Hinckley* trend in sentencing, a trend discussed earlier.

The general rejection of early cries for making mental abnormality irrelevant to defendants' guilt or innocence or for limiting that relevance to whether they entertained the required state of mind reflected a continuing perception that criminal conviction should be limited to those dangerous persons whose actions have demon-

strated their blameworthiness. Further, rejection of the *mens rea* approach strongly suggests recognition that the function of *mens rea* in assuring blameworthiness is not sufficient to accommodate all claims of abnormality. Instead, the aftermath of the *Hinckley* acquittal has left largely intact the traditional assumption of American criminal law that the need to assure blameworthiness requires a separate defensive doctrine to accommodate claims that, at the time of the conduct at issue, the accused was psychologically impaired.

Guilty but Mentally Ill Alternative

Another immediate but more widespread reaction to the *Hinckley* acquittal was an increased interest in the "guilty but mentally ill" alternative. This appears to be based in part at least upon the perception that the *Hinckley* acquittal reflected a distortion of insanity law by the jury to give some formal effect to the jurors' conclusion that Hinckley's impairment required some recognition in the verdict. If this consideration had been removed from the case by the availability of a verdict of guilty but mentally ill, it seems the reasoning would have been that the *Hinckley* jury would have rejected the insanity defense on its merits. A number of states enacted provisions for such verdicts (Alaska Laws, 1982; Georgia Laws, 1982; Indiana Laws, 1981; Kentucky Laws, 1982; New Mexico Laws, 1982).

To some extent, however, even this action reflected disenchantment with consideration of volitional impairment. Delaware, for example, had previously defined the insanity defense as available upon proof of lack of substantial capacity to appreciate the wrongfulness of the conduct or lack of sufficient willpower to choose whether to engage in conduct. The 1982 legislation adopting the guilty but mentally ill alternative, however, also limits the insanity defense to situations in which the accused experienced a lack of substantial capacity to appreciate the wrongfulness of his conduct. The trier of fact is directed to return a verdict of "guilty but mentally ill" if it determines:

that, at the time of the conduct charged, a defendant suffered from a psychiatric disorder which substantially disturbed such person's thinking, feeling or behavior and/or that such psychiatric disorder left such person with insufficient willpower to choose whether he would do the act or refrain from doing it, although physically capable. (Delaware Laws, 1982)

Elsewhere, adoption of the guilty but mentally ill alternative appeared intended in part to head off in advance any effort to expand the defense of nonresponsibility to include volitional impairment. Pennsylvania, for example, had previously embraced the right-wrong test as the insanity criterion. Legislation in 1982 specifically reaffirmed this. It also proceeded, however, to provide in terms similar to the Delaware statute for a verdict of guilty but mentally ill upon a determination of volitional impairment (Pennsylvania Laws, 1982).

The American Bar Association recommendations formally opposed enactment of statutes supplementing the retention of a defense of nonresponsibility with an alternative verdict of guilty but mentally ill (American Bar Association, 1983). A similar position was taken by the National Commission on the Insanity Defense. (National Commission on the Insanity Defense, 1983, pp. 32–34). Extreme skepticism concerning the approach was taken in the American Psychiatric Association's statement, which noted the danger that this approach would constitute a whitewash without fundamental progress on the underlying moral, legal, psychiatric and pragmatic problems (American Psychiatric Association, 1982, pp. 9–10). The Reagan Administration's Comprehensive Crime Control Act of 1983 contained no provision for a verdict of "guilty but mentally ill."

Abandonment of "Not Guilty" Terminology

Despite substantial reason to believe that the public reaction to the *Hinckley* acquittal was largely based upon offense taken to the verdict's symbolic designation of Hinckley as "not guilty," few of the proposed or actual reforms responded directly to this. The National Commission, however, recommended abandonment of "not guilty" by reason of insanity or nonresponsibility terminology. Instead, it urged, discussion (and apparently legislation) would minimize confusion and misunderstanding if the procedural consequences of a conclusion that an impaired offender was not culpable were expressed by use of the term, "not responsible by reason of insanity." Despite widespread use of "not guilty" phraseology,

the Commission's proposal was not new. Indiana, for example, provided in 1978 for a jury verdict directing exculpation to find the accused "not responsible by reason of insanity at the time of the crime" (Indiana Laws, 1978).

The Commission acknowledged that no meaningful legal difference exists between the terms "guilty" and "responsible." It suggested, however, that use of the term "not responsible" would reduce the risk of confusion as to whether the accused had been found to have committed the antisocial act at issue. It might also have added that many distressed over the *Hinckley* verdict might have been less offended if that verdict had specifically reflected the jury's conclusion that Hinckley engaged in the assaultive conduct charged.

Abandonment of the Volitional Impairment Prong of Insanity Criterion

The most amazing aspect of the *Hinckley* acquittal aftermath has been the coalescence of support for the proposition that the defense of insanity should be limited so as to preclude reliance upon impairment of volition. This view has already found its way into the statutory law of a number of American jurisdictions and seems likely to find increasing acceptance.

The American Psychiatric Association's statement avoided a definitive position on the insanity criterion itself. It did, however, tacitly approve a limited defense based on Bonnie (1983), that would require an inability on the part of the defendant to appreciate the wrongfulness of his conduct at the time of the offense.

The American Bar Association's House of Delegates' first resolution provided:

> That the American Bar Association approves, in principle, a defense of nonresponsibility for crime which focuses solely on whether the defendant, as a result of mental disease or defect, was unable to appreciate the wrongfulness of that defendant's conduct at the time of the offense charged. (American Bar Association, 1983)

The resolution also urged that the American Law Institute's formulation of a cognitive criterion further be narrowed by requiring an inability to appreciate the wrongfulness at issue, rather than merely loss of "substantial capacity." Such a narrowed standard, the Association's committee report argued, would give juries a "more concrete question" to resolve and would reduce the risk that juries would construe the defense "too loosely" (American Bar Association Standing Committee, 1982, p. 4).

In interesting contrast, the Association expressed approval of phraseology that would permit defendants, under a cognitive criterion, to avoid liability by establishing an inability to "appreciate" the requisite wrongfulness. This, it explained, would permit accommodation of emotional or affective dimensions of impairment and facilitate development before the jury of "a full clinical description of the defendant's perceptions and understanding." A test phrased in terms of the defendant's ability to "know" wrongfulness, it suggested, might not adequately serve these functions.

The Reagan Administration's Comprehensive Crime Control Act of 1983 proposed as a federal statutory responsibility standard a cognitive criterion similar to that urged by the American Bar Association (President of the United States, 1983). Legislation repealing what was previously the "volitional prong" of an insanity standard modeled on the Model Penal Code provision has already been enacted in several states (Alaska Laws, 1982; Delaware Laws, 1982; Texas Laws, 1983).

Despite the widespread acceptance of the Model Penal Code's formulation, it found few post-*Hinckley* defenders. The National Commission on the Insanity Defense, however, urged that the criterion should include both cognitive and volitional elements. The Commission did not undertake an extensive defense of exculpation on the basis of volitional impairment. Rather, it urged that the major objection to a volitional criterion—the risk of jury confusion and resulting improper acquittals—could be met by placing the burden of proof upon defendants seeking exculpation (National Commission on the Insanity Defense, 1983, p. 36).

Burden of Proof

There was widespread, although not universal, acceptance of the proposition that the *Hinckley* acquittal demonstrated a need for the burden of proof on nonresponsibility to be on the defendant

claiming that lack of responsibility. The National Mental Health Association's commission recommended that the burden of proof be on the defendant by a preponderance of the evidence (National Commission on the Insanity Defense, 1983, pp. 35–36). The Reagan Administration's bill proposed that the defendant carry the heavier burden of "clear and convincing" evidence (President of the United States, 1983).

The American Bar Association urged that those jurisdictions applying the Model Penal Code formulation of the insanity standard place on defendants the burden of proving insanity by a preponderance of the evidence. But it further suggested that those jurisdictions applying an insanity criterion embodying a cognitive right-wrong test place the burden on the prosecution to prove sanity beyond a reasonable doubt (American Bar Association, 1983). The American Psychiatric Association expressed reluctance to take a position on the matter, which it characterized as "clearly one for legislative judgment." But it called for more empirical study of the effect of various allocations of the burden (American Psychiatric Association, 1982, pp. 12–13).

Several state legislatures have acted on these proposals. Some have made nonresponsibility a matter to be proved by a preponderance of the evidence (Alaska Laws, 1982, codified as Alaska Statutes Sec. 12.47.010[a]; Hawaii Laws 1982, ch. 2290). But the suggestions that the defense should have the burden of proof by clear and convincing evidence has also found favor, as evidenced by Arizona legislation (Arizona Laws 1983, ch. 118).

The clear post-*Hinckley* trend towards placing the burden of proof on defendants claiming exculpation appears to reflect concern that juries are likely to be so confused by a vigorous claim of nonresponsibility that such confusion alone may give rise to what jurors perceive as reasonable doubt. The *Hinckley* jury, it was widely believed, fell into this trap. In response, the burden of proof had been with some frequency shifted to the defendant claiming exculpation.

Dispositional Procedures and *Jones v.* United States

Among the concerns stimulated by the *Hinckley* acquittal, of course, were those related to the processing of defendants found distinguishable from other defendants because of psychological abnormality. As discussed above, however, there has been widespread concern that federal constitutional considerations placed significant limits upon the manner in which such persons could be processed. The United States Supreme Court finally addressed this concern in an opinion handed down on June 29, 1983 in *Jones* v. *United States*.

Jones raised challenges to *some* aspects of the District of Columbia procedure for processing defendants acquitted of criminal charges on grounds of insanity. Such an acquittal requires that the defense establish, by a preponderance of the evidence, that the defendant was insane. Acquittal results in an automatic and indefinite commitment. The acquittee, however, is entitled to a hearing within 50 days of the initial commitment and again every 6 months thereafter. At these hearings, the acquittee bears the burden of establishing that he is no longer either mentally ill or "dangerous." If the defendant successfully carries the burden, he is entitled to discharge. Jones himself had been committed following his insanity acquittal of a charge of attempted petit larceny. The charged offense was a misdemeanor, punishable by a maximum term of 1 year incarceration. At the time of Jones' effort to obtain release, he had been hospitalized pursuant to the commitment for longer than a year.

In comparison with the issues raised in earlier lower court litigation, Jones' attacks upon his continued incarceration were quite limited. Jones emphasized that his commitment rested upon only a determination made in his criminal trial that a preponderance of the evidence showed that he was impaired at the time of the commission of the conduct amounting to his offense. In contrast, civil commitment in the District of Columbia requires proof by clear and convincing evidence that, at the time of commitment, the subject is mentally ill and dangerous. The finding implicit in the insanity acquittal, he urged, could not—under due process requirements—support a commitment at all or at least not a commitment lasting beyond the period of correctional incarceration to which he would have been subject had he been convicted of the crime charged. As a result, he argued, he was entitled to either be committed under the District's civil commitment procedure or to release.

Rejecting Jones' arguments, the Court's major-

ity concluded that Congress could reasonably have regarded an insanity acquittal as a determination of both mental illness and dangerousness adequate to justify commitment. Although the proof establishing insanity by a preponderance of the evidence might be less than the "clear and convincing evidence" required in a civil commitment case, the distinction was reasonable because the insanity evidence was presented by the defendant himself and established the commission of a criminal act. Given that Jones' initial commitment did not offend constitutional standards, its continuation beyond the period of possible correctional incarceration available upon conviction was also permissible. "The length of [an insanity] acquittee's hypothetical criminal sentence," the majority explained, ". . . is irrelevant to the purposes of his commitment." The Court summarized its holding:

> When a criminal defendant established by a preponderance of the evidence that he is not guilty of a crime by reason of insanity, the Constitution permits the Government, on the basis of the insanity judgment, to confine him to a mental institution until such time as he has regained his sanity or is no longer a danger to himself or society. (*Jones* v. *United States*, 1983, at 3052)

Because of the manner in which the issues were framed in *Jones*, a number of possible dispositional questions were not addressed. Specifically, the Court did not have occasion to consider whether federal constitutional considerations barred or limited legislatures' ability to subject committed acquittees to a more stringent standard for release than was imposed upon those civilly committed. Nor did the Court address the acceptability of subjecting acquittees to more stringent procedural requirements; it did not consider, for example, whether due process or equal protection would ever be offended by requiring judicial approval for release of committed acquittees but not those civilly committed. But *Jones* strongly suggests that the Court is willing to find substantial flexibility in the federal constitutional requirements applicable to the processing of insanity acquittees. At least some such distinctions are almost certain to survive federal constitutional scrutiny.

Jones, then, arguably reflects the Supreme Court's disapproval of at least some pre-*Hinckley* lower court decisions rigorously construing and applying federal constitutional requirements to the processing of insanity acquittees. But the exact scope of the due process and equal protection requirements here remains to be developed. Moreover, state tribunals remain free to construe state constitutional provisions as imposing more stringent limits upon the processing of such persons than are required under the federal provisions.

POST-*HINCKLEY* CHANGES

A variety of changes were made in state statutes between the *Hinckley* acquittal and the Supreme Court's decision in *Jones*. The Court's apparent receptivity in *Jones* to arguments in support of more stringent processing of nonresponsibility acquittees will quite likely stimulate further consideration of these matters. Two trends appear likely to develop; one would make discharge following responsibility acquittal a judicial matter, and the other would provide that the acquitting court have jurisdiction to address that matter.

First, there is a developing consensus that discharge (and perhaps even conditional release) of acquittees should be permissible only with judicial approval. Such acquittees, it is increasingly agreed, pose greater risks to community safety than other impaired persons compelled to submit to treatment. Moreover, treatment personnel cannot be trusted to have adequate sensitivity to this increased risk to community safety and thus cannot be given responsibility for the release decision.

Whether this will be constitutionally acceptable in jurisdictions in which civilly committed persons may be released or discharged at the discretion of treating authorities was not reached in *Jones* and remains to be resolved. *Jones*, however, suggests that the Court will uphold such schemes. The Court's opinion indicates that it will be receptive to the argument that the finding of criminal conduct on which acquittee-commitments are based provides a sufficient basis for regarding acquittees as distinguishably dangerous. This, in turn, may well support subjecting them to a more stringent procedure for release or discharge than is applied to civil committees. Whether these procedures may impose upon committed acquittees the burden of establishing in these procedures the appropriateness of release or discharge in jurisdictions where civilly committed persons must be periodically proven to still meet the commitment standard remains open. The "flavor" of *Jones*, however, is that a criminal trial in which the acquittee is proven beyond a reasonable doubt to

have engaged in criminal conduct may support even this major differentiation in the allocation of the burden of proof on long-term retention issues.

The second likely trend is for these judicial proceedings to be held in the acquitting court. Given court structures in many jurisdictions, those courts in which felony defendants are tried are often different courts than those with jurisdiction over civil commitment matters. Some states have provided for judicial post-acquittal proceedings of the sort that are likely to gain increased appeal, but for these proceedings to be in the same court with jurisdiction over civil commitment actions regarding impaired persons not involved in the criminal process. It is likely, however, that future schemes will give the court in which defendants are acquitted on responsibility grounds a type of "continuing jurisdiction" that includes authority to hold subsequent commitment and release proceedings.

This will eliminate what is sometimes perceived to be the lack of sufficient sensitivity to important issues on the part of courts that did not hear the evidence establishing the actual conduct in which the defendant engaged. If, on the other hand, those judges making retention and release decisions presided over the trials in which the details of the acquittees' conduct were developed, the presiding judge may harbor greater sensitivity to the risk posed by acquittees to societal safety.

The Reagan Administration's proposal for the processing of defendants acquitted in federal court embodies this latter approach. An acquitted defendant would have to be committed following a verdict of not guilty by reason of insanity. But a hearing would be held in the trial court within 40 days of the verdict. At this hearing, the committed defendant is to be indefinitely committed if, but only if, the court finds by clear and convincing evidence that he:

> is presently suffering from a mental illness or defect as a result of which his release would create a substantial risk of bodily injury to another person or serious damage to property of another. (President of the United States, 1983)

During commitment, an acquittee would be entitled to release if the director of the facility in which the acquittee is detained certifies that the acquittee no longer meets the standard set out above and the trial court finds, by a preponderance of the evidence, that the acquittee is no longer dangerous in the sense of the standard. The court would be authorized to conditionally release the defendant with a directive that he comply with a prescribed regimen of care or treatment if it determines that release under such a regimen would render the defendant no longer dangerous in the sense used by the statute.

The administration's proposal does not go as far in protection of societal safety as *Jones* held is constitutionally permissible. It would permit long-term detention of an acquitted defendant only upon affirmative proof after acquittal—and only upon "clear and convincing" proof—that the acquittee is still "dangerous." *Jones* holds that this is not constitutionally necessary; commitment can rest upon the acquittal verdict itself.

Summary

Despite the intensity of the reaction to the *Hinckley* acquittal and the extensive discussion stimulated by that reaction, little if anything has been added to American responsibility law by the episode. Comparison of post-*Hinckley* discussions with pre-*Hinckley* development of American responsibility law makes clear that no new proposals were developed. Abandonment of a defense of nonresponsibility in favor of reliance upon *mens rea* doctrine was again considered and almost uniformly rejected. Wider support developed for a guilty but mentally ill approach modeled upon the recent Michigan embodiment of that proposal. But the immediate post-*Hinckley* attractiveness of this appears to have diminished in light of further consideration. Placement of the burden of proof to establish nonresponsibility upon defendants and increased stringency of provisions for post-trial retention of defendants found nonresponsible also found legislative favor. Perhaps of greater long-run significance for American responsibility law, however, was the reinvigoration of the long-standing dispute as to the appropriate accommodation in responsibility analysis of defendants' claims of volitional impairment.

The reinvigoration of these disputes added little or nothing to the arguments that had traditionally been offered for and against the various positions. There was, however, a distinct flavor of increased emphasis on some traditional considerations. The major contribution of the post-*Hinckley* acquittal evaluation to American responsibility discussion, then, was a focus of attention on several matters long a part of the ongoing responsibility debate.

First, the post-*Hinckley* discussions resulted in or disclosed a widespread perception that "practical" problems in administering responsibility law should be given more weight in policymaking, even if this is inconsistent with the apparent implications of philosophical considerations. This was reflected in the demand for post-acquittal detention and retention procedures. In addition, many apparently concluded that the risk of jury confusion and resulting errors in response to claims of volitional impairment may justify a criterion providing for no opportunity for such claims, even if the philosophical demand for culpability suggests a need to accommodate volitional impairment.

Second, the discussion suggested that large segments of the population do not share the underlying philosophical foundation for provisions for exculpation and therefore that considerations based upon this foundation should be given less weight in policymaking. To some extent, the public reaction to the *Hinckley* acquittal can be attributed to a misunderstanding that the verdict suggested a conclusion that he did not engage in the assassination attempt. It can also, to some degree, be attributed to an apparently widespread failure to even consider the need for an attribution of guilt to rest upon a conclusion of moral culpability as well as commission of dangerous conduct. But the reevaluation also made clear that substantial portions of the public, after consideration, simply rejected the fundamental notion that there are important reasons why a finding of criminal liability should rest upon blameworthiness as well as dangerousness.

This increased emphasis upon considerations militating against accommodation of defendants' impairments has not persuaded many decision-makers to abandon the traditional American approach of providing for a "defense" of nonresponsibility. It is likely, however, to result in widespread narrowing of the criteria for resolving claims to such defenses. This narrowing may be of increased appeal because of the context in which post-*Hinckley* debate arose. American responsibility law had, quite recently in some cases, developed other methods of accommodating claims of abnormality. These alternatives included "diminished capacity," structured capital and other sentencing provisions, and the alternative of guilty but mentally ill. Claims of certain impairments— most importantly volitional impairment—might to some extent be partially accommodated through these alternative means. Narrowing the criteria for the defense of nonresponsibility there-fore appeared somewhat less costly to the un-derlying need to accommodate claims of nonculpability.

This trend towards abandonment of a nonre-sponsibility defense of volitional impairment may represent an adequately considered and well-based policy decision stimulated by the post-*Hinckley* discussion. It might, on the other hand, be an impulsive response to a single apparent "error" of the law as administered. The merits of a defense of volitional impairment require further consideration and are therefore addressed in the next section.

Discussion: Abandonment of the Volitional Impairment Defense

The post-*Hinckley* controversy regarding the ap-propriateness of providing a responsibility defense of volitional impairment, of course, merely con-tinued a traditional part of American responsibil-ity debate. But this stage of the debate is likely to result in a definitive shift in the direction of the law's development in this area. Four aspects of the post-*Hinckley* discussion leading to this shift sug-gest a need for further scrutiny: (1) the likely existence of volitional impairment in offenders who did not experience cognitive impairment suf-ficient to exculpate under right-wrong criteria; (2) the ability to conduct, with reasonable accuracy, inquiries into the existence and effect of particular defendants' volitional impairment; (3) the significance of volitional impairment under cogni-tive criteria; and (4) the bearing of other—and broader—concerns upon the wisdom of providing a defense of impaired volition.

Volitional Incapacity as an Independent Impairment

The pre-*Hinckley* trend—and the Model Penal Code position in particular—were based upon the assumption that mental disorders did with some frequency produce impairments of volition sufficient to require exculpation even in the ab-sence of cognitive impairment demanding the same result. This was not without dissent. Jerome Hall, for example, vigorously urged at the time of the formulation of the Code's position that in light of available information concerning the integra-tion of the personality, the existence of an inde-pendent impairment of volitional capabilities alone was simply not established (Hall, 1956, p.

775; Hall, 1958, p. 222).

This point was remade with emphasis by the American Psychiatric Association's post-*Hinckley* statement:

> Most psychotic persons who fail a volitional test for insanity will also fail a cognitive-type test when such a test is applied to their behavior, thus rendering the volitional test superfluous in judging them. (American Psy-chiatric Association, 1982, p. 12)

Again, however, the assertions on both sides are made exclusively on the basis of intuition. Vir-tually no "hard evidence" or useful research can be brought to bear on the matter.

Even if the existence of a volitional impairment defense would be determinative in only a few cases, that may not militate strongly against it. In many areas where legal criteria for decisionmak-ing must be developed, most cases are "easy" ones whatever the criteria. The criteria are necessary for decisionmaking only in the small minority of "hard" cases. If only a small group of defendants present viable cases for exculpation on the basis of impaired volition alone, this may not distinguish the matter from other legal issues nor constitute strong support for abandoning the defense of voli-tional impairment.

Inquiry into Volitional Impairment

A major contribution of the post-*Hinckley* furor to responsibility debate was the call for critical reassessment of the ability of the judicial system assisted by mental health professionals testifying as expert witnesses to determine, on a case-by-case basis, whether defendants' claims of volitional im-pairment sufficient to exculpate were meritorious. If this ability is seriously lacking, however, the appropriate response might not be to abandon the inquiry into volitional impairment but rather to impose a threshold requirement of a serious disor-der as a prerequisite to inquiry into the effect of any disorder upon volitional capacity.

PROFESSIONAL EXPERTISE IN VOLITIONAL CAPACITY

Proponents of a volitional defense harbored abid-ing faith that mental health professionals could assist in reliably identifying those situations where volitional impairment justified exculpation. The major rationale cited in post-*Hinckley* discussion for abandonment of volitional impairment as a defense was the mental health professions' failure to justify this faith. To the extent that such a failure occurred, it might be explained in large part by the failure of the professions to develop a conceptual framework for a professional evaluation of such matters.

Enthusiasm regarding a defense of volitional impairment appears to have been based in significant part upon optimism that dynamic personality theory would provide such a framework and therefore would assure high quality of testimony on defendants' claims of volitional impairment (Louisell & Diamond, 1965, p. 220). But there were doubts expressed in regard to this prior to the American Law Institute's acceptance of the proposed volitional test. Walder, a psychoanalyst, commented in 1952 that his discipline offered no criteria for deciding, when an impulse was one resisted by some persons and not others, whether any particular person could have resisted it.

Whether the optimistic expectations of dynamic personality theory were—and are—justified remains problematic. To the extent that dynamic personality theory embodies a completely deterministic assumption concerning behavior, of course, it holds little promise. But some saw—and still see—this conceptual framework as capable of assuming general free will and as positing certain abnormalities that, when present, sufficiently interfere with this free will so as to render the subject unable to exercise volition (Dix & Sharlot, 1973, pp. 1156–57).

Even those who observed the failure of dynamic personality theory to develop a conceptual framework that included free will and various pathological conditions which interfered with this remained optimistic. Louisell and Diamond (1965) best illustrated this. After noting the failure of psychoanalytic and other advances to bring about "really fundamental" insights into determinism and free will, they continued:

About the most we feel able to agree upon . . . is that there is ample evidence from psychoanalysis, psychiatry and the other behavioral sciences that the more free an individual is from the internal pressures of psychopathology and the less he is burdened with the detrimental forces of adverse social, economic and cultural conditions, the more he is able to make choices and decisions, to select among alternative patterns of behavior, in a manner

which appears to approximate our traditional notion of free will. (p. 221)

This, they concluded, "we think . . . enough for practical interprofessional cooperation" in inquiring into criminal defendants' responsibility.

The *Hinckley* acquittal has stimulated vigorous challenge to this conclusion. In the absence of a generally accepted conceptual framework for expert testimony that, first, assumes the general existence of free will and, second, identifies certain abnormalities that obstruct the exercise of free will in a manner that can be reliably measured or at least estimated, practical interprofessional cooperation is not possible. To the contrary, testimony lacking such a framework but offered in defense of volitional impairment may contribute nothing to the accurate resolution of that claim. In addition, it may so confuse matters as to detract from jurors' ability to resolve those issues that, otherwise, they would be capable of addressing effectively.

Several recent inquiries in American responsibility literature have challenged the actual and potential value of dynamic personality theory in criminal responsibility inquiries. Moore (1980) argued that psychoanalytic conclusions that behavior was influenced or caused by unconscious motivations simply do not address the responsibility issue. This is because—assuming the existence of a generally present ability to exercise conscious control—establishing that conduct was "caused" by unconscious factors does not address whether the person could have refrained from the conduct. Some have assumed that unconscious factors "compel" behavior in a manner negating responsibility if the actor, although he consciously experiences the influence (that is, he consciously perceives an expectation that certain behavior would be satisfying), does not consciously understand the full significance of that influence as revealed by psychodynamic insights (p. 1672). But there is simply no reliable evidence that this is correct.

Morse (1982) urged that given the absence of scientific verification for the underlying assumptions concerning human behavior, expert testimony based on psychodynamic psychology be inadmissible in criminal litigation. Further, he argues that even if this difficulty is overcome, individual assessments based upon psychodynamic theory are such as to require exclusion of expert testimony based upon such assessments. No acceptable method of externally verifying these assessments exists. Thus there is a high risk that any particular assessment will be unreliable. Further, admitting expert testimony based on such assessments often renders an unproductive "battle of the experts" likely to confuse the trier of fact, in Morse's words, "all but inevitable" (p. 1026).

It may well be that no skill in evaluating the "resistibility" of unconscious influences to engage in conduct has developed because there is little need to address the matter in therapeutic mental health practice. In the course of treatment it may be decided that an important treatment objective is the avoidance of certain conduct in the future. Pursuit of this objective, however, is unlikely to turn upon whether past conduct of the sort at issue reflected a failure to resist an influence that could have been resisted, on the one hand, or an influence that could not have been resisted, on the other. Mental health professionals may have little to offer in regard to whether a person could, by the exercise of conscious control, have avoided certain past behavior because they have little or no occasion to address such matters in the course of their therapeutic practices.

If claims of loss of volitional capacity are frequently supported by expert testimony based upon dynamic personality theory and if there are weighty reasons to doubt the value of such testimony, does this demand the abandonment of that aspect of the defense? Arguably not, for several reasons. First, it may be preferable to retain the defense but limit the admissibility of testimony. As Morse suggests, testimony based upon dynamic psychology or similarly suspect conceptual frameworks could simply be rejected when offered by defendants. Defendants, then, might retain the ability to raise impairment of volition but be more limited in the testimony that they could use for this purpose.

Dynamic personality theory, however, may provide the only available conceptual framework for expert inquiry into claims that an offender is entitled to exculpation solely because of volitional impairment. If testimony based upon this framework is excluded, then, the result may be to totally deprive the legal inquiry of useful—and perhaps necessary—assistance from mental health professionals.

But it seems likely the other conceptual frameworks provide some basis for identifying certain clinically observable conditions in which volition impairment is a major feature. The descriptively oriented *Diagnostic and Statistical Manual of* *Mental Disorders* (American Psychiatric Association, 1980), for example, identifies a number of what are called "disorders of impulse control." Discussion in the *Manual's* text, however, suggests that the subject's ability to resist the impulse was not of major interest in identifying or defining the disorders or in formulating diagnostic criteria for clinical practice. "Intermittent explosive disorder," for example, is described as involving "loss of control over aggressive impulse" resulting in serious assault or destruction of property (p. 295); the implication is that assaultive conduct resulting from such a clinical condition involves seriously impaired volition. But the next disorder, "Isolated Explosive Disorder," is described as involving a "failure to resist" an impulse leading to a single violent act (p. 297); the implication is that the impulse could have been resisted but was not. This strongly suggests that despite the use of terminology that suggests distinctions between inability and "blameworthy failure" to control, the drafters of the *Manual*—and probably the practitioners using it—in fact attach little clinical significance to the distinction.

In practice, it is likely that forensic mental health practitioners who do not use a dynamic personality theory framework work largely on a descriptive basis. This framework, however, provides little or no means by which to critically address volitional impairment or its degree and, most importantly, its impact in a particular situation. Steadman, Keitner, Braff, and Arvanities (1983) recently concluded that the major factor associated with a conclusion that an offender was not criminally responsible was a diagnosis of psychosis. If evaluations and testimony based upon dynamic frameworks are excluded, expert testimony may be based almost entirely upon an uncritical assumption that volitional impairment sufficient to render a defendant nonresponsible existed when, but only when, the subject's clinical condition at the time of the conduct justified a diagnosis of psychosis. If expert testimony concerning volitional deficiencies must rely heavily upon such assumptions, perhaps concern with volitional impairment should cease. Inquiry into volitional impairment ought to continue if, but only if, it can be made without the assurance of reliable expert advice from mental health professionals.

Permitting expert testimony on volitional impairment but screening out that based on dynamic personality theory may be an inadequate approach for another reason. The expectation that American trial judges will preview and screen defense testimony on the basis of the personality theory relied upon by the proffered defense expert may be unrealistic. Such screening would require fairly sophisticated distinctions to be drawn along lines that trial judges may be reluctant to develop. The risk of reversal on appeal for improper exclusion of defense testimony might discourage many judges from the sort of rigorous screening that would be necessary to accomplish the objective.

A second reason why defects in the established usefulness of dynamic personality theory may not constitute a persuasive argument against a defense of volitional impairment is that the matter may be an appropriate one for inquiry even if reliable expert testimony on the issue is not available. Whether or not "free will" has been incorporated by behavioral scientists into generally accepted theories of personality, it remains an operative part of criminal law. If the purposes of criminal responsibility demand inquiry into whether certain defendants have experienced loss of volitional capacity, triers of fact may be required to engage in a "common sense" inquiry into this even if useful expert testimony is unavailable. That a matter is not within the expertise of various professionals, in other words, does not necessarily render it inappropriate for inquiry during litigation.

RESTRICTING THE REQUIRED "DISORDER"

If there are serious problems with providing a defense of volitional impairment, the post-*Hinckley* discussions provide some basis for believing that these might be effectively dealt with by imposing stringent requirements concerning the disorder upon which a claim for exculpation must rest. Such an approach requires consideration as an alternative to elimination of a responsibility defense based on volitional impairment.

The American Bar Association committee report proposing the recommendations ultimately approved by the Association suggested that a volitional impairment defense was undesirable in large part because of the absence of any restriction upon the underlying impairment required:

The principle problem with continuing utilization of the volitional or "control" test is that the test is combined with vague or

broad interpretations of the term "mental disease." And it is the mixing of these ephemeral notions that results inevitably in unstructured expert speculation regarding the psychological causes of criminal behavior. This is the result especially in cases where defendants have a personality disorder, an impulse disorder or any other diagnosable abnormality short of clinically recognized psychoses. (American Bar Association Standing Committee, 1983, p. 5)

Apparently disparaging of any practical definition of disorder, however, the Association proposed the abandonment of inquiry into volitional impairment rather than limiting the inquiry by imposing a threshold requirement concerning the nature of the disorder.

The American Psychiatric Association, on the other hand, urged that responsibility law require defenses of nonresponsibility to be based on disorders that "grossly and demonstrably" impair the person's capacities. Usually, it continued, the defense should require that the underlying disorder "be of the severity (if not always of the quality) of conditions that psychiatrists diagnose as psychoses." (American Psychiatric Association, 1982, pp. 11–12). If effectively enforced, the requirement would apparently mean that a defense could appropriately be mounted only if the evidence showed that the defendant's unconsciously influenced behavior was part of a syndrome that included delusions, hallucinations, or other traditional psychotic symptoms. So limited, volitional defenses—even if based on dynamically oriented expert testimony—might not present pervasive problems of jury confusion and error.

On the other hand, it can be argued that such an approach undesirably ignores what mental health professionals sometimes have to offer. If dynamic personality theory has a sufficient basis to warrant relying upon it in making important forensic decisions, the proposed threshold requirement is artificial. A defendant may, for any of a variety of reasons, have exhibited no traditional symptoms other than thoughts and conduct related to the offense. Yet—and perhaps because of this—the offense may nevertheless, under dynamic personality theory, have been significantly influenced by unconscious factors that deprived the defendant of the ability to exercise conscious control over his action. In other words, a threshold requirement of a traditional serious mental illness may render unavailable expert testimony useful in resolving those "hard" cases that pose greatest difficulty.

Apart from the abstract desirability of such a threshold requirement, it is questionable whether such a requirement would be practically enforceable. Unless a workable standard for identifying those disorders that meet the requirement can be formulated, of course, trial judges cannot be expected to enforce the requirement. Formulation of such a standard may be impossible. The American Psychiatric Association was apparently unwilling to offer the concept of psychosis as a standard. It recommended a requirement that the disorder *usually*—not necessarily, however—be of the severity—but not *always* of the *quality*—of conditions diagnosed in practice as psychoses. Given the flexibility of the concept of psychosis, the Association's reluctance is understandable. But whether any reasonable alternative exists is uncertain. The Association's statement offers none.

Most importantly, it may be that any such threshold requirement as might be formulated would be so easily circumvented as to be ineffective. The proposals do not appear to require that the evidence of a disorder *apart from the defendant's activities related to the offense* constitute a serious disorder. Thus it remains open for a witness to argue that a defendant's conscious perception of an anticipated offense was so inconsistent with reasonableness or normality as to constitute evidence of an impairment of psychotic dimensions.

Hinckley's case provides an apt illustration. Some evidence was available tending to indicate that Hinckley believed that by killing the president he would assure himself of a relationship with Jodie Foster that would meet certain of his needs or desires. Whether that belief—or the thought processes that resulted in it—constituted a condition of the severity that mental health professionals diagnose as psychosis is sufficiently arguable that most trial judges would regard the testimony as raising the defense even under a legal standard including a threshold requirement of a serious disorder. At a minimum, a conscientious trial judge, anxious to avoid reversible error and uncomfortable with conflicting concepts of personality theory and diagnostic criteria, would not be likely to keep such a case from a trial jury on the ground that the defense testimony fails a threshold requirement of a serious disorder.

Volitional Impairments Under Cognitive Criteria

The impact of widespread rejection of a volitional impairment defense can only be evaluated by inquiring as to how this leaves responsibility law. Pre-*Hinckley* discussion included assertions that many if not all formulations of a cognitive criterion might be construed as to permit consideration of at least some volitional impairments. Post-*Hinckley* discussion returned to this possibility, and thus cast some doubt on the significance of abandonment of volitional impairment as a defense. The American Bar Association's endorsement of a criterion that places into issue a defendant's "appreciation" of the wrongfulness of his conduct was supported by the argument that this phraseology would allow or perhaps require trial judges to permit mental health professionals to testify as to all of their professional conclusions, including those concerning "emotional" or "affective" dimensions of defendants' impairment. In effect, the recommendation is apparently one of an especially flexible cognitive criterion that permits stretching to cover some volitional impairments. As was discussed earlier, the same construction can be given the requirement that the defendant "know" or "understand" as used in other and more traditional formulations of the cognitive standard. This construction of the remaining cognitive impairment defense, of course, would minimize the significance of abandoning the volitional defense. It also, however, raises other objections to such a course of action.

The effect of such a criterion might be best examined by considering the results of its application to the Hinckley litigation. At least some—and perhaps all—of the defense witnesses were prepared to acknowledge that Hinckley had an intellectual understanding of his conduct and its likely results, of the manner in which legal authorities would respond to it, and probably of its illegal status under the criminal law. But they were further prepared—as in many cases—to testify that because of his impairment he did not experience a "normal" emotional reaction to that intellectual awareness. This, in turn, rendered him—in their opinions—nonresponsible under a cognitive responsibility standard.

The factual conclusions on which these conclusions were based were the same conclusions the experts relied upon in offering the opinion that Hinckley was unable to control his conduct. Somewhat simplified, the defense testimony suggested that Hinckley approached the possible assassination of the president without the ability to respond in a "normal" emotional manner to the anticipation of that conduct and its results. Such an emotional reaction to potential conduct, the witnesses further suggested, is an integral part of exercising conscious control over possible future activity. Because Hinckley approached the choice of whether or not to kill President Reagan lacking this important foundation for exercising free choice, he lacked the "substantial capacity" to consciously and freely choose whether or not to engage in the conduct. The important characteristic of the testimony is that the same factual determination—that Hinckley did not respond "emotionally" in a normal fashion to the prospect of killing another human being—served as the basis for concluding that he was entitled to exculpation under either prong of the criterion. The determination was relied upon as establishing both that Hinckley lacked the cognitive capacity to "know" in a broad "appreciate" sense the wrongfulness of that conduct and that he lacked the volitional capacity to choose whether or not to engage in that conduct. Had *Hinckley* been litigated under a purely cognitive impairment criterion, it is quite likely that the testimony submitted to the jury would have been almost identical. The only likely difference would have been that the defense witnesses would not have expressly testified to professional opinions that Hinckley lacked the substantial capacity to conform to the legal prohibitions against the conduct at issue.

The end result, of course, is that litigation under many or all so-called cognitive criteria would involve most if not all of the defects of the volitional test. The trier of fact would hear extensive, conflicting and speculative testimony and would experience the same confusion. But unlike the situation where such a case is litigated under the volitional criteria, a trial conducted under a cognitive standard would most likely result in the jury being instructed in a manner that fails to give its members any guidance as to how to consider that testimony. Even if the trial judge instructed the jurors on the definition of "appreciate"—which is unlikely—that definition would almost certainly engender confusion regarding the significance that the jurors were expected to give to evidence that the defendant lacked the ability to control his conduct.

In practice, adoption of a cognitive standard might well increase the very undesirable characteristics of insanity litigation that stimulated the post-*Hinckley* concerns. This, of course, militates strongly against the wisdom of such modifications of present law.

The Issue in Broader Perspective

If inquiry can be made into defendants' claims of volitional impairment with reasonable accuracy or if there are important reasons for inquiring into the matter despite significant risks of inaccurate results, might there be countervailing considerations that nevertheless militate in favor of abandoning a volitional impairment defense? There is some reason to believe so.

DILUTION OF DETERRENCE

A broad defense of volitional impairment might affect the ability of the criminal justice system to accomplish its preventive function. Identification of nonmeritorious claims of volitional impairment may be possible in practice. But this ability may not be widely known or accepted. Thus the general deterrent effect of criminal punishment may be impaired. Unimpaired—and thus deterrable—persons may commit offenses under the firmly held—although incorrect—perception that they will be able to escape liability by claiming volitional impairment.

The post-*Hinckley* discussion, however, seldom addressed such considerations. Instead, discussion focused upon the legal system's ability to apply a volitional criterion in specific cases. Perhaps this reflects recognition that considerations involving the deterrent or preventive effect of criminal liability are pervasively controlled by imponderables and thus are of little help in resolving particular issues.

EFFECT ON PUBLIC PERCEPTION OF THE CRIMINAL PROCESS

Some broader considerations were, however, an important part of the post-*Hinckley* discussion. That discussion was frequently refreshing in its open recognition that the primary issue was not the actual processing of claims in which insanity is claimed. There was widespread acknowledgment that these cases were infrequent and when presented generally did not present significant problems. But those very infrequent cases in which a claim of nonresponsibility was made—often because of alleged volitional impairment—were characterized as widely publicized. Consequently, it was urged, their effect upon the public's perception of the criminal process was far more important than the actual outcome. Attorney General Smith, for example, asserted that the formulation of the insanity defense has a capacity to influence citizens' perception and acceptance of "the rationality, fairness and efficiency of the entire criminal justice process" (Smith, 1982, p. 606).

In effect, the argument goes, the public perceives the criminal justice system as unable to accurately resolve defendant's claims of volitional impairment and consequently as absolving from culpability many defendants who in fact acted in a blameworthy fashion. This perception, in turn, affects citizens' perception of the criminal justice system—and perhaps of the government as a whole—as deserving of support and compliance. Continued entertainment of claims of volitional impairment or perhaps even retention of a legal doctrine that permits such claims, then, will ultimately impair the ability of the legal system to maintain order by demanding and obtaining the voluntary cooperation of a vast majority of its citizens.

Whether these claims are meritorious or not seems impossible to address in other than speculative ways. The *Hinckley* acquittal does seem to have contributed some factual information, however. The reaction to the acquittal strongly confirms that substantial portions of the American population perceived the criminal justice system as unable to accurately evaluate Hinckley's claim of volitional impairment. There also appears to be reason to believe that this attitude is related to a broader disillusionment with the criminal justice system as a vehicle for community protection. Whether these "facts"—if they are accurate—will actually have a significant impact upon the ability of the American criminal justice system to function, however, remains at best problematic.

Conclusion

Viewed in historical perspective, the furor following the *Hinckley* acquittal added little of substance to American responsibility law debate. No new proposals or new considerations bearing upon previously made proposals were developed. The reaction to the acquittal did, however, suggest that the philosophically mandated need to exculpate offenders whose impairment rendered them nonblameworthy was not as widely shared as had been assumed. Moreover, the reaction also suggested a need for greater significance to be given to practical problems in administering the defense.

As a result of the post-*Hinckley* furor, changes in allocation of the burden of proof and in post-acquittal processing have begun and are likely to continue. Most significant for the long run development of American responsibility law, however, is the reversal of the traditional trend towards accommodating volitional impairment by providing for a complete defense to liability on this basis.

Hinckley is compelling reconsideration of some of the propositions upon which acceptance of a volitional impairment defense has been based. Little scientifically based support has been found. Specifically, little other than intuition is available concerning the extent to which volitional impairment sufficient to overcome "free will" occurs in the absence of serious cognitive deficiency. Nor can mental health professionals offer empirically-demonstrated effectiveness or reliability in assessing the effect of particular persons' impairments on their ability to exercise control over their conduct. The major issue developed by the post-*Hinckley* debate is whether this state of knowledge justifies foreclosing defendants from the opportunity to escape criminal liability by establishing impaired volition.

On balance, it does not. But the judgment is a difficult one because, as the post-*Hinckley* dispute has made so clear, it must be made largely on the basis of speculation or, at best, intuition. *Hinckley* is forcing American law to acknowledge that responsibility issues must be addressed as ones of general public policy rather than as matters of specialized expertise that can be resolved by uncritical acceptance of the recommendations of experts.

Conceptually, volitional and cognitive impairments are distinguishable and independently may affect whether persons' conduct justifies condemnation as blameworthy. Until reliable evidence to the contrary is developed, the law should regard them as independent and should extend to defendants the opportunity for exculpation on the basis of impairment of either a cognitive or a volitional nature.

Similarly, the unavailability of scientifically-based expertise in mental health professions concerning evaluation of particular persons' volitional impairments does not justify a refusal to inquire into the existence and effect of such impairments. Until and unless such expert assistance becomes available, the inquiries must be undertaken as are those others which are necessary to administration of the law. In the absence of expertise rightfully claiming deference, juries and trial courts must undertake the task as one of common sense intuition, aided insofar as possible by insights which mental health professionals have to offer.

Retention of a defense of volitional impairment despite the absence of reliable evidence supporting its assumptions is not inconsistent with practical reality. The realities of criminal litigation are that narrowing insanity criteria is unlikely to reduce the number of cases in which claims of nonresponsibility must be addressed by juries nor will it significantly affect the amount or content of the testimony that is given in support of such claims. Such action may, however, require that volitional impairment be addressed obliquely and prevent whatever guidance can be given to juries by realistic instructions from the presiding judge. It is far preferable to address the matter directly, with open recognition of the difficulties involved in the necessary inquiries. To retreat to purely cognitive standards in reaction to *Hinckley* would constitute an unwise and largely impulsive reaction to a single "hard case."

It is not unreasonable to hope for improvement. Mental health professionals may have so little to offer on volitional impairment because they have so little occasion to address it in their own endeavors. *Hinckley* has made clear that if mental health professionals are to materially aid in inquiries into volitional impairment, their techniques and analyses and perhaps their entire conceptual framework require reconsideration and refinement. If inquiries into volitional impairment continue after *Hinckley,* they will undoubtedly be affected by the increased skepticism that has developed after the *Hinckley* acquittal. This skepticism as translated into courtroom demands may result in more research and conceptualization and development of more effective evaluative skills. *Hinckley* and its aftermath hold some promise, then, of stimulating improved inquiries into volitional impairment and of higher quality expert assistance. This promise should not be prematurely abandoned by foreclosure of direct inquiry into criminal defendants' impaired volitional capacities.

Addendum

In December of 1983, the House of Delegates of the American Medical Association endorsed the abolition of the "special defense" of insanity and its replacement with provision for acquittal of defendants who, as a result of mental disease or defect, are found to have lacked the *mens rea* required by the offense charged ("AMA Would Severely Limit," 1984). The report of the Association's Committee on Medicolegal Problems supporting this position (American Medical Association Committee, undated) defended it on several grounds. Modern criminal law doctrine, it urged, has recently emphasized the promotion of social and public interests rather than the punishment of moral wrongdoing. Apparently the committee regarded this as evidencing a corresponding tendency to abandon moral fault as a prerequisite to imposing criminal liability. While abandonment of the defense might permit conviction of some nonblameworthy offenders, this would be consistent with what the report saw as the trend in criminal jurisprudence. In addition, however, the report characterized the insanity defense in application as arbitrarily selective and therefore an ineffective means of assuring conviction of only the blameworthy. Abandonment of the defense would not, it reasoned, abolish any effective existing relationship between criminal liability and blameworthiness. The Association's endorsement of the *mens rea* approach seems certain to increase the attention that this alternative will be given in further discussions.

References

Addington v. Texas, 441 U.S. 418 (1979).

AMA would severely limit use of insanity as defense. *Psychiatric News*, January 6, 1984, pp. 1; 35; 41.

American Bar Association. Report no. 1 of the Section on Criminal Justice and Recommendation. *Reports of the American Bar Association*, 1975, *100*(1).

American Bar Association. *Summary of action taken by the House of Delegates of the American Bar Association, 1983 midyear meeting* (Report No. 100). Chicago: American Bar Association, 1983.

American Bar Association Standing Committee on Association Standards for Criminal Justice and Commission on the Mentally Disabled. *Reports with recommendations to the House of Delegates, 1983 midyear meeting.* Chicago: American Bar Association, 1983.

American Law Institute. *Model penal code* (tentative draft no. 4). Philadelphia: Author, 1955.

American Law Institute. *Model penal code* (proposed official draft). Philadelphia: Author, 1962.

American Medical Association Committee on Medicolegal Problems. *Report of conclusions and recommendations regarding the insanity defense.* Undated mimeo.

American Psychiatric Association. *Diagnostic and statistical manual of mental disorders* (3rd ed.). Washington: American Psychiatric Association, 1980.

American Psychiatric Association. *American Psychiatric Association statement on the insanity defense.* Washington: American Psychiatric Association, 1982.

Alaska Laws, 1982, ch. 143, Sec. 27, codified as Alaska Stat. Sections 12.47.010(a), 12.47.030.

Arizona Laws, 1977, ch. 142, codified as Arizona Revised Statutes, Sections 13-502, 13-701, 13-702.

Arizona Laws, 1983, ch. 118, codified as Arizona Revised Statutes, Section 13-502.

Behman v. Edwards, 678 F.2d 511 (5th Cir. 1982).

Bonnie, R.J. The moral basis of the insanity defense. *American Bar Association Journal,* 1983, *69*(February), 194–197.

California Laws, 1981, ch. 404, codified as California Penal Code Sections 22, 26, 28, 29, 188, 189.

California Laws, 1982, ch. 893, codified as California Penal Code Sections 21, 22, 28.

Carnes v. State, 101 Tex.Cr.R. 273, 275 S.W. 1002 (1925).

Commitment following an insanity acquittal. *Harvard Law Review,* 1981, *94*(3), 605–625.

Criss, M.L., & Racine, D.R. Impact of change in legal standard for those adjudicated not guilty by reason of insanity 1975–1979. *Bulletin of the American Academy of Psychiatry and the Law,* 1980, *8*(3), 261–271.

Curry v. State, 611 S.W.2d 745 (Ark. 1981).

Delaware Laws, Vol. 63, ch. 328, 1982, codified as Delaware Code Annotated, Title 11, Sec. 401, 408.

Dershowitz, A. Abolishing the insanity defense: The most significant feature of the administration's proposed criminal code—An essay. *Criminal Law Bulletin,* 1973, *9*(5), 434–439.

Dix, G.E. Psychological abnormality as a factor in grading criminal liability: Diminished capacity, diminished responsibility, and the like. *Journal of Criminal Law, Criminology and Police Science,* 1971, *62*(3), 313–334.

Dix, G.E., & Sharlot, M.M. *Criminal law, cases and materials.* St. Paul, MN: West Publishing Co., 1973.

Enmund v. Florida, 102 S.Ct. 3368 (1982).

Fisher v. United States, 328 U.S. 463 (1946).

Florida Laws, 1972, ch. 72-72, codified as Florida Statutes Annotated, Sec. 921.141.

Furman v. Georgia, 408 U.S. 238 (1972).

Georgia Laws, 1968, p. 1270, codified as Georgia Code Annotated, Sec. 702.

Georgia Laws, 1982, p. 1474, codified as Georgia Code Annotated, Sec. 27–1503.

Goldstein, A.S. *The insanity defense.* New Haven: Yale University Press, 1967.

Gregg v. Georgia, 428 U.S. 153 (1976).

Gussfield, J.R. On legislating morals: The symbolic process of designating deviance. *California Law Review,* 1968, *56*(1), 54–73.

Hall, J. Psychiatry and criminal responsibility. *Yale Law Journal,* 1956, *65*(6), 761–785.

Hall, J. Mental disease and criminal responsibility—McNaghten versus Durham and the American Law Institute's tentative draft. *Indiana Law Journal,* 1958, *33*(1), 212–225.

Hawaii Laws, 1982, ch. 229, Section 1, codified as Hawaii Revised Statutes, Sec. 704-402(a).

Hendershott v. People, 653 P.2d 385 (Colo. 1982).

Hermann, D.J. *The insanity defense, philosophical, historical and legal perspectives.* Springfield, IL: Charles C. Thomas, 1983.

Hughes v. Matthews, 576 F.2d 1250 (7th Cir. 1978).

Idaho Laws, 1982, ch. 368, codified as Idaho Statutes Annotated, Section 18-207, 19-2513.

Illinois Laws, 1977, Public Act 80-1099, Section 3, pp. 3300–3301, codified as Illinois Annotated Statutes, chapter 38, Section 1005-5-3.1.

In re Winship, 397 U.S. 358 (1970).

Indiana Laws, 1978, P.L. 145, codified as Indiana Statutes Annotated, Section 35-36-2-3.

Indiana Laws, 1981, P.L. 198, codified as Indiana Statutes Annotated, Sections 35-36-1-1, 35-36-3-2, 35-36-2-5.

Ingber, W.J. Rules for an exceptional class: The commitment and release of persons acquitted by reason of insanity. *New York University Law Review,* 1982, *57*(2), 281–329.

Ingles v. People, 90 Colo. 51, 6 P.2d 455 (1931).

Jackson v. Indiana, 406 U.S. 715 (1972).

Jones v. United States, 103 U.S. 3043 (1983).

Keedy, E.R. Insanity and criminal responsibilty. *Harvard Law Review,* 1917, *30*, 535–560, 724–738.

Kentucky Laws, 1982, ch. 113, codified as Kentucky Revised Statutes Annotated, Sections 504.120, 504.130, 504.150.

Korsak v. State, 154 S.W.2d 348, 202 Ark. 921 (1941).

LaFave, W.R., & Scott, A.W., Jr. *Handbook on criminal law.* St. Paul, MN: West Publishing Co., 1972.

Leland v. Oregon, 343 U.S. 790 (1952).

Lockett v. Ohio, 438 U.S. 586 (1978).

Louisell, D.W., & Diamond, B.L. Law and psychiatry: Detente, entente, or concomitance? *Cornell Law Quarterly,* 1965, *50*(2), 217–234.

Lyles v. United States, 254 F.2d 725 (D.C.Cir. 1957), cert. denied, 356 U.S. 961 (1958).

M'Naghten's Case, 10 Cl. & F. 200, 8 Eng. Rep. 718 (1843).

Michigan Laws, 1975, Public Act 180, codified as Michigan Compiled Laws Annotated, Section 768.36, 330.1400a, 768.29a(2).

Mississippi Laws, 1928, ch. 75.

Missouri Laws 1977, Senate Bill 60, page 658, codified as Missouri Annotated Statutes, Article 562.086.

Montana Laws, 1967, ch. 713, codified as Montana Revised Codes Annotated, Section 46-14-101, 46-14-102, 46-14-301.

Montana Laws, 1977, ch. 196, Section 3, codified as Montana Revised Codes Annotated, Sections 46-14-101, 46-14-102.

Moore, M.S. Responsibility and the unconscious. *Southern California Law Review,* 1980, *53*(6), 1563–1675.

Morse, S.J. Failed explanations and criminal responsibility: experts and the unconscious. *Virginia Law Review,* 1982, *68*(5), 971–1084.

Mueller, G.O.W. McNaghten remains irreplacable: Recent events in the law of incapacity. *Georgetown Law Journal*, 1961, *50*(1), 105–120.

Mullaney v. Wilbur, 421 U.S. 684 (1975).

National Commission on Reform of Federal Criminal Laws. *Final report of the National Commission on Reform of Federal Criminal Laws*. Washington: U.S. Government Printing Office, 1971.

National Commission on the Insanity Defense. *Myths and realities: A report of the National Commission on the Insanity Defense*. Arlington, VA: National Mental Health Association, 1983.

New Mexico Laws 1982, ch. 55, codified as New Mexico Statutes, Sections 31-9-3, 31-9-4.

New York Department of Mental Hygiene. *A report to Governor Hugh L. Carey on the insanity defense in New York*. Albany: New York Department of Mental Hygiene, 1978.

New York Laws, 1965, ch. 1030, p. 1542, codified as New York Penal Law, Sec. 30.05.

Parsons v. State, 81 Ala. 577, 2 So. 854 (1887).

Patterson v. New York, 432 U.S. 197 (1977).

Pennsylvania Laws, 1982, P.L. 1262, No. 286, codified as Pennsylvania Statutes Annotated, Title 18, Sec. 314–315.

People v. Conley, 64 Cal.2d 310, 49 Cal.Reptr. 815, 411 P.2d 911 (1966).

People v. Drew, 22 Cal.3d 333, 149 Cal.Reptr. 275, 583 P.2d 1318 (1978).

People v. Henderson, 60 Cal.2d 482, 35 Cal.Reptr. 77, 386 P.2d 677 (1963).

People v. Mcquillan, 392 Mich. 511, 221 N.W.2d 569 (1974).

People v. Poddar, 10 Cal.2d 750, 111 Cal.Reptr. 910, 518 P.2d 342 (1974).

People v. Thompson, 591 P.2d 1031 (Colo. 1979).

People v. Wolff, 61 Cal.2d 795, 40 Cal.Reptr. 271, 394 P.2d 959 (1964).

Platt, A., & Diamond, B. The origins of the "right and wrong" test of criminal responsibility and its subsequent development in the United States: An historical survey. *California Law Review*, 1966, *54*(3), 1227–1260.

Powell v. Texas, 392 U.S. 514 (1968).

President of the United States. *Comprehensive Crime Control Act of 1983, message from the president of the United States transmitting a proposal for legisla-tion entitled the "Comprehensive Crime Control Act of 1983."* Washington: United States Government Printing Office (House Doc. No. 98-32), 1983.

Robinson, D. Consultant's report on criminal responsibility—Mental illness: Section 503. *Working Papers of the National Commission on Reform of Federal Criminal Laws,* 1970, *II*, 229–259.

Roby, A. Guilty but mentally ill. *Bulletin of the American Academy of Psychiatry and the Law*, 1978, *6*(4), 374–381.

Sinclair v. State, 161 Miss. 142, 132 So. 581 (1931).

Smith, G.A., & Hall, J.A. Evaluating Michigan's guilty but mentally ill verdict: An empirical study. *University of Michigan Journal of Law Reform*, 1982, *16*(1), 77–114.

Smith, W.F. Limiting the insanity defense: A rational approach to irrational crimes. *Missouri Law Review*, 1982, *47*(4), 605–619.

State v. Garrett, 391 S.W.2d 235 (Mo. 1965).

State v. Graimm, 156 W.Va. 615, 195 S.E.2d 637 (1973).

State v. Greenawalt, 128 Ariz. 150, 624 P.2d 828 (1981).

State v. Kaufman, 46 S.W.2d 843 (Mo.1932).

State v. Lange, 168 La. 958, 123 So. 639 (1929).

State v. Nuckolls, 273 S.E.2d 87 (W.Va. 1980).

State v. Strasberg, 60 Wash. 106, 110 P. 1020 (1910).

State v. Williams, 97 N.M. 634, 642 P.2d 1093 (1982).

Steadman, H.J., Keitner, L., Braff, J., & Arvanities, T.M. Factors associated with a successful insanity plea. *American Journal of Psychiatry*, 1983, *140*(4), 401–405.

Steele v. State, 97 Wis.2d 72, 294 N.W.2d 12 (1980).

Strickland v. State, 247 Ga. 219, 275 S.E.2d 29 (1981).

Taylor v. State, 440 N.E.2d 1109 (Ind. 1982).

Taylor v. United States, 222 F.2d 398 (D.C.Cir. 1954).

Texas Laws, 1983, codified as Texas Penal Code, Section 8.01.

United States Department of Justice. *Attorney general's Task Force on Violent Crime, final report*. Washington: U.S. Dept. of Justice, 1981.

Walder, R. Psychiatry and the problem of criminal responsibility. *University of Pennsylvania Law Review*, 1952, *101*(3), 378–390.

Weihofen, H. *Mental disorder as a criminal defense*. Buffalo: Dennis & Co., Inc., 1954.

Wharton, F., & Stille, M. *Medical jurisprudence* (5th ed.) (Vol. 1). Rochester: Lawyers' Cooperative Publishing Company, 1905.

2.
Informed Consent

Paul S. Appelbaum

ABSTRACT. Informed consent has become an instrument by means of which groups with widely divergent interests have sought to advance their ends. As a result of this process, the law of informed consent has been shaped in a series of compromises that leave advocates of any single point of view dissatisfied with the result.

The law of informed consent is most thoroughly developed in the United States. There the doctrine arose about 25 years ago from the previous doctrine of "simple consent." Whereas courts utilizing the older standard required physicians, in order to obtain patient consent and avoid liability for battery, to disclose only the nature of the medical interventions they planned to undertake, the doctrine of informed consent evolved to require disclosure of the consequences of the intervention, as well.

Three major forces have shaped the development of informed consent law. Most court decisions in the area have emphasized the importance of individual autonomy, and the consequent necessity of patients having sufficient information on which to base decisions about medical care. Concerns for health have played a more ambivalent role in consent law. Some decisions have argued that provision of information to patients will encourage rational decisions and greater cooperation in their care. Others, however, have adopted the view of many doctors that disclosure wastes valuable medical time and that allowing patients to make decisions encourages irrationality. The third major force has been the structure of negligence law. The inclusion of actions for failure to obtain informed consent under negligence law has limited patients' recourse to situations in which actual harm occurs, and in other ways made it more difficult for them to recover damages.

This chapter reviews how consent cases moved from battery to negligence law; ways in which standards of disclosure have been formulated; requirements for establishing causal relationships in informed consent cases; means of determining the competency and voluntariness of consent; exceptions to the requirement for informed consent; legislative initiatives on informed consent; and consent in special circumstances, including research, psychiatric facilities, and consent outside the United States, especially in Canada, England, and France.

Critiques of informed consent have generally emphasized one or another of the major interests accommodated by the doctrine. More radical critics tend to ignore the presence of competing interests, thus vitiating their chances of provoking substantive change in the doctrine. Moderate assessments, which recognize diverse interests, almost inevitably offer no more than suggestions for minor tinkering with the current equilibrium. Thus, although few people would describe themselves as satisfied with the present shape of the doctrine, fundamental changes are unlikely to occur in the near future.

This work was supported in part by Research Scientist Development Award No. 1-K01-MH00456-01 from the National Institute of Mental Health.

The author acknowledges the helpful comments of Loren Roth, M.D., M.P.H. and Alan Meisel, J.D. on an earlier draft of this chapter.

SOMMAIRE. Le consentement éclairé est devenu un instrument par lequel des groupes aux intérêts tout à fait divergents ont cherché à promouvoir leurs fins. Sous l'effet de ce processus, le consentement éclairé a donné lieu sur le plan du droit à une série de compromis qui mécontentent les avocats à tous points de vue.

C'est aux États-Unis que le régime du consentement éclairé est le plus développé, là où la doctrine est née il y a environ vingt-cinq ans à partir de l'ancienne doctrine du simple consentement. Alors qu'avec les anciennes méthodes, les tribunaux demandaient aux médecins de ne révéler que la nature des interventions médicales qu'ils avaient l'intention d'entreprendre pour obtenir le consentement du patient, afin d'éviter toute poursuite pour voies de fait, la doctrine du consentement éclairé a évolué et exige maintenant que soient aussi révélées les conséquences de l'intervention.

L'essor de la règle du consentement éclairé a été influencé par trois principaux facteurs. La plupart des décisions des tribunaux dans ce domaine ont accentué l'importance de l'autonomie de l'individu ainsi que la nécessité qui en découle pour les patients d'avoir suffisamment d'information pour pouvoir prendre une décision à propos du traitement. Les préoccupations de santé ont joué un rôle plus ambivalent dans le droit du consentement. Dans certaines décisions de jurisprudence, on a pu dire que le fait de donner des renseignements aux patients encouragerait les décisions rationnelles et une plus grande collaboration de leur part dans les soins. D'autres ont, cependant, soutenu comme de nombreux médecins que ce processus d'information constituait un gaspillage d'heures précieuses pour les médecins et que le fait de permettre aux patients de prendre les décisions encourageait l'irrationalité. Le troisième facteur essentiel a été le régime de responsabilité fondé sur la négligence. En faisant entrer les actions pour absence de consentement dans la responsabilité pour négligence, on a restreint les recours des patients aux cas de préjudice réel, et il est donc plus difficile pour ces derniers d'obtenir des dommages-intérêts en dehors de ces cas.

L'auteur montre comment la jurisprudence sur le consentement a évolué, de la catégorie des voies de fait à la catégorie de la négligence; il expose les différentes formulations données aux normes de divulgation, les exigences de l'établissement des relations de causalité dans les cas de consentement éclairé, les moyens de déterminer la compétence et le caractère volontaire du consentement, les exceptions à la règle du consentement éclairé, les initiatives législatives en matière de consentement éclairé et le consentement dans des cas particuliers, notamment la recherche et les établissements psychiatriques, et le consentement en dehors des États-Unis, plus particulièrement au Canada, en Angleterre et en France.

Les critiques du consentement éclairé ont, en général, mis l'accent sur l'un ou l'autre des principaux intérêts qui sont sauvegardés par la doctrine. Les critiques les plus radicaux tendent à faire fi des intérêts concurrents en présence, et ils menacent ainsi leurs chances de faire évoluer la doctrine de façon substantielle. Les modérés, qui tiennent compte, eux, des différents intérêts, n'offrent presque inévitablement que des suggestions de simple aménagement de l'équilibre actuel. Il est, par conséquent, peu probable que des changements fondamentaux ne se produisent dans un avenir proche, même si rares sont ceux qui se disent satisfaits de l'état actuel de la doctrine.

Introduction

The term "informed consent" is deceptive in its simplicity. On the surface, it appears to suggest no more than that patients should be making educated decisions about participation in medical treatment and research. Taken at this level its desirability is almost tautologic, and the enormous efforts of the last quarter-century to support, explicate, and extend the doctrine of informed consent, or alternatively to demonstrate its putative, pernicious impact on medical practice, seem inexplicable.

In fact, the many controversies generated about informed consent in the medical, legal, public policy, and ethical literature can only be seen in perspective when one recognizes that there is no unitary, widely-accepted concept of the term. Informed consent has become an instrument by means of which groups with widely divergent interests have sought to advance accordingly diverse ends. The result has been a series of compromises whereby the law of informed consent, as well as its practice, has been molded.

This process of accommodating differing and often conflicting interests accounts for the nearly universal dissatisfaction displayed in the professional literature with informed consent law. By hewing to no single theoretical rationale and seeking no single end, the doctrine of informed consent remains susceptible to assault by anyone with a consistent ideological position.

The goal of this discussion is to avoid the easy task of assessing the law of informed consent from a single point of view and, inevitably, finding it wanting. Rather, an attempt will be made to reflect the multifaceted nature of the doctrine, illuminating the conflicting forces at work, assessing their success in attaining their own goals, and highlighting the tensions that make this such a difficult area of interaction between medicine and law.

Since informed consent is largely a product of American law and medical practice, the discussion will focus primarily on developments in the United States. Some attention will be given, however, to analogous developments in Canada, England, and other jurisdictions. The chapter will begin with an overview of the evolution of informed consent in American law. In the second part of the chapter, the varying interests accommodated will be identified. The third section will outline in greater detail the current law of informed consent and will apply the analysis of competing interests to major issues in contemporary practice. This will be followed by a review of informed consent law in special situations, including consent to research, consent in psychiatry, and consent in other countries. In the final pages of the chapter, an overview of critical approaches and suggested changes in the law and practice of informed consent will be presented.

Historical Evolution of the Doctrine of Informed Consent in American Law

Consent to Treatment

The principle that consent is required prior to medical interventions can be traced back through American common law to its English progenitor. Although unconsented touchings have long been viewed as compensable events, the first reported application of this principle to the medical profession dates from the English case of *Slater* v. *Baker & Stapleton* in 1767. In that decision, the court held a surgeon, who had rebroken the improperly healed leg of his patient without either the patient's prior knowledge or consent, liable for civil

damages for the "trespass" thereby committed.

The usual view of the history of consent law is that in the 190 years between *Slater* and the first modern informed consent case, *Salgo* v. *Leland Stanford Jr. University Board of Trustees* (1957), the rules governing consent to medical treatment remained narrowly focused and constant: Medical procedures (almost always invasive, surgical procedures) undertaken without the patient's consent, or following a consent induced under fraud or duress, left the practitioner liable for damages for battery. On the other hand, as long as the essential nature of the procedure had been revealed to an uncoerced patient, no further questions were asked. The consent involved here could be called "simple consent." The situation in 19th-century law was actually somewhat more complex than this (Pernick, 1982), but the notion of "simple consent" provides a useful heuristic starting point for a consideration of the development of informed consent law.

Mohr v. *Williams*, a 1905 Minnesota case, presents a good illustration of the application of the doctrine of simple consent. The plaintiff Mohr had consulted Dr. Williams, a specialist in diseases of the ear, about problems with her right ear. She gave consent for surgery on that ear, but once she was placed under anesthesia, an examination of her left ear revealed that it was even more severely diseased and in need of intervention. Dr. Williams then "skillfully performed" the surgery on the left ear, without awakening the patient to obtain her consent. The patient later sued Dr. Williams, contending *inter alia* that the unauthorized surgery constituted an assault and battery.

The court in *Mohr* dismissed the possibility of criminal liability by noting that "the case is unlike a criminal prosecution for assault and battery, for there an unlawful intent must be shown." Dr. Williams, however, despite his beneficent intentions, was found liable for civil damages, since "every person has a right to complete immunity of his person from physical interference of others, except insofar as contact may be necessary under the general doctrine of privilege; and any unlawful or unauthorized touching of the person of another, except it be in the spirit of pleasantry, constitutes an assault and battery."

As in almost all of the pre–1957 consent cases, the focus in *Mohr* was on the failure of the physician to portray accurately to the patient the nature and character of the procedure (*Meisel*, 1977; *Plant*, 1968). The dramatic transition from simple consent to informed consent, which began with *Salgo* in 1957, reflected a shift in judicial attention from this focus on what the patient was told about the *nature* of the procedure to what was revealed to the patient about the *consequences* of the procedure. There was a concomitant shift in the legal category under which these cases were handled, from battery to negligence (*Plant*, 1968).

Salgo involved a patient with intermittent claudication of the legs who was the subject of an aortogram, a radiologic assessment of the patency of the aorta, the body's largest artery. At that time, the procedure required general anesthesia and involved a transcutaneous puncture of the aorta from the lumbar region of the patient's back, followed by injection of a radiopaque contrast medium. The physician had "called on the plaintiff in his hospital room and informed him that he was to do the aortography and would do it the next afternoon. He explained that he would inject some material into the aorta and take films at that time to see if they could ascertain the precise condition of plaintiff's circulatory system." Having obtained the patient's consent following this disclosure, the physician had clearly satisfied the historic standard of simple consent exemplified by *Mohr*.

Not long after the procedure, however, and most likely as a result of it, the patient developed a permanent paralysis of his lower extremities. There was some dispute as to whether the procedure had been performed negligently or not, but the California Court of Appeals found, distinct from the performance issue, that a physician involved in any procedure "violates his duty to his patient and subjects himself to liability if he withholds any facts which are necessary to form the basis of an intelligent consent by the patient." Later in the opinion, the court described this as a duty to obtain an "informed consent," the first known use of that term.

This judicial hint of a new obligation on the part of physicians—the duty to disclose risks and other facts important to the patient's decision making, in addition to the previously required disclosure of the nature of the procedure—was seized upon and elaborated three years later in the Kansas case of *Natanson* v. *Kline* (1960). Subsequently, a flood of informed consent cases emanated from the appellate courts. They vary in their particulars, but the classic and most widely discussed exposition of the doctrine of informed consent, the 1972 decision of the District of Columbia Circuit Court of Appeals in *Canterbury* v.

Spence, offers a concise summary of the state of informed consent law today. It should be noted that although not every aspect of *Canterbury* has been adopted in every jurisdiction, as will be elaborated below, the decision addresses all of the major aspects of informed consent law.

Judge Robinson in *Canterbury* began his analysis from the "root premise," enunciated 45 years previously by New York's Chief Judge Cardozo, that " 'every human being of adult years and sound mind has a right to determine what shall be done with his own body . . .' True consent to what happens to one's self is the informed exercise of a choice, and that entails an opportunity to evaluate knowledgeably the options available and the risks attendant upon each." Consequently, Robinson held that physicians were obligated to disclose all risks "material" to the patient's decision. (This has come to be known as a "materiality" standard.) These included "the inherent and potential hazards of the proposed treatment, the alternatives to that treatment, if any, and the results likely if the patient remains untreated." A risk was material if a "reasonable person, in what the physician knows or should know to be the patient's position, would be likely to attach significance to the risk or cluster of risks in deciding whether or not to forego the proposed therapy."

The *Canterbury* court had also to consider when the failure to abide by this standard of disclosure left a physician open to liability. Applying traditional ideas of negligence law, the court held that the plaintiff must prove that the failure to disclose had in fact led to the injury which was the source of the complaint. This requirement could be satisfied by demonstrating that "a prudent person in the patient's position" would have decided not to undergo the treatment or procedure administered had the missing information been revealed.

Two elements of those described above from the *Canterbury* decision, which is otherwise representative, lack universal acceptance. First, not all courts have adopted a materiality standard for disclosure. In fact, although the situation is in constant flux, it appears that the majority of jurisdictions in the United States require physicians to disclose only that information which the average responsible practitioner would disclose, rather than all that would be material to the "reasonable person's" decision (LeBlang, 1983). Some states, opting for neither of these choices, have actually specified by legislation or regulation either the type of information to be disclosed or the specific facts to be revealed (Meisel & Kabnick, 1980). Second, a few jurisdictions (and a far larger number of legal commentators) believe that the link between the missing disclosure and the injury should be demonstrated by proving that the patient himself (not "a prudent person in the patient's position") would have declined to proceed with treatment had the information been revealed (see, e.g., Trichter & Lewis, 1980). (These issues will be addressed in greater detail in a later section of this chapter.)

A useful model has been developed by Meisel, Roth, and Lidz (1977) to characterize the state of post-*Canterbury* informed consent law. They point to five elements of a legally valid decision. The first of these is the provision of information, the area addressed most thoroughly in judicial opinions on informed consent. In addition, however, patients must make their decisions voluntarily, without overt coercion or constraint, and they must be legally competent to make a binding choice. Meisel et al. also note that the courts implicitly assume that the competent patient who is presented with the proper information will develop an understanding of the necesssary facts for a rational decision. This assertion is controversial and will be examined at length later in this chapter. Finally, a patient must actually make an identifiable decision as the end product of the informed consent process. When compared with pre–1957 consent law, this model highlights the fact that provision of information (with or without resulting understanding) is the area in which the major developments have taken place, while the associated concepts of voluntariness, competency, and the formulation of a decision have remained relatively constant.

Consent to Research

Given the intimate relationship between medical treatment and research, and the intuitive observation that both areas are likely to raise similar issues concerning patient consent, it is remarkable that the law governing informed consent to research has developed almost entirely independently of the law on informed consent to treatment. Instead of evolving largely as the result of court decisions addressing cases in which patients have suffered injury, the rules for obtaining consent to research have evolved almost entirely as a matter of ethical codes and administrative regulation.

Prior to 1947, there was almost no law governing the conduct of medical research in general, or the procedures for obtaining consent in particular (Annas, Glantz, & Katz, 1977). Retrospective writings make clear that there was considerable variation in practices, but that subjects were often told little about either the procedures involved or their risks; in fact, it appears that in some medical settings research was not clearly labeled as such for patient-subjects, many of whom were led to believe they were undergoing therapeutic procedures (McCance, 1963).

In 1946, the International Military Tribunal sitting at Nuremberg heard the case of Nazi physicians who were accused of committing crimes against humanity by virtue of the "experiments" they performed on concentration camp inmates and others during World War II (Ivy, 1977; *U.S. v. Brandt*, 1947). Searching for acknowledged standards of conduct on which to base their decisions, the judges found an almost complete absence of professional guidelines concerning research with human subjects. Standards rapidly developed by a consultant, Dr. Andrew Ivy, and approved by the American Medical Association were forwarded to the Tribunal and found their way, conceptually intact, into the resulting decision the following year. The 10 principles of conduct in human experimentation laid down by the court have come to be called the "Nuremberg Code." Eight of the 10 principles were designed to minimize the possibility of harm resulting to research subjects; these addressed such issues as the competency of the experimenter and the design of the research. Two provisions, however, dealt with the question of consent by subjects. The first principle, although lengthy, is worth quoting in full in this regard:

> The voluntary consent of the human subject is absolutely essential. This means that the person involved should have legal capacity to give consent, should be so situated as to be able to exercise free power of choice without the intervention of any element of force, fraud, deceit, duress, over-reaching, or other ulterior form of constraint or coercion and should have sufficient knowledge and comprehension of the elements of the subject matter involved as to make an understanding and enlightened decision. This latter element requires that before the acceptance of an affirmative decision by the experimental subject there should be made known to him the nature, duration, and

purpose of the experiment; the method and means by which it is to be conducted; all inconveniences and hazards reasonably to be expected; and the effects upon his health or person which may possibly come from his participation in the experiment. (Reiser, Dyck, & Curran, 1977)

A later provision called for a subject to have the right to leave any experiment "if he has reached the physical or mental state where continuation of the experiment seems to him to be impossible."

Despite the clearly stated requirements for consent enumerated in the Code, its impact on the world research community was limited, because the declaration was not enforceable under the law of individual nations. Nonetheless, it stimulated considerable world-wide discussion, and the production of similar codes by national organizations, such as the Medical Research Council of the United Kingdom (Frenkel, 1977). Most of these codes were less restrictive than Nuremberg, permitting consent to be dispensed with under certain circumstances, such as when experimental trials were intended to have therapeutic benefit for the subject or significant harm was unlikely. The separate paths of development of informed consent to treatment and research are thrown into stark constrast when one realizes that many of these standards for consent to research would not have met even the long-standing requirements for "simple consent" to treatment derived from Anglo-American common law.

The development of codes for researchers culminated in the Declaration of Helsinki, adopted by the World Medical Association in 1964 (Reiser et al., 1977). This document, like many of its predecessors, distinguished "clinical research combined with patient care"—for which the patient's informed consent or the consent of a guardian was desirable, but not required—from non-therapeutic research—for which informed consent was essential. But, like all of the other codes, the Declaration of Helsinki had no binding authority. The real significance of the codes lies in the impetus they gave to the development of enforceable regulations.

This process began in the United States in 1953 with the formulation of guidelines for internal programs at the National Institutes of Health (NIH). In accord with many of the codes being developed at the time, the NIH guidelines distinguished between therapeutic and non-therapeutic research, exempting the former from controls external to "the doctor-patient relationship"; even for research conducted with normal volunteers, however, written consent was required only when there was the possibility of an unusual hazard (Frankel, 1975). Research funded by NIH but conducted by other institutions was left unregulated.

A number of factors led to a gradual change in this position (Curran, 1970). The controversy evoked by the births of hundreds of deformed children in Europe following the introduction of the drug thalidomide provoked Congressional hearings on the adequacy of American procedures for testing new drugs prior to their approval (Lasagna, 1963). The resulting legislation, passed in 1962, tightened screening procedures and, in the process, required the consent of subjects who were involved in the testing of new medications (Kelsey, 1963). Most biomedical research was not covered by this legislation, but NIH action was already underway. Stimulated by several instances of irresponsibility on the part of investigators, including the scientifically-unjustified transplantation of a monkey's kidney into a human patient and the injection of live cancer cells into chronically ill patients without their knowledge or consent, the NIH funded a survey of institutional controls on research practices, which found an almost complete absence of meaningful guidelines (Frankel, 1975).

In response, in 1966 the Public Health Service (the parent body of NIH) formulated policies requiring institutions receiving grants to:

provide prior review of the judgment of the principal investigator or program director by a committee of his institutional associates. This review should assure an independent determination: (1) of the rights and welfare of the individual or individuals involved, (2) of the appropriateness of the methods used to secure informed consent, and (3) of the risks and potential benefits of the investigation. (Curran, 1970)

This simple formulation, which represented the first firm, nationwide requirement for informed consent in research, developed, by 1981, into the current, complex document, whose description required seven pages of small print in the Federal Register, with 20 pages of accompanying explication. The control of consent procedures remains lodged in the hands of a decentralized system of review boards at each grantee institution. But the boards operate under detailed guidelines that specify the scope of their responsibilities, their composition, the criteria to be considered prior to approval of research protocols, the records to be kept, and the nature of the informed consent to be obtained from subjects. In most research involving human subjects a detailed written consent is required, but under some circumstances "short form" written consents or oral consents may be permitted. Review boards are given some leeway in altering consent requirements when the research in question presents no more than minimal risk to subjects and some additional requirements have been met.

Current regulations specify in detail what is to be contained in an informed consent disclosure, whether written or oral (U.S. Department of Health and Human Services, 1981a). The "eight basic elements of informed consent" are identified as: (1) a statement that the study constitutes research, an explanation of its purposes and the expected duration of subject involvement, and a description of the procedures involved, with experimental procedures identified as such; (2) a description of risks and discomforts that are "reasonably foreseeable"; (3) a description of possible benefits to subjects and others; (4) disclosure of appropriate alternative treatments, if any; (5) a statement describing the extent of confidentiality of records generated; (6) an explanation of whether compensation or treatment will be available if injuries occur; (7) a note as to who can be contacted with questions or reports of injuries; and (8) a statement as to the voluntary nature of participation and the subject's right of withdrawal at any time. In addition, the regulations list six optional elements of informed consent that may be included as appropriate. These are: (1) a statement that unforeseen risks may arise; (2) a description of circumstances in which subjects' participation may be terminated without their consent; (3) a note as to any additional costs to the subject as a result of participation; (4) a description of the consequences of premature withdrawal; (5) a statement that subjects will be informed of any findings that may affect their willingness to continue; and (6) a notation of the number of subjects to be involved in the research.

It is immediately obvious that the regulatory approach taken to informed consent to research has resulted in much more detailed guidelines than has the judicial process largely responsible

for shaping the contours of consent to treatment. Although these regulations nominally apply only to research funded by the Department of Health & Human Services (which adopted the Public Health Service–NIH model for all of its funded programs in 1969), recipient institutions have often insisted that all research performed under their auspices conform to the federal standards. Thus, the regulations effectively cover almost all of the biomedical and behavioral research performed in the United States today. (In 1981, the Food and Drug Administration, which oversees development and testing of new pharmacologic agents, amended its regulations to conform to those of the rest of the U.S. Department of Health and Human Services [1981b].)

Despite the domination of regulatory law in this area, the courts have not been altogether silent about the issues involved in consent to experimentation. A handful of cases have reached the courts since the mid–1960s, involving patients who suffered harm as a result of research procedures. The courts almost uniformly have applied an analysis similar to those developed in cases involving consent to treatment, and have required similar informed consents to be provided (Annas, Glantz, & Katz, 1977). The rarity of these cases, however, and the much greater specificity of regulatory law in this area, have made the judicial decisions much less influential than they are in the treatment arena.

Forces Shaping the Evolution of Informed Consent Law

Simply to trace the development of informed consent law offers little insight into the powerful, and often competing, factors that molded the doctrine into its current form. It is evident that contemporary consent law represents a compromise among a number of interests, such that no one theoretical orientation has emerged predominant. The two most potent factors involved in this process have been the interest in promoting individual autonomy and the interest in health (President's Commission, 1982a). While proponents of these two factors have been jockeying for dominance in the substantive law of informed consent, a third set of factors, the traditional procedures for redressing wrongs offered by the legal system, has defined the framework within which the struggle has been taking place. Ironically, this last consideration has often had a more powerful influence on the law and practice of informed consent than either considerations of autonomy or health.

Autonomy

Of the major court decisions establishing the doctrine of informed consent, those that gave any rationale at all for their ruling tended to emphasize the importance of informed consent for the autonomy of the individual (White, 1983). Many of the decisions quoted Cardozo's famous dictum, "Every human being of adult years and sound mind has a right to determine what shall be done with his own body" (*Schloendorff* v. *Society of New York Hospital*, 1914). Once the importance of individual autonomy had been asserted, the usual argument that followed is exemplified by the line of reasoning found in *Canterbury*:

> True consent to what happens to one's self is the informed exercise of a choice, and that entails an opportunity to evaluate knowledgeably the options available and the risks attendant upon each. The average patient has little or no understanding of the medical arts, and ordinarily has only his physician to whom he can look for enlightenment with which to reach an intelligent decision. From these almost axiomatic considerations springs the need, and in turn the requirement, of a reasonable divulgence by physician to patient to make such a decision possible. (*Canterbury* v. *Spence*, 1972)

Other than citing Cardozo, however, the court decisions made little effort to develop a systematic justification for the position accorded the value of autonomy in their reasoning. That gap has been filled by an enormous body of literature on consent that has been generated by the newly-emerged field of bioethics. Although other justifications for informed consent may be offered by the bioethicists, autonomy is the primary principle on which their argumentation rests.

The argument offered by Beauchamp and Childress (1979) is typical of the approach in much of the bioethical literature. They locate their discussion of informed consent in a chapter entitled, "The Principle of Autonomy." Drawing first from the work of Kant, the authors note the importance of autonomous decision making in his system of thought. For Kant, autonomy meant "governing oneself, including making one's own choices, in accord with moral principles which are one's own and which are universalizable." Kant emphasized the importance of rationality in the choice-making process; choices directed by passion rather than by reason were considered a capitulation to heteronomy, the antithesis of autonomy.

While Kant was primarily concerned with the autonomy of will, John Stuart Mill's philosophy focused on the autonomy of action. As Beauchamp and Childress note, "Mill argues that social and political control over individual actions is legitimate only if necessary to prevent harm to other individuals affected by those actions." Thus, the combined effect of the work of Kant and Mill is to mandate respect for the choice of other individuals, at least insofar as they are capable of making autonomous decisions. Informed consent advances these interests both by permitting patients themselves to make choices about whether to receive treatment, and by providing sufficient information to permit those choices to be rational—and therefore, in Kant's sense, autonomous—acts. To the extent that it is sound public policy to promote autonomy, courts and legislatures should require informed consent.

This abstract argument for the importance of autonomy can be made in more prosaic terms. Medical treatment is less often curative than ameliorative, and rarely is only one approach to treatment possible. Patients are often faced with choices between degrees of improvement at costs of differing levels of risk of side effects and untoward events. Since patients are the persons most affected by these choices, and different persons are likely to accept varying degrees of risk to achieve the goals they desire, both a sense of basic fairness and a desire to optimize decision-making (in the sense of selecting means that are most likely to attain desired ends) point towards encouraging autonomous decision-making by patients.

Discussions of the ethical basis of informed consent often complement their descriptions of the importance of autonomy as a guiding principle with mention of other, related but distinct, justifications for patient consent. Among those frequently mentioned are: the protection of the patient's status as a human being (Katz & Capron, 1975), which is sometimes referred to in this sense as "respect for persons" (Lebacqz & Levine, 1977), but which is closely related to the principle of respecting the autonomy of others: the avoidance of fraud and duress (Katz & Capron, 1975), which again is a different way of saying that one desires to respect autonomy; protection of the patient from harm (Veatch, 1976); the encouragement of self-scrutiny by the physician or investigator (Katz & Capron, 1975); the fostering of rational decision making (Katz & Capron, 1975; Strong, 1979), which, as noted above, is subsumed under a Kantian notion of autonomy; and the involvement of the public in medical research and practice (Katz & Capron, 1975). Despite this multitude of justifications for informed consent, advocates of an autonomy-directed model clearly indicate that autonomy is the prime justification. In the event of a conflict between autonomy and some other value in shaping informed consent policy, considerations of autonomy should prevail (Beauchamp & Childress, 1979; Veatch, 1976).

Those who would base the doctrine of informed consent on an autonomy-directed model vary somewhat in their willingness to consider the accommodation of conflicting interests. Some theorists, including philosophers (Veatch, 1976) and lawyers (Goldstein, 1978), view autonomy as so important a value that they would strongly resist any compromise with competing interests. Other writers in this area are more willing to acknowledge the desirability or necessity of integrating other concerns into their model (President's Commission, 1982a). But even in the latter cases, the focus of the doctrine of informed consent is seen to be the enhancement of individual autonomy.

The autonomy-directed model can be summarized in the following way. Its a priori assumption is that autonomy is an extremely important, if not supreme, value for the regulation of human affairs. The preferred means of implementing this value in health care is to give patients and research subjects maximal decision-making power and a large amount of information (perhaps all they do or should desire) with which to make their decisions. The ends sought are rational, autonomous decisions, whether or not such decisions would be judged to be in the patient's best interests by an outside observer.

Health

Concern for the promotion of health is the second factor that has played a major role in shaping the law of informed consent, but in a much less coherent fashion than considerations of autonomy. Most discussions of the influence of health-related concerns in consent law have pointed to the way in which these interests can be used to argue

against the practice of informed consent (Meisel, 1979). To the extent that decision-making power remains lodged in the hands of physicians, these arguments contend, the goal of health is most forcefully advanced. Offering patients the opportunity to learn about their conditions and make ultimate decisions about their care, opens the door to factors such as fear, irrational prejudice, ignorance, and hopelessness as influences on the course of treatment. Thus, in this simplistic view, health is seen as an interest contrary to the interest of autonomy and to the practice of informed consent.

There is no question that beliefs of this sort have prompted judges to limit the scope of disclosure required in informed consent decisions and to define circumstances in which the value of health is so likely to be compromised by considerations of autonomy that the need for informed consent is abrogated. Legislatures, too, in their efforts to limit the extent of informed consent requirements, have undoubtedly been affected by this perceived need to redress the balance between interests of autonomy and health (Meisel & Kabnick, 1980).

It would be wrong, however, to think that interests in health serve only to stifle the development of informed consent. One way in which these interests might be seen as advancing informed consent is exemplified by an approach that views health more broadly under the rubric of "well-being" (President's Commission, 1982a). Since many illnesses are susceptible to treatment, but not to cure, and may be treated in a variety of ways, each of which has its own peculiar benefits and risks, individual preferences are seen as playing a valid role in the selection of alternative forms of medical care. If individual preferences are ignored, one may purchase objectively-defined health only at the cost of a subjective sense of discomfort and unhappiness. This means that patients' well-being is sacrificed when their personal values are not allowed to affect the decision-making process. Autonomous decision-making comes to be seen as an important element of overall well-being, and thus of health. The conflict between autonomy and health disappears. To date, however, this formulation has had relatively little influence on the evolution of consent law.

Another way in which interests in health have stimulated informed consent draws on elements of each of the two preceding arguments. The potential is recognized for patients who are provided with information and encouraged to make their own choices about health care to choose unwisely and thereby impair both their health and well-being. On the other hand, it is also acknowledged that in the absence of sufficient information to permit patients to participate actively in implementing, if not choosing, a course of medical treatment, cooperation, and thereby efficacy, is likely to be compromised.

The beliefs underlying this approach to health-related interests pre-date by centuries the development of formal consent law. Physicians have long recognized the utility of providing information to patients as a means of encouraging their cooperation with care. Hippocrates advised physicians to:

Perform all things calmly and adroitly, concealing most things from the patient while you are attending to him. Given encouragement to the patient to allow himself to be treated [precise translation in doubt] with cheerfulness and serenity, turning his attention away from what is being done to him. (Reiser et al., 1977)

Pernick (1982) has recently reviewed medical attitudes toward information disclosure, with a particular focus on 19th-century practices. For a time in the early 1800s, among a group of "medical democrats," ancient and medieval injunctions to manipulate patients for their own good by selectively revealing information were cast aside in favor of more open disclosure. The rationale for this practice was the belief that informed liberty of choice would, in a holistic sense, have a positive effect on the health of the organism as a whole. Even here, however, information was not viewed as enabling a patient to choose in conflict with the physician's recommendation, merely to choose to cooperate with it. Later in the century, as the science of medicine evolved and a clearer understanding of pathophysiology was obtained, physicians abandoned these ideas in favor of a return to more manipulative practices.

In the 20th century, the development of effective medications for the treatment of a variety of illnesses brought an interest in better means of obtaining patient compliance. DiMatteo and DiNicola (1982) have exhaustively reviewed the literature on compliance, pointing to studies that demonstrate the generally poor state of doctor-patient communication, and the reasons to believe that enhanced communication will improve doctor-patient rapport, compliance with treat-

ment, and, ultimately, outcome. Many of the same studies have been cited by advocates of informed consent as evidence that more detailed disclosure to patients is required to improve medical care (Note, 1970; Simpson, 1981).

There is an uneasy tension among those who promote informed consent on these grounds. In general, the physicians are concerned primarily with revealing information needed to achieve the desired goal of compliance. Although that may require substantial disclosure, the decision as to how much to reveal remains in medical hands. As a corollary to this, if information is likely to be harmful to the patient's health, perhaps even if it would lead to refusal of needed treatment, there would appear to be some justification for withholding it (Meisel, 1979). Others, however, including some legal commentators (Note, 1970; Simpson, 1981), for whom this is usually a secondary justification for informed consent, have taken the argument one step further. They reason implicitly that if some amount of disclosure will benefit patient care, then the greater degree of disclosure envisioned by considerations of autonomy should be even more facilitative of patient cooperation. Thus, they reach a similar conclusion about the scope of disclosure as do those who argue from autonomy.

To summarize the effect of health-related factors on informed consent, the assumption that health is a value that ought to be promoted by the law can result in widely different conclusions about the desirable amount of disclosure and the optimal nature of the decision-making process. Health can be seen as a factor that conflicts with interests of autonomy and thus limits the development of informed consent, or as an interest that is entirely coterminous with the interest of autonomy. Alternatively, the interest in health might demand a doctrine of consent law which calls for disclosures that are carefully tailored to promote patient cooperation, but not necessarily independent decision-making.

The Structure of Negligence Law

As described above, informed consent to treatment developed almost entirely within the context of court cases in which harm was alleged as a result of the failure to obtain informed consent. Cases in this area have generally come to be considered under the category of actions in negligence. Consequently, regardless of the models of informed consent that might be suggested by considerations of autonomy or health, the shape of informed consent law is heavily influenced by the traditional approaches of the legal system to the law of negligence. This has consequences for the way in which the requirements of disclosure are defined, how those cases in which sanctions are to be applied are selected, and the sanctions that may be employed.

These issues will be discussed at length in the following section, but one indication of the impact of legal considerations on informed consent law that can be examined here is the manner in which failure to obtain informed consent can lead to sanctions against the practitioner.

The characteristics of negligence litigation make it inevitable that only those cases in which actual harm occurred to the patient, allegedly as the result of a failure to obtain informed consent, will be addressed by the law. As will be demonstrated below, this does not have to be the case if informed consent cases are treated as actions in battery, where infringements of the patient's autonomy in itself might provide a basis for compensation. In practice, however, although the absence of informed consent might infringe a patient's autonomy or impair his cooperation with measures designed to advance his health, negligence law will not sanction intervention unless harm resulted. Even in the case of harm, according to the rules of negligence law, intervention would be warranted only when the negligently obtained consent was sufficiently closely related to the harm to have been deemed a "proximate cause."

Again, *Canterbury* provides a classical statement of this point of view:

No more than breach of any other legal duty does nonfulfillment of the physician's obligation to disclosure alone establish liability to the patient. An unrevealed risk that should have been made known must materialize, for otherwise the omission, however unpardonable, is legally without consequence. Occurence of the risk must be harmful to the patient, for negligence unrelated to injury is non-actionable. And, as in malpractice actions generally, there must be a causal relationship between the physician's failure to adequately divulge and damage to the patient. (*Canterbury* v. *Spence*, 1972)

Another important consequence of the usual legal rules for handling such cases is that the primary means of enforcing the law of informed consent becomes damages assessed against physicians in cases in which harm has resulted. This may be a relatively weak enforcement mechanism, given the rarity of malpractice suits in which informed consent is the pivotal issue, the difficulty of plaintiffs' winning such cases, and the small percentage of negligent maloccurrences that progress to the level of a suit in the first place.

The President's Commission for the Study of Ethical Problems in Medicine recently pointed to a number of other ways in which the litigation process has influenced the shape of informed consent law (President's Commission, 1982a). These include the fact that the courts' experience is limited to contact with unhappy patients who in fact have suffered harm, in cases in which undisclosed risks *have* materialized and reasonableness of behavior must be judged retrospectively. All of these factors may contribute to the construction of more rigorous standards for physician behavior than if the courts were able to take into account the entire spectrum of doctor-patient interactions. In addition, the courts tend to rely heavily on documentary evidence, accounting in part for the ubiquitous presence of written consent forms, and to focus proceedings on the best-insured defendant, resulting in the burden of disclosure being placed on the physician, to the virtual exclusion of other members of the health care team.

The impact of legal traditions in the development of consent law is remarkably underplayed in most writing on the subject. Yet, these considerations have had fully as important a role as the more frequently debated issues of autonomy and health.

The Effect of the Multiple Influences on the Law of Informed Consent

The influences presented here represent the three major factors that have shaped the law of informed consent. Most advocates of informed consent, as well as most critics, fail to acknowledge how these influences affect their reasoning, often ending up in internally inconsistent postures as a result. Not surprisingly, courts and legislature have behaved similarly, for example, offering the rhetoric of autonomy as a basis for informed consent, finding their remedies circumscribed by the traditional limits of tort law, and simultaneously attempting to temper the end product by accommodating the interests of health.

As suggested in the introduction to this chapter, one result of this conceptual stew has been the failure of informed consent law in practice to resemble the theoretical models of any ideologically pure school of thought. This means that ideologically-based criticism is remarkably easy to generate and, on its own terms, usually convincing. A blending of interests, however, is not necessarily illegitimate, as long as the underlying values are genuinely worth fostering. Conversely, if one believes that consent law should primarily enhance autonomy, but unknowingly adopts the means of a legal system not designed for that end, the only certain result is confusion. To a large extent this has been the situation in both theoretical discussions and implementation of laws governing informed consent.

The following section will examine several of the key areas of informed consent with the intent of demonstrating how the various influences on informed consent have contributed to shaping the law.

Contemporary Informed Consent Law: Effects of Competing Interests Form of Action: Battery vs. Negligence

Under early English common law, the precise terminology that a litigant used to describe his complaint was of immense importance, since improper labeling would ordinarily lead to a dismissal of the case regardless of the merits (Epstein, Kalven, & Gregory, 1977). In modern times, a relaxation of judicial rules has lessened the importance of selecting the proper rubric for a plaintiff's allegations. Nonetheless, whether informed consent cases were to be treated by courts as actions in battery—i.e., as unconsented touchings—or in negligence—i.e., as failures to conform to established standards of care—was one of the earliest and hottest controversies engendered by the new doctrine.

There are a number of practical aspects of this question. If informed consent cases are pursued under a theory of battery, expert testimony will not be needed to establish that a negligent act has occurred, actual harm need not be shown for recovery to take place (see discussion of *Mohr* v. *Williams* above), the statue of limitations might be briefer, and defense of the action and indemnity

for damages might not be covered by a physician's malpractice insurance policy. On the other hand, if such cases are considered as a type of negligence, expert testimony might be required to establish a deviation from the standard of care, the action might be covered by state regulations requiring arbitration or review of malpractice claims, a more complex standard of causation applies, and punitive damages will ordinarily not be available (Ludlam, 1978; Plant, 1968; Somerville, 1981).

One approach to distinguishing between cases that might be tried in battery versus those appropriately considered under negligence allocates to the former instances in which the essential nature of the procedure has been withheld or distorted, and to the latter cases in which only the risks have remained undisclosed (Plant, 1968). The problem with this attempt to draw a "bright line" around these causes of action is its susceptibility to the argument that in some circumstances failure to disclose risks may so distort the patient's perception of the procedure as to leave its "essential nature" obscured (Somerville, 1981).

Recognizing this peril, courts have tended to draw the line around negligence more broadly: In most courts, total failure to obtain consent gives rise to an action in battery, while partial consent is more likely to sound in negligence (*Cobbs* v. *Grant*, 1972; Meisel, 1977). Although this formulation, too, fails to eliminate all borderline cases, it does shift the vast bulk of consent cases into negligence law. Legal justification of this move has been weak in most decisions, but the courts' motivation probably relates to the decreased necessity for confronting the issue if almost all cases fall into the negligence category, and the desirability of the move on a number of policy grounds: informed consent allegations can be handled within the context of ordinary malpractice cases, of which they are often integrally a part; coverage by malpractice insurers will be available both to defendants and plaintiffs; and the stigma of having committed an intentional tort will not be placed on the physicians involved, who generally have not desired to harm the patient (although an intentional tort need not involve an act committed with an intent to harm).

The debate about the proper cause of action for failures to obtain informed consent may appear to involve only technical, legal considerations, but represents a good example of how the legal framework can affect substantive issues. The decision to categorize these cases as negligence is responsible for the previously discussed situation in which physical harm must result from the failure to obtain informed consent before a case can be brought and compensation can be obtained.

If autonomy were to be defended most forcefully, any failure to obtain informed consent, not just those that result in physical harm, should leave the practitioner liable. Some commentators have noted that this elimination of "dignitary harms" from the scope of informed consent law thus undercuts the value of autonomy that the law is ostensibly designed to uphold (Goldstein, 1975; J. Katz, 1977).

Standard of Disclosure

The expansion of consent law beyond the boundaries of simple consent raised a new set of issues concerning the scope of disclosure required of physicians. If the medical profession were to face potential liability for deficiencies in this area, essential notions of fairness seemed to demand that their responsibilities be outlined with some degree of clarity. Unfortunately, the early cases were somewhat vague in this regard. In *Salgo* (1957), for example, the court held only that, "A physician violates his duty to his patient and subjects himself to liability if he withholds any facts which are necessary to form the basis of an intelligent consent by the patient to the proposed treatment." The court did not say how the physician might judge which of many categories of facts might be relevant to the patient. For example (to choose some categories that have generally not been required to be disclosed in subsequent opinions), should the patient be told about the cost of procedure, the physician's training (or lack of it) in this area of medicine, or the physician's intention to leave the region in the near future and thus be unavailable for follow-up care? Although the language of the *Salgo* standard is clearly supportive of patient autonomy in the broadest sense of the term, the ambiguities it contained suggested from the beginning just how difficult it would be to define the standard of disclosure.

Subsequent decisions went much further in delineating the type of information that ought to be disclosed. The *Canterbury* court held that, "The topics importantly demanding a communication of information are the inherent and potential hazards of the proposed treatment, the alternatives to that treatment, if any, and the results likely if the patient remains untreated." These subjects are now generally accepted as constituting the elements required in an informed consent disclosure along, of course, with the earlier requirement for a description of the nature and perhaps the purpose of the procedure to be performed.

Still, the mere enumeration of the categories of facts that ought to be disclosed does not settle the issue. Procedures can be described in varying degrees of detail and complexity, and the universe of possible adverse effects is enormous. In surgery, for example, every procedure carries the risk of numerous complications, up to and including death. Most medications used today can cause dozens of side effects, although many of them are quite uncommon. "Complete disclosure," even if theoretically possible, would be extraordinarily time-consuming, and might end up with patients more confused than they were prior to disclosure.

The approach of the courts to this problem has fallen into one of two categories. The first looks to the usual guideline embodied in malpractice law: whether the physician abided by the standard of care of the profession in formulating his disclosure. The standard offered in *Natanson* v. *Kline* (1960) is the most frequently cited example of this approach: "The duty of the physician to disclose is limited to those disclosures which a reasonable medical practitioner would make under the same or similar circumstances." This has come to be called a "professional standard" of disclosure, and in one of a number of forms (Ludlam, 1978), is still apparently in effect in a majority of American jurisdictions (LeBlang, 1983; Miller, 1980).

The term "professional standard" as applied to *Natanson*, however, is something of a misnomer. Although the *Natanson* court attempted to keep the newly-defined duty to obtain informed consent within the bounds of traditional negligence law by referring to the behavior of a "reasonable medical practitioner," the opinion in fact went further than this phrase might suggest. Apparently recognizing that it was unlikely that the medical profession was disclosing much information to patients at the time, the court itself defined the framework within which medical discretion might operate (Weyandt, 1965–1966). The court not only described the areas that the physician's disclosure was required to cover (the nature of the illness and proposed treatment, the probability of success and of "unfortunate results and unforeseen consequences," and the alternative treatments available), but also required that the disclosure be "sufficient to assure an informed consent," and that it be made "in language as simple as necessary." These terms represented a potentially significant limitation on the medical profession's capacity to set its own standards. If the usual medical practice were to explain operations to patients in highly technical terms, or to limit disclosure severely, this would presumably not provide an adequate defense to a charge of negligence under *Natanson*.

Thus, the approach of the Natanson court might better be called a "modified professional standard" (Miller, 1980). As in *Natanson*, courts do, from time to time, assume the power to establish reasonable standards of professional or commercial practice when an entire profession or industry has been derelict in monitoring its practices (see the classic example of *Helling* v. *Carey*, 1974; *The T.J. Hooper*, 1932). Despite the failure of the opinion in *Natanson* to own up to this approach, it is clear that this is the course it took.

Nonetheless, there are courts and state legislatures (Miller, 1980) that have adopted genuine professional standards of disclosure. In *Bly* v. *Rhoads* (1976), for example, the Supreme Court of Virginia required plaintiffs to show "that prevailing medical practice requires disclosure of certain information," without limiting professional practices in any way. Thus, the professional standard of disclosure really embodies two different standards, depending on whether the courts have left the issue entirely in medical hands or have established the perimeters within which medical opinion may be determinative.

The most popular alternative to one of the professional standards of disclosure is adoption of a "materiality standard." This approach was popularized by *Canterbury* and the 1972 California case of *Cobbs* v. *Grant*. According to one frequently relied upon formulation, "A risk is material [and therefore should be disclosed] when a reasonable person, in what the physician knows or should know to be the patient's position, would be likely to attach significance to the risk or cluster of risks in deciding whether or not to undergo the proposed therapy" (Waltz & Scheuneman, 1970). The materiality standard rejects professional practices as the determinant of disclosure, looking instead to the individual patient's need for "adequate information to enable an intelligent choice" (*Cobbs* v. *Grant*, 1972).

The materiality standard, too, has two variants. A small number of jurisdictions have adopted a "subjective" materiality standard, in which that information material to the patient's own decision making is required to be disclosed (see, e.g., *Scott* v. *Bradford*, 1979). Most courts, however, have followed the lead of *Canterbury* and Cobbs in utilizing an "objective" standard: Only that information which would be material to a reasonable person's decision making (sometimes the phrase "in the patient's position" is added) must be disclosed.

Two other possible standards of disclosure should be mentioned. LeBlang (1983) has noted a tendency for some courts to combine the professional and materiality standards by requiring disclosure to meet both standards. Although he refers to this as a "hybrid" standard, it seems likely that in practice it would have the same effect as the most demanding of its components, the materiality standard; it would be an odd court that would rule that anything physicians ordinarily disclosed would not be material to the decision of a reasonable person.

A final option, which will be discussed in greater detail below in the section on legislative action, is for some independent body to enumerate in such detail the required components of disclosure as to remove any discretion from the physician or patient. Neither professional nor materiality standards would apply in such a circumstance. Some statutes have adopted this approach.

The choice of a standard of disclosure, which has been largely a judicial function, has probably attracted more attention from legal commentators than any other aspect of the law of informed consent. The controversies, which reflect starkly the competing interests involved in shaping the doctrine, have had two focal points: the dispute between those who favor a professional standard and those who prefer a materiality standard, and the dispute between champions of an objective and a subjective test of materiality.

Advocates of a professional standard are strongly influenced by traditional legal approaches to negligence, according to which courts should be wary of substituting their own judgments for the rules that have been developed over time by the professions. In addition, the professional standard requires the testimony of expert witnesses to establish reasonable practice within the profession, a requirement many courts view as desirable. The court in *Bly* v. *Rhoads* (1976) noted, "The matters involved in the disclosure syndrome [sic] more often than not are complicated and highly technical. To leave the establishment of such matters to lay witnesses [as would be the case under a materiality standard, in which the plaintiff's testimony about materiality might be determinative], in our opinion, would pose dangers and disadvantages which far outweigh the benefits and advantages" of a materiality standard.

Given that the professional standard makes recovery more difficult for the plaintiff, who must find an expert willing to characterize the behavior in question as a deviation from a usually amorphous standard of professional care, courts may have other motives for advocating this approach. "Undoubtedly such a [materiality] rule would cause further proliferation of medical malpractice actions in a situation already approaching a national crisis. This is a result which, if at all possible consonant with sound judicial policy, should be avoided" (*Bly* v. *Rhoads*, 1976).

Health-related interests may also be perceived as weighing in on the side of a professional standard. To the extent that it is believed that disclosure of information is a sensitive matter that needs to be carefully adapted to each situation lest harm result to the patient, there is a strong incentive to allow considerable professional discretion in determining the scope of disclosure. The *Salgo* court acknowledged that excessive disclosure "may well result in alarming a patient who is unduly apprehensive and who may as a result refuse to undertake surgery in which there is in fact minimal risk; it may also result in actually increasing the risks by reason of the physiological results of the apprehension itself." Instead, the court chose "to recognize that each patient presents a separate problem, that the patient's mental and emotional condition is important and in certain cases may be crucial, and that in discussing the element of risk a certain amount of discretion must be employed."

The professional standard's durability, and the widespread acceptance of the arguments that support it, is particularly noteworthy in light of the furious assault to which it has been subjected. In a large part this assault has been launched by proponents of greater autonomy for patients, although it is often supported by those offering more practical arguments, as well.

To consider the practical arguments first, the most obvious grounds for attacking the use of a professional standard, particularly early in the evolution of informed consent law in a given jurisdiction, is that in many situations no such standard exists. Professional practice may not have crystallized sufficiently that any set of practices are widely enough accepted to constitute a standard of care (Dalrymple, 1976; Rosoff, 1981). Alternatively, the standard may be so low (perhaps requiring no disclosure at all) as to be utterly inadequate (Ludlam, 1978). There is evidence suggesting that even today disclosure consistent with informed decision-making, particularly in hospital settings, is extraordinarily rare (Appelbaum & Roth, 1982b; Lidz & Meisel, 1982). Some courts, of course, have recognized this difficulty, and as was seen in *Natanson*, have devised a way around it that does not require sacrifice of a professional standard. In the modified professional standard approach, the courts themselves lay out the minimum requirement for adequate disclosure, allowing the profession to fill in the details.

A second practical objection addresses the "conspiracy of silence" that many observers believe exists among members of the medical profession (Dalrymple, 1976). The difficulty of finding an expert who is willing to testify against a fellow physician may effectively deprive the plaintiff of a chance to prove his or her case, particularly in jurisdictions in which the locality rule, requiring the expert to come from the same or a similar locality, is applied. This consideration has proved influential in leading some courts to reject the professional standard (see, e.g., *Canterbury* v. *Spence*, 1972; *Cooper* v. *Roberts*, 1971). On the other hand, as advocates of the professional standard have pointed out, plaintiffs almost always will need expert witnesses to testify to the likelihood of certain risks arising and to the link between the intervention and the harm suffered (*Bly* v. *Rhoads*, 1976). Although it may at times be easier to find experts willing to testify about this latter set of issues, it seems unlikely that a materiality standard will ordinarily ease the plaintiff's problems in obtaining experts.

The strongest arguments for a materiality standard, however, derive from those who believe that this approach is essential if meaningful support is to be given to the notion of patient autonomy in decision-making. J. Katz (1977) has pointed out that courts effectively undercut their broad language about self-determination when they allow the medical profession to set the standard for the information to be divulged. "Unlimited discretion in the physician," noted the court in *Cobbs* v. *Grant* (1972), "is irreconcilable with the basic right of the patient to make the ultimate informed decision regarding the course of treatment to which he knowledgeably consents to be subjected." The rapid acceptance of the materiality standard in a large number of jurisdictions (Miller, 1980) is testimony to the power of concerns about patient autonomy in judicial (and to lesser extent, legislative) reasoning.

Even among supporters of a materiality standard, there is a serious split between those who favor an objective and subjective test. The objective test, which requires disclosure of all information that would be material to the decision of a reasonable person (but not necessarily all that would be desirable for *this* patient's decision), has been adopted by most materiality jurisdictions. The motivation for this approach again derives from traditional legal concerns, this time dealing with questions of fairness in tort litigation. Rejecting the subjective standard, the *Canterbury* court commented that it "would summon the physician to second-guess the patient, whose ideas on materiality could hardly be known to the physician . . . *No less than any other aspect of negligence*, [emphasis added] the issue on nondisclosure must be approached from the viewpoint of the reasonableness of the physician's divulgence in terms of what he knows or should know to be the patient's informational needs."

Theorists who are unwilling to see the value of autonomy diluted by historic legal approaches are strongly critical of this compromise. "To the extent that, given a particular revelation, a patient would have declined the procedure and a reasonable person in like circumstances would have undergone the procedure, the patient's right of self-determination is lost" (Seidelson, 1976). J. Katz (1977) asks why the courts do not merely require the physician to ask patients what information—or type of information—they desire? He comments, "The [*Canterbury*] court's preoccupation with the physicians' plight in determining what to disclose prevented it from considering the patient's plight and proceeding further to protect his right of choice . . . Physicians need not 'sense' how the patient will react or 'second-guess' him;

instead, they should explore what questions need further explanation."

Just as the widespread adoption of a materiality standard (although still apparently in a minority of jurisdictions) demonstrates the strength of arguments for autonomy, the rejection of the pleas of Katz and others for a subjective test of materiality points out the tenacity with which traditional tort law approaches are maintained.

A final issue that must be addressed under the heading of disclosure is the difference between disclosure and understanding. Although it has been claimed that the assumption that patients understand the information revealed is implicit in the doctrine of informed consent (Meisel, Roth, & Lidz, 1977), many of the leading court cases have explicitly disavowed this contention. "As we later emphasize," wrote Judge Robinson in *Canterbury*, "the physician discharges the duty when he makes a reasonable effort to convey sufficient information although the patient, without fault of the physician, may not fully grasp it." The motive for this stance would appear to be a fear of placing too great a burden on the physician, by compelling repeated disclosure and efforts to educate an uncomprehending patient, to the detriment of patient care. There may also be an underlying fear that some patients may be so refractory to education, yet unwilling to waive their rights in this area, as to frustrate completely their medical care.

As might be expected, proponents of maximal autonomy for patients have difficulty accepting this justification (Simpson, 1981). Although one cannot "compel" patients to understand information presented, it is argued that much greater requirements can be placed on physicians to identify areas of misunderstanding and attempt to correct them. This, of course, is precisely what the courts are unwilling to do, for fear of sacrificing health-related values linked to physicians' time commitments. As in the dispute over the objective-subjective test of materiality, autonomy interests here are again subordinated to other values.

Causation

The arguments about establishing causation in informed consent cases resemble those concerning the proper standard of disclosure, with one important difference: Whereas disclosure is an inherent aspect of the consent process, causation arises as an issue only by virtue of the way in which the legal system has chosen to deal with failures to obtain informed consent.

With the assumption of informed consent cases into negligence law, plaintiffs are required to prove that the injury suffered was proximately caused by the negligent failure to disclose. The courts have held that the necessary causal links are established when it is demonstrated that the patient would have rejected the treatment had disclosure taken place. (Of course, the patient must also demonstrate that the treatment in question was a "proximate cause" of the harm that resulted.)

As in determining the standard of disclosure, the standard of causation is susceptible to two tests, one subjective and the other objective. Under the subjective test, if the plaintiff can prove that *he or she* would not have submitted to the treatment or procedures had the risk in question been disclosed, causation is established. Under the objective test, the plaintiff must prove that a *reasonable person* would not have proceeded with treatment under those circumstances.

The objective test, which is the more widely adopted of the two, again comports most closely with traditional notions of fairness in tort cases. It avoids the problems, in the words of the *Canterbury* decision, of placing "the physician in jeopardy of the patient's hindsight and bitterness," and of placing "the factfinder in the position of deciding whether a speculative answer to a hypothetical question is to be credited." The objective test would "ease the fact-finding process and better assure the truth as its product."

As might be expected, commentators who are loathe to see the interests of autonomy sacrificed again to traditional legal values have opposed vigorously the use of the objective test. If the concern of informed consent law is to protect the autonomy of the individual, they argue, that person's probable behavior, not the behavior of a hypothetical reasonable or prudent person, should form the basis for an analysis of causation (Goldstein, 1975; J. Katz, 1977). Seidelson (1976) goes even further, challenging the assumption of the *Canterbury* court that an objective test will clarify the decision-making process. He argues that even with a subjective test, juries will be well aware of the potentially self-serving nature of the plaintiff's testimony as to whether consent would have been forthcoming with additional disclo-

sure, and that they will be able to take this factor into account, as they do in many other trial settings (see also Meisel, 1977). These arguments, though, have been rejected in most jurisdictions, leaving the objective test as the norm for establishing causation.

Competency

As noted above, the nearly exclusive focus on issues related to disclosure in consent law has deflected attention from other important aspects of the problem. The question of competency to provide consent is one of these aspects, and the changes accompanying the rise of informed consent have markedly increased its centrality.

Competency to provide consent has long been recognized as a necessary component of a valid consent. Cardozo's much-quoted formulation in *Schloendorff* (1914), it will be recalled, held out the promise of autonomy only for those "of adult years and sound mind." Yet, despite the integral role that competency plays in conceptualizations of the consent process, careful consideration of what attributes comprise a competent state have been largely lacking in court decisions, statutes, and even academic commentary (Appelbaum & Roth, 1982a). This is true despite the fact that issues of competency reach far beyond consent law, arising as well in litigation over contracts, wills, waivers of rights, and criminal procedure.

Persons are ordinarily presumed to be competent, obviating the need in everyday practice for any careful analysis of the concept (Roth, 1982). Yet, if consent is obtained from an incompetent person, without concurrence from a legally-recognized proxy decision maker, the physician may be held liable for mal-occurrences (and even for battery), as if no consent had been obtained. Distinguishing between competent and incompetent patients thus becomes an issue of some moment. Three key questions must be addressed concerning competency to consent: how is competency to be determined? who should make decisions and provide consent when the patient or research subject is incompetent to do so? and what standard should be utilized in reaching those decisions?

A recent review of the literature on competency revealed that the many suggestions for standards by which it might be measured fell into four broad categories, which form a roughly hierarchical order (Appelbaum & Roth, 1982a). The most basic standard of competency requires only that the individual be able to evidence a choice of conduct, that is, to indicate whether he or she desires to consent to the treatment or procedure. The next most rigorous standard inquires into the individual's understanding of the facts that are deemed relevant to the decision. Since the law has generally not required *actual* understanding of disclosed information in informed consent cases, this standard should probably focus on the individual's *ability* to understand information of the type in question.

The third standard looks beyond factual understanding to the person's ability to manipulate rationally the information provided. Finally, the most rigorous standard demands that the individual appreciate the relevance of the information and the consequences of the decision, as they relate to that person's own situation. Means of testing for each of these standards have been outlined (Appelbaum & Roth, 1981, 1982a). An additional standard that might be utilized, although it does not fit neatly into the hierarchical conceptualization, is whether the person has the ability to make an autonomous decision, that is, whether he or she can resist expectable levels of coercion.[1]

Once again, outlining possible standards fails to resolve the controversy as to which standard should be applied. A variety of factors might affect that decision, and they operate in complex ways (Appelbaum & Roth, 1982a). Commentators concerned with autonomy, for example, might argue that the lowest possible standard of competency—the ability to evidence a choice—should be employed to enable the maximum number of people to make their own decisions (Goldstein, 1978). Yet, if one adopts a Kantian notion of autonomy (Beauchamp & Childress, 1979), which looks to rational decision making as the *sine qua non* of autonomy, a higher standard incorporating the ability to manipulate information rationally might be required (Roth, Appelbaum, Sallee, Reynolds, & Huber, 1982).

Health-related concerns might act to raise or lower the standard of competency, depending on the prevailing assumption about whether or not most people are reasonable decision makers and on the identity of substitute decision makers. Many physicians believe that patients are less capable of deciding about their care than is a member of the medical profession. This might induce physicians to use high standards of competency when patients produce decisions that fail to conform to physicians' preferences, thus effectively removing patients' power to decide about their own care. This might be especially likely to occur if the physicians can act as the substitute decision makers, or if their recommendations are likely to be accepted by whomever fills that role.

The paucity of court decisions on which standard of competency is to be adopted means that relatively little attention has been given to concerns about the traditional legal approaches and procedures that have proven so influential elsewhere in consent law. Nonetheless, arguments have been offered in favor of standards of competency such as "evidencing a choice" and "factual understanding" because of the ease with which a fact-finder can apply them (Barnhart, Pinkerton, & Roth, 1977; Freedman, 1975). Other factors may also play a role in determining the standard selected, especially when competency to consent to research is considered; these may include ideas of justice and the desire to encourage investigation (Appelbaum & Roth, 1982a).

Rather than focusing on single standards, or some combination of standards, for determining competency, some commentators have suggested that a sliding scale be applied, with the stringency of the standard adjusted according to the likely harm to the patient if an incompetent decision is reached[2] (President's Commission, 1982a). This is an attempt to strike an accommodation between interests of autonomy and health, but one in which autonomy plays a clearly subordinate role, yielding whenever the patient's well-being is truly endangered. There is reason to believe that this suggestion resembles the process by which decisions about patient competency are actually made in medical hospitals. Only when an incompetent patient's decision is likely to result in serious harm do physicians ordinarily challenge the patient's capacity to offer an opinion and seek substituted consent elsewhere (Roth, Meisel, & Lidz, 1977).

This, of course, raises the question of who should be making judgments about treatment for incompetent patients. In many instances it appears that physicians arrogate to themselves this right, avoiding any formal determination of the patient's competency in a court of law. This is

---

[1]Dix, G. Personal communication, July 2, 1981.
[2]Drane, J. Unpublished manuscript, January, 1983.

particularly true when patients are willing to comply with treatment, but also occurs when patients resist (Appelbaum & Roth, in press-a). These practices are designed to maximize the interest in health (narrowly defined), but sometimes only at the cost of patients' interests in avoiding unnecessary pain or particularly distressing side effects, and taking part in pleasurable activities while they still retain the capacity to do so.

The traditional approach to substitute decision-making for incompetents modifies physicians' judgments with the input of close family members. This presumably protects patients' idiosyncratic interests, of which physicians would not be likely to be aware, at the same time as it promotes their health. There have been renewed calls recently for formal acknowledgment of a patient's family, along with the physician, as the appropriate decision makers (President's Commission, 1982a). This approach also avoids the necessity of invoking formal legal proceedings, although that option remains if family members are unavailable or in disagreement among themselves. Very real family interests in a patient's care are thereby acknowledged, as well. On the other hand, to the extent that final power is lodged in family members, who may lack an appreciation of the medical issues involved or be deficient in dedication to the patient's best interests, on occasion neither interests in health nor other interests may be satisfied (Gutheil & Appelbaum, 1980).

More recently there has been a tendency to require both formal adjudications of incompetency and substitute decision making by either a legal guardian or the court itself (*In re Grady,* 1981; *In re Quinlan,* 1976; *In re the Guardianship of Richard Roe III,* 1981; *Rogers* v. *Okin,* 1979; *Superintendent of Belchertown State School* v. *Saikewicz,* 1977). Although this is sometimes justified as offering protection for the patient's autonomy, the underlying rationale appears to be the belief that the court (or the legal guardian) will be best able to protect the incompetent patient's well-being, broadly conceived, from narrowly-focused attempts by the medical profession to treat at any cost (Appelbaum & Gutheil, 1981). The controversy about the results of this approach has been sharpest when the question of treating allegedly incompetent psychiatric patients has been discussed. It has been claimed that the procedures designed to protect autonomy and the assignment of decision-making power to non-medical personnel have compromised patients' interests in health (Gill, 1982; Gutheil, Shapiro, & St. Clair, 1980). The enormously complex issues raised by this debate are beyond the scope of this chapter to address in detail.

Assuming that competency (or more precisely incompetency) can be determined and a substitute decision maker appointed, a final issue remains: On what basis should that person decide whether treatment should proceed? There are two competing standards that might be used, and they correspond to the objective vs. subjective distinctions that have been confronted previously. The subjective approach would be to decide the issue as the patient would, if he or she retained the capacity to make a decision; this is usually denominated the "substituted judgment" approach. Alternatively, one could decide objectively, depending on what was viewed as being in the patient's best interests.

Substituted judgment has been advocated as a means of preserving some vestige of patient autonomy even in the face of incompetency. It has been attacked, however, as being difficult to implement and as being as susceptible to manipulation, both conscious and unconscious, on the part of the decision maker as is the best interests approach (Gutheil & Appelbaum, 1980). The latter, of course, is advocated as protecting patients' health-related interests at a time when it is meaningless to speak of their interest in autonomy. A compromise position that may provide the benefits of both approaches calls for a substituted judgment to be made when it is clear what the patient would have desired; otherwise, a best interests determination is made (President's Commission, 1982a). One court has adopted a permutation of this approach, allowing the substituted judgment when one can be made meaningfully, but at least in the case of a proposed termination of life-sustaining medication in an incurable case of cancer, requiring maximal treatment to be undertaken when the patient's wishes could not be known (*Eichner* v. *Dillon,* 1981; *In re Storar,* 1981). This approach again accommodates the interest in health (though not necessarily well-being in the broader sense) unless a clear interest in autonomy is involved.

Voluntariness

The third leg of the triad on which informed consent rests, in addition to disclosure and competency, is voluntariness. Patients and research subjects must be free of coercion in reaching their decisions if the consent is to be legally valid. As with competency, this requirement derives from the traditional law of consent that predates the development of informed consent.

Relatively little has been written about voluntariness, perhaps because it is so difficult to conceptualize and measure. The matter might seem simple indeed if any consent given in the absence of overt coercion—that is, clear-cut threats of physical or other harm—is to be deemed voluntary. This was the approach of the law prior to the development of the doctrine of informed consent. But with the new emphasis on patient autonomy in decision-making, more subtle forms of coercion, including the provision, as well as the withholding, of rewards, have been deemed to cast doubt on the voluntariness of patients' and subjects' decisions.

This debate has focused primarily on residents of total institutions, such as prisons and mental hospitals. The argument is made that such institutions are inherently coercive, because residents are dependent on the institutional staff for fulfillment of all their needs and therefore dare not refuse anything they are asked to do. In addition, if consent, particularly to research or to behavior-modifying treatment, may play some role in the ultimate decision about the person's release, it may be seen as coerced, even if staff members do not intend to apply coercion in this way (Bach-y-Rita, 1974).

The most significant legal case in this area was *Kaimowitz* v. *Department of Mental Health* (1973). Here a sexually-disoriented offender involuntarily hospitalized for nearly two decades following a rape-murder was offered the opportunity to undergo experimental psychosurgery designed to control his aggression. Following review of the procedure by independent scientific and human rights committees, the patient gave his consent. An independent legal aid group then brought suit to stop the procedure, based in part on the assertion that legally adequate consent could not be given in such circumstances. The court's decision enjoined the proposed surgery, in large part because, "It is impossible for an involuntarily detained mental patient to be free of ulterior forms of restraint or coercion when his very release from the institution may depend upon his cooperating with the institutional authorities and giving consent to experimental surgery."

The ruling in *Kaimowitz* has been subjected to a good deal of adverse criticism. Stone (1978) pointed out that the logic of the decision can be extended to hold that no involuntarily confined patient or inmate is capable of providing informed consent in any situation. The philosopher Murphy (1979) concurred, noting in addition the imprecision in the court's analysis, specifically as it implicitly categorized all potentially coercive situations as unfair. There might, Murphy argues, be situations in which the possibility of a "reward" for desirable outcomes is both coercive in the sense in which the *Kaimowitz* court used the word and yet generally accepted as fair. He distinguishes between predicating a prisoner's release on his willingness to consent to psychosurgery, which is coercive and unfair, and basing his release on his ability to function in society, an attribute that might be improved by surgery, which is not unfair, but may still be construed as coercive. Murphy's reasoning is an attempt to demonstrate that *Kaimowitz* should not lead to the conclusion that all prisoners and mental patients should be prevented from making any decisions that might affect their welfare. Nonetheless, following *Kaimowitz*, the Federal Bureau of Prisons prohibited all research with prisoners in federal facilities, and some states have followed suit (Levine, 1981).

Since the flurry of concern aroused by *Kaimowitz* subsided, voluntariness has again become a neglected component of informed consent, largely because the inherent coerciveness of custodial settings has been downplayed. A variant of coercion that has been labeled "manipulation," though, has attracted some attention (President's Commission, 1982a). Manipulation refers to the interpersonal maneuvers that all of us use, often without conscious awareness, to get other people to go along with our desires. This may be as prevalent in medical settings as elsewhere, and may be helped along by the inherent status differences between doctors and patients. When the interests of patient-subjects and caregivers are likely to diverge, as in research settings, the potential for manipulation is especially great (Roth & Appelbaum, in press). It is difficult, however, to see how this behavior can be regulated by external controls. The law "can do little about subtle manipulations without incurring severe disruptions of private relationships by intrusive policing, and so the duty of physicians (to avoid manipulation) is best thought of primarily in ethical terms" (President's Commission, 1982a).

Exceptions to the Requirement for Informed Consent

As informed consent law has evolved, the courts have recognized circumstances in which a strict application of the doctrine would be undesirable as a matter of policy. "These exceptions reflect the strong emphasis that society generally and the medical profession in particular place on health and upon the responsibility of the medical profession to promote health" (Meisel, 1979). The usual exceptions involve emergencies, incompetents, waiver of the right to informed consent, and a doctrine known as "therapeutic privilege," and they all constitute some limitation on individual autonomy. These exceptions may also be termed "defenses" to an informed consent action, in that physicians may attempt to prove their presence in an effort to refute charges of negligence in disclosure.

Before examining these exceptions, a group of factors often classified as constituting exceptions needs to be addressed. Courts have held, with varying degrees of uniformity, that minor or remote risks, or those that should be known to the patient or could not have been known to the physician need not be disclosed (Miller, 1980). These items do not constitute exceptions to the requirement for informed consent so much as they define the scope of the disclosure requirement (Meisel & Kabnick, 1980). Allegations that a materialized risk falls into one of these categories, however, may well be useful in the defense of informed consent litigation.

The first exception to the requirement for informed consent involves emergencies. In these situations, efforts to obtain informed consent may consume precious seconds, at a time when survival may depend upon the speed with which treatment is administered. The law has been willing to assume that most people in such situations would consent to treatment and has therefore allowed physicians to rely on this "implied consent." It is important to recognize that a medical emergency alone does not call this exception into play; there are many emergent situations in which sufficient time exists to obtain patients' consent. The need to begin treatment immediately is the decisive factor (Meisel, 1979).

A second exception, incompetency, has been discussed previously as a situation in which normal consent procedures need not (in fact, cannot) be followed. Yet, as distinct from emergencies, incompetency does not result in an implied consent for treatment. Rather, consent must be obtained from a legally-authorized, substitute decision maker. The ambiguity of the law in specifying when formal adjudications of incompetency are required and who should serve as a proxy for the incompetent patient has been alluded to earlier. In many emergencies, of course, the patient will also be incompetent, for example, a patient who arrives comatose in the emergency room. There the emergency exception will be operative.

Children constitute a group of persons who are *de jure* incompetent, regardless of their actual functional capacity (Roth, 1982). Many states are now lowering the age at which children are deemed competent to give consent as a matter of law, with cut-offs ranging down to 12 years of age and often varying for different medical procedures (Wadlington, 1983). Children who have lived apart from their parents for specified periods of time may, as a matter of either common or statutory law, be deemed "mature minors" and permitted to give consent. If the minor is not "mature" and is not statutorily entitled to consent, however, practitioners should ordinarily obtain consent from parents or the patient's legal guardian, unless an emergency exists. Even statutes lowering the age of consent do not eliminate all problems. Although a minor might have the legal right to offer a consent, the physician is still left to determine whether the patient actually has the capacity to do so (Wadlington, 1983). In the absense of capacity, it is unclear what value enabling legislation may have.

Waiver of the right to informed consent is analogous to waiver of other personal rights (Meisel, 1979). This exception accepts the desirability of the patient being able to tell the physician that he or she desires to proceed with treatment without hearing the disclosure that would ordinarily be required. There may be sound psychological reasons to permit patients this option. Patients may not want to assume the burden of decision-making, or particularly in the case of potentially fatal conditions, may not want to hear the details of their diseases and proposed treatments (Almquist, 1980). There has been little formal legal analysis of waiver of informed consent. Specifically, it is unclear if such a waiver must meet the "knowing and voluntary" requirements of waivers of constitutional rights (Meisel, 1979).

The most controversial of the exceptions is the "therapeutic privilege." As explicated in *Canterbury*, this privilege selectively to withhold information arises when it is feared that patients may "become so ill or emotionally distraught on disclosure as to foreclose a rational decision, or complicate or hinder the treatment, or perhaps even suffer psychological damage." The *Canterbury* court's use of multiple disjunctives is indicative of the difficulty courts have had in defining the extent of the privilege. There are few data to suggest how often these problems might arise, and some commentators allege that they are almost never seen, but advocates of the therapeutic privilege believe that "these possibilities are recognized assumptions in medical practice and must be accorded consideration in any formulation of disclosure principles" (Waltz & Scheuneman, 1970).

The obvious problem with a therapeutic privilege is that if it is broadly construed (as it often is in court decisions such as *Nishi* v. *Hartwell*, 1970) it threatens to vitiate the disclosure requirement in most situations, since physicians can always claim they feared the patient would have rejected the treatment if the risks had been revealed (*Canterbury* v. *Spence*, 1972). The only reasonable construction of the privilege, therefore, is that it is not legitimately invoked when the harm feared to the patient would arise solely as a result of his or her rejection of the proposed treatment. Instead, it must be the case that the disclosure itself would produce significant harms (Rice, 1974). J. Katz (1977) has also noted perceptively that therapeutic privilege allows a partial adoption of a professional standard (albeit with burden of proof on the physician), at least in extreme cases, even in jurisdictions that have formally taken the materiality approach.

Another idiosyncratic attempt to identify an exception to informed consent, unlike the others, does not relate to the balancing of interests in autonomy and health. A Pennsylvania court has held that informed consent is not required for the administration of medication, because the doctrine applies only to surgical procedures (*Malloy* v. *Shanahan*, 1980). As the dissent notes, this approach interprets treatment following a failure to obtain informed consent as a battery, and holds that in the absence of an actual unconsented touching (i.e., an invasive procedure) no liability accrues. This decision has been criticized as inconsistent with trends in most states, as well as with certain aspects of Pennsylvania law, and has been followed by no other court (Heckert, 1982). What makes it of more than passing interest is evidence indicating that physicians in hospital-based practices actually operate in much the same way as *Malloy* suggests should be the law. That is, consents are carefully obtained for operative and other invasive procedures, but consents for medication are rarely solicited; in fact, patients may not even be told that medications have been prescribed, much less given an opportunity to decide about their desirability (Lidz & Meisel, 1982). *Malloy* may therefore constitute a legal anomaly, but at the same time accurately reflect clinical practices. Physicians who engage in such practices, however, may be at risk of liability for failure to obtain consent in the majority of jurisdictions that would not embrace *Malloy*'s approach.

Legislative Initiatives on Informed Consent

The law of informed consent to treatment has been shaped primarily by judicial decisions, but more recently state legislatures have become involved in the area. Legislative action might be thought particularly useful when the resolution of diverse, competing interests is required, because of the limited ability of courts to address issues and consider implications that transcend the facts of the cases brought before them. Legislatures might, for example, be expected to be less concerned with legal tradition as a constraint on the development of consent law and thus more willing to endorse approaches that radically enhance individual autonomy; or on the contrary, since they need not be exclusively concerned with cases in which malpractice is alleged, they might be more interested in promoting the social value of health, which might make them more willing to allow leeway to the medical profession in setting disclosure practices (Plant, 1978).

In fact, legislatures have elected for the most part not to become involved in altering substantive aspects of consent law, or in trying to achieve a new synthesis of interests. They have chosen instead to tinker with existing rules in their states in relatively small ways. Among the changes wrought by the statutes have been establishment of a presumption of valid consent if certain risks have been disclosed and a consent form signed; classification of informed consent as an action in negligence; promulgation of a standard of disclosure (usually a professional or modified professional standard); clarification of the burden of proving causation and the standard to be utilized; recognition of particular exceptions to informed consent; establishment of a requirement for expert testimony; and promulgation of various procedural rules (Ludlum, 1978; Magnet, 1981; Meisel & Kabnick, 1980; Miller, 1980).

The most extensive analysis to date of legislative approaches to informed consent has been undertaken by Meisel and Kabnick (1980). They note that the motivation for most legislation in this area has been the desire to cope with the perceived "crisis" in malpractice claims, to which it is believed informed consent cases are contributing. While this represents one way in which legislatures might legitimately take into consideration issues that would not ordinarily be addressed by the courts, it explains why tinkering with existing law—rather than substantially new approaches to informed consent—have been the result of most legislative efforts. Ironically, Meisel and Kabnick point out, most statutes have done little to alter the law of consent in a way that substantially diminishes patient-plaintiffs' likelihood of recovery.

One unique contribution of legislation in several states has been the adoption of an administrative approach to the standard of disclosure issue, which resembles in some ways the regulatory control that has been exercised over consent to research. A number of statutes enumerate either the type of risks that must be disclosed (e.g., "death, brain damage, quadriplegia, paraplegia, the loss or loss of function of any organ or limb, or disfiguring scars" (Iowa Code Ann. Sec. 147.137, cited in Miller, 1980) or provide mechanisms, as do the statutes in Texas and Hawaii, for an advisory body to detail exactly which risks must be disclosed for each type of procedure. In Texas, a "Medical Disclosure Panel" has been created to develop specific lists of disclosable risks and to designate treatments (generally surgical procedures) for which no disclosure is required (Curran, 1979).

Due to the emphasis of many of the statutes on particular elements of disclosure and on the wording of consent forms, one effect of their adoption has been to focus physicians' attention on written means of obtaining consent. To the extent that attempts to get the patient's signature on a consent form come to take the place of genuine disclosure, the interest in autonomy is undercut and health interests related to the cooperation of understanding patients suffer, as well (Lidz & Roth, 1981). This is undoubtedly an unintended effect of many statutes, but points out once again the difficulty of satisfying any single interest in this area without infringing on some other value.

Consent in Special Circumstances
Consent to Research:
Prospective vs. Retrospective Review

The preceding discussion of those factors that have shaped informed consent law has focused largely on consent to treatment, rather than on consent to research. As noted previously, despite considerable similarity in the interests involved, the mechanisms governing consent in these two settings evolved separately and have come to differ greatly. The most important difference is that informed consent in the research setting is primarily regulated prospectively, as opposed to the retrospective controls that are exerted on consent to treatment. That is, whereas consent to treatment is reviewed after the fact to determine if lapses in procedures have resulted in compensable harms to patients, consent to research is reviewed in advance to prevent such lapses from occurring. (Of course, this does not preclude later retrospective review, although to date that has been infrequent, see Annas, Glantz, & Katz, 1977.)

The reasons for this divergence in approach relate in part to the different emphasis each system must give to protecting the values of autonomy and health. In the treatment setting, it can usually be presumed that the physician's goal is to promote the patient's health to the best of his or her ability (Fried, 1974). In fact, physicians are thought to be so single-minded about advancing health interests (narrowly conceived) that they are likely to overwhelm the patient's autonomous decision-making. Thus, a primary purpose of informed consent to treatment is to allow patients to temper physicians' therapeutic zeal.

In contrast, in the research setting there may often be a conflict of interest between the physician-investigator, who must be concerned with recruiting and retaining subjects and carrying out the research project, and the patient-subject, whose therapeutic interests may take second place

(Appelbaum, Roth, & Lidz, 1982; Fried, 1974). Cases of subjects whose health was sacrificed for the attainment of scientific knowledge are unfortunately easy to cite (see, e.g., Beecher, 1966). Regulation of research, therefore, must focus on protecting patients' interests in receiving appropriate treatment (and, for non-patient subjects, on protecting their interests in avoiding actual harm), in addition to promoting the autonomy of their decision-making.

This additional factor in the regulation of research is a potent argument for a prospective model of review, one that insures that potentially harmful investigations will not be permitted to proceed. Since a prospective system for protection from harm appeared desirable, it was logical that review of informed consent practices would be incorporated into it. Prospective review of consent practices has both advantages and disadvantages when compared with a retrospective approach. Given that harms to research subjects occur rarely (President's Commission, 1982b), prospective review allows more effective control to be exerted over researchers who otherwise might not be persuaded to alter their disclosure practices by the remote possibility of litigation. It also insures the rapid establishment of a uniform body of practice; because of the idiosyncracies in the individual cases that arise for review under a retrospective system, substantial periods of time may be required before the scope of required practices is clearly defined. On the other hand, prospective review imposes substantial costs on the research process in terms of the personnel and money required to carry out the review, and the time lost awaiting approval.

Just as the approaches and imperatives of tort law played a substantial role in shaping the law of consent to treatment, the requirements of regulatory law were influential in determining the final form of the law of consent to research. The initial problem in the United States was how jurisdiction might be established over a diverse body of researchers whose actions had not yet raised questions of either civil or criminal liability. As noted previously, the approach taken was to require prospective review and conformance to specified standards of consent as a prerequisite to funding of research by agencies of the federal government, primarily those in the Department of Health and Human Services. Institutions receiving federal grants, which dominate funding in the field of

biomedical research, were required to give assurances that such review would be carried out, and that even research not funded by the federal government would be reviewed according to prespecified (though possibly differing) standards (U.S. Department of Health and Human Services, 1981a). It has been most convenient for institutions to apply uniform standards of review to all research, with the result that federal requirements have come to dominate the prospective review process, regardless of the funding source.

From the issuance of the first Public Health Service regulations in 1966, the decision was made to decentralize the review process. Institutional review boards (IRBs) were established at each institution receiving federal research funds. The most recent set of regulations require IRBs to have at least five members, and to be diverse culturally, sexually, and professionally (U.S. Department of Health and Human Services, 1981b). At least one member must be unaffiliated with the institution, one must have primary concerns in nonscientific areas, and one must be primarily concerned with subjects' welfare. It is possible for all of these roles to be filled by a single individual.

IRBs are charged with determining that: (1) risks to subjects are minimized; (2) risks to subjects are reasonable in relation to anticipated benefits; (3) selection of subjects is equitable; (4) informed consent will be sought in accordance with the regulations; (5) informed consent will be appropriately documented; (6) the research plan makes adequate provision for monitoring the data to insure the safety of subjects; (7) there are adequate provisions to protect the privacy of subjects; and (8) where some or all of the subjects are likely to be vulnerable to coercion or undue influence, additional safeguards are included for their protection. As can be seen from this list, in which only items (4), (5), and (8) deal with informed consent, the primary emphasis of the review process is on the protection of subjects from harm.

Extant research (Appelbaum & Roth, in press-b; Gray, 1975; Gray, Cooke & Tannenbaum, 1978), as well as anecdotal accounts (Levine, 1983) of the performance of IRBs, suggests that their review of informed consent practices has been shaped largely by the imperatives of the regulatory process. Review and suggestions for changes tend to focus almost entirely on the content of the consent form, to the exclusion of such other potentially relevant matters as the timing of consent, the identity of the person soliciting consent, the exclusion of incompetent subjects, and assuring that subjects actually understand the material that has been disclosed. Efforts to monitor actual consent practices, although explicitly authorized under the current regulations, are almost unheard of (Appelbaum & Roth, in press-b). This probably relates to the ease with which written disclosure can be reviewed and the difficulty of examining other aspects of the consent process.

Informed Consent in Psychiatry

Although it is frequently asserted that informed consent in psychiatric practice raises different issues than in the rest of medicine (Dyer, 1978; Macklin, 1982; Stone, 1979), and by implication that the doctrine itself should be modified to address these issues, the similarities between the informed consent processes in psychiatry and in general medicine vastly outweigh the differences. There is little question that informed consent law is generally relevant to psychiatric practice. Outpatients and voluntary inpatients, who constitute the overwhelming majority of patients treated (NIMH, 1983), have the same legal right to be free of somatic treatment (including medications and electroconvulsive therapy) without their informed consent as medical and surgical patients.

The situation for involuntary inpatients, however, is somewhat anomalous in this regard. From the inception of formal involuntary commitment in the second quarter of the 19th century, committed inpatients were treated as if they represented an exception to the legal requirement for simple consent. This practice was probably based on the universal assumption that the "insane" were globally incompetent to make decisions on their own behalf (Dain, 1964), and the usually unstated belief that commitment was a sufficient legal prerequisite to the exercise of substitute decision making by the treatment staff. At times, commitment statutes were explicit about this de facto declaration of incompetency, often transferring the power of consent to the superintendent of the facility (Brakel & Rock, 1971). Even in the absence of explicit authorization for involuntary treatment, however, such practices represented the norm, and continued after the rise of informed consent.

The first challenges to the assumption that involuntary commitment constituted an "excep-tion" to the requirement for consent arose in the early 1970s, in the context of a broader movement seeking to define and extend the scope of mental patients' rights. The ensuing litigation over what came to be called "the right to refuse treatment" remains unsettled as of this writing (Appelbaum, 1983; Bonnie, 1982). Several state and federal courts have held that committed patients have a right to refuse treatment, on either state law (*Goedecke v. State*, 1979), or constitutional grounds (*Davis v. Hubbard*, 1980; *In re the Mental Health of K.K.B.*, 1980; *Rennie v. Klein*, 1979; *Rogers v. Okin*, 1979). All courts to consider the issue have acknowledged exceptions to this right to refuse, but the extent of the exceptions and the procedures by which patients' refusals can be overridden have varied widely. Some courts have ruled that except in emergencies, when the patient or others face imminent danger unless treatment is instituted, the usual rules of informed consent apply and treatment cannot proceed absent a judicial finding of incompetency and the appointment of a substitute decision maker (*Rogers v. Okin*, 1979). Other decisions have granted treating facilities the power to determine incompetency without resort to the courts, and then to institute treatment, or to treat on the basis of some other combination of factors without consideration of patient competency (*Anderson v. State of Arizona*, 1982; *Project Release v. Prevost*, 1982; *Rennie v. Klein*, 1979, 1981).

Part of the reason for the continuing ambiguity in this area has been the reluctance of the U.S. Supreme Court to address the question of a right to refuse treatment definitively (Appelbaum, 1983). The court has indicated that patients do possess some constitutionally protected interests in not being treated involuntarily (*Rodgers v. Okin* sub nom *Mills v. Rogers*, 1982), but it has also hinted that these interests may be satisfied by the determination of a mental health professional that treatment is in fact necessary (*Rennie v. Klein*, 1982). Given that the issue has been framed largely in federal constitutional terms, any clear-cut resolution of the conflicting, lower-court opinions will almost inevitably have to await Supreme Court action.

An ultimate failure of the Supreme Court to endorse the right to refuse treatment on constitutional grounds, however, would not preclude the issue from being pursued in state courts on either state constitutional (Meisel, 1982) or common law grounds. Resolution of the issue may depend on the courts' willingness to recognize the problems inherent in committing patients to psychiatric facilities and then allowing them to stymie all efforts at treatment (Appelbaum, 1983; Stone, 1979). (Readers are referred to recent reviews of this complex subject for further details; see, for example, Brooks, 1980; Gutheil, 1982.)

The feeling of many psychiatrists that informed consent ought not to be applicable to their specialty may derive in part from this traditional exception accorded the treatment of involuntary inpatients. Thus, the claim is often made that psychiatric patients as a group demonstrate such impairment of their competency that informed consent is a meaningless exercise and that psychiatrists should be permitted to treat them on the basis of simple consent alone. While this belief is often tenaciously held, it has not yet been supported unequivocally by empirical investigation. Some studies have demonstrated poor functioning in a number of relevant areas among newly admitted psychiatric patients, suggestive of substantial levels of incompetency (Appelbaum, Mirkin, & Bateman, 1981; Olin & Olin, 1975; Palmer & Wohl, 1972). Other studies have shown psychiatric patients to be unaware of the nature of their treatment (Geller, 1982), particularly when compared with medical patients (Soskis, 1978). All of these studies suffer, however, from a failure to control or to standardize disclosure of information, leaving one uncertain whether psychiatric patients are incapable of assimilating information or simply are never told the details of their treatment. On the other hand, preliminary studies comparing the judgments made about participation in research by medical and psychiatric patients have shown few differences between the two groups (Stanley, Stanley, Lautin, Kane, & Schwartz, 1981). Thus, even if psychiatric patients are less than optimal decision makers, it is unclear that they are any worse than most medical patients.

Macklin (1982) has suggested that psychiatric patients may also be less capable of voluntary consent than other people. Since psychiatric illness is often characterized by high levels of dependency on care-takers or family members and difficulties in individuation, it is argued that the ability of the mentally ill to decide independently about treatment may be compromised. Again, however, it is not clear if this situation is unique to

psychiatric practice. Many people without psychiatric diagnoses have unresolved dependency problems, and even "normal" individuals are likely to find themselves feeling quite dependent and helpless when serious medical decisions need to be made. Comparisons of medical and psychiatric populations along these dimensions are entirely lacking.

Even if the arguments about competency and voluntariness ultimately prove valid—that is, higher levels of impairment of each of these functions are found in psychiatric populations—such data would not necessarily constitute a justification for abandoning informed consent law in psychiatry. Patients who retain adequate capacities in these areas presumably are as deserving as anyone else of exercising their right to informed consent. Patients lacking such capacities could, following the usual procedures, have substitute decision makers appointed for them. If the latter group constitutes a substantial portion of the psychiatric patient population, there might be practical difficulties in obtaining such decision makers (Gutheil, Shapiro, & St. Clair, 1980), but institutionalized solutions are possible ("Exercising Judgment," 1979). In any event, it is difficult to make a strong theoretical argument for the inapplicability of informed consent law to voluntary psychiatric patients.

Granting that informed consent is required, then, one must determine the proper scope of disclosure for consent to the administration of psychotropic—particularly antipsychotic—medications. A number of commentators have suggested that patients should not be told at the inception of treatment with antipsychotic medications about the risk of developing tardive dyskinesia (TD). TD is a syndrome characterized by involuntary movements, especially in the orofacial area and in the extremities (American Psychiatric Association, 1979). It usually develops slowly, after months to years of antipsychotic drug administration, and can be masked temporarily by increasing the dosage. The syndrome often reverses spontaneously if the medications can be discontinued, but many cases are permanent. No effective treatment exists. TD is usually mild to moderate in severity, producing movements of which the patient may not even be aware. Sometimes, however, severe muscular dysfunction may result in interference with chewing, swallowing, breathing, and walking. While such extreme cases are rare, they lend dramatic emphasis to the arguments of those who urge that patients be informed of the risk of TD before treatment is begun.

In contrast to this approach, a number of authors in the psychiatric literature have suggested waiting for up to several months before discussing the risk of TD with patients (Devaugh-Geiss, 1979; Sovner, DiMascio, Berkowitz, Randolph, 1978). Their assumption appears to be that mention of TD when antipsychotic medications are first prescribed, which is generally when patients are acutely disturbed, will induce patients disproportionately and unreasonably to reject treatment. The justification offered for delaying disclosure of the risk of TD is that the syndrome is unlikely to occur soon after the implementation of antipsychotic drug therapy, and therefore does not constitute a risk at the time that consent is first obtained. It is reasoned that after some months of therapy patients will be able more rationally to decide whether the risk of TD is worth the benefits of continued treatment.

In jurisdictions in which a professional standard of disclosure is adopted, this procedure may be acceptable as a reflection of common professional practice. Where a materiality standard is employed, however, the practice, despite its appeal for psychiatrists, is likely to run into problems. It appears to be based on a misunderstanding of two of the previously-discussed exceptions to the requirement for informed consent—incompetency and therapeutic privilege. Proponents of delayed disclosure argue that the patient's state at the time medication is begun is such that he or she is unlikely to be able to make a reasoned decision about treatment. If this is true, however, a substitute consent should be sought, as is usually required in cases of incompetency. Alternatively, it is maintained that patients will suffer harm because disclosure of the risk of TD will lead them to reject needed treatment. Therapeutic privilege, however, is not generally construed to encompass situations in which harm to the patient will result from rejection of treatment based on a consideration of the risks. Neither of the commonly offered bases for this practice, therefore, is theoretically sound.

Further, for a large number of patients who have been treated previously with neuroleptics, it is *not* true that the period of risk does not begin until several months after the initiation of treatment. The risk of TD is now believed to be (at least in part) a function of the total lifetime dose of antipsychotic medication (American Psychiatric Association, 1979). Even the first dose, therefore, in someone who has been treated previously, incrementally increases the risk. Finally, there is something inherently deceptive about treating someone with an effective medication on which they may come to rely, only to reveal to them, after stabilization has occurred, a new set of risks of which they were previously ignorant (Appelbaum, in press).

Consent for somatic treatment is not the only difficult area in psychiatry; psychotherapy also presents unique problems of consent. Although the general practice is not to obtain explicit informed consent for psychotherapy, soliciting consent has been advocated as appropriate in light of the potential risks of the treatment (Schutz, 1982). These risks include the possibility of adverse outcomes, or simply of a failure to achieve a therapeutic response, and the risk of breach of confidentiality of the intimate disclosures that usually attend dynamic psychotherapy. On the other hand, many psychotherapists, particularly those with a Freudian orientation, view any explicit statement of risks and benefits, and any description of psychotherapeutic procedures as destructive to the therapeutic process. According to this view, a state of ambiguity ought to be deliberately created to allow the patient to develop a relationship with the therapist (the "transference") that is characteristic of his or her usual mode of relating to others. This process opens up to exploration those aspects of the patient's functioning that are usually most problematic, allowing therapeutic resolution of the underlying issues.

The rationale for limiting disclosure in psychotherapy to that sufficient for simple consent (which often means no disclosure, since therapists assume that patients who seek their services already have sufficient knowledge of what is involved in treatment to meet the simple consent standard) is strongest for Freudian, psychoanalytically-oriented psychotherapy. In other forms of treatment, in which resolution of the transference may play less of a role, the argument for obtaining informed consent is stronger. There is, to date, almost no case law on this subject, and thus it is difficult to predict in which direction the courts will lean.

A final issue concerning informed consent in psychiatry concerns the ulterior motives that sometimes dominate regulation of the consent process. Some forms of somatic treatment, particularly electro-convulsive therapy, have aroused ardent opposition from certain patients' rights groups. Attempts have been made to establish consent procedures that are so onerous (for example, requiring the consent of a relative before electroconvulsive therapy can be administered) as to severely limit the use of such treatments (Stone, 1979). Although control over certain forms of treatment may be called for, using the informed consent process to discourage patient consent, rather than openly regulating the treatment in question, distorts informed consent law, thereby diminishing its legitimacy in other settings. Psychiatry has not been alone in witnessing such practices; explicit depictions of the consequences of an abortion for the fetus have been required as part of disclosures preceding abortions in attempts to dissuade women from terminating their pregnancies (*Akron* v. *Akron Center for Reproductive Health*, 1983).

The application of informed consent to psychiatry, to be sure, raises some interesting issues, but it bears repeating that, for the most part, the law and practice of informed consent apply equally to psychiatric and other forms of medical care.

Informed Consent in Other Countries

The law of informed consent, although not uniquely American, clearly has received its greatest elaboration in the United States. No other country can match, either in quantity or intricacy, the outpouring of commentaries, statutes, and court decisions that have characterized discussion of the issue in the United States over the past quarter-century. Nonetheless, other nations have made efforts in this area, and their approaches will now be reviewed. This discussion is by no means exhaustive; it relies entirely on English-language literature on informed consent, and thus is intended to provide an introduction to, rather than a definitive summary of, the subject.

Canada, as might be expected by virtue of geographical proximity and cultural similarity, has most closely approximated the United States in the development of its consent law. Until 1980, Canada's law of informed consent had developed slowly, relying explicitly on American precedents, but reaching approximately the same level of development as American law had in the early 1960s. Many of the major questions—battery vs.

negligence, professional vs. lay standard of disclosure, objective vs. subjective tests of disclosure and causation—had been answered differently by the provincial courts that had addressed the subject, or remained largely unasked.

This situation changed dramatically in 1980 as a result of two decisions of the Supreme Court of Canada, *Hopp* v. *Lepp* and *Reibl* v. *Hughes*, which between them adopted a framework of consent law that closely resembles that enunciated by *Canterbury* v. *Spence*. *Reibl* is the more comprehensive of the cases, dealing with a Hungarian immigrant who consented to surgery designed to relieve a blockage in his carotid artery. Although testimony differed, it appears that Mr. Reibl was told only that he would be more likely to suffer harm if he failed to have the procedure than if he went through with it. In the version of the evidence accepted by the court, it appeared that no formal discussion of risks was undertaken. Reibl suffered a stroke as a post-operative complication of the surgery, which left him disabled just 1½ years before his pension would have vested.

The decision of the Supreme Court of Canada has been widely discussed in the Canadian legal literature (see, e.g., Picard, 1981; Somerville, 1981). The court first clarified the appropriate cause of action: suits must be brought in negligence, not battery. Drawing on its previous decision in *Hopp* v. *Lepp*, the court next adopted a materiality standard of disclosure, but one that differs from the standard in *Canterbury* in an important way. If the physician has reason to believe that the patient might not understand the information being communicated, a situation that arose in this case because of the patient's relative unfamiliarity with English, the *Reibl* court required the physician to insure that, in fact, understanding was attained. The decision in *Hopp* v. *Lepp*, reiterated in *Reibl*, also made explicit a requirement that appears to have been taken for granted in many United States' cases: The physician must respond to the best of his or her ability to any questions asked by the patient.

Causation was also decided along the lines of *Canterbury*. An objective test of causation—what a reasonable person would have done if the information had been provided—was adopted, muted by the requirement that the reasonable person be construed as being in the same circumstances as the patient. Given that Mr. Reibl was asymptomatic and a short time away from vesting his pension, this subjective shading of the objective test made an important contribution to the ultimate decision of the case on behalf of the defendant. The *Reibl* court also explicitly recognized the exceptions to the informed consent requirement of waiver and therapeutic privilege. In summary, there are now few differences in informed consent law between Canada and the United States.

The decision in *Reibl*, of course applies to the common law Canadian provinces, excluding the civil law province of Quebec, whose law is closely related to that of France. French law has required, at least since 1970, as part of the contractual obligations the physician is deemed to owe the patient, that the patient be informed of the potential risks of the treatment or procedure (Carbonneau, 1980). Failure to undertake adequate disclosure, however, "is not actionable *per se*, but only if the doctor is at fault in making a decision which has untoward consequences, when he is liable for damages caused by this fault, which is aggravated by the fact that he took this decision alone" (Somerville, 1979). The scope of required disclosure has not been subjected to the minute analysis given it in common law jurisdictions and remains somewhat unclear (Somerville, 1979).

European countries generally have doctrines requiring consent for treatment, but have failed to elaborate on these requirements (Giesen, 1976). The principle of prospective review of research projects, presumably including consent procedures, has been adopted in a number of countries around the world, but details on the functioning of these systems are sparse (Gutteridge, Bankowski, Curran, & Dunne, 1982). The British system is the best described (Allen, Waters, & McGreen, 1983; Ethical Committee, University College Hospital, 1981; "Ethical Committees," 1981; "Research Ethical Committees," 1983; Thompson, French, Melia, Boyd, Templeton, & Potter, 1981). The committees are highly decentralized, serving areas, districts, hospitals, and clinical divisions. They address primarily issues of risk and consent, and may not have ultimate authority in their jurisdiction. Many committees function only in an advisory capacity. No clearcut set of guidelines delimits their responsibilities or powers (Thompson et al., 1981).

One of the more interesting situations with regard to informed consent exists in England. The origins of American and Canadian law in English common law might lead one to expect England to have taken a similar approach to the question of informed consent as have the former North American colonies. Judged by recent controversies concerning consent to research, however, this has not been the case. Following the death of a research subject in a randomized trial of potentially toxic cancer chemotherapy, it became clear that the patient, and many others in her position, were being placed in these trials without their knowledge or consent (Brahams, 1982b; "Secret Randomized Clinical Trials," 1982). The argument that ensued over proper consent procedures made it apparent that only a "simple consent" standard is adhered to in ordinary medical practice (Elkeles, 1982), and perhaps even a less stringent standard in research (Brahams, 1982a, 1982b). Of particular interest is the fact that the experimental trials that provoked the controversy had been approved by a number of "ethics committees," which had agreed that consent could be foregone. Recent court cases concerning consent to treatment also reveal the reluctance of English courts to require disclosure of risks beyond what the physician thinks appropriate, although it is evident that the law of consent is not yet settled (Brahams, 1983; Robertson, 1981).

Critical Approaches to Informed Consent

The law of informed consent, in part because of the variety of interests that were accommodated in its evolution, has been subjected to a good deal of criticism from a number of perspectives. Many of these critiques are offered in tones that suggest the anger of those who feel betrayed by the failure of the doctrine single-mindedly to advance their primary objectives. This review of critical writings will focus, insofar as possible, on those commentators who have offered positive suggestions about what alternative form consent law might take, since it is here that the goals of the critics and the consequences of their approaches are most apparent.

The Autonomy-Based Critique

Several authors have pointed, quite correctly, to the numerous ways in which current consent law compromises patient autonomy in decision-making. J. Katz (1977) has been the most eloquent of these critics. Informed consent's "frequently articulated underlying purpose—to promote patients' decisional authority over their medical fate—has been severely compromised from the beginning," he writes. As evidence, Katz points to: the use of objective, rather than subjective standards of materiality and causation; therapeutic privilege as an exception to the requirement for informed consent; and reliance on negligence law, with its requirements for proximate cause (i.e., requiring both that the patient suffer physical harm before redress is available, and that the patient prove that disclosure would have averted the occurrence of the harm) and, in many cases, for professional standards and expert testimony. He concludes, "Judges toyed briefly with the idea of patients' self-determination and largely cast it aside."

Katz has never formulated a comprehensive alternative to the current system, but he has indicated the directions that such an effort should take (Katz, 1977). He would return consent law at least partially to the realm of battery by recognizing the possibility of dignitary injuries; the physician's failure to disclose would be construed as an assault on the dignity of the patient as a human being. Such dignitary harms would give rise to an independent cause of action in which the patient would not have to prove either that phsyical harm occurred or that consent would not have been withheld had appropriate disclosure been made. There is, of course, a problem with this suggestion that arises from the primacy given to actual, physical harms in determining compensation. "Unless nominal damages are greatly increased or punitive damages or damages for mental suffering freely awarded, allowing plaintiffs to sue for dignitary harms will have little practical significance (J. Katz, 1977). Further, Katz is not necessarily willing to dispense with the requirement, where physical harms are concerned, that the plaintiff demonstrate that consent would have been withheld in the face of full disclosure. He would, however, adopt a subjective standard of causation.

Others have been led to reason along the same lines as Katz as to the desirability of recognizing dignitary harms (Note, 1970). They have been similarly confronted with the difficulty of finding sufficiently punitive means of deterring the physician from curtailing disclosure when damages are limited to compensation for overt injuries. A suggested alternative, which would transcend the limitations of tort law, would be for "the legislature . . . [to] fashion sanctions other than damages for injury, such as fines, probation, loss of license or other administrative penalties, which could be imposed on a sliding scale, depending on the gravity of the offense" (Note, 1970). As Riskin (1975), who makes a similar proposal for a system of "non-insurable tort-fines," recognizes, the primary difficulty with such an approach would be to motivate patients to pursue these actions, when they no longer have the prospect of substantial recovery of damages.

Riskin (1975), whose concern "is based primarily on a commitment to human dignity as a value transcending even physical health," offers two other possible ways of diminishing legal obstacles to the enhancement of autonomy. The first of these would, in essence, adopt a partial battery approach to informed consent cases by eliminating the requirement for causation as it is currently interpreted. Any undisclosed risk that materialized would warrant the assessment of damages. Alternatively, he would reduce the standard of causation to require that the plaintiff show only that he or she *might* not have consented had full disclosure been made. Each of these suggestions would cut deeply against the negligence theory on which informed consent law has been based to date, and would approximate a system of strict liability for undisclosed risks (Meisel, 1977).

Some commentators have focused more on means of regulating disclosure as a technique for increasing patient autonomy. Simpson (1981) argues that if patients are to be able to "engage in the informed decision-making originally contemplated by the [informed consent] doctrine . . . the courts should go beyond [merely requiring disclosure] to consider whether the physician has taken reasonable measures to ensure that the patient *understands* [emphasis in original] the information disclosed." This might be construed as a Kantian approach to autonomous decision-making, in which rationality is the *desideratum* and understanding the crucial step toward that goal.

Surprisingly, after a lengthy discussion of the importance of comprehension, Simpson backs away from suggesting a system that would pursue it. Fearful that patients who cannot comprehend the nature and risks of treatment or who choose to remain ignorant might thereby be deprived of medical care (the possibility of waiver by the patient in such a situation is not mentioned), Simpson decides to base his "comprehension" standard on a detailed listing of those items physicians are required to disclose. In a complete turnaround from his original argument, if disclosure is complete, he would presume comprehension.

Goldstein (1975) arrives at a similar solution from very different premises. In what might be called an anti-Kantian mode, Goldstein argues that an emphasis on patients' comprehension would only serve to undercut their autonomy. If comprehension is the touchstone, Goldstein fears that uncomprehending patients (or those who simply desire not to comprehend) will have their decisions made for them by others. Even "irrational" patients should have the right to determine their own medical care (see Goldstein, 1978). He would therefore focus entirely on the disclosure by the physician, shunning any assessment of comprehension, and allowing (in some unspecified way) for compensation for dignitary harms.

Those critics offering an autonomy-based approach are generally attempting to undercut the influence of either health-related interests or the traditional approaches of negligence law. As opposed to those who would merely tinker with some aspect of existing law (e.g., as by utilizing subjective standards whenever possible), they seek some more basic restructuring of the current system. Yet, despite the emphasis given autonomy in the theoretical literature on informed consent, it is impressive how few fully thought-out proposals have been offered for restructuring the system in this way, and how slight the impact of existing proposals appears to have been on courts and legislatures.

The Health-Based Critique

As has been demonstrated, health-related interests lead to divergent approaches to the issue of informed consent, depending on the preconceptions of the people involved. Most critiques of current informed consent law that purport to be promoting the value of health, however, come at the question from a similar perspective: Informed consent is seen as a stumbling block to effective health care because its places decision-making power in the hands of those—namely patients—least capable of exercising it.

Unlike proponents of other critical approaches to informed consent law, those who offer a health-based critique have attempted to employ empirical data on a large scale to substantiate their argument. This probably relates to the empirical/scientific background of most of these persons, which leads them to confer legitimacy primarily on positions that can be supported with actual data. The result of this approach has been the publication of a large number of papers that either make some effort to measure the efficacy of informed consent in a naturalistic setting, or manipulate disclosure in an artificial setting and measure relevant variables. These studies have recently been reviewed as a group (Meisel & Roth, 1983), and subjected to serious criticism on a variety of methodologic grounds. This section is less concerned with the validity of the data, however (although readers are cautioned that many of these studies are seriously flawed), than with the way the data are used to support suggestions for changes in the law of informed consent.

Meisel and Roth (1983) note five areas in which empirical work has been undertaken; these include studies of disclosure, understanding, competency, voluntariness, and the decision-making process. Data from each area are used to demonstrate that the informed consent process does not work, and sometimes by implication and sometimes explicitly, to suggest that it ought to be abandoned. Examples of empirically-based argumentation in each of these five areas will be examined.

There are a few naturalistic studies of physician *disclosure*, but several that do exist suggest that the scope of disclosure anticipated by the doctrine of informed consent, under either a mixed professional or materiality standard, does not comport with actual (in-hospital) practices (Appelbaum & Roth, 1982b; Applebaum & Roth, 1983; Lidz, Meisel, Zerubavel, Ashley, Sestak, & Roth, in press; Lidz & Meisel, 1982). Further, the reasons for such dramatic constriction of disclosure relate to the structure of hospital-based care, in which decision-making by physicians precedes and shapes disclosure to the patient. Many decisions about treatment and diagnostic procedures, for example, are reached during discussions between physicians on daily rounds; these decisions may be implemented before even a physician who desired to discuss the issues with the patient would have an opportunity to do so. Since many of these practices have been adopted for reasons of efficiency, it is maintained that serious efforts to insure greater levels of disclosure would require both restructuring medical care in hospitals and increasing available resources to compensate for the time involved (Appelbaum & Roth, 1982b; Lidz & Meisel, 1982). Similar arguments can be made for office-based practice, in which reallocation of time can have immediate and significant effects on practitioners' income, but empirical support in this setting is lacking. In either setting, it is argued, in the absence of greater resources, time for consent transactions would presumably have to be taken from other functions that are important for the treatment of patients' illnesses.

Patient (and research subject) *understanding* of disclosed material has probably been the subject of the most intensive investigation. Most, though not all, studies demonstrate poor ability to recall information at some time after disclosure. A typical study was conducted by Schultz, Pardee, and Ensinck (1975), who tested 50 patients who had been admitted to a Clinical Research Center, "within an hour or two of their admission to the Center and their consent interview with the physician-investigator." All subjects had just consented to a clinical research project, which involved reading and signing a consent form (although 22% of subjects failed to read the form in its entirety). Of the patient-subjects, 52% were judged to be adequately informed, based on a 19-item questionnaire. Only 34% were adequately informed about procedures, 22% about the purpose of the study, and 20% about the risks. In assessing the reasons for this poor performance, the authors pointed to the format and content of the consent forms, the manner of presentation, and the circumstances in which the patient-subjects were situated.

This study suffered from the common defects of most investigations of understanding: disclosure was neither observed nor standardized, and therefore the authors were forced to assume that the information, the comprehension of which they were measuring, was actually conveyed. In addition, ability to recall information is not necessarily equivalent to understanding information at the time of disclosure. These authors were rather more sophisticated than many in pointing to multi-factorial causes of poor understanding, and in suggesting improvements in consent practices rather than totally rejecting the idea of informed consent.

Data of this sort, however, which has been generated repeatedly by different research groups (see references in Meisel & Roth, 1983), is often used as the basis for the argument that understanding *cannot* be achieved. The classic statement of this position was offered by Ingelfinger (1972). "The chances are remote," Ingelfinger wrote, "that the subject really understands what he has consented to." Not only will the subject have difficulty comprehending the true import of discomforts and risks associated with any procedure, but, "it is moreover quite unlikely that any patient-subject can see himself accurately within the broad context of the situation, to weigh the inconveniences and hazards that he will have to undergo against the improvements that the research project may bring to the management of his disease in general and to his own case in particular." Although Ingelfinger directed his argument toward the research subject, similar assertions could be made about patients who are asked to consent to therapeutic treatment.

Blanket statements such as Ingelfinger's to the effect that understanding can never be achieved would appear to be refuted by some studies demonstrating good comprehension in certain populations (see, for example, Bergler, Pennington, Metcalfe, & Freis, 1979; Howard, DeMets, & the BHAT Research Group, 1981). A more reasonable conclusion might be that understanding is at least sometimes possible, but a number of factors, including the difficulty that lay people have appreciating the significance of medical information (on which Ingelfinger relies so heavily), enter into the picture. One of the most important of these factors may be the complexity of the information provided. Grundner (1980), Cassileth, Zupkis, Sutton, Smith, and March (1980) and Morrow (1980) have demonstrated that most informed consent forms are written for those with at least a college-level education. There may, however, be two limits on the degree of simplification possible: (1) the material may sometimes be inherently complex; and (2) simplification usually requires more words to explain concepts that can otherwise be condensed in jargonesque language. Epstein and Lasagna (1969) demonstrated that length of consent forms is inversely related to comprehension, suggesting real limits on the possibility of simplification.

A final attack on the issue of understanding is based not on the difficulty of achieving that goal, but on the potential side effects of comprehension. A number of rather sensational case reports have purported to show instances in which patient understanding of risks led to untoward results, including cardiac problems, unjustified refusal of treatment, and death, either self-inflicted or as the result of the untreated disease process (Kaplan, Greenwald, & Rogers, 1977; Katz, 1977;

Patten & Stump, 1978). The conclusions drawn from these anecdotal accounts are that more patients are being harmed than helped by informed consent disclosures. "I would propose," suggests one author, "that we provide patients with reasonable explanations of what we feel is appropriate and not permit lawyers or administrators to set the rules" (R.L. Katz, 1977).

Studies of patients' and subjects' *competency* have focused mainly on psychiatric patients, the group thought most likely to demonstrate a high incidence of incompetency. Some investigators have identified incompetency as an important explanation for the failure of these patients to understand disclosed information. Appelbaum, Mirkin, and Bateman (1981), for example, estimated the competency of patients who had recently admitted themselves to a psychiatric hospital. Using a number of different standards of competency, they found a majority of patients would be deemed incompetent. This led them to call into question an informed consent model for voluntary psychiatric hospitalization. Conversely, data from Stanley et al. (1981), looking at responses to hypothetical research projects among psychiatric and medical patient groups, showed each group reaching similar conclusions. This led these investigators to conclude that psychiatric patients could participate as well as "normals" in the informed consent process. Little research has been done in this area, due in part to the difficulty of formulating methodologically adequate designs for the assessment of competency.

Voluntariness has also been neglected in empirical assessments of informed consent, but there have been some relevant studies. Lidz, et al. (in press) demonstrated the presence of pressures from family members on the consent of psychiatric patients. Ketai, Minter, Brandwin, and Brode (1981), again looking at psychiatric patients, found that in more than one-half of their schizophrenic research subjects' "relatives attempted to become excessively involved in the patient's decision-making." The inferences which can be drawn from a small number of studies with specialized populations are weak, but this has not stopped some commentators from claiming that pressures on patients and subjects are so widespread as to vitiate the value of consent. Ingelfinger (1972) wrote of "the thumbscrews of coercion [being] most relentlessly applied . . . [to] the most used and useful of all experimental sub-

jects, the patient with disease." Other physicians have claimed that they can obtain an informed consent from any patient for any procedure they desire to perform, presumably because of the coercive aspects of the status differential between doctors and patients (see, e.g., Beecher, 1966).

The final set of empirical studies has concerned the *decision-making process*. Here some very sophisticated arguments have been made to show that the model of decision-making implicit in the doctrine of informed consent does not resemble the way, in reality, patients make decisions. The informed consent model presupposes that, after being provided with information, patients will mull the relative risks and benefits of possible course of action and select the one course that most comports with their personal values. This sequence has been shown to be inaccurate for a number of reasons.

First, the structure of medical care and research may be such that the patient is required to make a decision prior to being presented with information. This is true for medical and surgical patients, who may first commit themselves to hospitalization, and by implication the diagnostic procedures and treatment that will accompany it, before learning of the risks of those procedures or even their identity (Appelbaum & Roth, 1982b; Lidz & Meisel, 1982). A similar process may take place with research subjects, who may come to identify with the researchers or the goal of research and commit themselves to participation before disclosure of relevant information occurs (Fellner & Marshall, 1970); in fact, disclosure may be timed to occur only after psychological commitment has taken place (Appelbaum & Roth, in press-b).

Second, the presentation of information may have relatively little impact on the patient's or subject's decisional process. This may be because of patient preconceptions about desirable and undesirable forms of treatment (Faden & Beauchamp, 1980); because of the primacy of emotional factors in the decision (Fellner & Marshall, 1970); or because the patient is most comfortable assuming the "sick role," in which the doctor makes the decisions while the patient passively acquiesces.

Third, the process of rational deliberation may be interfered with by psychopathological or psychological factors. For a small group of patients, primarily those in psychiatric treatment, overt delusions, hallucinations, psychotic ambivalence, and other symptoms of psychiatric illness may preclude rational consideration of the presented information. More common psychological processes, however, may interfere with the deliberations of a much larger number of patients. A substantial body of work in cognitive psychology, looking in detail at the decision-making process, has shown that a wide variety of extraneous, but predictable, influences distort everyday decision-making (Thompson, 1982). A recent attempt was made to apply the techniques of this research directly to patient decision-making. McNeil, Pauker, Sox, and Tyversky (1982), showed that minor differences in the way in which consent disclosures were constructed (whether or not treatments were explicitly identified, and whether the outcomes were described in terms of the probability of survival or the probability of death) produced substantial differences in the choices made by patients, physicians, and students.

All of these factors, it can be argued, interfere sufficiently with the rational deliberation that is at the core of at least some autonomy-related conceptions of informed consent that the purpose of the doctrine is vitiated. Informed consent then comes to be considered a "myth" (Fellner & Marshall, 1970), which can only act as an impediment to the delivery of health care without producing any benefits of its own.

The health-based critiques of informed consent may include one or more of these arguments, and their reasoning may stem from the empirical data or from "common knowledge." The conclusion that informed consent is of little value to patients may be explicitly drawn or only implied. Common to almost all of the health-based critiques, however, is a failure to consider practical alternatives to the current system. Many physicians appear to be arguing for a system in which physicians make decisions for patients, which they believe represents a return to the "old days." Others argue for increased (sometimes total) physician discretion as to the scope of disclosure. But in almost no case is any recognition given to legitimate interests of autonomy or to powerful traditions of tort law which would prevent a return to absolute physician discretion in either the selection or description of treatments. To this extent, much of the health-based critique of informed consent has been a theoretical failure. Nonetheless, it has probably influenced some legislators and judges to restrict the scope of the informed

consent doctrine, although not to the extent urged.

The Interactionist Critique

Burt (1979) has recently attempted to alter the focus of the debate on informed consent from the outcomes (e.g., health, autonomy) to the process. His work is probably the only comprehensive effort that has been made to re-think the rationale for informed consent and to offer a carefully thought-through alternative to the current system. Despite some important flaws in Burt's proposals, therefore, they warrant careful examination.

Burt is skeptical of autonomy as a goal of informed consent law because he sees autonomous, rational decision-making as unattainable in the usual medical setting. Demands for patient autonomy, just like corresponding demands for physician dominance in decision-making, he believes, reflect the failure of each side to recognize that neither can act independently of the other. Both patients and physicians are driven to demand control of the relationship, however, because an acknowledgment by either party that they are not in control would force them to confront such frightening realities as dependency, impotence, and death. Once control is obtained, the dominant party then seeks to remove the other party from the interpersonal scene in order to destroy any challenge to the assumption of absolute control.

This attempt to understand in psychodynamic terms the wellsprings of the enormous controversy over informed consent leads Burt to a very different view of the role of law in this situation. Rather than supporting one side or the other in the consent interaction (perhaps under the guise of promoting autonomy or health), Burt would have the legal system act only to force each party to continue to talk with the other, and thus to acknowledge shared power and powerlessness, until a mutual agreement on a course of action was reached. Maximal vagueness in the laws governing informed consent would be required to achieve this goal. In place of presumptions of consent if forms are signed, and detailed lists of risks that must be disclosed, Burt would require only that physicians obtain patients' consent for treatment. The reasonableness of the process by which the consent was obtained would be evaluated after the fact on grounds of which neither party would be certain. This, Burt believes, would force both parties to continue interacting with each other until mutual satisfaction (which would minimize the risk of future litigation) was achieved.

Burt's analysis has evoked considerable response, primarily from the legal profession. Most commentators have avoided criticizing his view of the dynamic basis of the doctor-patient relationship, which is sophisticated and probably accurate in large measure, and instead have targeted his proposed solution for their comments. There would clearly be enormous legal difficulties in implementing Burt's scheme. Law thrives on certainty, not uncertainty, and has elevated certainty to constitutional proportions. A situation in which neither side could know with assurance the consequences of their behavior would strike many legal theorists as manifestly unfair. In addition, it is difficult to imagine how that uncertainty might be maintained, that is, how one could prevent precedent from developing and a body of rules from emerging. A statute that would implement Burt's proposal is almost unimaginable.

The value of Burt's work lies not in its practicality, but in the provocation to thought that it offers. Viewing informed consent law as a defense against uncertainty, and refocusing attention on the process of the transaction should provide a stimulus for future efforts to re-think the basis of the doctrine of informed consent.

Conclusion

The law of informed consent, as should by now be evident, is a hybrid. It has evolved its current form in an attempt to accommodate several, often conflicting interests. The apparently random sacrifice of autonomy or interests in health, often for the sake of conforming to traditional legal approaches, gives informed consent law the ungainly shape of a building designed by a team of architects, none of whom were permitted to view the plans drawn up by their collaborators. Informed consent law thus accomplishes many goals in part, reaches no end in full, aggravates all, and satisfies none.

Seeing how this situation has come about, one is led inevitably to question whether it might be susceptible to change. A review of the extant critiques of the doctrine of informed consent suggests that significant change, in the sense of structural alterations of the doctrine, is most unlikely. Radical critiques almost always ignore valid counter-

vailing interests, thus destroying their chances of being adopted. More moderate critiques, which recognize the legitimacy of opposing interests, are forced to acknowledge the necessity for compromise and to restrict their suggestions to tinkering with the particular accommodations that have been made. Consideration of the diverse interests involved leads one to an almost fatalistic sense of determinism about the overall shape of the law of consent: If the interests could have been accommodated differently, this would already have taken place.

Yet, this is not to suggest permanency for the current form of the doctrine. Law reflects a dynamic equilibrium in which the strengths of different interests wax and wane. Informed consent law owes its birth to such a process: the extraordinary growth of interest in autonomy of the individual, particularly relative to relationships with professionals and other specialists. With time, this interest may wane, professional behavior may change, or some other factor— perhaps a massive change in the economic structure of health care—may force a reaccommodation. Consent law is therefore likely to remain in a state of flux, and though substantial short-term changes are unlikely, the picture is much less certain over the long haul.

References

Akron v. Akron Center for Reproductive Health, No. 81–746 (U.S. June 15, 1983).

Allen, P.A., Waters, W.E., & McGreen, A.M. Research ethical committees in 1981. *Journal of the Royal College of Physicians of London*, 1983, *17*, 96–98.

Almquist, N.J. When the truth can hurt: Patient-mediated informed consent in cancer therapy. *UCLA-Alaska Law Review*, 1980, *9*, 143–196.

American Psychiatric Association. *Tardive dyskinesia*. Washington, DC: Author, 1979.

Anderson v. State of Arizona, No. 1–CA–CIV–5946, Dept. A. (Ariz. Ct. App. 1982).

Annas, G.J., Glantz, L.H., & Katz, B.F. *Informed consent to human experimentation: The subject's dilemma*. Cambridge, MA: Ballinger Publishing Company, 1977.

Appelbaum, P.S. Refusing treatment: The uncertainty continues. *Hospital and Community Psychiatry*, 1983, *34*, 11–12.

Appelbaum, P.S. Legal and ethical aspects of psychopharmacologic practice. In J.S. Bernstein (Ed.), *Clinical psychopharmacology*. Littleton, MA: PSG Publishing Co., in press.

Appelbaum, P.S., & Gutheil, T.G. The right to refuse treatment: The real issue is quality of care. *Bulletin of the American Academy of Psychiatry and the Law*, 1981, *9*, 199–202.

Appelbaum, P.S., Mirkin, S.A., & Bateman, A.L. Empirical assessment of competency to consent to psychiatric hospitalization. *American Journal of Psychiatry,* 1981, 9, 1170–1176.

Appelbaum, P.S., & Roth, L.H. Clinical issues in the assessment of competency. *American Journal of Psychiatry,* 1981, 138, 1462–1467.

Appelbaum, P.S., & Roth, L.H. Competency to consent to research: A psychiatric overview. *Archives of General Psychiatry,* 1982, 39, 951–958.(a)

Appelbaum, P.S., & Roth, L.H. Treatment refusal in medical hospitals. In President's Commission for the Study of Ethical Problems in Medicine and Biomedical and Behavioral Research, *Making health care decisions: The ethical and legal implications of informed consent in the patient-practitioner relationship. Volume two: Appendices.* Washington, DC: U.S. Government Printing Office, 1982.(b)

Appelbaum, P.S., & Roth, L.H. Patients who refuse treatment in medical hospitals. *Journal of the American Medical Association,* 1983, 250, 1296–1301.

Appelbaum, P.S., & Roth, L.H. Involuntary treatment in medicine and psychiatry. *American Journal of Psychiatry,* in press.(a)

Appelbaum, P.S., & Roth, L.H. The structure of informed consent in psychiatric research. *Behavioral Sciences and the Law,* in press.(b)

Appelbaum, P.S., Roth, L.H., & Lidz, C. The therapeutic misconception: Informed consent in psychiatric research. *International Journal of Law and Psychiatry,* 1982, 5, 319–329.

Bach-y-Rita, G. The prisoner as an experimental subject. *Journal of the American Medical Association,* 1974, 229, 45–46.

Barnhart, B.A., Pinkerton, M.L., & Roth, R.T. Informed consent to organic behavior control. *Santa Clara Law Review,* 1977, 17, 39–83.

Beauchamp, T.L., & Childress, J.F. *Principles of biomedical ethics.* New York: Oxford University Press, 1979.

Beecher, H.K. Ethics and clinical research. *New England Journal of Medicine,* 1966, 274, 1354–1360.

Bergler, J.H., Pennington, A.C., Metcalfe, M., & Freis, E.D. Informed consent: How much does the patient understand? *Clinical Pharmacology and Therapeutics,* 1979, 4, 435–440.

Bly v. Rhoads, 222 S.E. 2d 783 (Vir. 1976).

Bonnie, R.J. The psychiatric patient's right to refuse medication: A survey of legal issues. In A.E. Doudera & J.P. Swazey (Eds.), *Refusing treatment in mental health institutions—Values in conflict.* Ann Arbor, MI: AUPHA Press, 1982.

Brahams, D. Consent to randomized treatment. *Lancet,* 1982, II, 1050–1051.(a)

Brahams, D. Death of a patient who was unwitting subject of randomized controlled trial of cancer treatment. *Lancet,* 1982, I, 1028–1029.(b)

Brahams, D. Informed consent does not demand full disclosure of risks. *Lancet,* 1983, II, 58.

Brakel, S., & Rock, R. (Eds.). *The mentally disabled and the law* (Rev. ed.). Chicago: University of Chicago Press, 1971.

Brooks, A.D. The constitutional right to refuse antipsychotic medications. *Bulletin of the American Academy of Psychiatry and the Law,* 1980, 8, 179–221.

Burt, R.A. *Taking care of strangers: The rule of law in doctor-patient relations.* New York: The Free Press, 1979.

Canterbury v. Spence, 462 F. 2d 772 (D.C. Cir. 1972).

Carbonneau, T.E. The principles of medical and psychiatric liability in French law. *International and Comparative Law Quarterly,* 1980, 29, 742–765.

Cassileth, B.R., Zupkis, R.V., Sutton-Smith, K., & March, V. Informed consent—Why are its goals imperfectly realized? *New England Journal of Medicine,* 1980, 16, 896–918.

Cobbs v. Grant, 104 Cal. Rptr. 505, 502 P.2d 1 (1972).

Cooper v. Roberts, 220 Pa. Super. 260, 286 A.2d 647 (1971).

Curran, W.J. Governmental regulation of the use of human subjects in medical research: The approach of two federal agencies. In P.A. Freund (Ed.), *Experimentation with human subjects.* New York: George Braziller, Inc., 1970.

Curran, W.J. Informed consent, Texas style: Disclosure and non-disclosure by regulation. *New England Journal of Medicine,* 1979, 300, 482–483.

Dain, N. *Concepts of insanity in the United States, 1789–1865.* New Brunswick, NJ: Rutgers University Press, 1964.

Dalrymple, G. Informed Consent: A new standard for Texas. *St. Mary's Law Journal,* 1976, 8, 499–513.

Davis v. Hubbard, 506 F. Supp. 915 (W.D. Ohio 1980).

Devaugh-Geiss, J. Informed consent for neuroleptic therapy. *American Journal of Psychiatry,* 1979, 136, 959–962.

DiMatteo, M.R., & DiNicola, D.D. *Achieving patient compliance: The psychology of the medical practitioner's role.* New York: Pergamon Press, 1982.

Dyer, A.R. Reflections on the doctor-patient relationship. In J.P. Brady & H.K.H. Brodie (Eds.), *Controversy in psychiatry.* Philadelphia: W.B. Saunders, 1978.

Eichner v. Dillon, 52 N.Y.2d 263, 420 N.E.2d 64 (1981).

Elkeles, A. Informed consent in clinical trials. *Lancet,* 1982, I, 1189.

Epstein, L.C., & Lasagna, L. Obtaining informed consent. *Archives of Internal Medicine,* 1969, 123, 682–688.

Epstein, R.A., Kalven, H., Jr., & Gregory, C.O. *Cases and materials on torts.* Boston: Little, Brown & Company, 1977.

Ethical Committee, University College Hospital. Experience at a clinical research ethical review committee. *British Medical Journal,* 1981, 283, 1312–1314.

Ethical committees. *Lancet,* 1981, II, 1432.

Exercising judgment for the disabled: Report of an inquiry into limited guardianship, public guardianship and adult protective services in six states. Washington, DC: American Bar Association, 1979.

Faden, R.R., & Beauchamp, T.L. Decision-making and informed consent: A study of the impact of disclosed information. *Social Indicators Research,* 1980, 7, 314–336.

Fellner, C.H., & Marshall, J.R. Kidney donors—The myth of informed consent. *American Journal of Psychiatry,* 1970, 9, 79–85.

Frankel, M.S. The development of policy guidelines governing human experimentation in the United States: A case study of public policy-making for science and technology. *Ethics in Science & Medicine,* 1975, 2, 43–59.

Freedman, B. A moral theory of informed consent. *Hastings Center Report*, 1975, 5 (August), 32–39.

Frenkel, D.A. Human experimentation: Codes of ethics. *Legal Medical Quarterly*, 1977, *1*, 7–14.

Fried, C. *Medical experimentation: Personal integrity and social policy.* Amsterdam: North-Holland Publishing Company, 1974.

Geller, J.L. State hospital patients and their medication—Do they know what they take? *American Journal of Psychiatry*, 1982, *139*, 611–615.

Giesen, D. Civil liability of physicians for new methods of treatment and experimentation. *International and Comparative Law Quarterly*, 1976, *25*, 180–213.

Gill, M.J. Side effects of a right to refuse treatment lawsuit: The Boston State Hospital experience. In A.E. Doudera & J.P. Swazey (Eds.), *Refusing treatment in mental health institutions—Values in conflict.* Ann Arbor, MI: AUPHA Press, 1982.

Goedecke v. State, 603 P.2d 123 (Colo. 1979).

Goldstein, J. For Harold Lasswell: Some reflections on human dignity, entrapment, informed consent, and the plea bargain. *Yale Law Journal*, 1975, *84*, 683–703.

Goldstein, J. On the right of the "institutionalized mentally infirm" to consent to or refuse to participate as subjects in biomedical and behavioral research. In National Commission For the Protection of Human Subjects of Biomedical and Behavioral Research, *Research involving those institutionalized as mentally infirm. Appendix.* Washington, DC: U.S. Government Printing Office, 1978.

Gray, B.H. An assessment of institutional review committees in human experimentation. *Medical Care*, 1975, *13*, 318–328.

Gray, B.H., Cooke, R.A., & Tannenbaum, A.S. Research involving human subjects. *Science*, 1978, *201*, 1094–1101.

Grundner, T.M. On the readability of surgical consent forms. *New England Journal of Medicine*, 1980, *302*, 900–902.

Gutheil, T.G. The right to refuse treatment. In L. Grinspoon (Ed.), *Psychiatry 1982: The American Psychiatric Association annual review.* Washington, DC: American Psychiatric Press, 1982.

Gutheil, T.G., & Appelbaum, P.S. Substituted judgment and the physician's ethical dilemma: With special reference to the problem of the psychiatric patient. *Journal of Clinical Psychiatry*, 1980, *41*, 303–305.

Gutheil, T.G., Shapiro, R., & St. Clair, R.L. Legal guardianship in drug refusal: An illusory solution. *American Journal of Psychiatry*, 1980, *137*, 347–352.

Gutteridge, F., Bankowski, Z., Curran, W., & Dunne, J. The structure and functioning of ethical review committees. *Social Science and Medicine*, 1982, *16*, 1791–1800.

Heckert, L. Informed consent in Pennsylvania—The need for a negligence standard. *Villanova Law Review*, 1982, *28*, 149–172.

Helling v. Carey, 83 Wash.2d 514, 519 P.2d 981 (1974).

Hopp v. Lepp, 4 W.W.R. 645, 22 A.R. 361, 13 C.C.L.T. 66 (S.C.C 1980).

Howard, J.M., DeMets, D., & the BHAT Research Group. How informed is informed consent? The BHAT experience. *Controlled Clinical Trials*, 1981, *2*, 287–303.

Ingelfinger, F.J. Informed (but uneducated) consent.

New England Journal of Medicine, 1972, 9, 465–466.

In re Grady, 85 N.J. 235, 426 A.2d 476 (1981).

In re Quinlan, 70 N.J. 10, 355 A.2d 647, cert. denied sub nom. Garger v. New Jersey, 429 U.S. 922 (1976).

In re Storar, 52 N.Y.2d 266, 420 N.E.2d 64 (1981).

In re the Guardianship of Richard Roe III, 421 N.E.2d 40 (Mass. 1981).

In re the Mental Health of K.K.B., 609 P.2d 747 (Okla. 1980).

Ivy, A.C. Nazi war crimes of a medical nature. In S.J. Reiser, A.J. Dyck, & W.J. Curran (Eds.), *Ethics in medicine: Historical perspectives and contemporary concerns.* Cambridge, MA: MIT Press, 1977.

Kaimowitz v. Michigan Department of Mental Health, Civil Action 73–19434–AW (Wayne County, Mich., Cir. Ct. 1973), in A.D. Brooks (Ed.), *Law, psychiatry and the mental health system.* Boston: Little, Brown & Co., 1974.

Kaplan, S.R., Greenwald, R.A., & Rodgers, A.J. Neglected aspects of informed consent. *New England Journal of Medicine*, 1977, *19*, 1127.

Katz, J. Informed consent—A fairy tale? Law's vision. *University of Pittsburgh Law Review*, 1977, *39*, 137–174.

Katz, J., & Capron, A.M. *Catastrophic diseases: Who decides what?* New Brunswick, NJ: Transaction Books, 1975.

Katz, R.L. Informed consent—Is it bad medicine? *Western Journal of Medicine*, 1977, *126*, 426–428.

Kelsey, F.O. Patient consent provisions of the Federal Food, Drug, and Cosmetic Act. In I. Ladimer & R.W. Newman (Eds.), *Clinical investigation in medicine: Legal, ethical, and moral aspects.* Boston: Law-Medicine Research Institute, 1963.

Ketai, R., Minter, R., Brandwin, M., & Brode, M. Family influence in the recruitment of schizophrenic research subjects. *American Journal of Psychiatry*, 1981, *3*, 351–354.

Lasagna, L.C. Drug panic and its aftermath. In I. Ladimer & R.W. Newman (Eds.), *Clinical investigation in medicine: Legal, ethical, and moral aspects.* Boston: Law-Medicine Research Institute, 1963.

Lebacqz, K., & Levine, R.J. Respect for persons and informed consent to participate in research. *Clinical Research*, 1977, *25*, 101–107.

LeBlang, T.R. Informed consent—Duty and causation: A survey of current developments. *The Forum*, 1983, *2*, 280–289.

Levine, M. IRB review as a "cooling out" device. *IRB*, 1983, *4*, 8–9.

Levine, R.J. *Ethics and regulation of clinical research.* Baltimore: Urban & Schwarzenberg, 1981.

Lidz, C.W., & Meisel, A. Informed consent and the structure of medical care. In President's Commission for the Study of Ethical Problems in Medicine and Biomedical and Behavioral Research, *Making health care decisions: The ethical and legal implications of informed consent in the patient-practitioner relationship. Volume two: Appendices.* Washington, DC: U.S. Government Printing Office, 1982.

Lidz, C.W., Meisel, A., Zerubavel, E., Ashley, M., Sestak, R., & Roth, L.H. *Informed consent: A study of decisionmaking in psychiatry.* New York: Guilford Press, in press.

Lidz, C.W., & Roth, L.H. The signed form—Informed consent? In R.F. Boruch, J. Ross, & J.S. Cecil (Eds.),

Solutions to legal and ethical problems in applied social research. New York: Academic Press, 1981.

Ludlum, J.E. *Informed consent.* Chicago: American Hospital Association, 1978.

Macklin, R. Some problems in gaining informed consent from psychiatric patients. *Emory Law Journal,* 1982, *31,* 345–374.

Magnet, S.R. Legislating for an informed consent to medical treatment by competent adults. *McGill Law Journal,* 1981, *26,* 1056–1067.

Malloy v. Shanahan, 280 Pa. Super. 440, 421 A.2d 803 (1980).

McCance, R.A. The practice of experimental medicine. In I. Ladimer & R.W. Newman (Eds.), *Clinical investigation in medicine: Legal, ethical, and moral aspects.* Boston: Law-Medicine Research Institute, 1963.

McNeil, B.J., Pauker, S.G., Sox, H.C., Jr., & Tversky, A. On the elicitation of preferences for alternative therapies. *New England Journal of Medicine,* 1982, *21,* 1259–1262.

Meisel, A. The expansion of liability for medical accidents: From negligence to strict liability by way of informed consent. *Nebraska Law Review,* 1977, *56,* 51–152.

Meisel, A. The "exceptions" to the informed consent doctrine: Striking a balance between competing values in medical decision-making. *Wisconsin Law Review,* 1979, 413–488.

Meisel, A. The rights of the mentally ill under state constitutions. *Law and Contemporary Problems,* 1982, *45,* 7–40.

Meisel, A., & Kabnick, L.D. Informed consent to medical treatment: An analysis of recent legislation. *University of Pittsburgh Law Review,* 1980, *41,* 407–564.

Meisel, A., & Roth, L.H. Toward an informed discussion of informed consent: A review and critique of the empirical studies. *Arizona Law Review,* 1983, *25,* 265–346.

Meisel, A., Roth, L.H., & Lidz, C.W. Toward a model of the legal doctrine of informed consent. *American Journal of Psychiatry,* 1977, *134,* 285–289.

Miller, L.J. Informed consent. *Journal of the American Medical Association,* 1980, *244,* 2100–2103, 2347–2350, 2556–2559, 2661–2662.

Mohr v. Williams, 95 Minn. 261, 104 N.W. 12 (1905).

Morrow, G.R. How readable are subject consent forms? *Journal of the American Medical Association,* 1980, *244,* 56–58.

Murphy, J.G. Therapy and the problem of autonomous consent. *International Journal of Law and Psychiatry,* 1979, *2,* 415–430.

Natanson v. Kline, 186 Kan. 393, 350 P.2d 1093; rehearing denied 187 Kan. 186, 354 P.2d 670 (1960).

NIMH (National Institute of Mental Health). Unpublished data, 1983.

Nishi v. Hartwell, 52 Haw. 188, 473 P.2d 116 (1970).

Note. Restructuring informed consent: Legal therapy for the doctor-patient relationship. *Yale Law Journal,* 1970, *79,* 1533–1576.

Olin, G.B., & Olin, H.A. Informed consent in voluntary mental hospital admissions. *American Journal of Psychiatry,* 1975, *132,* 938–941.

Palmer, A.B., & Wohl, J. Voluntary-admission forms: Does the patient know what he's signing? *Hospital*

and Community Psychiatry, 1972, *23,* 250–252.

Patten, B.M., & Stump, W. Death related to informed consent. *Texas Medicine,* 1978, *74,* 49–50.

Pernick, M.S. The patient's role in medical decisionmaking: A social history of informed consent in medical therapy. In President's Commission for the Study of Ethical Issues in Medicine and Biomedical Research, *Making health care decisions: The ethical and legal implications of informed consent in the patient-practitioner relationship. Volume three: Appendices. Studies on the foundations of informed consent.* Washington, DC: U.S. Government Printing Office, 1982.

Picard, E. Consent to medical treatment in Canada. *Osgoode Hall Law Journal,* 1981, *19,* 140–151.

Plant, M.L. An analysis of "informed consent." *Fordham Law Review,* 1968, *36,* 639–672.

Plant, M.L. The decline of "informed consent." *Washington and Lee Law Review,* 1978, *35,* 91–105.

President's Commission for the Study of Ethical Problems in Medicine and Biomedical and Behavioral Research. *Making health care decisions: The ethical and legal implications of informed consent in the patient-practitioner relationship. Volume one: Report.* Washington, DC: U.S. Government Printing Office, 1982.(a)

President's Commission for the Study of Ethical Problems in Medicine and Biomedical and Behavioral Research. *Compensating for research injuries: The ethical and legal implications of programs to redress injured subjects. Volume One: Report.* Washington, DC: U.S. Government Printing Office, 1982.(b)

Project Release v. Prevost, No. 78–CV–1467 (ERN) (E.D.N.Y. November 24, 1982).

Reibl v. Hughes, 33 N.R. 361, 14 C.C.L.T. 1 (S.C.C. 1980).

Reiser, S.J., Dyck, A.J., & Curran, W.J. *Ethics in medicine: Historical perspectives and contemporary concerns.* Cambridge, MA: MIT Press, 1977.

Rennie v. Klein, 462 F. Supp. 1131 (D.N.J. 1978), 476 F. Supp. 1294 (D.N.J. 1979), aff'd in part, 653 F.2d 836 (3rd Cir. 1981), vacated and remanded, 102 S.Ct. 3506 (1982).

Research ethical committees. *Lancet,* 1983, *I,* 1026.

Rice, N. Informed consent: The illusion of patient choice. *Emory Law Journal,* 1974, *23,* 503–522.

Riskin, L.L. Informed consent: Looking for the action. *University of Illinois Law Forum,* 1975, 580–611.

Robertson, G. Informed consent to medical treatment in England. *Law Quarterly Review,* 1981, *97,* 102–126.

Rogers v. Okin, 478 F. Supp. 1342 (D. Mass. 1979), aff'd in part, 634 F.2d 250 (1st Cir. 1980), vacated and remanded sub nom Mills v. Rogers, 102 S.Ct. 2442 (1982).

Rosoff, A.J. *Informed consent: A guide for health care providers.* Rockville, MD: Aspen Publications, 1981.

Roth, L.H. Competency to consent to or refuse treatment. In L. Grinspoon (Ed.), *Psychiatry 1982: The American Psychiatric Association annual review.* Washington, DC: American Psychiatric Press, 1982.

Roth, L.H., & Appelbaum, P.S. Obtaining informed consent for research with psychiatric patients—The controversy continues. In R. Sadoff (Ed.), "Forensic psychiatry," *Psychiatric clinics of North America.* Philadelphia: W.B. Saunders, in press.

Roth, L.H., Appelbaum, P.S., Sallee, R., Reynolds,

C.F., & Huber, G. The dilemma of denial in the assessment of competency to refuse treatment. *American Journal of Psychiatry,* 1982, *139,* 910–913.

Roth, L.H., Meisel, A., & Lidz, C.W. Tests of competency to consent to treatment. *American Journal of Psychiatry,* 1977, *134,* 279–284.

Salgo v. Leland Stanford Jr. University Board of Trustees, 154 Cal. App.2d 560, 317 P.2d 170 (1957).

Schloendorff v. Society of New York Hospital, 211 N.Y. 125, 105 N.E. 92 (1914).

Schultz, A.L., Pardee, G.P., & Ensinck, J.W. Are research subjects really informed? *Western Journal of Medicine,* 1975, *1,* 76–80.

Schutz, B.M. *Legal liability in psychotherapy.* San Francisco: Jossey-Bass, 1982.

Scott v. Bradford, 606 P.2d 554 (Okl. 1979).

Secret randomized clinical trials. *Lancet,* 1982, *I,* 78–79.

Seidelson, D.E. Medical malpractice: Informed consent cases in "full-disclosure" jurisdictions. *Duquesne Law Review,* 1976, *14,* 309–347.

Simpson, R.E. Informed consent: From disclosure to patient participation in medical decisionmaking. *Northwestern University Law Review,* 1981, *76,* 172–207.

Slater v. Baker & Stapleton, C.B. Eng. Rptr. 860 (Michelmas Term, 8 Geo. III, 1767).

Somerville, M.A. *Cosent to medical care.* Ottawa, Canada: Law Reform Commission of Canada, 1979.

Somerville, M.A. Structuring the issues in informed consent. *McGill Law Journal,* 1981, *26,* 741–808.

Soskis, D.A. Schizophrenic and medical inpatients as informed drug consumers. *Archives of General Psychiatry,* 1978, *35,* 645–647.

Sovner, R., DiMascio, A., Berkowitz, D., & Randolph, P. Tardive dyskinesia and informed consent. *Psychosomatics,* 1978, *19,* 172–177.

Stanley, B., Stanley, M., Lautin, A., Kane, J., & Schwartz, N. Preliminary findings on psychiatric patients as research participants: A population at risk? *American Journal of Psychiatry,* 1981, *5,* 669–671.

Stone, A.A. The history and future of litigation in psychopharmacologic research and treatment. In D.M. Gallant & R. Force (Eds.), *Legal and ethical issues in human research and treatment: Psychopharmacologic considerations.* New York: Spectrum Publications, Inc., 1978.

Stone, A.A. Informed consent: Special problems for psychiatry. *Hospital and Community Psychiatry,* 1979, *30,* 321–327.

Strong, C. Informed consent: Theory and policy. *Journal of Medical Ethics,* 1979, *5,* 196–199.

Superintendent of Belchertown State School v. Saikewicz, 373 Mass. 728, 370 N.E.2d 417 (1977).

The T.J. Hooper, 60 F.2d 737 (2d Cir. 1932).

Thompson, I.E., French, K., Melia, K.M., Boyd, K.M., Templeton, A.A., & Potter, B. Research ethical committees in Scotland. *British Medical Journal,* 1981, *282,* 718–720.

Thompson, W.C. Psychological issues in informed consent. In President's Commission for the Study of Ethical Problems in Medicine and Biomedical and Behavioral Research, *Making health care decisions: The ethical and legal implications of informed consent in the patient-practitioner relationship. Volume three: Appendices.* Washington, DC: U.S. Government Printing Office, 1982.

Trichter, J.G., & Lewis, P.W. Informed consent: The three tests and a modest proposal for the reality of the patient as an individual. *South Texas Law Journal,* 1980, *21,* 155–170.

U.S. v. Brandt, United States Adjutant General's Department, Trials of War Criminals Before Nuremberg Military Tribunals Under Control Council Law No. 10 (October, 1946–April, 1949), The Medical Case (Vol. 2). Washington, DC: U.S. Government Printing Office, 1947.

U.S. Department of Health and Human Services. Final regulations amending basic HHS policy for the protection of human research subjects. *Federal Register.* January 26, 1981, *46*(16), 8366–8392.(a)

U.S. Department of Health and Human Services. Final regulations amending basic HHS policy for the protection of human subjects. *Federal Register.* January 27, 1981, *46*(17), 8942–8980.(b)

Veatch, R. Three theories of informed consent: Philosophical foundations and policy implications. In National Commission for the Protection of Human Subjects of Biomedical and Behavioral Research, *The Belmont report.* Washington, DC: U.S. Government Printing Office, 1976.

Wadlington, W.J. Consent to medical care for minors: The legal framework. In G.B. Melton, G.P. Koocher, & M.J. Saks (Eds.), *Children's competence to consent.* New York: Plenum Press, 1983.

Waltz, J.R., & Scheuneman, T.W. Informed consent to therapy. *Northwestern University Law Review,* 1970, *64,* 628–650.

Weyandt, C.J. Valid consent to medical treatment: Need the patient know? *Duquesne University Law Review,* 1965–1966, *4,* 450–462.

White, W.D. Informed consent: Ambiguity in theory and practice. *Journal of Health Politics, Policy and Law,* 1983, *8,* 99–119.

3.
Sexual Aggression: Studies of Offenders Against Women

Vernon L. Quinsey

ABSTRACT. *Comparative data indicate that coercive male mating strategies are common in a variety of animals, including primates. Because coercive mating can result in differential male reproductive success, it may have been related to the evolutionary development of greater male size and aggressiveness. Competition among males for females has undoubtedly favored the same evolutionary result.*

Male competition for females is related to warfare among preliterate societies. In general, the more warlike the society, the higher the frequency of rape. Groups of men who exert power through the application of force are characteristic of these societies. Male dominance in itself, however, is not a sufficient condition for high rape frequency.

Studies of men in Western society reveal marked individual differences in their self-reported proclivity to rape, their sexual arousability to rape descriptions, and their attitudes toward rape. Rapists themselves often engage in other criminal activities, are more sexually aroused by descriptions of rape, and frequently have other sexual deviations. Sadistic rapists are commonly obsessed with aggressive sexual imagery and exhibit marked sexual arousal to descriptions of rape. There is evidence that violent sexual pornography may be conducive to the development of an interest in sexual aggression.

Clearly, learning plays an important role in both appropriate and aggressive sexual behaviors. Learning is involved in the acquisition of sexual behaviors, sexual attitudes and, more importantly in the present context, sexual arousal patterns. The acquisition of an interest in aggressive sexual imagery is, therefore, a central problem in this area of research. Progress in understanding this issue may well hinge on discovering the genesis of "normal" sexual fantasies.

There are few differences between rapists and other nonsexual offenders in personality, intelligence, drug addiction, testosterone levels, or social competence. Rapists may, however, more frequently have assertive deficits but more data are needed on this point. Alcohol appears to be related both to the propensity to rape and to inflict physical damage on the victim. Attitudes toward women do not appear to be strongly related to rape but specific attitudes toward rape may be more important.

With respect to the treatment of rapists, there are, unfortunately, no comparative evaluative studies of different treatment types. Behavioral methods of treatment appear very promising and antiandrogen treatment may be effective with hypersexual rapists but there are no longterm followup data relevant to either treatment method. Castration appears to be related to low recidivism rates but is ethically problematic.

This review was supported by grant 847 from the Ontario Mental Health Foundation. I wish to thank G. Harris, A. Maguire, M. Rice and D. Upfold for comments on an earlier draft of this paper and M. Quinsey for bringing many of the anthropological studies to my attention.

Both treatment and research suffer from the absence of a demonstrably valid typological scheme for rapists. Rapists are a heterogeneous group; they vary in their sexual responsiveness to rape and sadistic imagery, their social competence, their level of criminality, and the degree to which alcohol is related to their offense pattern. In addition, there are great differences in the offense patterns themselves (frequency, degree of violence, and so on). Rapists who engage in multiple offender rapes, for example, are different from solitary offenders on a variety of measures. Clearly, a taxonomy is required to bring order to the repeatedly observed individual differences among rapists. These individual differences among rapists undoubtedly obfuscate comparisons of rapists with non-sex offenders and hinder rational treatment programming.

Research on etiologically relevant differences among rapists is thus indicated. More importantly, however, an understanding of the development of male sexual interest in both consenting and aggressive sexual activities is required before any definitive theories of rape can be formulated in the future.

SOMMAIRE. Des données comparatives montrent que les stratégies d'accouplement coercitif du mâle sont répandues chez différents animaux, notamment les primates. Comme l'accouplement coercitif peut avoir des résultats différents pour le succès de la reproduction, il se peut qu'il ait entraîné une évolution caractérisée par la taille et l'agressivité accrue du mâle. La concurrence entre les mâles pour posséder les femelles a sans aucun doute favorisé le même phénomène d'évolution.

Dans les sociétés primitives, la concurrence des hommes pour les femmes est liée à la guerre. En général, plus la société est guerrière, plus l'incidence du viol est fréquente. Dans ces sociétés, ce sont des groupes d'hommes qui exercent le pouvoir par la force. Toutefois, la prédominance du mâle n'est pas, en soi, une condition suffisante pour que le viol soit très fréquent.

L'étude des hommes dans la société occidentale révèle des différences individuelles marquées quant à la propension déclarée au viol, à l'excitation sexuelle devant des descriptions de viol et aux attitudes en matière de viol. Les auteurs de viol eux-mêmes ont souvent d'autres activités criminelles, sont plus vite excités sexuellement par des descriptions de viol et souffrent, très souvent, d'autres déviations sexuelles. Les violeurs sadiques sont très souvent obsédés par des images d'agression sexuelle, et ils manifestent une excitation sexuelle marquée face à des descriptions de viol. Il est prouvé que la pornographie violente peut être la cause du développement d'un goût pour l'agression sexuelle.

Il est sûr que l'apprentissage joue un rôle important sur le comportement sexuel, tant approprié qu'agressif. L'apprentissage intervient dans l'acquisition du comportement sexuel, des attitudes sexuelles et, ce qui est plus important dans le présent contexte, dans les modèles d'excitation sexuelle. L'acquisition d'un goût pour les images sexuelles agressives est, par conséquent, un problème crucial dans ce domaine de la recherche. Tout progrès dans la compréhension du problème dépendra peut-être surtout de la découverte de la genèse des fantasmes sexuels normaux.

Il existe peu de différences entre les coupables de viol et les autres délinquants non sexuels eu égard à la personnalité, à l'intelligence, à l'accoutumance aux drogues, aux niveaux de testostérone ou à la compétence sociale. Toutefois, le violeur peut plus fréquemment avoir un "déficit d'assertion," mais il faudrait davantage de données sur ce point. L'alcool semble être lié à la propension, à la fois, à violer et à infliger des blessures à la victime. Les attitudes à l'égard des femmes ne semblent pas être fortement liées au viol, mais il se peut que des attitudes spécifiques vis-à-vis du viol aient plus d'importance.

Quant au traitement des coupables de viol, il n'existe malheureusement aucune étude comparative sur l'évaluation des différents types de traitement. Les méthodes de traitement behavioriste semblent très prometteuses et le traitement antiandrogène peut s'avérer efficace auprès des violeurs hypersexués, mais il ne se trouve aucune donnée de suivi à long terme qui traitent de l'un ou l'autre de ces méthodes. La castration semble avoir causé une diminution du taux de récidive, mais elle pose un problème déontologique.

Tant le traitement que la recherche souffrent de l'absence d'un modèle typologique valable pour les cas de viol. Les violeurs constituent un groupe hétérogène; ils varient dans leurs réactions sexuelles aux images de viol et de sadisme, dans leur compétence sociale, leur niveau de criminalité et eu égard à l'incidence de l'alcool sur leurs types de délinquance. De plus, on remarque des différences très nettes dans les modèles de délinquance (fréquence, degré de *violence, etc.). Les violeurs qui se livrent à des viols collectifs, par exemple, ne sont pas les mêmes que ceux qui opèrent tout seuls, à de multiples égards. Il est clair qu'il faut établir une classification afin de mettre en ordre les différences individuelles maintes fois observées entre les violeurs. Ces différences individuelles entre ces délinquants nuisent sans aucun doute aux comparaisons entre les violeurs et les délinquants non sexuels, et empêchent aussi l'instauration d'un traitement rationnel.*

Il convient, par conséquent, de se livrer à une recherche sur les différences pertinentes, d'ordre étiologique, entre les violeurs. Cependant, il est primordial de comprendre le développement de l'intérêt sexuel du mâle dans les activités sexuelles tant volontaires qu'agressives, avant de tenter de formuler à l'avenir toute théorie définitive à propos du viol.

Introduction

Rape is of increasing concern in contemporary society. This concern has been reflected in and promoted by a great deal of attention from the popular media; fortunately, it has also motivated a large amount of scholarly activity in a heretofore ignored area. The purpose of this chapter is to organize and interpret this large amount of recent literature and to suggest lines of further inquiry.

Rape is often defined as the vaginal penetration of an unwilling female. Unfortunately, this definition excludes a number of coercive sexual activities that are closely related (e.g., anal intercourse, forced fellatio, and so on); in addition, there are legal offenses in many jurisdictions such as "indecent assault" and "statutory rape" which may or may not involve rape as more strictly defined. These vagaries of the law make it exceedingly difficult to count the number of rapes. Partly because of these difficulties in definition, the Law Reform Commission of Canada (1978) has successfully recommended that "rape" be replaced by "sexual assault" in the criminal code. A sexual assault is sexual contact with another person (including the touching of the sexual organs of another or the touching of another with one's sexual organs) without that person's consent. The Law Reform Commission suggested that circumstances involving violence and/or penetration be taken into account only in sentencing. In this review, the term "rape" will be used interchangeably with the term "sexual assault."

The focus of the present paper is on sexual assaulters of adult women: Sexual assaults on children (Quinsey, 1977) and adult males (Groth & Burgess, 1980) will be excluded, as will be issues of prevention and rape resistance (e.g., Bart, 1981; Brodsky, 1976; Wright, 1980). The

more coercive and violent the sexual behavior is, the more it will be emphasized in the present review, both because very aggressive behavior is more serious and of more concern to society and the victim (Ellis, Atkeson, & Calhoun, 1981; Kilpatrick, Resick, & Veronen, 1981) and because it is more easily studied. Very violent acts are more likely to be reported, less likely to suffer from definitional variance, and more likely to be viewed by various social groups in the same light.

This review is primarily substantive in that it attempts to determine what is known about sexual assaulters and sexual violence, and is not a critique of the literature per se. Although the literature is improving, all reviewers have lamented its scientific weakness. There is no need to document this scientific inadequacy further, particularly since several methodological critiques have already been published (Bentler & Abramson, 1981; Dietz, 1978; Schwartz, 1980). Methodological comments, therefore, will be made only when necessary for an understanding of the material. On a more positive note, however, we have come a very long way from the state of almost complete ignorance documented over 20 years ago (Wheeler, 1960).

This chapter is organized in sections which reflect the disparate areas of investigation subsumed under the topic of sexual assault. Immediately following this introduction, background information is presented from biological and cross-cultural perspectives and the incidence of sexual assault in Western societies is examined. A final subsection deals with relevant data obtained from non-sexual assaulters. The next major section reviews studies of known sexual assaulters and presents data derived from comparisons of these men with various non-sex offender groups; this is followed by a section on treatment. Using the material presented in the earlier sections, the penultimate section evaluates various ways of explaining sexual assault. The last section provides a brief overview and conclusions.

Perspectives on Sexual Assault

Sexual Assault in Biological Perspective

A biological perspective involves evolutionary or physiological concepts. From an evolutionary point of view, it is apparent that coercive intercourse can increase the relative reproductive success of males and under certain, less likely, conditions, females as well. Comparative behavioral data can provide important information about these various conditions (Beach, 1976). However, it is important to remember in attempting to extrapolate from non-human species to man that even among our closest relatives, the primates, there are wide variations in mating strategies and that, even within a species, the relations between the sexes vary with habitat (Goy & McEwen, 1980; Jensen, 1973); indeed, humans are unique among mammals in that females do not advertise their peak periods of fertility with estrus (Symons, 1979). Human capacity for language, in particular, makes generalization from animals to man hazardous. In addition, evolutionary arguments arc "ultimate" rather than "proximate;" that is, they involve the history of natural selection in a given species and not the mechanisms currently in operation which determine the behaviors. These caveats aside, observations of other species are at least useful heuristics and some common features are indeed observed in a variety of species.

Coercive intercourse has been described in a wide variety of species from insects to mammals (Crawford, 1982). Among insects, forced insemination of unwilling females has been described in detail among *Panorpa* scorpionflies (Thornhill, 1980). In nonforced mating, female scorpionflies are attracted by males who exude a pheromone and present a nuptial offering which the female eats during copulation. Females' preferences for offerings, in descending order, are large dead insects, smaller dead insects, and a salivary mass. The males risk predation by gathering the insects (especially from spider webs) and guarding their nuptial offerings. Males without offerings assault passing females using a specially developed notal organ on their wings to restrain

the females' wings and a pair of muscular abdominal claspers. Thornhill hypothesizes that this behavior and the physical structures which make it possible have evolved because the male requires control of significant resources to attract females. As resource control is risky and not always possible, natural selection favors the development of an alternative method of fertilization on the part of males. It is of significance that the reproductive interests of the males and females do not coincide in forced mating; both sexes, however, prefer non-forced mating.

Attempts at forced copulation are very common among mallards and most often involve multiple male attackers (Titman & Lowther, 1975). The attempts are not preceded by courtship behavior and the female is frequently injured and sometimes even killed. If a male's pair bond partner has been raped, he sometimes copulates with her immediately thereafter, thereby increasing the chances that the offspring will be his. The relative social dominance of males influences coercive mating and reproductive success. Dominant drakes successfully protect their pair bond partners with threat displays, although the likelihood of the male pair bond partner's intervention has been shown to vary inversely with the number of attackers. More aggressive males often interrupt subordinate males during mating attempts. The subordinates have little success in defending their mates and often make no attempt to do so (Barash, 1977).

McKinney, Derrickson, and Mineau (in press) have reviewed the literature on forced copulation among waterfowl (family *Anatidae*) and concluded that forced copulation is an important but less common method of insemination than pair bonding. The frequency of forced copulation varies with species and increases with crowding, as reflected in the dispersal of nesting sites. Another important variable is the extent to which male territory guarding and mate guarding behaviors are incompatible with forced copulation strategies. These data on waterfowl as well as those on scorpionflies illustrate clearly that the optimal mating strategies of males and females are not always complementary, as coercive mating frequently involves physically damaging females.

Turning to primates, coercive mating has been described among several primate species (Crawford, 1982). Among orangutans, subadult males commonly force intercourse on females who are not in estrus but the adaptive significance of this behavior is unknown. Male chimpanzees have also been observed to coercively copulate with females. Because chimpanzees are our closest relatives extant, their mating habits are of considerable interest. Groups of males are highly territorial and social; they patrol the borders of their territory and attempt to kill members of other bands. Females are more solitary and live within the defended territory; thus, the larger the territory a group of males controls, the more females who are available. Groups of males serially copulate with females who are in estrus but there is evidence that male status is positively correlated with reproductive success and high ranking males inhibit males of lower status from breeding. Individual males attempt to separate females who are in estrus from the group in order to form pair bonds; the male forces the female to follow with threat displays but higher ranking males interrupt this process when possible (Symons, 1979). Clearly, male chimpanzees aggressively compete for females both within and between groups.

Coercive mating among mammals in general and primates in particular is related to a variety of gender-related differences in dominance, physiology, and the development of sexual behavior. In most mammalian species, males are larger, more aggressive, and more socially dominant than females (Goy & McEwen, 1980). These differences between genders have been linked to fetal brain organization and post-pubertal testosterone levels (Gadpaille, 1980; Michael, 1964), although the relationship between androgens and aggression is complex and affected by a variety of variables (Goldstein, 1974). Goy and McEwen (1980), in a thorough review of the literature on sexual dimorphism, have concluded that testosterone masculinizes the fetal brain in mammals at a critical period. This masculinization is reflected among juvenile rhesus monkeys, for example, in a high frequency of "rough and tumble" play and high frequencies of mounting which are not dependent on post-natal testicular secretions. Females exposed to androgens prenatally exhibit the same behaviors. Prenatal masculinization of the brain is positively related to subsequent dominance rank. There is also evidence in man that prenatal androgenization of the brain alters female prepubertal gender role behavior.

It is of interest that, in many species of mammals, the hormones involved in male sexual behavior are those involved in aggression and dominance and, furthermore, that sexual and aggressive behaviors can be elicited from common areas of the brain (Blumer, 1970; MacLean, 1973; Prentky, 1982, 1984). Among squirrel monkeys, for example, the striatal complex appears to be the neural area for genital displays used in greeting, courtship, and aggression (MacLean, 1973). Among rhesus monkeys, the copulatory behavior of less dominant males is inhibited by the presence of more dominant males (Jensen, 1973). Marler and Hamilton (1967) conclude that the courtship of many species is a modified version of their fighting behavior which involves elements of both aggression and withdrawal.

Humans, like many other species, form pair bonds for reproduction where the paternity of offspring is relatively certain and both parents invest time and effort in the rearing of their young. Pair bonding occurs in societies which practice polygyny (serial or not), polyandry, and monogamy. An abundance of correlational data relate the stability and strength of pair bonds to reproductive success in man and in other species (Rasmussen, 1981). Because organisms are "programmed" to achieve reproductive success (Dawkins, 1978), a variety of reproductive strategies can be expected to occur given particular circumstances. Male reproductive success can be achieved by forming a pair bond with one or more healthy, young (but reproductively mature) females, avoiding being cuckolded, and if the risks (including those of competition for resources) are not too high, fathering as many children by sexual assault or seduction as possible outside the pair bond. Symons (1979) has argued that men lust after a variety of female partners for precisely this reason; whereas females, who can produce a strictly limited number of offspring, do not. Given that reproductively successful men inevitably supplant their less successful fellows, we might wonder why sexual assault is not more common than it is. Although it must be remembered that reproductive success means having children that themselves survive to reproduce and, therefore, that simply having a lot of offspring is not necessarily a viable strategy, there is, in many instances, little cost to males in having children that someone else will care for, providing the male helps to take care of the offspring from his own pair bond(s).

An additional impetus to forced mating exists where females discriminate among potential male partners. Such female discrimination exists among non-human primates (Beach, 1976) and has been well documented in the beagle (Beach & LeBoeuf, 1967). Clearly, males who are unattractive and cannot secure a partner have an evolutionary incentive for forced mating. Sexual dimorphism in which males are larger than females could well have arisen in this context as well as in the context of inter-male competition (Dawkins, 1978).

For females, the results of a coercively produced pregnancy are quite different; if the male who sexually assaults her does not have "good genes" her own offspring are less likely to reproduce. In addition, if she is not in a pair bond, she will have fewer resources with which to raise the child. Furthermore, if she is in a pair bond, the "infidelity" may lead to its dissolution (Rasmussen, 1981). An optimal female strategy would be to form a pair bond with a reproductively capable male who has control over significant resources, and, if the male turns out to be infertile, to cuckold him or form another pair bond.

In summary, biological data indicate that forced mating strategies are common in a wide variety of species, that optimal male and female reproductive strategies do not always coincide, and that there may well be heritable tendencies for males to engage in forced mating under certain conditions. These considerations have been elaborated in a sociobiological theory of sexual assault to be considered later.

Cross Cultural Perspective on Sexual Assault

We have seen that, among primates, sexual behavior patterns vary with ecology, experience, and species; it is no surprise, therefore, that these patterns vary widely over human cultures as well (e.g., Carstairs, 1964; Gadpaille, 1980). With respect to sexual assault, there are great difficulties in obtaining incidence data over various cultures; firstly, one must depend on the respondents' reports rather than on frequency data and, secondly, "rape" is socially defined and this definition is in fact different in different cultures (Chappell, 1976). Despite these methodological difficulties, however, it does appear that frequencies of sexual assault vary markedly over cultures. Sexual assault has been reported to be rare or absent

among such disparate societies as the peace-loving pygmies of the Ituri forest (Turnbull, 1961), the reprehensibly exploitative and loveless Ik of the African mountains (Turnbull, 1972), and the Trobriand islanders in their tropical paradise (Malinowski, 1929). In contrast, sexual assault has been extremely common among certain societies, for example, the Gusii of Kenya, and, in fact, appeared to be the most common form of sexual interaction among them whether the interaction was perceived by them as legitimate or not (LeVine, 1959). LeVine has argued from his study of the Gusii that four factors are related to high rape frequency: (a) severe restrictions on non-marital female sexual activity, (b) female sexual inhibition, (c) prolonged bachelorhood of males, and (d) an absence of physical segregation between the sexes. A study of a single culture can, however, only yield hypotheses and other interpretations of these data can be offered, perhaps most notably concerning the importance of the conception among the Gusii that all sex involves coercion and violence.

Several interesting attempts have been made to examine differences in sexual assault frequency among cultures in a systematic way with somewhat comparable results. Otterbein (1979) studied 135 non-literate societies using data from the Human Relations Area Files; of these societies, there were data for 43 on rape frequency and for 32 on punishment for this crime. Rape frequency was coded on a 7-point scale ranging from 1 (concept absent or rape reported not to occur) to 7 (all sexual relations viewed as aggressive). Punishment was rated from 1 (death) to 7 (none). In addition to punishment severity, two further variables were coded. The first was the existence of fraternal interest groups, which are power groups of biologically-related men who resort to aggression in order to defend their members' interests. The existence of fraternal interest groups was measured by patrilocality, a marital residence pattern in which the family lives with the groom's relatives, or by a residence pattern in which the males live together and apart from the family. The second variable was feuding, defined as blood revenge in response to a homicide.

Significantly higher rape frequencies were found in societies characterized by patrilocality and feuding. There was an inverse relationship between rape frequency and punishment severity. An interesting relationship among these two findings emerged: Punishment severity was related to rape frequency only when there were no fraternal interest groups but societies with no punishment for rape had high frequencies whether there were fraternal interest groups or not.

Sanday (1981) examined 156 tribal societies from a standard cross-cultural sample. Inter-rater agreement on the 21 variables selected was high and rape frequency data were found for 75 societies. Rape incidence was classified as (a) rare or absent, (b) present but no data on frequency or said to be not atypical, or (c) rape-prone (where used as punishment or as a threat against women, as part of a ceremony, or where rape was clearly of moderate to high frequency). Eighteen percent of the societies were rape-prone and 47% rape-free. Variables related to sexual repression (e.g., attitudes toward premarital sex and age of males at marriage) were not significantly related to rape frequency. However, variables relating to interpersonal violence were correlated with rape frequency; these variables were: (a) raiding other groups for wives, (b) degree of interpersonal violence, (c) ideology of male toughness, and (d) war. Similarly, variables related to the ideology of male dominance correlated with rape frequency: (a) lack of female power and authority, (b) lack of female political decision-making, (c) negative attitudes toward women as citizens, (d) the presence of special places for men, and (e) the presence of special places for women. The largest of these correlations, however, were found for degree of interpersonal violence and the ideology of male toughness. This finding relates well to the fraternal interest group theory of Otterbein (1979).

The fierce Yanomamo of South America offer a classic example of a rape-prone society (Chagnon, 1977); the Yanomamo are obsessed with male toughness. Fights within villages and wars between villages are very common and male mortality due to warfare is high; both fights and wars are primarily over women. Dominant males and villages possess more women than those less dominant. Symons (1979) suggests that warfare was very common among nonliterate groups before contact with state societies, that it was motivated by competition for women, and that it resulted in 25% of adult male mortality. We can conclude that rape among nonliterate societies must be viewed in the context of male competition for women.

These considerations make it appear that warfare among groups of men over women is the phenomenon most predictive of rape frequency. It is therefore, unfortunate that the Sanday paper does not include the intercorrelations among the variables used to predict rape frequency or, even better, a regression analysis, as we are left to suspect that after degree of interpersonal violence is partialled out, there is no variance left in the other variables to correlate with rape frequency. Thus, a plausible interpretation of these data is that rape frequency is only related to gender dominance and sexual separation as a byproduct of a warlike culture; the correlations between rape frequency and variables such as female lack of authority thus being epiphenomenal. This interpretation agrees in part with that of Sanday but suggests that an ameliorative course would involve addressing the issue of interpersonal violence in general rather than the issue of gender dominance. In support of this position, there are societies, such as the Hutterites, where there is complete male dominance, no machismo ideology, no war, and little or no rape (Hostetler & Huntington, 1980).

Incidence and Variation in Western Societies

Statistics Canada (1981) reports that in 1981 there were 3,625 rapes reported to the police, of which 1,066 were classified as unfounded. Of the 2,559 remaining, 1,050 were cleared by charges (1,119 adult males were charged, 2 adult females, and 75 juveniles). There were, in addition, 7,370 indecent assaults on females reported, of which 647 were classified as unfounded (without basis). To put the statistics in perspective, the total of "founded" sexual assaults on females (9,282) is much larger than the number of homicides (657) and much smaller than the number of non-sexual assaults (121,076). There were 56,370 forcible rapes recorded in the U.S. during 1976; indicating a rape rate at least twice that of Canada.

Scanlon (1982), using Statistics Canada information, has reported that rapes per 100,000 Canadian population have increased from 3.1 in 1962 to 8.6 in 1978. In the U.S., the Uniform Crime Report indicates a steadily increasing trend since 1933 (Bowker, 1979). How much of the increase is due to increases in rape frequency or is simply a function of variation in victim reporting probability or police reporting practices is a matter of contention. Scanlon (1982) has argued that, although there are real problems in using rape statistics because of differences in local definition, regional disparities are obscured in broad national samples and can be used in static situations to measure changes in the same location. Regional disparities are indeed a real problem: Chappell (1976), for example, found that the Los Angeles police used a very liberal set of criteria in defining rape whereas the Boston police used a very restrictive one and concluded that sophisticated comparisons of different geographical localities were unsound.

With respect to the reporting of rapes, Bowker (1979) cites data from the National Opinion Research Centre victimization polls which show that rape is the most underreported crime of personal violence; the self-report rate was almost 4 times the Uniform Crime Report rate of the FBI. Although other victimization studies show the reporting rate to be higher (40%) and to be the same as for other crimes of violence against the person (Scanlon, 1982), it is clear that underreporting is a serious problem. More serious sexual assaults, particularly those involving personal injury, are, however, more likely to be reported (Monahan, 1981). It is, however, one thing to have various estimates of the degree of underreporting but it is quite another to find that reporting rates vary with victim variables. In the most comprehensive study relevant to this issue, Feldman-Summers and Ashworth (1981) interviewed 100 women in each of Asian, Black, Hispanic or White ethnic groups in Seattle. Each participant was interviewed by a woman of the corresponding ethnic group. The intention to report a hypothetical rape was related to the perceived likelihood and evaluation of each of a variety of outcomes and the perceived expectations of various social referents with which the respondent was motivated to comply (e.g., husband). Ethnic differences were most marked in the likelihood of reporting to the police or a rape crisis center; not surprisingly, white women were more likely to say they would report to these public agencies. The results of this study, therefore, support the idea that the underreporting of sexual assault is markedly biased.

One of the variables most closely related to the decision to report a sexual assault is the relationship of the victim to the rapist. In most jurisdictions, sexual assault within the context of marriage is not even a criminal offense. Sexual assault which occurs in a dating context is also very unlikely to be reported. Kirkpatrick and

Kanin (1957) reported that, in the previous academic year, 56% of women students at Ohio State University had been offended by sexual aggression, 21% by forceful attempts at intercourse, and 6% by attempts involving threats or the infliction of physical pain. Similar results were found by Kanin (1957) who gathered reports concerning women's experiences in their last year of high school: Of 163 offended women, two reported the attack to the police. Although these data are striking and important, the majority of the assaults were, of course, fairly minor.

These data underscore the difficulties inherent in using officially-gathered statistics on the incidence of sexual assault; it appears that the official statistics are both gross and biased underestimates, particularly in cases where there is no physical injury. "Sexual assaults" or "rapes" are socially defined behaviors; behaviors which "look" like sexual assault, i.e., which involve actual or attempted coercive intercourse and the infliction of pain, are not always labeled as sexual assaults, as, for example, in the Gusii wedding night activities or in the dating activities of Western society.

It is important to realize that the issue in Western society is whether a particular instance is classified as a sexual assault; once such a label is applied, there is a consensus about the seriousness of the act—i.e., people agree about the seriousness of the behavior once it is classified as rape. Akman and Normandeau (1967), using a ratio scaling technique in which subjects rated the seriousness of 14 offenses in comparison to a standard offense, found that French and English university students in several Canadian provinces, white collar workers, judges, and police officers agreed very well with each other and a Philadelphia sample on the relative seriousness of the index offenses. Forcible rape (without physical injury or intimidation with a weapon) was seen as very serious; specifically, to put the matter into concrete (if strange) perspective, it was 1.43 times as serious as being hurt to the extent of requiring hospitalization, equal to a property loss or destruction of between $62,501.00 and $100,000.00, and as 2.8 times less serious than homicide.

The classical study on sexual assault was conducted by Amir in Philadelphia (Amir, 1965, 1971). Using police files, data were gathered on 646 victims and 1,292 offenders involved in 370 single-rapes, 105 pair-rapes and 171 group rapes. The results of this large study can be summarized very briefly as follows: Rape was found to be primarily intra-racial and of higher frequency among blacks, in more than a third of the cases the victim and offender knew each other (if only slightly), the participants typically lived in the same neighborhood, the offenses often occurred in the home of one of the participants, three-quarters of the rapes were planned, 50% of the victims did not resist, 43% of the rapes involved more than one rapist, most rapes occurred on weekend evenings, most participants were of lower socioeconomic status, and finally, alcohol was associated with increasing amounts of violence used by the offender.

Dietz (1978) has critically summarized a large number of sociological studies of rape. He begins by noting that, in the U.S., only 16% of reported forcible rapes lead to any conviction (cf. Abel, Becker, & Skinner, 1980; Peterson, Braiker, & Polich, 1980) and that the probability of reporting, arrest, and conviction are probably all strongly related to social status and race; thus Dietz reaffirms the position taken earlier on the biases inherent in studies of sexual assault. Sexual assaulters available for study come differentially from low socioeconomic backgrounds and are poorly educated. Similarly, blacks are disproportionally represented (cf. Schiff, 1973). Lester (1974) has also found that there is a small correlation between the proportion of blacks in a state and the incidence of rape. Data on temporal and spatial patterning from a variety of European and American studies indicate that rapes are more common in the evening, in the summer, and on weekends. With respect to locale, the rapist typically breaks into the victim's residence (or uses a ruse to effect the same purpose) or entices or forces her to accompany him to a convenient location (Dietz, 1978).

Considerable light is thrown on the nature of sexual assault by a study of rape frequency before, during and after a transit strike in Toronto (Geller, 1977). During the 23-day strike, the number of sexual offenses against female hitchhikers increased 9 times to 13% of all sex offenses (as compared to 1.6% in a comparable pre-strike period and 0% in a comparable post-strike period). The total number of sexual assaults, however, was unaffected by the strike. The most plausible interpretation of these data appears to be that sexual assaulters were looking for accessible victims and opportunistically changed the place where they ordinarily found them.

There are a number of interesting differences between multiple offender and solitary offender rapes (Dietz, 1978): Multiple offender rapes: (a) are more sharply clustered on weekends, summers, and evenings; (b) involve younger offenders from lower status ethnic groups in communities with pronounced ethnic hierarchies; (c) more often involve alcohol; (d) involve offenders who less frequently have previous offenses against the person or sex offenses; (e) more often involve offenders from the same neighborhood as the victim and the crime; (f) more often begin in the street, less often occur in the residence of the participants, and more often in an automobile; (g) less often involve intimates; and (h) involve greater force. Peterson, Braiker and Polich (1980) have supported these results in a study of California inmate self-reports; gang membership was found to be associated with high rates of all types of violent crime, including rape. These findings are reminiscent of the cross-cultural data pertaining to societies which use rape in pubertal rites, as well as to fraternal interest group theory, and the influence of machismo ideology.

Variations in the rates of sexual assault have been studied within Western societies but in view of the softness of the data have to be viewed with extreme caution (Chappell, 1976; Geis & Geis, 1979). Schiff (1974) concludes that Greece, Italy, Spain, and Switzerland have lower incidents of forcible rape than the U.S. Geis and Geis (1979) present data indicating that Stockholm has the same incidences as comparably-sized cities in the U.S. and much higher incidences than London, for example. They argue that sexual permissiveness in Sweden leads occasionally to misunderstandings on the part of (especially foreign) men in dating situations.

The incidence of rape and attempted rape does not appear to vary with increased penalties upon conviction. In a Philadelphia study, Schwartz (1968) found that large increases in the duration of incarceration for rape and attempted rape had no effect on the seriousness or number of sexual assaults. This is not to argue, of course, that criminal sanctions have no deterrent effect, only that an increase in an already severe sanction had no increased effect (cf. Otterbein, 1979).

In summary, data on the incidence and variation of sexual assault in Western societies are subject to discrepancies in police definitions and victim reporting practices. Nevertheless, there are some indications that rape is increasing in rate over time in many locations; that, in the U.S., rape is more common in slum conditions and black communities with adolescent gangs (note that the rates are higher and victims *less* likely to report); that rapists are predatory and opportunistic; and that rapists involved in multiple offender rapes are different from solitary rapists.

Variations in the Proclivity to Sexual Assault

This section reviews studies of men who are not identified as sexual assaulters. In addition to providing a general context for the evaluation of data on sexual assaulters, several issues can be addressed by these studies: most notably, the identification of attitudes and behaviors which are conducive to sexual assault and the identification of individual differences among "normal men" in their proclivity to rape. If we were to assume that some or all rapists were in some way different from men who never rape, they would be differentially recruited from subgroups of men or boys with certain characteristics. If this is so, there must be variation in theoretically- or, better, empirically-relevant variables within the population of non-sex offenders.

Among these variables are beliefs concerning sexual assault itself. It would not strain our credulity to believe that men who think that certain women deserve or "look for" sexual assault would be more likely to engage in such behavior; or, perhaps, more to the point, that men who think that women's resistance is invariably coyness or that women cannot be forced into intercourse against their will would be more likely to commit a sexual assault. Note that the truth or falsity of these beliefs is irrelevant, as is their *logical* relationship as to whether women *should* be sexually assaulted. The assertion here is only that there is an intuitively appealing link for a relationship between these sorts of beliefs and a predilection for sexual assault (cf. Gager & Schurr, 1976), although the direction of causality presumed by this assertion has not been established.

Some of the beliefs mentioned above are surprisingly common. Consider Heller's (1969) views on victim precipitation: "The victim herself may contribute unwittingly to her demise by masochistic provocation. . . Among common fatal attitudes or 'games' played by female victims are provocativeness of dress, posture or gait accompanied by a rigid, stubborn defense of genital 'integ-

rity'. When rape is inevitable, these same women act as though they would rather be dead than in bed, and are tragically accommodated."

In an important study on beliefs about rape (Burt, 1980), a large sample of adults in Minnesota, of whom 60% were women, were interviewed by female interviewers concerning a variety of attitudes toward sexual behaviors and relations between the sexes. Subjects were selected at random to yield representative age and sex distributions. A variety of scales were used to measure: (a) Own sex role satisfaction; (b) Self-esteem; (c) Romantic self-image; (d) Sex role stereotyping (e.g., "A woman should be a virgin when she marries."); (d) Adversarial sexual beliefs (e.g., "In a dating relationship a woman is largely out to take advantage of a man."); (f) Sexual conservatism (e.g., "People should not have oral sex."); (g) Acceptance of interpersonal violence (e.g., "Being roughed up is sexually stimulating to many women."); and (h) Rape myth acceptance (e.g., "A woman who is stuck-up and thinks she is too good to talk to guys on the street deserves to be taught a lesson.").

In the male sample the following variables were correlated (in descending order) with the Acceptance of Rape Myths Scale: sex role stereotyping, acceptance of interpersonal violence, sexual conservatism, education (negative), adversarial sexual beliefs, and age. Very similar zero order (simple) correlations were obtained in the female sample. Burt developed a model based on these relationships in which acceptance of interpersonal violence was the best predictor of scores on the Acceptance of Rape Myths Scale, but, although this relationship is plausible, it was unfortunately contaminated by overlap in content between the two scales. The most important result of Burt's survey, however, was the finding of the great prevalence of mistaken ideas about rape: for example, over half the sample believed that 50% or more of reported rapes result from a woman trying to get back at a man because she was angry or attempting to cover up an illegitimate pregnancy.

Briere, Malamuth, and Check (1981) administered a questionnaire containing Burt's Rape Myth, Adversarial Sexual Beliefs, and Acceptance of Interpersonal Violence items, together with others concerning issues such as use of pornography and sexual inhibitions, to a large sample of male undergraduates. These items were then subjected to factor analysis, a procedure which determines the degree to which items form homogeneous clusters by correlating with each other and not with other items. The Rape Myth Acceptance Scale was found to contain four independent factors: disbelief of rape claims, victim responsibility for rape, rape reports as manipulation, and rape can be resisted. These unidimensional factors appear more useful for future research than the Rape Myth Scale and, in addition, do not bear value laden titles. The Adversarial Sexual Beliefs scale was comprised of two factors: male dominance is justified, and adversarial sexual beliefs. Finally, the Acceptance of Interpersonal Violence scale contained two interpretable factors: women enjoy sexual violence, and acceptance of domestic violence. These 9 new scales were related to the sexuality variables using multiple regression. The tendency not to believe victim rape reports was predicted by pornography use, perceived importance of sex, self-reported sexual knowledge, an absence of serious relationships with women, and little sexual experience. The beliefs that women enjoy sexual violence and are responsible for their own rapes were correlated with self-reported sexual inhibition. These data illustrate the complex multidimensional nature of attitudes toward rape and emphasize the importance of male individual differences in sexual inhibition and actual sexual experience.

In a series of studies, Malamuth and his associates (Malamuth, 1981c) directly dealt with individual differences in the self reported proclivity to commit sexual assault by asking college students to rate on a 5-point scale how likely they were to rape if they could be assured of not being caught. Approximately 35% of the sampled men rated their likelihood as "2" or higher and 20% as "3" or higher. Individuals rating themselves as likely to rape have been found to endorse more callous attitudes toward rape and to endorse mistaken ideas about rape to a greater extent. In addition, such individuals, when mildly insulted by a female confederate in a contrived laboratory aggression situation, reported more anger toward the female, reported more desire to hurt her, and used higher intensities of aversive noise to correct her errors in a bogus learning task. It should be noted in this context that male aggression toward females in laboratory paradigms is ordinarily strongly inhibited (Donnerstein & Barrett, 1978); for example, Taylor and Smith (1974) found, using a bogus reaction time competitive task with liberal profeminist and traditional male undergraduates, that the traditional subjects gave higher shocks than profeminist men but that both groups gave lower intensity shocks to female, relative to male, "opponents."

In addition to attitudes which may contribute to the likelihood of a male committing a sexual assault, it would seem that the degree to which he finds rape-related stimuli sexually arousing would be related to the probability of such behaviors. Malamuth and Check (1980a) exposed 75 male undergraduates to either an audiotaped description of mutually-consenting sexual activity, a rape in which the victim became sexually aroused, or a rape in which the victim continued to abhor the assault. The first story presentation was followed by another rape description, the criterion rape story. Subjects' ratings of their degree of sexual arousal were obtained and, in addition, their penile tumescence changes in response to the stories were measured with a mercury in rubber strain gauge. Penile tumescence increases are indicative of male sexual arousal; measurement of penis size is sometimes called "phallometry." Subjects were significantly less sexually aroused, as measured by changes in penile circumference, by the rape-abhorrence story than by the rape-arousal story and a similar trend was found in the self-report data. Interestingly, subjects who heard the rape-arousal and mutually desired stories first showed larger circumference changes in response to the criterion rape story than those who heard the rape-abhorrence scenario. Subjects who heard the rape-arousal story first rated less victim trauma in the criterion rape story than other subjects. These findings suggest that pornography can strongly influence subjects' ideas about rape.

In the questionnaire data, subjects' self-reported proclivity to rape was correlated positively with the beliefs that women would enjoy victimization, the woman derived pleasure from the criterion rape story, and the woman shares responsibility. Self-reported proclivity to rape was positively correlated with self-reported sexual arousal to the rape abhorrence story and to the rape criterion story if it followed either of the rape stories. A small but significant correlation was obtained between the belief that women derive pleasure from rape and both penile tumescence and self report measures of arousal to the criterion rape description. In a questionnaire study of undergraduate males, Malamuth and Check (1980b) replicated the finding of lowered self-reported sexual arousal to descriptions of a rape in which the victim experienced disgust.

Malamuth (1981a) used a bogus extrasensory perception task in which male undergraduates "helped" a female confederate by delivering aversive noise as punishment for incorrect responses to study the influence of sexual arousal to rape stimuli and attitudes on aggression towards females. All 42 subjects were exposed to audiotaped scenarios sometime before the ESP task. Subjects were angered by the female before the task began. The difference between their penile responses to the rape and to the mutually consenting intercourse stories as well as high scores on Burt's Rape Myth Acceptance and Acceptance of Interpersonal Violence Toward Women scales predicted the intensity of noise that subjects gave the confederate. Although some subjects suspected the anger manipulation and the data analysis was rather sophisticated for the number of subjects, the results support the links between attitude, sexual arousal, and aggression towards women.

In the final study of this series, Malamuth and Check (1983) found that male undergraduates who rated themselves as likely to rape were more sexually aroused (as indicated by self-report and penile tumescence responses) by rape descriptions when the victim was described as sexually aroused than by a mutually-consenting sex description. Subjects who rated themselves as unlikely to rape showed equal amounts of arousal to the two story types; all subjects were less aroused to descriptions of rape where the victim showed disgust. Self-reported sexual arousal to the rape depictions was positively correlated with self-reported likelihood of raping, Eysenck's psychoticism and neuroticism scales, and Nelson's "power motivation" for sexual activity scale (sample item: "I enjoy the conquest."). Sexual arousal to rape depictions was negatively correlated with sexual experience.

The research reviewed so far in this section clearly indicates that there are individual differences among men in their self-reported proclivity to sexually assault females. In addition, those men who claim that they are relatively likely to rape show greater arousal to rape cues, are less sexually experienced, and endorse more callous attitudes toward rape. The studies which follow have addressed the issue of whether there are situational variables which appear to increase the probability of sexual assault. It is, of course, clear that gross societal disorganization (as in wartime) and marked social inequities (as in slavery) increase the frequencies of sexual assault (Brownmiller, 1975) but the studies to be reviewed below

deal with issues involving "everyday" sorts of variables.

Perhaps the most obvious variable which may be related to sexual assault is the ingestion of alcohol. In a series of studies of male undergraduates (Briddell & Wilson, 1976; Wilson & Lawson, 1976), it has been found that penile responses to erotic films decline as a function of blood alcohol level and are increased by the expectation that alcohol has been received, regardless of whether subjects have received no alcohol or a low alcohol dose. Lansky and Wilson (1981) reported that alcohol expectancy increased penile responses to erotic audiotaped stories among subjects who were high in sex guilt.

Of greater relevance to the present review, however, are similar studies which include sexual assault descriptions as stimuli. Unfortunately, the results of these studies are inconsistent. Briddell, Rimm, Caddy, Krawitz, Shotis, and Wunderlin (1978) studied undergraduate male social drinkers using a placebo-alcohol design; the placebo condition involved subjects being led to believe they had ingested alcohol when in fact they had not. Subjects were exposed to audio descriptions of consenting sex, rape, and nonsexual violence toward women. The alcohol expectancy condition was associated with increased arousal (penile tumescence changes) to the rape and nonsexual violence scenarios but alcohol itself was not related to sexual arousal. There were, however, methodological difficulties with this study; the most important of these is the possibility of a ceiling effect on the responses to consenting sex which makes it impossible to conclude whether there is an overall increase in sexual arousal to all stimuli with alcohol expectancy or a differential increase in arousal to deviant stimuli. Barbaree, Marshall, Lightfoot, and Yates (in press) did not replicate these findings with a similar design. These investigators found no effect of alcohol expectancy but did find an effect of alcohol itself: Subjects who had consumed alcohol did not increase their discrimination between rape and consenting sex scenarios upon second testing whereas sober subjects did. Unfortunately, the expectancy manipulation in the Barbaree et al. study was not completely successful. Essentially, the results of laboratory studies on alcohol, alcohol expectancy, and sexual arousal to deviant and non-deviant stimuli are equivocal.

Another variable which may be involved in sexual assault is anger; indeed, sexual assault is often viewed as a crime of anger and hostility. Yates, Barbaree, and Marshall (unpublished manuscript) examined the effects of an anger-producing insult on penile responses to rape cues among 24 university students. Subjects' arousal was measured to consenting and nonconsenting sexual intercourse descriptions in the first session; in the second session the subjects were assigned to three conditions: an exercise condition in which subjects pedalled on a bicycle ergometer before testing, an exercise and insult condition in which a female confederate made derogatory comments on the subject's exercise performance, or a no exercise and no insult control condition. Sexual arousal measurements were then repeated; subjects were told the purpose of the study was to determine the effects of exercise on sexual arousal. Pilot data indicated that the insult condition was credible and resulted in increased aggression in a bogus laboratory strategic game. In initial testing, all groups showed less arousal to the rape than to the consenting stimuli; for the exercise and control groups, this discrimination was sharper upon the second testing. The angered subjects, however, showed less response to the mutually-consenting episodes and more arousal to the non-consenting sexual activity. Anger, therefore, apeared to make males more likely to rape.

What can be concluded from these studies of non-sex offenders? First, although sexual assault of adult women (particularly in its less violent and brutal forms) is very common, men show great individual variation in their self-reported propensity to sexually assault. Men who claim they are more likely to sexually assault are more likely to have mistaken beliefs about rape and endorse more callous attitudes toward rape, are more hostile towards women, show greater sexual arousal to descriptions of sexual assault where the victim is depicted as sexually aroused than to descriptions of mutually-consenting sex, and are relatively sexually inexperienced. Angered men would appear more prone to sexual assault but the effects of alcohol are equivocal.

The studies reviewed in this section suffer from obvious limitations; none involve comparisons with rapists, most involve college populations, many use laboratory tasks in which demand characteristics and ecological validity issues cause difficulties in interpretation, and most deal with attitudes or self-report rather than behaviors. The authors of these studies are, of course, well aware of these limitations and never intended them to stand alone in the manner in which they have been presented here. This research on normal subjects acquires significance in connection with studies of known sexual assaulters which are presented below.

Studies of Known Sexual Assaulters

The advantage of studying normal populations is that random sampling techniques can be employed, whereas the disadvantage is that it is unknown whether any sexual assaulters are in the sample. College student samples, however, are more problematic because they are hardly randomly selected. In addition, even if minor sexual assaults are common among them, there is no way to know whether those students who claim they may rape under certain circumstances in fact ever do. Studying groups of known sexual assaulters avoids these problems but raises others. We have seen that rapes are under-reported in a biased manner. One cannot assume, therefore, that known sexual assaulters are representative of sexual assaulters in general. In particular, on the basis of victim data, we would expect that known sexual assaulters would be more likely to have white, middle-class victims and victims who were not well known to them. It should be noted that bias or selection increases with each step in the criminal justice process from arrest to incarceration.

The representativeness problem is not, however, as severe as it may appear. For certain issues, representativeness is irrelevant; most notably, in treatment research only sexual assaulters who can be identified can be treated, so that the question of the treatability of unidentified sexual assaulters does not arise. Moreover, the principal reason that assaults are not reported is lack of seriousness of the crime (Monahan, 1981); the more serious the offense, particularly in terms of personal injury, the more likely it is to be reported to the police. Perhaps more importantly, offenders who have been convicted of one sexual assault are many times more likely than the general population to have committed similar offenses for which they were not arrested (Monahan, 1981). Thus, known offenders in fact make up an appreciable number of the "unknown" sexual assaulters. Known sexual assaulters are, therefore, a biased sample in part because they are likely to have committed more serious offenses and more frequent offenses than non-apprehended sexual assaulters. In short, known sexual assaulters tend to be those in whom we should be most interested.

General Descriptions and Typologies

There is a large literature of varying quality which describes the general characteristics of sexual assaulters. Among these papers are articles written for laypersons which are often directed toward dispelling myths about sex offenders (Cohen & Boucher, 1972; Kozol, 1971; Littner, 1974; Rada, 1977) and those which are largely or exclusively transcripts of interviews with sexual assaulters (Levine & Koenig, 1980; Parks, 1974). A further category of articles describes groups of sexual assaulters in mental hospitals, prisons, or outpatient clinics; these descriptions are sometimes accompanied by a classification scheme or typology (Anderson, Kunce, & Rich, 1979; Brancale, Ellis, & Doorbar, 1952; Cohen, Garofalo, Boucher, & Seghorn, 1971; Henn, Herjanic, & Vanderpearl, 1976; McCaldon, 1967; Pacht & Cowden, 1974; Peterson, Braiker, & Polich, 1980; Rada, 1978; West, 1965; Wile, 1941). Some of the more influential studies of this type are reviewed below.

In the most ambitious description of sexual offenders, Gebhard, Gagnon, Pomeroy, and Christenson (1965) interviewed 1,356 men convicted of a sexual offense, 888 convicted of a nonsexual offense, and 477 controls. Official records were also examined. One hundred and forty men in this sample were convicted of sexual contact accompanied by force or threat with females aged 16 years or older who were not their daughters; these were called "heterosexual aggressors against adults." By age 26, 66% of these men had spent at least one year in prison for a single offense and 87% had been convicted of some crime other than the index offense; about half of the convictions were for sex offenses. Only 33% of the men had *only* previous sex offenses. The most common previous sexual offenses, aside from aggression against adult women, were offenses (such as statutory rape) against willing females (27%), exhibition (21%), and peeping (19%). Langevin, Paitich, and Russon (in press) have also reported the presence of various sexual deviations among rapists and a history of a variety of nonsexual offenses.

Heterosexual aggressors against adults reported being sexually aroused by pictures or stories concerning sadomasochistic activity more than any other group of sex offenders save heterosexual aggressors against minors but the proportion was small (15%). More reported sadomasochistic dreams than any other sex offender group but again the proportion was small (4%). Most (70%) of the offenses were premeditated but many of the offenders (39%) were drunk at the time of the offense and a further 15% had been drinking. More of these offenders than any other group (13%) used violence which was designed to inflict physical injury rather than to obtain coitus.

Gebhard et al. assigned the heterosexual aggressors against adults to seven categories. The "assaultive offenders" constituted between 25 and 33% of the sample. Typically, they committed their offenses alone against unknown women, often used weapons, made no or little attempt at seduction, were not discriminating as to the appearance of the victim, and often stole their victim's money. The assaultive offender appeared to be sadistic and used unnecessary violence. Often there was erectile dysfunction during the offense. Less common categories were: amoral delinquents, drunks, explosive assaulters (who exhibited inexplicable and out-of-character aggression), double standard assaulters (who believed that force applied to bad girls after failed seduction was appropriate), psychotics, and mental defectives. About one-third of the sample did not fall clearly into any of the categories and appeared to be mixtures.

Gebhard et al. also assigned the heterosexual aggressors against adults into incidental ($N = 83$) and patterned offender categories ($N = 57$). Patterned offenders were those who committed the same offense repeatedly. In comparison to incidental offenders, patterned heterosexual aggressors against adults completed more years of schooling, more frequently reported not getting along with their father as a teenager, reported more prepubertal sex play of all types, and more often reported sadomasochistic fantasy (20% as compared to 0%). This is the first study of sexual assaulters which hints at the importance of sadistic fantasies. Given the legal status of the inmate respondents, it is likely that many of those who claimed not to have these fantasies, in fact entertained them.

Cohen, Garofalo, Boucher, and Seghorn (1971) have presented a clinical classification of rapists developed during their assessment and treatment of offenders in the Bridgewater prison hospital setting. The first pattern is labelled "rape-aggressive aim," in which the offender's sexual behavior is in the service of aggression and his purpose is to humiliate and hurt the victim. In the "rape-sexual aim" pattern the rapist is primarily interested in sex and uses only as much violence as is required. The final pattern is "rape-sex aggression defusion" in which the offender requires violence in order to become sexually aroused. Rapists of the first type have been shown to be more popular with other patients than other types in a maximum security setting (Cohen, Seghorn, & Calmas, 1969).

Groth and his associates (Groth & Birnbaum, 1979; Groth, Burgess, & Holmstrom, 1977) have used victim and rapist accounts of rapes to establish a typology. Groth asserts that rape is never primarily a matter of sex but is a pseudosexual act. "Power assault" rapists seek to control their victims through intimidation: the power-assertive rapist uses rape to express his virility, whereas the power-reassurance rapist uses the offense to offset doubts about his masculinity. In "anger rape" the victim is beaten and degraded; the anger-excitation rapist is sadistic and his aggression eroticized.

Unfortunately, these taxonomies are unsatisfactory both methodologically and conceptually. With respect to method, some taxonomies rely heavily on interview data; such data are useful but there are important limitations on offenders' self-reports. As MacDonald (1971) has observed: "The conscious confessions of criminals and a statement of the circumstances of the crime, be it ever so complete, will never sufficiently explain why the individual in the given circumstances had to commit just that act. External circumstances very often do not motivate the deed at all, and the doer, did he wish to be frank, would mostly have to acknowledge that he really did not himself exactly know what impelled him to do it; most often, however, he is not so frank, not even to himself, but subsequently looks for and finds explanation of his conduct." A further problem with these classification schemes is that no investigators have presented inter-clinician reliability data; we cannot know, therefore, whether the category descriptions are specific enough to permit agreement or how discrete the categories are. One would think that a classification scheme could best be arrived at through clustering algorithms or factor analytic techniques rather than intuition.

In addition, theoretical issues such as the relative contributions of "sex," "power," and so on, to sexual assault cannot be resolved by examining a series of cases. The collection and description of case material is, of course, important and necessary but it must be accompanied by rigorous analysis before theory can proceed.

Such a clustering approach to a taxonomy of sexual aggressors has recently been attempted and the results, although yet preliminary, indicate the promise of this strategy. Knight, Prentky, Schneider, and Rosenberg (1982) examined a large amount of file data on 41 child molesters and 78 rapists who had been committed to the Bridgewater institution as sexually dangerous. Separate factor analyses on family characteristics, childhood behavior, adult behavior and offense characteristics led to the identification of 15 factors which were used in subsequent regression and path analyses. There were a number of differences between the rapists and child molesters but only the rapists' results will be reported here. Childhood social and academic incompetence predicted both adult social incompetence and severe adult psychopathology and sexual pathology. Childhood antisocial behavior predicted adult antisocial behavior, indicating long-term stability of this behavior. Offense frequency (unfortunately, both sexual and nonsexual) was predicted by childhood psychiatric system contact, adult academic and vocational incompetence and adult antisocial behavior. Degree of violence was associated only with adult alcohol abuse. Two major paths appeared to originate in family instability: The first involved juvenile antisocial behavior, adult antisocial behavior, and frequent criminal offenses; whereas the second involved juvenile psychiatric system contact and frequent criminal offenses. Thus there appear to be impulsive, antisocial rapists, incompetent rapists with no evidence of early conduct disorder (both groups with high adult offense frequencies) and, by implication, a third group of "normal" men with low offense frequencies.

Further work on these data have been reported by Rosenberg (1981). Briefly, five factors (substance abuse, social competence, antisocial behavior, impulsivity in sexual offenses, and sexual aggression) were used in a cluster analysis of 114 rapists or child molesters. Eleven clusters emerged, the most noteworthy of which were: (a) explosive-aggressive rapists, controlled type, characterized by high competence, low general antisocial behavior and high sexualized aggression; (b) explosive-aggressive rapists, impulsive type, comprised of persons with high sexual aggression and impulsivity; and (c) disturbed antisocial-aggressive rapists characterized by substance abuse, general antisocial behavior, and sexualized aggression. Although the validity of these clusters must be established in future research using independent information, such an effort appears justified and would put a taxonomic scheme on a firm empirical foundation.

In summary, the descriptions of known sexual assaulters, despite their methodological inadequacies, indicate a degree of offender heterogeneity which must be taken into account in any theory of rape. This heterogeneity is consistent with studies of non-sex offenders who show variation in variables potentially related to sexual assault. In particular, several variables appear potentially useful in assigning sexual assaulters to types: the presence of aggressive sexual fantasies, alcohol abuse, general antisocial criminal behavior, and degree of violence in the offense.

Descriptions of Sexual Murderers

Sexual homicides and sadistic murders are extremely rare (Swigert, Farrell, & Yoels, 1976) but receive a great deal of media attention. These murders are distinguished by sexual assault and mutilation or deliberate efforts to cause pain. Because of the infrequency of this type of crime, the literature on sadistic murderers is sparse and consists primarily of psychoanalytically-oriented case descriptions (Howell, 1972; Thornton & Pray, 1975; Williams, 1964, 1965) or psychoanalytic theory (Glover, 1964). Revitch (1965) reviewed nine cases of sexual murder and 34 of sexual assault. "Dynamic factors" in these cases were speculated to be: hostility to women, preoccupation with maternal sexual conduct, incestuous preoccupations, guilt over sex, rejection of sex as impure, feelings of sexual inferiority, and the need to possess the victim or what she represents. It is noteworthy in this connection that sexual guilt is strongly associated with sexual inexperience in normal samples (DiVasto, Pathak, & Fishburn, 1981). Revitch hypothesized that fetishism of female underwear, previous instances of solo breaking-and-entering, sadistic fantasies, minor assaults on females, and mutilation of animals may

be important prognostic signs.

Brittain (1970) has described the characteristics of sadistic sex murderers based upon his clinical experience. Such offenders are commonly introspective and withdrawn, appear studious, are mild mannered and timid, are tidy in their personal habits and are most likely to offend after a loss of self-esteem (particularly in a sexual context). They are often prudish about sexual matters, hypochondriacal, and considered to be a little "weird" by their associates. Many appear somewhat effeminate or perhaps overpolite. Typically, they are daydreamers who imagine sadistic scenes and are interested in such things as Nazi atrocities. Their sexual contacts are very limited; they are modest, and often feel physically inadequate. Often, there have been no previous offenses but, if there are, they involve minor offenses such as stealing women's underwear or voyeurism. Their occupational record is usually not good and may include such trades as that of a butcher; many are fascinated by weapons. They are often "Mama's boys." Transvestism is common, as is cruelty to animals. Many sadistic murderers are interested in anatomy, forensic medicine, and sadistic pornography. Such offenders are typically model prisoners.

These descriptions of sadistic murderers are, of course, only impressions but can be useful in providing hypotheses for future research. Several elements are found in each of the descriptions in the literature: sexual murderers tend to be shy and passive, have dependent relations with their mothers, are hostile to women, and have extremely sadistic fantasies. Fortunately, there are some data which relate to this latter point. Langevin, Paitich, and Russon (in press) have reported that the amount of force used in rapists' sexual assaults was correlated with more frequent sadistic and more frequent masochistic fantasies. Abel and his associates (Abel, Barlow, Blanchard, & Guild, 1977; Abel, Becker, Blanchard, & Djenderedjian, 1978) found that sadistic offenders showed very high penile responses to audio descriptions of rape scenes relative to their responses to descriptions of consenting sex and, in addition, showed marked arousal to scenes depicting nonsexual violence against women.

Quinsey and Chaplin (1982) studied the penile responses of 44 rapists to audiotaped narrations describing neutral heterosexual activities, mutually-desired intercourse, rape, and nonsexual violence towards women. A ratio formed for each rapist by dividing the average response to nonsexual violence narratives by the average response to consenting sex was significantly related to whether or not the rapists had seriously injured their victims. The relationship between sexual arousal to nonsexual violence and victim damage was not large enough to provide much help in making release decisions but would appear to be useful in identifying targets for treatment. The small number of offenders who show large amounts of sexual arousal to nonsexual violence against women are of considerable theoretical and practical interest. In particular, such arousal to sadistic themes offers the opportunity to do research on sadistic individuals as only the most extreme sadists can reliably be differentiated from aggressive sexual assaulters on the basis of their history and offense description (e.g., Quinsey & Chaplin, 1982).

Recidivism Studies

Studies of recidivism are vital to understanding sexual assaulters. If, for example, sexual assaulters commit a wide variety of offenses of which sexual assault is but one, we are dealing with general criminality and specialized treatment and research efforts concerning sexual assaulters themselves are unwarranted because sexual recidivism would be extremely rare. Recidivism studies are also central to attempts to predict subsequent dangerousness and to evaluate treatment programs. There is a large general literature on the prediction of dangerousness and future violence which will not be reviewed here; but, in general, the evidence indicates that clinicians are not very accurate in their appraisals (e.g., Quinsey & Ambtman, 1978, 1979) and tend to overpredict dangerousness (Monahan, 1981). Despite these findings, however, accurate prediction is theoretically possible under certain conditions (Quinsey, 1980; Monahan, 1978).

A number of articles have appeared which describe methods of making release decisions concerning sexual offenders in various prison and hospital settings (Andriola, 1966; Kozol, Cohen, & Garofalo, 1966; Roberts & Pacht, 1965), and also offer lists of criteria which are used in making predictions. Unfortunately, none of these lists have been evaluated by relating them to follow-up data specifically concerning sex offenders of adult women. There are well-known and large differences among the recidivism rates of different types of sexual offenders (Christiansen, Elers-Nielson, LeMaire, & Sturup, 1965; Frisbie, 1965; Gray & Mohr, 1965) which make follow-ups of undifferentiated sex offenders difficult to interpret. In addition, the clinical, or case conference, method of making predictions, although representing the state of the art, is inaccurate under the best conditions because of poor inter-clinician agreement (Quinsey & Ambtman, 1978) and the suboptimal manner in which the case conferences address the issue of dangerousness (Dix, 1975).

The literature on sexual assaulters of adult females has been reviewed by West, Roy, and Nichols (1978) who conclude that recidivism rates vary with the characteristics of the sample studied and that there is a small number of sexual assaulters against adult females who repetitively offend. Unfortunately, there are fewer data on rapists than on other sexual offenders. The major studies are reviewed below.

As part of a large follow-up study of sex offenders treated and released from the Atascadero institution in California, Frisbie and Dondis (1965) followed 70 sexual aggressors (defined as men who committed sexual acts on females 18 years of age or older which were accompanied by threats or force). After adjusting for opportunity to reoffend, sexual aggressors were found to have the highest sexual recidivism rate during their first post-release year. The cumulative 5-year recidivism rate was 36%, interestingly, higher than that of heterosexual child molesters. The new sex offenses tended to be of the same type.

The Cambridge study examined a large number of sex offenses committed in England during 1951 (Radzinowicz, 1957). Of 22 men convicted of rape and attempted rape, only 9% had been convicted of a previous sex offense although many had committed other crimes. During a 4-year follow-up, 10% of 40 men convicted of a sex offense against adult women committed another sex offense. A positive association was found between alcohol and the amount of violence used in the index offense.

In another English study, Soothill, Jack, and Gibbens (1976) found that of 86 men convicted of rape or attempted rape in 1951, 6% were reconvicted of rape, 9% of other sexual offenses, 27% of violence toward the person, 15% of burglary or robbery, and 64% of other offenses within 22 years. The proportion of violent offenses declined with age but the proportion committing sex offenses before and after the 1951 index offense remained the same. A remarkable finding was the length of time during which reoffending of all kinds continued to occur. The six rapes (committed by five offenders) occurred 3, 5, 10, 13, 16, and 17 years after the index offense. The investigators also followed up 23 men who were acquitted in 1951; of these, 30% had subsequent convictions and 22% of the total had reconvictions for a sexual offense (one person for rape). A number of other investigators have also found sexual aggressors against women to have relatively high rates of non-sexual offenses of a variety of kinds (Christiansen et al., 1965; Frisbie, 1965; Gebhard et al., 1965).

The differences in recidivism across these studies is truly remarkable; clearly, by selectively contemplating the various studies one can conclude anything one wants. Taken as a group, however, the follow-up studies make an important, if simple, methodological and theoretical point: Sexual aggressors are heterogeneous. If one chooses a sample where subjects have been convicted of an offense, one gets a very different picture than if one chooses persons judged to be sexually dangerous (as in the Atascadero study) or persons with a history of repeated sexual assaults. This point may at first seem trivial but is responsible for many of the disagreements and much of the confusion in the literature. Investigators tend to speak of "rapists" or "the rapist" and to design research studies with this view in mind, even though, as we have seen, there have been a number of typologies described (but not validated) which imply marked heterogeneity among these offenders.

One must also remember in interpreting these data, that reports of convictions or arrests underestimate the amount of reoffending which actually occurs. There are small numbers of sexual assaulters who commit large numbers of offenses for which they are seldom charged. In a sample of 25 outpatients whose primary sexual arousal pattern involved rape themes, the average number of self-reported rapes and attempted rapes was 21; among four subjects whose arousal pattern involved sadism, the average was 46 (Abel, Becker, & Skinner, in press).

The Search for Unique Attributes of Sexual Assaulters

This section reviews studies which explicitly com-

pare sexual assaulters with a comparison group. When the comparison group is from the same institution and convicted of a criminal offense, some of the difficulties of biased sampling are avoided and clearer inferences may be drawn.

ATTITUDES TOWARDS WOMEN

In view of the frequent clinical observations that sexual assaulters have negative attitudes toward women and endorse various peculiar ideas about rape, it is surprising that so few investigators have studied these relationships. The only published investigation on this topic is that of Feild (1978). Data were gathered from 528 males and 528 female citizens, 254 patrol police officers, 118 female counselors in rape crisis centers, and 20 rapists at a state mental hospital. Each respondent completed the Attitudes Towards Rape Questionnaire, the Rape Knowledge Test, and the Attitudes Towards Women Scale (Spence, Helmreich, & Stapp, 1973). Factor analysis of the Attitudes Towards Rape Questionnaire yielded eight factors. Rape counselors and rapists were significantly different on all eight but citizens and police officers (the most appropriate comparison group) were more similar to rapists than counselors. In comparison to the police officers on the individual factors, rapists were more likely to endorse the views that rape was primarily a woman's responsibility, rapists should not be punished severely, victims precipitate rape, and women should not resist during rape. Rapists and police officers did not differ in their opinions on sex as motivation for rape, power as motivation for rape, the desirability of a raped woman, or the normality of rapists. These data make manifest rapists' relatively pro-rape and self-serving attitudes.

Among the citizen groups, Feild (1978) found that liberal or profeminist scores on Attitudes Towards Women Scale correlated with anti-rape attitudes; gender differences were similar. Among the rapists, however, there was no significant correlation of rape attitudes with the Attitudes Towards Women Scale. Similarly, using the same scale, Stermac and Quinsey (submitted for publication) found that sexual assaulters of adult women were not differentiated by their attitudes towards women from non-sex offenders sampled from the same maximum security psychiatric institution or unemployed males from the local community. Thus it appears that specific attitudes concerning rape are related to sexual assault but not necessarily more general attitudes concerning women; however, comparisons between rapists and non-sex offender criminal groups on both attitudes towards rape and attitudes towards women will be required for a definitive conclusion. Unfortunately, it is not yet apparent whether pro-rape beliefs are antecedent to rape or vice versa.

PORNOGRAPHY USE

There is great controversy over the effects of pornography and at least some of this concern is politicized. Early research into pornography (Lipton, 1973) found no association between pornography and sexual crimes or delinquency. These conclusions, are, however, now being challenged, chiefly because of the shift in pornography over recent years from depictions of explicit sex to depictions of more violent and deviant activities.

Sex offenders have been found to have been exposed to less pornography than normal control subjects of various types (Cook, Fosen, & Pacht, 1971). Data specifically concerning men who have sexually assaulted adult women are of more interest in the present context and have been presented by Goldstein and his colleagues (Goldstein & Kant, 1973; Goldstein, Kant, Judd, Rice, & Green, 1971). These investigators interviewed 20 rapists in a maximum security mental hospital (Atascadero), 53 control subjects, 78 heavy pornography users, 20 heterosexual child molesters, 20 homosexual child molesters, 13 transsexuals, and 37 homosexuals.

In contrast to controls, rapists were exposed to less erotica in adolescence and adulthood; however, a variety of findings indicate that the effect of erotica on rapists was different than on normals. Rapists reported that their most exciting (peak) experience with erotica occurred at an earlier age, was more likely to be either inhibited or enhanced by the presence of friends, and more often wanted to imitate the erotic activities but less often tried to do so. Rapists more often reported arousal and disgust; they relied heavily on masturbation and more often daydreamed about the content of the erotic stimulus. As adults, the rapists more often had a peak experience with erotica alone, daydreamed more about sex, thought more about erotica in their daydreams, masturbated more to thoughts of erotica, and reported more negative affect concerning the content of their daydreams. Rapists' adult daydreams more often concerned sadistic acts and homosex-

ual activities but they reported finding sadistic material disgusting. It was curious that the rapists described depictions of heterosexual intercourse most exciting. Goldstein and Kant (1973:137) conclude:

> They reported oral-genital, homosexual, and transvestite daydreams, as well as fantasies involving aggression and sadism—themes that disgust and upset them—in greater profusion than the controls. This contrasts sharply with their reports that the erotica they find most stimulating involves depictions of heterosexual intercourse. . . It would seem that the rapist is beset with a variety of self-generated fantasies, which he finds distasteful but cannot control. Rather than being cathartic, these daydreams apparently lead him further toward action. Pornography, however, is neither stimulating nor cathartic, instead serving as a means of warding off anxiety, disgust, and guilt about his disturbing daydreams.

There have been dramatic increases in the amount of violent sexual imagery in both soft core (Malamuth & Spinner, 1980) and hard core pornography (Dietz & Evans, 1982) available in North America; similar trends have occurred elsewhere (Court, 1976). In Denmark, where these changes have been most marked, there appear to have been declines in some categories of minor sex offenses (Court, 1976; Kutchinsky, 1976) but apparent increases in the frequencies of rape and attempted rape (Court, 1976). Court has examined rape and attempted rape statistics from England, Sweden, the United States, Australia, and New Zealand. In each of these countries, rape rates increased with the availability of sadistic pornography; in Singapore, there was no increase in rape rates; the government there, however, had strictly controlled pornography.

These data on the effects of violent pornography suffer from the methodological problems of official crime statistics but the results appear consistent. Fortunately, these criminological data are supported by laboratory demonstrations of effects which would be expected if violent pornography did in fact cause men to rape. Donnerstein and his colleagues (Donnerstein, 1980; Donnerstein & Barrett, 1978; Donnerstein & Berkowitz, 1981) found that aggressive erotic films increased males' aggression in a laboratory task toward a female confederate who had angered them; in a second study, it was shown that, among nonangry subjects, only films depicting erotic aggression with a positive outcome were associated with increased aggression toward the female confederate.

Malamuth, Haber, and Feshbach (1980) exposed college students to a sadomasochistic or nonviolent sexual story and then to a rape depiction. Males who read the sadomasochistic story reported more sexual arousal to the rape story. In a further study (Malamuth, Heim, & Feshbach, 1980), males were found to report equal amounts of sexual arousal to rape stories as to consenting sex stories when the victim of rape was portrayed as being involuntarily aroused. Males were most aroused when the rape victim was described as having an orgasm and experiencing pain. In a "field experiment" Malamuth and Check (1981) found that viewing regular movies which portrayed sexual violence as having positive consequences increased males' acceptance of rape myths.

In the final study of this series (Malamuth, 1981b), 29 male college students (of which 13 reported that they found the idea of force somewhat or very attractive and/or thought they might engage in coercive sex) were exposed to either a rape or consenting sexual story and later to a rape story. Force-oriented subjects created more arousing fantasies (by self-report) after the rape stories whereas non-force-oriented subjects showed the reverse pattern. All subjects created more violent fantasies after the rape version than the mutually-consenting version.

In summary, rape rates vary positively with the availability of violent pornography. It appears that rapists are more strongly affected by pornography than normals. Rapists often report violent sexual fantasies. Among normal subjects, descriptions of female sexual arousal disinhibits male sexual arousal to rape stories; violent sexual descriptions encourage violent fantasies and force-oriented subjects are differentially aroused by rape depictions. Although the interpretation of these findings must be tentative, it seems fair to conclude that certain individuals are made more likely to rape by violent pornography.

PSYCHOMETRIC VARIABLES

The data on the personality characteristics as shown by psychological testing has been reviewed by Langevin (1983), Lester (1975), and Rada

(1978c). These reviewers concur that few personality variables have been found to reliably differentiate rapists from other offenders and that the literature is weak scientifically. The most common methodological problems in this literature are the use of inappropriate control groups such as college students (e.g., Marsh, Hilliard, & Liechti, 1955), small sample size (e.g., Ruff, Templer, & Ayers, 1976), and the use of heterogeneous groups of sex offenders (e.g., Fisher & Rivlin, 1971; Marsh, Hilliard, & Liechti, 1955).

There have been a number of studies which have compared rapists with other populations on various measures of intelligence (Langevin, 1983; Langevin, Paitich, & Russon, in press; Perdue & Lester, 1972; Ruff, Templer, & Ayers, 1976; Stermac & Quinsey, submitted for publication; Vera, Barnard, & Holzer, 1979). Although some of these studies have presented data indicating that rapists score lower on standard tests of intelligence than control groups of offenders, the majority, and, in particular, the better-designed studies with larger samples, have not found such differences.

Projective testing of personality traits has not shown differences between rapists and other offenders (e.g., Jensen, Prandoni, & Abudabbeh, 1971; Perdue & Lester, 1972). Objective testing has typically involved the MMPI. Data collected on the MMPI indicate that rapists score highly on the Psychopathic Deviate Scale, as do many institutionalized populations. Although some differences between rapists and other offenders have been reported (Armentrout & Hauer, 1978; Rader, 1977), these differences are small and, in general, one must be impressed by the similarity in MMPI profile between rapists and other groups of offenders, from addicts to nonsexual assaulters (Quinsey, Arnold, & Pruesse, 1980). Langevin (1983) and Quinsey, Arnold, and Pruesse (1980) found that rapists did not differ from various other offender groups on any MMPI scale, including Megargee's Overcontrolled-Hostility Scale.

TESTOSTERONE LEVELS

Folklore has it that sexual assaulters are simply "oversexed" and, although clinical observation (e.g., Walker & Myer, 1981) reveals that some sexual assaulters are hypersexual (as indicated by extremely high masturbatory frequencies), there have been very few studies of the issue. Rada, Laws, and Kellner (1976) provide the only published data on plasma testosterone levels among rapists. They compared 52 rapists from Atascadero with male employees from the same institution. There were no differences in plasma testosterone levels between the two groups but the five rapists with the greatest amount of violence in their index offense were all above the testosterone average for the rapist group. These findings, particularly the relationship between violence and testosterone, should be replicated with a larger sample. Studies of sexual arousability and hypersexuality, which both can be relatively independent of testosterone level, are also needed.

SOCIAL COMPETENCE

Sexual assaulters are often deemed to be heterosocially inept (Abel, Blanchard, & Becker, 1978) and many treatment programs incorporate social skill training components (e.g., Whitman & Quinsey, 1981). Despite clinical observations, however, there has been little systematic study of sexual assaulters' heterosocial skills. If it were assumed that heterosocial deficits played an etiological role in sexual assault, sexual assaulters should exhibit more social deficits than other offenders, particularly in difficult interactions with women.

Stermac and Quinsey (submitted for publication) examined these hypotheses by comparing 20 sexual assaulters against adult women with 20 non-sexual offenders from the Oak Ridge maximum security psychiatric institution in Ontario and 20 low socioeconomic status normal controls. Subjects were audiotaped in unstructured brief conversations with a male and a female partner, separately. Audiotapes were also made of subjects' responses to prerecorded standard heterosocial and heterosexual situations which varied from rude rejection to a sexual overture; subjects were required to complete each of the interactions at the sound of a tone by taking the part of one of the participants (always a male who had made a social overture).

The audiotapes were rated on dimensions of social skillfulness by raters who were blind to subjects' group assignment. Subjects rated their own performance and completed a number of questionnaires. Behavioral measures of social competence (including self-ratings) did not differentiate the two offender groups but did indicate that the normal controls were superior in hetero- and homosocial skills. The only variables to differentiate the sexual assaulters from both other groups were the General Assertiveness and Heterosexual Assertiveness scales of the Callner-

Ross Assertiveness Questionnaire (Callner & Ross, 1976); rapists reported themselves to be less assertive than both other groups.

It is noteworthy that Langevin, Paitich and Russon (in press) found somewhat similar results using rapists' self-reports. In their study, rapists, as well as sexually-deviant men, reported more frequently than normal controls and nonsexually assaultive men that they wished to be more forceful and more athletic, that they felt they were unattractive to women and that they were more often thought of as sissies. Similarly, Fisher and Rivlin (1971) found rapists to be less self-assured, aggressive and independent than other offenders on the Edwards Personal Preference Schedule.

Stermac and Quinsey's data indicate that rapists are unlikely to have unique heterosocial deficits, although they are less skilled than normals. With respect to treatment, this study implies that although improvement of heterosocial skills may be ameliorative or even necessary, it cannot be considered sufficient. Theoretically, these results similarly suggest that social competence, if involved with the causation of sexual assault at all, acts in concert with other variables. Deficits in rapists' assertion (or perhaps their self-perceived assertion) deserve further study.

ALCOHOLISM AND DRUG ADDICTION

Rada (1975) collected autobiographical information from 77 rapists hospitalized at Atascadero. Thirty-five percent of the subjects were classified as alcoholics by direct admission or evidence of serious alcohol problems in their histories and 51% were drinking (mostly drinking very heavily) at the time of the offense. Very few offenders were using other drugs at the time of the offense. Knight, Prentky, Schneider, and Rosenberg's study of rapists at the Bridgewater institution (1983) found that the only variable related to the degree of violence in the offense was adult alcohol abuse; an association between alcohol and violence has also been reported several other times in the literature (Amir, 1971; Gebhard et al., 1965; Radzinowitz, 1957). Langevin, Paitich, and Russon (in press) confirmed Rada's results in a study of 40 rapists; 54% had a chronic drinking problem and 60% were drinking at the time of the offense. In contrast to other studies however, there was no significant relation between use of alcohol at the time of the offense and the amount of force used.

Although these data must be viewed with some caution because rapists may well claim alcohol use as an exculpatory strategy, it does appear as a significant problem in the history of many rapists and deserves further study, particularly in the context of physical violence, as well as attention in therapy programs for rapists.

SEXUAL AROUSAL PATTERNS

Individual differences in sexual arousal patterns among non-sex offenders lead one to expect that rapists would come differentially from the most rape-prone groups—i.e., we would expect rapists to find rape cues sexually exciting. Rapists, however, are often reluctant to volunteer descriptions of aggressive sexual imagery for legal reasons; outpatients, on the other hand, are more likely to do so but only when directly questioned. Walker and Meyer (1981) have found that 80% of their rapists report primarily or exclusively deviant sexual fantasies. Abel and his co-workers (Abel, Becker, & Skinner, in press) have also found that a large proportion of their outpatient sample of sexual assaulters report aggressive sexual fantasies. Even in maximum security settings, such as Oak Ridge, sexual assaulters who are motivated for treatment sometimes describe an astonishing preoccupation with aggressive and sadistic sexual themes. These data, of course, indicate the sexual nature of rape; claims that rape is not a sexual crime are based primarily on reports of sexual dysfunction during the act. However, sexual dysfunction can occur for a variety of reasons, for example, anxiety or distraction, and is not useful in identifying the motive for an assault. A sexual assault committed by an individual examined at our Oak Ridge laboratory nicely confirms this point. Prior to the index offense (an attempted sexual murder) this man stalked a young woman with the intent to rape her; as he grabbed her from behind, however, he had an orgasm. Thus thwarted in his aim, he threw her down and ran away.

Psychophysiological study has confirmed that sexual assaulters tend to be more responsive to depictions of coercive sex than non-assaulters. Early work in this area was methodologically weak and produced negative results (Kercher & Walker, 1973). More recent research, however, has produced the expected results. Abel, Barlow, Blanchard, and Guild (1977) monitored the penile tumescence responses of 13 rapists and seven other sexual deviants to audiotaped descriptions of consenting sex, rape, and nonsexual violence. A rape index formed by dividing the average response to the rape stories by the average response to depictions of consenting sex differentiated the rapists from nonrapists and was related to rape frequency among the rapists. Rapists responded less to descriptions of nonsexual violence but their arousal to these stimuli was correlated with their responses to rape depictions. Following this initial study, Abel and his associates (Abel, Becker, Blanchard, & Djenderedjian, 1978; Abel, Becker, & Skinner, 1980) gathered more data using similar procedures. Briefly, they found that (a) nonrapists do not respond to rape cues where rapists do, (b) nonrapists' subjective reports parallel their physiological data whereas rapists' reports underestimate their arousal to rape cues, (c) the rape index correlates with victim injury and rape frequency, and finally, (d) sadists show large erectile responses to nonsexual violence.

The basic finding of Abel's group that rapists can be differentiated from nonrapists with measures of erectile responses to rape and consenting sex stories has been replicated several times. Barbaree, Marshall, and Lanthier (1979) compared 10 incarcerated rapists and 10 graduate students. Because their results indicated that mutually consenting sex descriptions elicited comparable levels of arousal in both groups, but that rape cues elicited less arousal among nonrapists, they hypothesized that force and violence may not produce arousal among rapists but rather fail to inhibit the arousal generated by the sexual elements in the rape stories.

Wydra, Marshall, Earls, and Barbaree (in press) attempted to determine whether the differential arousal of rapists to rape depictions was a result of their inability to discriminate appropriate from inappropriate sexual behavior. Using the same stories as in their initial study, subjects were asked to press a button as soon as they detected what type of story (i.e., rape or consenting) it was. Latency data were comparable for rapists, nonrapist offenders, and non-offenders for consenting stories and the less aggressive rape stories; on the most aggressive rape story, however, rapists took longer to identify its category than other subjects. Thus, rapists appear to have discrimination difficulties where they would be least expected, on the most extreme rape descriptions. The interpretation of this result is unclear. In a second experiment (Wydra, Marshall, Earls, & Barbaree, in press), rapists and normals were found to differentially respond to rape stimuli as in previous research; however, when subjects were asked to inhibit their penile response to a tone occurring where subjects in the first experiment detected the stimulus category, both groups were able to inhibit their arousal to both types of rape. Rapists appear, therefore, to be able to control their sexual arousal, at least in a laboratory setting.

Quinsey, Chaplin, and Varney (1981) examined the sexual arousal patterns of 20 rapists, 10 non-sex offender patients from a maximum security mental hospital and 20 nonpatient (primarily unemployed) volunteers from the local community. Penile responses to audiotaped descriptions of neutral (i.e., nonsexual) heterosocial interactions, consenting sex, rape, and nonsexual violence were recorded. Half of the non-offender subjects were instructed that sexual arousal to "unusual" sexual cues was common and expected among non-sex offenders in order to examine the effects of demand characteristics in the testing session. Rapists were differentiable from non-sex offender subjects as in previous work; subjects given permissive instructions responded more to rape and consenting sex descriptions but the relative relationship between the average response to these two categories was the same as in the other non-sex offender groups (i.e., more response to consenting sex than rape).

Quinsey and Chaplin (1984) attempted to determine what aspects of the rape stimuli were responsible for the differential responses of rapists and non-sex offenders. Fifteen rapists and 15 nonrapists (community volunteers or non-sex offender patients) served as subjects. In addition to consenting sex stories, rape stories were included and varied in a 2×2 factorial design where the variables were initial victim resistance strategy (pleading for mercy or assertive refusal) and ultimate response to the assault (pain or involuntary arousal). These categories were selected because of Marques' (1979) demonstration that rapists were more sexually aroused by a pleading for mercy strategy than assertive refusal, attempts to establish a relationship, or no verbal resistance strategies and Malamuth and Check's (1980a, 1980b) finding that non-sex offenders showed more arousal to rape scenes where the victim enjoyed as opposed to when she abhorred the assault. Rapists responded equally to all of the categories whereas non-sex offenders responded most to the consenting sex narrations, less to the rape stories where the victim became aroused, and least to the rape stories where the victim experienced pain. These results support the idea that non-consent and violence fail to inhibit rapists' sexual arousal.

Freund and his colleagues (Freund, Scher, Campbell, Hucker, Ben-Aron, & Heasman, in preparation; Freund, Scher, & Hucker, in press) have approached these issues from an ethological perspective. They note that normal male sexual activity involves location and choice of a partner, pretactile integration, tactile integration, and effecting genital union. Sexual deviations are hypothesized to be courtship disorders in which there is an exaggeration of one of these normal phases. Respectively, the disorders or deviations of each phase are: voyeurism, exhibitionism, toucheurism, or frotteurism, and the preferential rape pattern. Toucheurism involves touching the breasts of an unknown female and, frottage, rubbing the genitals against the buttocks of an unknown female. Preferential rapists are those who are more sexually aroused by rape than consenting sexual intercourse. Preferential rapists, in turn, are hypothesized to fall into at least three sub-categories those (mentioned above) in whom the precopulatory sequence is vestigial, those who exhibit the hyperdominance syndrome (that is, who are excited by female fear), and sadists (who are sexually excited by inflicting pain).

The idea that rapists may exhibit a courtship disorder suggests that they are similar to voyeurs, exposers, frotteurs, and toucheurs. Rapists are, in fact, often found to have multiple sexual deviations (cf. Abel, Becker, & Skinner, in press; Langevin, 1983). In support of this similarity, Freund has shown that exhibitionists show greater penile volume responses to audiotaped descriptions of voyeuristic activities than normals, although the exhibitionists denied any interest in voyeurism; similarly, voyeurs were more sexually aroused than normals to descriptions of exposing. Rapists, unlike normal controls, showed as much sexual arousal to descriptions of voyeuristic and toucheuristic activities as to intercourse; rapists did not, however, show arousal to indecent exposure. Similarly to other studies, rapists were found to respond as much to intercourse with a fearful woman as to intercourse with a cooperative woman, whereas normal subjects were more aroused by the cooperative partner description.

In summary, rapists have been shown to be differentiable from nonrapists on the basis of their penile responses to audiotaped descriptions of consenting and forced intercourse in studies employing different stimuli, instructions, rapist samples (outpatient, correctional, maximum security mental hospital) and comparison groups (sexual deviants, college students, non-sex offender inmates, non-sex offender security hospital patients, and low socioeconomic status volunteers given normal or permissive instructions). Although it appears firmly established, despite certain criticisms (Krisak, Murphy, & Stalgaitis, 1981; Langevin, 1983), that a large proportion of rapists respond differently than non-sex offenders in phallometric assessment, the interpretation of these data is more at issue. One theoretical interpretation, as mentioned earlier, is that rapists are aroused by sex and violence and the other is that they are aroused by sex but not inhibited by violence. A number of studies support the latter view (Barbaree, Marshall, & Lanthier, 1979; Freund et al., in preparation, Quinsey & Chaplin, 1984; Quinsey, Chaplin, & Varney, 1984). The studies of Abel and his associates do not permit clear interpretation on this issue. Although the average responses of rapists are roughly the same to consenting sex and rape as the theory requires, more detailed analysis indicates that the situation is more complex than either theory suggests. First, some rapists (probably sadistic individuals) are more sexually aroused by rape scenes than by consenting sex stories; similarly, some rapists (often the same individuals) show marked arousal to scenes of nonsexual violence (Quinsey & Chaplin, 1982).

An example of a sexual murderer tested in our laboratory at Oak Ridge is illuminating. This individual showed no arousal to depictions of consenting sex but large penile responses to both rape and nonsexual violence stories. When asked how he had sex with his wife, he replied that he fantasized strangling her. These extremely sadistic rapists are not common but are of considerable interest. It would appear, therefore, that populations of rapists are comprised primarily of individuals who are not particularly aroused by violence but are not inhibited by it, and to a much lesser extent, of sadistic individuals for whom violence is arousing, at least in a sexual context. In support of this interpretation, Quinsey, Upfold, and Chaplin (in preparation) have recently found that rapists who respond to descriptions of nonsexual violence involving females do not respond to nonsexual violence involving males; the gender of the victim appears to be a sufficient context.

The important elements in rapists' sexual fantasies have, however, just begun to be explored. To date, the elements or features of sexual fantasies which have been manipulated include coercion, physical violence, female sexual arousal, female pain, female fear, and victim gender. Other elements may be equally or more important in generating sexual arousal; in particular, humiliating the victim (Darke, Marshall, & Earls, in press) or expressing power over her (Groth & Birnbaum, 1979). These features are common in rapists' explanations of their offenses but one often wonders whether these elements have been suggested to them in therapy. In order to clarify these issues, the stimulus control of rapists' sexual arousal requires much further work and such research will probably lead to the identification of idiosyncratic arousal patterns. An interesting and unusual such pattern was reported by a rapist who was tested in the Oak Ridge laboratory and asked to write the most arousing sexual fantasy of which he could think. His elaborate fantasy, which elicited large erectile responses, involved capturing rich and beautiful enemy women whom he would enslave, embarrass, and degrade. It is of interest that the actual sexual activities in this fantasy were almost incidental and the cues eliciting sexual arousal appeared to be "contextual" and related to dominance and humiliation. Rapists are, of course, no more interested in identifying specific cues which arouse them than anyone else. If they have an exciting fantasy they use it and don't apply Mill's method of agreement to systematically vary the content of the fantasies in order to determine the critical elements. Unaided self-report, therefore, is not the best method of identifying idiosyncratic sexually-arousing stimuli. Abel, Blanchard, Barlow, and Mavissakalian (1975) have described a phallometric technique to identify such stimuli which appears very promising for future research. In view of the idiosyncratic nature of the sexual fantasies reported by sex offenders whom we have treated, it is all the more surprising that differences in sexual arousal to standard stimulus sets have been found between non-sex offenders and rapists.

In conclusion, studies of sexual arousal have found large differences among men in their relative preferences for mutually-consenting sex and rape. Variation occurs within non-sex offender groups, although most non-sex offenders clearly prefer consenting sexual activity. Rapists' sexual arousal patterns appear to be further along the continuum and they exhibit little or no discrimination between rape and consenting sex. Sadistic rapists occupy the end of the continuum characterized by greater sexual arousal to sexual violence than consenting sex.

Treatment of Sexual Assaulters

The literature on the treatment of sexual assaulters is conspicuously casual and few convincing evaluative studies exist (Pacht, 1976; West, Roy, & Nichols, 1978). There are many fewer articles on the treatment of rapists than there are on the treatment of less serious sex offenders (Langevin, 1983). In part, this lack of attention is understandable because, as we have seen, many convicted rapists do not commit further sex crimes; however, for repetitive offenders, the lack of research on treatment efficacy is most unfortunate. Moreover, many sexual assaulters do, in fact, receive treatment and it is sometimes lengthy (Brecher, 1978).

There are many descriptions of treatment programs: Most of these deal with undifferentiated groups of sex offenders of various kinds, do not precisely describe their methods of treatment (i.e., do not allow for the possibility of replication), do not present acceptable data on short-term changes, and do not include follow-up data. Of those programs for which follow-up data are provided, comparison conditions are seldom included and the descriptions of treatment are usually inadequate. In addition, there has been little scientific attention paid to potential differences in the treatability of sexual assaulters, although there is little doubt that such differences exist and are important (Pacht, 1976). Konecni, Mulcahy, and Ebbesen (1980) found that previous sex offenses best predicted whether sex offenders were sent to a mental hospital for treatment instead of a prison; psychiatric diagnosis and testimony, courtroom variables, previous non-sex offenses, and probation officers' reports were irrelevant once the history of previous sex offenses was taken into account. Given current knowledge, this may well be a good, if simple, method of selecting persons with actual sexual problems, although it does not address the issue of differential responsiveness to treatment.

Most treatment programs for rapists use a variety of methods (Brecher, 1978) but emphasize group psychotherapy, behavior therapy, or techniques for reducing androgens. Abel, Blanchard, and Becker (1976, 1978) point out that five major components are included (at least minimally) in most treatment programs for rapists: establishing an empathic relationship, confronting them with their responsibility, training in heterosocial skills, increasing sexual arousal to adult women, and decreasing arousal to rape urges.

Group Psychotherapy

The most common form of therapy for sexual assaulters is group therapy but, unfortunately, the criticisms listed above apply most clearly to descriptions of group psychotherapy programs (Brancale, Vuocolo, & Prendergast, 1972; Cabeen & Coleman, 1961; Cohen & Kozol, 1966; Costell & Yalom, 1972; MacIndoe & Pengelly, 1976; Marcus, 1966; Pacht, Halleck, & Ehrmann, 1962; Peters & Roether, 1972; Peters & Sadoff, 1971; Sarafian, 1963; Silver, 1976; Smith, 1968), although some papers have dealt exclusively with the treatment of rapists and recognize different treatment needs among them (Cohen, Garofalo, Boucher, & Seghorn, 1971; Groth & Cohen, 1976; West, Roy, & Nichols, 1978).

Brecher (1978) has reviewed group psychotherapy programs for sex offenders in the United States. None of these have been convincingly evaluated and few involve rapists as a separate entity. Common elements of treatment involve the offender confronting his own behavior, accepting responsibility for it, and making a commitment to change. In addition, most of the programs attempt to improve the self-esteem of the participants.

Although the emphasis of this review is on scientific evidence and evaluation (subjects which the group therapy literature fails abysmally to address), it should be noted that the lack of evidence cannot be used to infer that these programs do not work. Moreover, although the ultimate criterion of success is lowered sexual recidivism, treatment programs, particularly in maximum security settings, can serve demonstrably valuable functions, such as providing a humane system of inmate or patient management and functioning as a morale building tool for both patients and staff (cf. Quinsey, 1983).

Castration

Surgical castration as a treatment for sex offenders in Denmark has been described as highly successful (Orno, 1965; Ortmann, 1980; Sturup, 1968, 1972); it involves enucleation of the testes and their replacement with a suitable substance. A lengthy follow-up of 900 castrated Danish offenders indicates a sexual recidivism rate of about 2% and a low frequency of serious psychological or physical sequelae. Sturup (1968) has concluded that the treatment is indicated for adult sex offenders who cannot control their sexual urges, are likely to recidivate, suffer guilt about their crimes, and are not psychotic. Of 11 rapists who were castrated and followed for a minimum of 13 years, five recidivated with nonsexual difficulties; one offender, however, who obtained testosterone from a physician, was charged with a new sex offense and committed suicide.

Careful management of the cases and prolonged aftercare is advocated by Sturup because depression can result from the procedure (2% of the castrates commit suicide) and various physical symptoms can occur. Patients report that their sexual fantasies and interests decline and that they are less responsive to sexual stimuli but about a third report engaging in post-operative sexual intercourse with understanding partners (Sturup, 1968; Heim, 1981).

Although no comparison data from similar untreated subjects are available because the cases are carefully selected and the mechanism of therapeutic action is unclear (possible variables include: aftercare procedure, hormone change, motivation for change, and cognitive dissonance, among others), castration does appear to be related to low rates of sexual recidivism despite methodological criticisms (Heim & Hursch, 1979). Castration is, however, not always effective and there is at least one case reported of a postoperative sadistic rape and other cases of sexual reoffending (Sturup, 1972).

The strongest arguments against castration are ethical. Castration can, of course, be viewed as punishment instead of treatment and because it is an irreversible procedure it presents special difficulties. If castration is viewed as treatment, patient consent should be obtained without coercion. Unfortunately, coercion is extremely difficult to preclude as the state can give long life sentences, arrange harsh institutional living conditions, or place special restrictions on parole or release in order to induce sex offenders and their families to comply with it. This state of affairs is most unfortunate for there are small numbers of hypersexual and sadistic individuals for whom castration appears beneficial (Freund, 1976), ethically justifiable, and, at present, the most likely way of reducing the length of their incarceration.

Fortunately, however, "chemical castration" may offer an equally effective, more humane, and more practical alternative (Ortmann, 1980).

Antiandrogen Medication

Investigators agree that libido-reducing drugs do not alter the direction of sexual interests but affect their strength. In studies of the effects of cyproterone acetate in sexual deviants (Bancroft, Tennent, Loucas, & Cass, 1974) and studies of testosterone replacement therapy for hypogonadal men (Bancroft & Wu, 1983), it has been shown that arousal generated by sexual fantasy is much more susceptible to modification than erectile responsiveness to strong sexual stimuli (e.g., movies). Thus it appears possible to have sex offenders who receive antiandrogens enjoy sexual intercourse but not fantasize obsessively about sex.

Medroxyprogesterone acetate and cyproterone acetate have been used in the treatment of a variety of sex offenders (Berlin & Meinicke, 1981; Langevin et al., 1979; Laschet, 1973; Rubin & Henson, 1979; Spodak, Falck & Rappeport, 1978; Walker & Meyer, 1981) but the literature has been criticized on methodological grounds, especially for short follow-up periods (Ortmann, 1980). Reports on the effectiveness of these treatments are extremely variable, with recidivism rates following treatment ranging from 50% downwards. Patient dropout is often reported to be a significant problem. Treatment failures with these chemical interventions have been attributed to noncompliance, drug and alcohol abuse, sexual impulsivity, sociopathy, histories of violence, psychosis, senile dementia, and neurotic fixation of pedophilia (Berlin & Meinicke, 1981; Laschet, 1973). It is at present unclear how serious the various side effects of these medications are, particularly with long term administration. For a review of the side effects of these drugs see Bradford (1983).

Despite these reservations and restrictions, there have been enough clinical demonstrations of beneficial effects to permit therapeutic optimism with respect to selected cases. Perhaps the most important variable determining the usefulness of antiandrogens is hypersexuality (as defined by extremely high masturbatory frequencies and obsessive fantasies) because that problem involves strength of sexual interest, not direction. Cooper (1981) reported very favorable results in a placebo-controlled trial of cyproterone acetate with hypersexual men. Further research is required to evaluate the effectiveness of these drugs with hypersexual rapists. Future improvements in the drugs themselves and refinements in clinical techniques may offer a palatable alternative to castration, particularly when the drug administration is coupled with techniques designed to produce more lasting change. Further theoretical work on the effects of drugs on sexual behavior is clearly needed (Rubin & Henson, 1979).

Behavior Modification

Behavior modification programs for sexual assaulters share several characteristics: brief intervention, separate focused assessment of a particular problem area, individualized treatments depending on assessment results, the use of training as a form of treatment, and pre- and post-treatment measurement of change (Abel, Becker, & Skinner, in press; Abel, Blanchard, & Becker, 1976, 1978; Marshall & Barbaree, 1978; Marshall, Earls, Segal, & Darke, in press; Turner & Van Hasselt, 1979). The problem areas which have been studied most extensively are: inappropriate sexual arousal (including responsiveness to aggressive imagery and hyporesponsiveness to non-coercive sexual imagery), heterosocial skill deficiencies, assertive deficits, and lack of sexual knowledge.

A wide variety of techniques, such as electrical aversion therapy, covert sensitization, and olfactory aversion, have been used to reduce inappropriate sexual arousal (Quinsey & Marshall, 1983). Each of these techniques associates inappropriate arousal with unpleasant stimuli. Although many of these techniques can effectively reduce sexual arousal to aggressive cues as measured by changes in penile responses, there are variations in effectiveness which are not well-understood. Satiation therapy, in which sadistic or aggressive fantasies are extensively rehearsed in a non-aroused state, has also been shown to reduce inappropriate arousal (Marshall & Barbaree, 1978). Improvements in heterosocial skill are readily produced by modeling, coaching, and videotape feedback and not surprisingly, sexual knowledge can be markedly improved through sex education (Whitman & Quinsey, 1981).

Unfortunately, there are no behavioral treatment studies of rapists, other than case reports, which include follow-up data. Thus, the promise offered by short-term improvement, even though

impressive, has yet to be verified. Clearly, the greatest need in the treatment literature is for outcome studies of a variety of treatments offered to similar clients, and studies of the prediction of recidivism from measures of therapeutic change. At present, it cannot be concluded unequivocally whether any of the forms of treatment reviewed are differentially effective with different sorts of sexual assaulters or effective at all in the long term. On the other hand, both the behavioral and somatic treatments appear promising.

Theories of Sexual Assault

There are no comprehensive theories of sexual assault. From the literature reviewed above, we know that a variety of classes of variables are relevant: biological, sociological, cultural, and psychological. These classes of variables appear to be differentially related to different types of sexual assault: gang rape, sexual aggression in dating contexts, repetitive predatory sexual assaults, and sexual sadism. Because theories of sexual assault tend to focus on certain variables and types of assault and to ignore others, there may or may not be contradictions among widely different theories purporting to explain the "same" phenomena. In addition, there is confusion between the ultimate and proximate causes of sexual assault. A further but related issue is that different theories are pitched at different levels of explanation: we would suppose, if perfect knowledge were available, that biological, sociological, and psychological theories would all exist for sexual assault and all be compatible with each other. In fact, there are, in principle, explanations of sexual assault at the subatomic level. Unfortunately, our knowledge is imperfect and it is often difficult to compare theories at different levels of explanation; few opportunities exist, therefore, for quantitative and rigorous comparisons because of the incompatible levels of explanation, vagueness of the theories and the mushiness of much of the data.

In view of the state of the theoretical art, it would perhaps be best to think of the theories to be described as invitations to conceptualize sexual assault in particular ways. The relative value of these alternate conceptualizations can sometimes be assessed only by determining which lead to interesting research questions or practical implications. Inference research which compares alternative predictions for identical data sets is seldom a possibility.

Brodsky (1976) has suggested that lay explanations of sexual assault blame sexual assaults on victims, offenders, and/or situations. *Victim blame* models in their strong form assert that women provoke sexual attacks. However, popular beliefs aside (Burt, 1980; Toner, 1977), there is an abundance of disconfirming evidence for this proposition (e.g., Hursch, 1977). Victim behavior is, however, undoubtedly involved in some sexual assaults (Amir, 1972) but appears to be a minor factor because of the large percentage of assaults involving weapons, complete strangers, and premeditation (Amir, 1965; Gager & Schurr, 1976; Wright, 1980). Data suggesting that sexual assaults are predatory and opportunistic (Geller, 1977) point to the same conclusion.

Attribution of fault to victims shows strong gender effects. Calhoun, Selby, and Warring (1976) presented 64 male and 64 female undergraduates with an identical videotape of a mock rape victim interview. Background information on the "case" was varied systematically over subjects: The victim was raped before or not, the rapist was in the victim's class previously or not, and there had been zero or seven other rapes in the area recently. In comparison to females, males tended to see the rape as being caused by the victim's personality traits and behavior and thought the rape was more the victim's fault. Female blameability has also been shown to be a function of her "respectability" (Jones & Aronson, 1973).

Turning to *offender blame*, explanatory accounts often focus on why a man would choose to rape when consenting sexual activity is, in the eyes of the explainer, more fun, more honorable, and less risky. One explanation is that sexual assaulters cannot engage in consenting sexual behavior because they are less attractive and more heterosocially unskilled. Unfortunately, for this approach, many sexual assaulters are married (Gebhard et al., 1965) and they have not been found to be less attractive or heterosocially skilled than other offenders (Stermac & Quinsey, submitted for publication). Another similar explanation involves lack of opportunity as reflected by imbalanced sex ratios. Lester (1974), however, found no relation between sex ratio and rape frequency. In addition, it must be remembered that because of male desire for a variety of sexual partners, females are always a scarce resource (Symons, 1979). Sex ratios may be a factor under extreme conditions but these are not found in Western societies.

A further variation on this theme is that there is something wrong with the offender's judgment. He may be psychotic, retarded, or drunk and simply not know what he is doing. None of these pass muster. Very few sexual assaulters are psychotic (e.g., Quinsey & Chaplin, in press; Quinsey, Chaplin, & Varney, 1984) and as we have seen there is little difference in intelligence between rapists and other offenders. Alcohol does appear to be important but its role is unclear (giving the offender courage, providing an excuse for the offense, disinhibition of inappropriate sexual interests, pathological intoxication, and so on). In a similar manner, sexual assaulters are sometimes said to be psychopaths (i.e., have defective moral judgment) and certainly most are diagnosed as personality disordered; the diagnosis is not sufficient, however, as personality disordered nonsexual offenders can be differentiated from rapists on the basis of their sexual interests (Quinsey & Chaplin, in press; Quinsey, Chaplin, & Varney, 1984). This is not to argue, however, that general criminality or psychopathy is not involved, particularly in gang rapes.

Situational blame has also been invoked, and as we have seen, forceful seduction often occurs in a dating context. Nevertheless, the predatory nature of rape makes such an explanation lose force (e.g., Geller, 1977). Rapists too frequently create opportunities to rape by breaking and entering, or following women, for this explanation to have much value.

Freudians have not attempted to theorize about rape in any systematic fashion (Brownmiller, 1975; Langevin, 1983). There have been a few case reports and some speculation (e.g., Glover, 1964; Kardener, 1975; Williams, 1964, 1965) but little in the way of research or evaluation. Berlin and Meinicke (1981:602) summarize the situation aptly:

Psychodynamic theory generally assumes that sexually deviant behaviors occur because of unresolved unconscious conflicts, and treatment is directed at uncovering such conflicts. . .To our knowledge there have been no well-controlled clinical trials to demonstrate that any of the individual or group psychodynamic methods result in sustained behavioral change in these conditions, and achieving insight into how they develop does not necessarily alter them. In point of fact, most of us have little understanding about why particular things arouse us sexually.

Feminists have argued that "rape stems from a fundamental conflict in our competitive, aggressive society, justified by the sexist notion that males should control and dominate a woman's sexual being as well as the economic life. The fear of rape, as well as the way rape is prosecuted in our courts serves to maintain social control over the entire feminine population and to maintain the domination of men over women. Our social and economic structure generates rape and does nothing to discourage it" (Kasinsky, 1975). Brownmiller (1975) has gone further, asserting that rape is "nothing more or less than a conscious process of intimidation by which *all men* keep *all women* in a state of fear."

Although there is little doubt that our society is sexist, and that the fear of rape troubles women and restricts their behavior (Riger & Gordon, 1979; Riger, Gordon, & LeBailly, 1982), the nature of the relationship between sexism and sexual assault is less clear. If the feminist argument is simply that all men are rapists, it must fail. All men, of course, are potential rapists in the same sense that they are potential murderers or mountain climbers but data on non-sex offenders clearly indicate large variations in male proclivity to rape. Some of these differences are consistent with a feminist analysis, that is, that men who hold anti-women views tend to be those more likely to rape. The effects appear stronger, however, when specific attitudes toward rape are examined as opposed to more general attitudes concerning women. As the cross-cultural data indicate, sexism is not necessarily connected with high rape rates.

Sociobiological theories are in a sense complementary to feminist theories in that they emphasize the different reproductive interests of males and females. Thornhill and Thornhill (in press) have presented the most complete formulation of a sociobiological theory of rape. Briefly, they argue that, evolutionarily, humans have been in a polygynous situation where men compete for females (cf. Chagnon, 1977; Symons, 1979). Males who lose this competition and cannot secure mates resort to other strategies, including forced mating. Thus, rape victims should be those who are most fertile and rapists those men who are disadvantaged (e.g., poor) and who are competing most strongly for mates (i.e., prior to first

marriage). Support for the theory is provided by a disproportionate representation of young and poor men among rapists and a close correspondence between female fertility values (based on age) and rape victimization rates of women of varying ages. Unfortunately, the correspondence between fertility and victimization, although reasonable at the adult and older age ranges, is very problematic at the prepubescent age ranges. There are, of course, many sex offenses against female children; many of these are not classified as rape or attempted rape simply because of labelling policies; moreover, rape is in many cases physically impossible with young children. Thus, plotting rapes as a function of age is grossly misleading at prepubescent ages.

In addition to these methodological problems, sociobiological theories of sexual behavior have a variety of potentially-problematic phenomena to explain. Perhaps most importantly they must explain why some men do not rape and why many rapists engage in fellatio or anal intercourse instead of vaginal intercourse. Child molestation and homosexuality, in addition, appear to be extremely wasteful forms of sexual activity and their existence, particularly in their exclusive forms, provides a problem for a baldly stated evolutionary theory. This is not to argue, however, that genetic explanations for such phenomena as familially transmitted homosexuality may not be forthcoming in the future (Pillard, Poumadere, & Carretta, 1981, 1982). The evolutionary explanation of sexual assaults of adult females (which do not result in murder), however, does not suffer from a prima facie implausibility; nevertheless, until theories of natural selection purporting to explain human sexual assault can specify heritable *mechanisms* which are currently in operation, they will be extremely difficult to test rigorously in any direct fashion.

In the long run, however, a complete theory of sexual behavior and sexual assault must involve natural selection as a crucial element. As Dawkins (1978) has argued, current reproductive strategies have inevitable consequences for the behavior and characteristics of succeeding generations. It is of no use to argue that sexual behavior is learned in man, and therefore, highly variable, as any genetic mechanism which is associated with unsuccessful reproduction (e.g., learning the wrong preferences) will be inevitably bred out of the population, *ceteris paribus*. One could only assume the doubtful proposition that there is no genetic variance in the mechanisms under discussion to be acted upon by natural selection or that the mechanisms are linked to others which are very helpful.

The issue of mechanism is critical for the development of a theory of sexual assault and sexual behavior in general. Observation of human sexual behavior reveals extreme diversity; most male sexual behavior is clearly adaptive in an evolutionary sense but some is very plainly not. A mechanism must be sought which encompasses both sets of observations. Specifically, in regard to sexual assault, such a mechanism must be able to explain individual differences in the amount of arousal occasioned by sadistic imagery. The most obvious candidate for such a mechanism is some variety of learning.

There is a great deal of evidence that learning is involved in the sexual behavior of a wide variety of animal species. This learning appears to be of two sorts: learning associations between certain environmental cues and sexual arousal and learning specific copulatory behavior sequences. Considering the first type of learning, recent studies of quails, sticklebacks, and pigeons (Hollis, 1982) have shown that male courtship behavior can be elicited by and directed toward a stimulus associated with copulation or, in sticklebacks, the sight of a gravid female. In the latter case, the courtship behavior directed toward the conditional stimulus (a rod) interfered with the male performing the biting response on the rod which was required to obtain a view of the female. This Pavlovian or classical conditioning process clearly produces an animal analog to a human fetish.

The prefiguring hypothesis (Hollis, 1982) asserts that the biological function of classically conditioned responding is to enable the organism to optimize interactions with a biologically important event, thus, the conditional response serves to prepare the animal to deal with the unconditional stimulus. In support of this view, presentation of a conditional stimulus (associated with the sexual activity) reduces copulating latency in the quail and the rat. Among quails, in particular, fast copulation is very adaptive for males in the natural mating context because of competition from other males. Thus the unfortunate capacity to learn the wrong things from an evolutionary perspective may be the inevitable consequence of the actual phenomenon of learning helpful (but sometimes arbitrary) things most of the time. Parenthetically, this explanation very naturally accounts for the fact that human fetish objects are usually associated with female sexuality and change with fashion (Gebhard, 1969).

Turning to sex offenders, McGuire, Carlisle, and Young (1965) have argued from case history data that sexual deviations are acquired through masturbation to deviant sexual imagery. The original source of the imagery can be a real event or something fictional but the erotic value of the stimulus is maintained and strengthened through its association with masturbation. Unfortunately, there are no convincing data one way or the other on this theory, although it is, in broad outline, compatible with what is known.

Learning is also involved in establishing appropriate copulatory behaviors and its importance is greatest among mammalian species. This learning can sometimes go awry. It is known that male sexual performance among mammals is more easily disrupted by traumatic learning experiences, cortical lesions, and distraction than is female sexual behavior (Gadpaille, 1980). Among rhesus monkeys, sex play with juvenile peers is crucial in establishing normal adult sexual behaviors but the effects of depriving juveniles of this experience is only irreversible in the male (Gadpaille, 1980).

Taken together, these lines of evidence have possible implications for human sexual behavior and suggest that learning an association between sexual arousal and "peculiar" stimuli is quite possible, as is the learning of inappropriate sexual behaviors. It appears as though early learning is important. Despite the importance of learning in sexual behavior, it seems implausible that it is unconstrained by genetic influences because of its great relevance to reproductive success. Genetic influence could occur in a variety of ways. The most obvious of these is the establishment of unconditional stimuli involved in classical conditioning or reinforcers involved in instrumental learning; orgasm is one such event and we may speculate that youthful female body shape is another. Another form of influence is on the ease with which certain connections are learned. What is being suggested here is a "preparedness" type notion whereby certain sorts of associations are much more easily acquired than others.

Some support for a preparedness theory is provided by studies on classically conditioned sexual arousal. Rachman (1966) and Rachman and Hodgson (1968) found that penile responses to pictures of female high heeled boots could be acquired through the experimental association of the boot slides with pictures of nude women. Much weaker classical conditioning was found by Langevin and Martin (1975) who used patterns of low association value as conditional stimuli. One can argue, therefore, that non-arbitrary stimuli which are associated with women may be more easily conditionable (Marks, 1976).

Among potentially easily acquired associations, the ultimate link between sex and violence is the most important in the present context. It is plausible that such an association is easily acquired because of the presumed genetic benefits of forced mating strategies in evolutionary history, the close association of neural structures mediating sex and aggression, the intimate association of dominance hierarchies and mating success, and the likely phylogenetic association of inter-male aggression and sexual behavior. This account is conjectural, of course, but does agree with what is known.

Conclusions

Although the literature is far from definitive, there are interpretations which can be made and these may be useful both in organizing the literature and in a heuristic manner. It is in this spirit that the following conclusions are offered.

The literature indicates that all or at least most men are capable of rape but that its frequency varies with cultural variables such as the prevalence of male warlike behavior and the extent of social upheaval (most commonly found in wartime). In Westernized societies, most men prefer consenting sex to rape but there are large individual differences among them in the extent to which they consider rape to be legitimate and the extent to which they find the thought of it sexually exciting. Many males, although preferring consenting sex, will use forceful seduction strategies in an opportunistic, if half-hearted, fashion. The likelihood of such forceful seduction behaviors is related to the presence of alcohol, attitudes relating to women and sexuality, the amount of sexual experience the man has had, appropriate opportunities, and the female's behavior. Such attempts do not usually end in rape.

Rapists tend to be individuals who are more sexually aroused by rape than non-rapists. They often engage in nonsexual criminal activities as well. In particular, gang rapes appear to reflect a criminal or delinquent lifestyle, rather than inappropriate sexual interests (although this proposition requires direct testing). Rapists who are repetitive or commit extremely brutal crimes appear to be erotically attracted to this type of behavior; they fantasize about it, stalk women, and use rape fantasies in masturbation. This obsession with violent sex reaches its apogee among sadistic murderers. Thus, considering individual difference variables, it appears there are two relevant and independent continua in the proximate causation of rape: criminality and an erotic attraction to violent sexuality. Situational variables appear to be more important among rapists who do not have inappropriate sexual interests.

Thus there are two phenomena which require explanation; the first of these is criminality and the second is the acquisition of an erotic attraction toward violent sexuality. Turning first to criminality, the association between rape and the commission of a variety of other offenses appears reasonable in a broad evolutionary context. Symons (1979) has cogently argued that males have been selected to desire a large number of sexual partners. Among the arguments supporting the idea that male desire is stimulated by novelty is the "Coolidge effect" observed in many mammalian species where the substitution of new female partners potentiates the male sexual responses and the differences in partner choice between male and female homosexuals. Symons suggests with respect to homosexuality, that sexual relations within genders allow us to see what male and female sexuality is like when compromises do not have to be made with the opposite sex. Male homosexuals tend to have very large numbers of partners and partner choice is determined by physical attractiveness, particularly youthfulness. Female homosexuals, on the other hand, tend to form enduring relationships and to have few sexual partners. Evolution, being concerned with reproductive success, is indifferent to frustration in heterosexual men and disappointment among heterosexual women.

Given the plausibility of Symon's thesis, we must be impressed by the role of socialization in male sexual behavior. When socialization fails, as, for example, when men do not feel "appropriate" guilt or do not emulate "responsible" role models, we may expect not only a high frequency and variety of criminal activities but also the occasional sexual assault. Poorly socialized or criminal individuals would be expected to rape when the costs are low and an appropriate opportunity occurs. We would expect that the sexual arousal of such men would not be inhibited by victim suffering or nonconsent and the research on the sexual arousal patterns of rapists supports this expectation. The finding that rapists are differentiable on the basis of their sexual responsiveness to rape cues from other personality disordered offenders probably indicates that some rapists are erotically attracted to sexual sadism and that poor socialization does not always entail poor sexual socialization. The socialization argument allows us to predict that rapists should resemble other offenders in personality and that alcohol should be related to the commission of rape. Callous attitudes towards rape may reflect this specific failure of socialization.

Turning to the acquisition of an erotic attraction toward violent sexuality, in an earlier section it was argued that such an association might be easily learned. Now, we must inquire as to what sorts of individuals would be most likely to learn it. One would expect those most likely to develop sadistic interests to be those individuals who are: (a) socially isolated, as they would elaborate sexual fantasies without interruption, would not have realistic ideas about sexual behavior and would have few real-life exemplars of consenting sexual behavior to serve as stimuli to masturbation; (b) hypersexual, as hypersexuals would engage in a great deal of masturbatory activity; (c) exposed to violent pornography, as such material may appear to legitimize such thoughts, as well as serving as a masturbatory stimulus; and (d) hostile towards women, as such hostility and anger would be paired with sexual thoughts, particularly if the hostility was in a sexual context (e.g., rejection). These ideas lead one to predict the observed high frequencies of other sexual deviancies among sadistic assaulters.

A wide variety of topics offer interesting opportunities for further investigation: typologies of rapists, testosterone and sexual aggression, rapists' attitudes toward women, alcohol and rape, comparative evaluative studies of different treatment methods, assertive deficits among rapists, and hypersexuality. Research on the development of both "normal" and inappropriate sexual interests is, however, the most important and is fundamental to theory development, prevention, and treatment interventions.

References

Abel, G.G., Barlow, D.H., Blanchard, E.B., & Guild, D. The components of rapists' sexual arousal. *Archives of General Psychiatry*, 1977, *34*, 895–903.

Abel, G.G., Becker, J.V., Blanchard, E.B., & Djenderedjian, A. Differentiating sexual aggressives with penile measures. *Criminal Justice and Behavior*, 1978, *5*, 315–332.

Abel, G.G., Becker, J.V., & Skinner, L.J. Aggressive behavior and sex. *Psychiatric Clinics of North America*, 1980, *3*, 133–151.

Abel, G.G., Becker, J.V., & Skinner, L.J. Treatment of the violent sex offender. In L.H. Roth (Ed.), *Clinical treatment of the violent person*. Crime and delinquency issues: A monograph series, in press, Washington, DC: National Institute of Mental Health.

Abel, G.G., Blanchard, E.B., Barlow, D.H., & Mavissakalian, M. Identifying specific erotic cues in sexual deviations by audiotaped descriptions. *Journal of Applied Behavior Analysis*, 1975, *8*, 247–260.

Abel, G.G., Blanchard, E.B., & Becker, J.V. Psychological treatment of rapists. In M.J. Walker & S.L. Brodsky (Eds.), *Sexual assault: the victim and the rapist*. Toronto: Lexington Books, 1976.

Abel, G.G., Blanchard, E.B., & Becker, J.V. An integrated treatment program for rapists. In R.T. Rada (Ed.), *Clinical aspects of the rapist*. New York: Grune and Stratton, 1978.

Akman, D.D., & Normandeau, A. The measurement of crime and delinquency in Canada: A replication study. *British Journal of Criminology*, 1967, *7*, 129–149.

Amir, M. *Patterns in forcible rape with special reference to Philadelphia*. Doctoral Dissertation, University of Pennsylvania, 1965.

Amir, M. *Patterns of forcible rape*. Chicago: University of Chicago Press, 1971.

Amir, M. The role of the victim in sex offenses. In H.L.P. Resnik & M.E. Wolfgang (Eds.), *Sexual behaviors: social, clinical and legal aspects*. Boston: Little, Brown, 1972.

Anderson, W.P., Kunce, J.T., & Rich, B. Sex offenders: Three personality types. *Journal of Clinical Psychology*, 1979, *35*, 671–676.

Andriola, J. Criteria for success or failure in the treatment of hospitalized sex offenders. *Corrective Psychiatry and Journal of Social Therapy*, 1966, *12*, 323–326.

Armentrout, J.A., & Hauer, A.L. MMPIs of rapists of adults, rapists of children, and non-rapist sex offenders. *Journal of Clinical Psychology*, 1978, *34*, 330–332.

Bancroft, J., Tennent, T.G., Loucas, K., & Cass, J. The control of deviant sexual behaviour by drugs: Behavioural change following oestrogens and antiandrogens. *British Journal of Psychiatry*, 1974, *125*, 310–315.

Bancroft, J., & Wu, F.C.W. Changes in erectile responsiveness during androgen replacement therapy. *Archives of Sexual Behavior*, 1983, *12*, 59–66.

Barash, D.P. Sociobiology of rape in mallards (*Anas platyrhynehos*): Responses of the mated male. *Science*, 1977, *197*, 788–789.

Barbaree, H.E., Marshall, W.L., & Lanthier, R.D. Deviant sexual arousal in rapists. *Behaviour Research and Therapy*, 1979, *17*, 215–222.

Barbaree, H.E., Marshall, W.L., Lightfoot, L.O., & Yates, E. Alcohol intoxication and deviant sexual arousal in male social drinkers. *Behaviour Research and Therapy*, in press.

Bart, P.B. A study of women who both were raped and avoided rape. *The Journal of Social Issues*, 1981, 37, 123–137.

Beach, F.A. Cross-species comparisons and the human heritage. *Archives of Sexual Behavior*, 1976, 5, 469–485.

Beach, F.A., & LeBoeuf, B.J. Coital behaviour in dogs. I. Preferential mating in the bitch. *Animal Behaviour*, 1967, 15, 546–558.

Bentler, P.M., & Abramson, P.R. The science of sex research: Some methodological considerations. *Archives of Sexual Behavior*, 1981, 10, 225–251.

Berlin, F.S., & Meinicke, C.F. Treatment of sex offenders with antiandrogenic medication: Conceptualization, review of treatment modalities, and preliminary findings. *American Journal of Psychiatry*, 1981, 138, 601–607.

Blumer, D. Changes of sexual behavior related to temporal lobe disorders in man. *Journal of Sex Research*, 1970, 6, 173–180.

Bowker, L.H. The criminal victimization of women. *Victimology: An International Journal*, 1979, 4, 371–384.

Bradford, J. The hormonal treatment of sex offenders. *Bulletin of the American Academy of Psychiatry and the Law*, 1983, 11, 159–169.

Brancale, R., Ellis, A., & Doorbar, R.R. Psychiatric and psychological investigations of convicted sex offenders: A summary report. *American Journal of Psychiatry*, 1952, 109, 17–21.

Brancale, R., Vuocolo, A., & Prendergast, W.E. The New Jersey Program for sex offenders. In H.L.P. Resnik & M.E. Wolfgang (Eds.), *Sexual behaviors: social, clinical, and legal aspects*. Boston: Little, Brown, 1972.

Brecher, E.M. *Treatment programs for sex offenders*. Washington, DC: U.S. Government Printing Office, 1978.

Briddell, D.W., Rimm, D.C., Caddy, G.R., Krawitz, G., Sholis, D., & Wunderlin, R.J. Effects of alcohol and cognitive set on sexual arousal to deviant stimuli. *Journal of Abnormal Psychology*, 1978, 87, 418–430.

Briddell, D.W., & Wilson, G.T. Effects of alcohol and expectancy set on male sexual arousal. *Journal of Abnormal Psychology*, 1976, 85, 225–234.

Briere, J., Malamuth, N., & Check, J. *Sexuality and pro-rape beliefs*. Paper presented at the Canadian Psychological Association meeting, Toronto, June 1981.

Brittain, R.P. The sadistic murderer. *Medicine, Science and the Law*, 1970, 10, 198–207.

Brodsky, S.L. Prevention of rape: Deterrence by the potential victim. In M.J. Walker & S.L. Brodsky (Eds.), *Sexual assault: The victim and the rapist*. Toronto: Lexington, 1976.

Brodsky, S.L. Sexual assault: perspectives on prevention and assailants. In M.J. Walker & S.L. Brodsky (Eds.), *Sexual assault: The victim and the rapist*. Toronto: Lexington, 1976.

Brownmiller, S. *Against our will: Men, women and rape*. New York: Simon and Schuster, 1975.

Burt, M.R. Cultural myths and supports for rape. *Journal of Personality and Social Psychology*, 1980, 38, 217–230.

Cabeen, C.W., & Coleman, J.C. Group therapy with sex offenders: Description and evaluation of group therapy program in an institutional setting. *Journal of Clinical Psychology*, 1961, 17, 122–129.

Calhoun, L.G., Selby, J.W., & Warring, L.J. Social perception of the victim's causal role in rape: An explatory examination of four factors. *Human Relations*, 1976, 29, 517–526.

Callner, D.A., & Ross, S.M. The reliability and validity of three measures of assertion in a drug addict population. *Behaviour Therapy*, 1976, 7, 659–667.

Carstairs, G.M. Cultural differences in sexual deviation. In I. Rosen (Ed.), *The pathology and treatment of sexual deviation: A methodological approach*. London: Oxford University Press, 1964.

Chagnon, N.A. *Yanomamo: The fierce people* (2nd ed.). Toronto: Holt, Rinehart and Winston, 1977.

Chappell, D. Cross-cultural research on forcible rape. *International Journal of Criminology and Penology*, 1976, 4, 295–304.

Christiansen, K.O., Elers-Nielson, M., LeMaire, L., & Sturup, G.K. Recidivism among sexual offenders. In K. Christiansen (Ed.), *Scandinavian studies in criminology*. London: Tavistock, 1965.

Cohen, M.L., & Boucher, R.J. Misunderstandings about sex criminals. *Sexual Behavior*, 1972, 56–62.

Cohen, M.L., Garofalo, R., Boucher, R., & Seghorn, T. The psychology of rapists. *Seminars in Psychiatry*, 1971, 3, 307–327.

Cohen, M.L., & Kozol, H.L. Evaluation for parole at a sex offender treatment center. *Federal Probation*, 1966, 30, 50–55.

Cohen, M.L., Seghorn, T., & Calmas, W. Sociometric study of the sex offender. *Journal of Abnormal Psychology*, 1969, 74, 249–255.

Cook, R.F., Fosen, R.H., & Pacht, A. Pornography and the sex offender: Patterns of previous exposure and arousal effects of pornographic stimuli. *Journal of Applied Psychology*, 1971, 55, 503–511.

Cooper, A.J. A placebo-controlled trial of antiandrogen cyproterone acetate in deviant hypersexuality. *Comprehensive Psychiatry*, 1981, 22, 458–465.

Costell, R., & Yalom, I. Institutional group therapy. In H.L.P. Resnik & M.E. Wolfgang (Eds.), *Sexual behaviours: Social, clinical and legal aspects*. Boston: Little, Brown, 1972.

Court, J.H. Pornography and sex crimes: A re-evaluation in the light of recent trends around the world. *International Journal of Criminology and Penology*, 1976, 5, 129–157.

Crawford, C. *Infra-human rape in evolutionary perspective*. Paper presented at Canadian Psychological Association meeting, Montreal, June 1982.

Darke, J.L., Marshall, W.L., & Earls, C.M. Humiliation and rape: A preliminary inquiry. In G.G. Abel (Ed.), *Social factors in sexual aggression*. Elmsford, NY: Pergamon Press, in press.

Dawkins, R. *The selfish gene*. London: Paladin, 1978.

Dietz, P.E. Social factors in rapist behavior. In R.J. Rada (Ed.), *Clinical aspects of the rapist*. New York: Grune and Stratton, 1978.

Dietz, P.E., & Evans, B. Pornographic imagery and prevalence of paraphilia. *American Journal of Psychiatry*, 1982, 139, 1493–1495.

DiVasto, P.V., Pathak, D., & Fishburn, W.R. The

interrelationship for sex guilt, sex behavior, and age in an adult sample. *Archives of Sexual Behavior*, 1981, *10*, 119–122.

Dix, G.E. Determining the continued dangerousness of psychologically abnormal sex offenders. *Journal of Psychiatry and Law*, 1975, *3*, 327–344.

Donnerstein, E. Pornography and violence against women: Experimental studies. *Annals of the New York Academy of Science*, 1980, *347*, 277–288.

Donnerstein, E., & Barrett, G. Effects of erotic stimuli on male aggression toward females. *Journal of Personality and Social Psychology*, 1978, *36*, 180–188.

Donnerstein, E., & Berkowitz, L. Victim reactions in aggressive erotic films as a factor in violence against women. *Journal of Personality and Social Psychology*, 1981, *41*, 710–724.

Ellis, E.M., Atkeson, B.M., & Calhoun, K.S. An assessment of long-term reaction to rape. *Journal of Abnormal Psychology*, 1981, *90*, 263–266.

Feild, H.S. Attitudes toward rape: A comparative analysis of police, rapists, crisis counselors, and citizens. *Journal of Personality and Social Psychology*, 1978, *36*, 156–179.

Feldman-Summers, S., & Ashworth, C.D. Factors related to intentions to report a rape. *The Journal of Social Issues*, 1981, *37*, 53–70.

Fisher, G., & Rivlin, E. Psychological needs of rapists. *British Journal of Criminology*, 1971, *11*, 182–185.

Freund, K. Diagnosis and treatment of forensically significant anomalous erotic preferences. *Canadian Journal of Criminology and Corrections*, 1976, *18*, 181–189.

Freund, K., Scher, H., Campbell, K., Hucker, S., Ben-Aron, J., & Heasman, G. *The preferential rape pattern*, in preparation.

Freund, K., Scher, H., & Hucker, S. The courtship disorders. *Archives of Sexual Behavior*, in press.

Frisbie, L.V. Treated sex offenders who reverted to sexually deviant behavior. *Federal Probation*, 1965, *29*, 52–57.

Frisbie, L.V., & Dondis, E.H. *Recidivism among treated sex offenders* (Mental Health Research Monograph, No. 5). Sacramento: California Department of Mental Hygiene, 1965.

Gadpaille, W.J. Cross species and cross-cultural contributions to understanding homosexual activity. *Archives of General Psychiatry*, 1980, 37, 349–356.

Gager, N., & Schurr, C. *Sexual assault: Confronting rape in America*. New York: Grosset, and Dunlap, 1976.

Gebhard, P.H. Fetishism and sadomasochism. In J. Masserman (Ed.). *Dynamics of deviant sexuality*. New York: Grune and Stratton, 1969.

Gebhard, P.H., Gagnon, J.H., Pomeroy, W.B., & Christenson, C.V. *Sex Offenders: An analysis of types*. New York: Harper and Row, 1965.

Geis, G., & Geis, R. Rape in Stockholm. Is permissiveness relevant? *Criminology*, 1979, *17*, 311–322.

Geller, S.H. The sexually assaulted female: innocent victim or temptress? *Canada's Mental Health*, 1977, 25, 26–29.

Glover, E. Aggression and sado-masochism. In I. Rosen (Ed.), *The pathology and treatment of sexual deviation: A methodological approach*. London: Oxford University Press, 1964.

Goldstein, M. Brain research and violent behavior. *Archives of Neurology*, 1974, *30*, 1–35.

Goldstein, M.J., & Kant, H.S. (1973). *Pornography and sexual deviance*. Berkeley: University of California Press, 1973.

Goldstein, M., Kant, H., Judd, L., Rice, C., & Green, R. Experience with pornography: Rapists, pedophiles, homosexuals, transsexuals, and controls. *Archives of Sexual Behavior*, 1971, *1*, 1–15.

Goy, R.W., & McEwen, B.S. *Sexual differentiation of the brain*. Cambridge, MA: The MIT Press, 1980.

Gray, K.G., & Mohr, J.W. Follow-up of male sexual offenders. In R. Slovenko (Ed.), *Sexual behavior and the law*. Springfield, IL: Thomas, 1965.

Groth, A.N., & Birnbaum, H.J. *Men who rape: The psychology of the offender*. New York: Plenum, 1979.

Groth, A.N., & Burgess, A.W. Male rape: offenders and victims. *American Journal of Psychiatry*, 1980, *137*, 806–810.

Groth, A.N., Burgess, A.W., & Holmstrom, L.L. Rape: Power, anger and sexuality. *American Journal of Psychiatry*, 1977, *134*, 1239–1243.

Groth, A.N., & Cohen, M.L. Aggressive sexual offenders: diagnosis and treatment. In A.N. Burgess & A. Lazare (Eds.), *Community mental health: Target populations*. Englewood Cliffs, NJ: Prentice-Hall, 1976.

Heim, N. Sexual behavior of castrated sex offenders. *Archives of Sexual Behavior*, 1981, *10*, 11–20.

Heim, N., & Hursch, C.J. Castration for sex offenders: Treatment or punishment? A review and critique of recent European literature. *Archives of Sexual Behavior*, 1979, 8, 281–304.

Heller, M.S. The mentally ill offender—The question of dangerousness. *Prison Journal*, 1969, *6*, 6–12.

Henn, F.A., Herjanic, M., & Vanderpearl, R.H. Forensic psychiatry: Profile of two types of sex offenders. *American Journal of Psychiatry*, 1976, *133*, 694–696.

Hollis, K.L. Pavlovian conditioning of signal-centered action patterns and autonomic behavior: A biological analysis of function. *Advances in the Study of Behavior*, 1982, *12*, 1–64.

Hostetler, J.A., & Huntington, G.E. *The Hutterites in North America*. Toronto: Holt, Rinehart and Winston, 1980.

Howell, L.M. Clinical and research impressions regarding murder and sexuality perverse crimes. *Psychothera. Psychosom.*, 1972, *21*, 156–159.

Hursch, C.J. *The trouble with rape*. Chicago: Nelson Hall, 1977.

Jensen, D.E., Prandoni, J.R., & Abudabbeh, N.N. Figure drawings by sex offenders and a random sample of offenders. *Perceptual and Motor Skills*, 1971, *32*, 295–300.

Jensen, G.D. Human sexual behavior in primate perspective. In J. Zubin & J. Money (Eds.), *Contemporary sexual behavior: Critical issues in the 1970s*. Baltimore: Johns Hopkins University Press, 1973.

Jones, C., & Aronson, E. Attribution of fault to a rape victim as a function of respectability of the victim. *Journal of Personality and Social Psychology*, 1973, *26*, 415–419.

Kanin, E.J. Male aggression in dating-courtship relations. *American Journal of Sociology*, 1957, *63*, 197–204.

Kardener, S.H. Rape fantasies. *Journal of Religion and Health*, 1975, *14*, 50–57.

Kasinsky, R.G. Rape: A normal act? *The Canadian Forum*, 1975, *55*, 18–22.

Kercher, G.A., & Walker, C.E. Reactions of convicted rapists to sexually explicit stimuli. *Journal of Abnormal Psychology*, 1973, *81*, 46–50.

Kilpatrick, D.G., Resick, P., & Veronen, L. Effects of a rape experience: A longitudinal study. *The Journal of Social Issues*, 1981, *37*, 105–122.

Kirkpatrick, C., & Kanin, E. Male sex aggression on a university campus. *American Sociological Review*, 1957, *22*, 52–58.

Knight, R., Prentky, R., Schneider, B., & Rosenberg, R. Linear causal modeling of adaptation and criminal history in sex offenders. In K. Van Dusen & S. Mednick (Eds.), *Antecedents of antisocial behavior*. Boston: Marlinus Nijhoff Co., 1983.

Konecni, V.J., Mulcahy, E.M., & Ebbesen, E.G. Prison or mental hospital: Factors affecting the processing of persons suspected of being "mentally disordered sex offenders." In P.D. Lipsitt & B.D. Sales (Eds.), *New directions in psychological research*. Toronto: Van Nostrand, 1980.

Kozol, H.L. Myths about the sex offender. *Medical Aspects of Human Sexuality*, 1971, *5*, 50–62.

Kozol, H.L., Cohen, M.I., & Garofalo, R.F. The criminally dangerous sex offender. *New England Journal of Medicine*, 1966, *275*, 79–84.

Krisak, J., Murphy, W.D., & Stalgaitis, S. Reliability issues in the penile assessment of incarcerants. *Journal of Behavioral Assessment*, 1981, *3*, 199–207.

Kutchinsky, B. Deviance and criminality: The case of voyeur in a peeper's paradise. *Diseases of the Nervous System*, 1976, 145–151.

Langevin, R. *Sexual strands: Understanding and treating sexual anomalies in men*. Hillsdale, NJ: Erlbaum, 1983.

Langevin, R., & Martin, M. Can erotic responses be classically conditioned? *Behavior Therapy*, 1975, *6*, 350–355.

Langevin, R., Patich, D., Hucker, S., Newman, S., Ramsay, G., Pope, S., Geller, G., & Anderson, C. The effects of assertiveness training provera and sex of therapist in the treatment of genital exhibitionism. *Journal of Behavior Therapy and Experimental Psychiatry*, 1979, *10*, 275–282.

Langevin, R., Patich, D., & Russon, A. Are rapists sexually anomalous, aggresive or both? *Archives of Sexual Behavior*, in press.

Lansky, D., & Wilson, G.T. Alcohol, expectations and sexual arousal in males: An information processing analysis. *Journal of Abnormal Psychology*, 1981, *90*, 35–45.

Laschet, U. Antiandrogen in the treatment of sex offenders: mode of action and therapeutic outcome. In J. Zubin & J. Money (Eds.), *Contemporary sexual behavior: Critical issues in the 1970s*. Baltimore: Johns Hopkins University Press, 1973.

Law Reform Commission of Canada. *Sexual offences* (Working paper 22). Ottawa, Canada: Author, 1978.

Lester, D. Rape and social structure. *Psychological Reports*, 1974, *35*, 146.

Lester, D. *Unusual sexual behavior: the standard deviations*. Springfield, IL: Thomas, 1975.

LeVine, R.A. Gusii sex offences: A study in social control. *American Anthropologist*, 1959, *61*, 965–990.

Levine, S., & Koenig, J. (Eds.). *Why men rape: Interviews with convicted rapists*. Toronto: Macmillan, 1980.

Lipton, M.A. Fact and myth: The work of the commission on obscenity and pornography. In J. Zubin & J. Money (Eds.), *Contemporary sexual behavior: Critical issues in the 1970s*. Baltimore: Johns Hopkins University Press, 1973.

Littner, N. The psychology of the sex offender: causes, treatment, prognosis. *Police Law Quarterly*, 1974, *3*, 5–31.

MacDonald, J.M. *Rape: Offenders and their victims*. Springfield, IL: Thomas, 1971.

MacIndoe, I., & Pengelly, E. (1976). *The behavioral, emotional and attitudinal development program* (Research Report). St. Peter, MN: Minnesota Security Hospital, 1976.

MacLean, P.D. New findings on brain function and sociosexual behavior. In J. Zubin & J. Money (Eds.), *Contemporary sexual behavior: Critical issues in the 1970s*. Baltimore: Johns Hopkins University Press, 1973.

Malamuth, N.M. Attitudes and sexual arousal as predictors of aggression against women: A structural equation analysis. Paper presented at the Canadian Psychological Association meeting in Toronto, June 1981.(a)

Malamuth, N.M. Rape fantasies as a function of exposure to violent sexual stimuli. *Archives of Sexual Behavior*, 1981, *10*, 33–48.(b)

Malamuth, N.M. Rape proclivity among males. *The Journal of Social Issues*, 1981, *4*, 138–156.(c)

Malamuth, N.M., & Check, J.V.P. Penile tumescence and perceptual responses to rape as a function of victim's perceived reactions. *Journal of Applied Social Psychology*, 1980, *10*, 528–547.(a)

Malamuth, N.M., & Check, J.V.P. Sexual arousal to rape and consenting depictions: The importance of the woman's arousal. *Journal of Abnormal Psychology*, 1980, *89*, 763–766.(b)

Malamuth, N.M., & Check, J.V.P. The effects of mass media exposure on acceptance of violence against women: A field experiment. *Journal of Research in Personality*, 1981, *15*, 436–446.

Malamuth, N.M., & Check, J.V.P. Sexual arousal to rape depictions. Individual differences. *Journal of Abnormal Psychology*, 1983, *92*, 55–67.

Malamuth, N.M., Haber, S., & Feshbach, S. Testing hypotheses regarding rape: Exposure to sexual violence, sex differences and the "normality" of rapists. *Journal of Research in Personality*, 1980, *14*, 121–137.

Malamuth, N.M., Heim, N., & Feshbach, S. Sexual responsiveness of college students to rape depictions. Inhibitory and disinhibitory effects. *Journal of Personality and Social Psychology*, 1980, *38*, 399–408.

Malamuth, N.M., & Spinner, B. A longitudinal content analysis of sexual violence in the best-selling erotic magazines. *The Journal of Sex Research*, 1980, *16*, 226–237.

Malinowski, B. *The sexual life of savages in North-Western Melanesia*. New York: Eugenics Publishing Co., 1929.

Marcus, A.M. A multi-disciplinary two-part study of those individuals designated dangerous sexual offenders held in federal custody in British Columbia, Canada. *Canadian Journal of Corrections*, 1966, *2*, 90–103.

Marks, I.M. Management of sexual disorders. In H. Leitenberg (Ed.), *Handbook of behavior modification and behavior therapy.* Englewood Cliffs, NJ: Prentice-Hall, 1976.

Marler, P., & Hamilton, W.J. *Mechanisms of animal behavior.* New York: Wiley, 1967.

Marques, J.K. *Effects of victim resistance strategies on the sexual arousal and attitudes of violent rapists.* Paper presented at the 11th International conference on behavior modification, Banff, Alberta, March 1979.

Marsh, J.T., Hilliard, J., & Liechti, R. A sexual deviation scale for the MMPI. *Journal of Consulting Psychology*, 1955, *19*, 55–59.

Marshall, W.L., & Barbaree, H.E. The reduction of deviant arousal: Satiation treatment for sexual aggressors. *Criminal Justice and Behavior*, 1978, *5*, 294–303.

Marshall, W.L., Earls, C.M., Segal, Z., & Darke, J.L. A behavioral program for the assessment and treatment of sexual aggressors. In K. Craig & R. McMahon (Eds.), *Advances in clinical behavior therapy.* New York: Bruner/Mazel, in press.

McCaldon, R.J. Rape. *Canadian Journal of Corrections*, 1967, *9*, 37–59.

McGuire, R.J., Carlisle, J.M., & Young, B.G. Sexual deviation as conditioned behavior: A hypothesis. *Behaviour Research and Therapy*, 1965, *2*, 185–190.

McKinney, F., Derrickson, S.R., & Mineau, P. Forced copulation in waterfowl. *Behaviour*, in press.

Michael, R.P. Biological factors in the organization and expression of sexual behaviour. In I. Rosen (Ed.), *The pathology and treatment of sexual deviation: A methodological approach.* London: Oxford University Press, 1964.

Monahan, J. Prediction research and the emergency commitment of dangerous mentally ill persons: A reconsideration. *American Journal of Psychiatry*, 1978, *135–201*.

Monahan, J. *The clinical prediction of violent behavior.* Rockville, MD: National Institute of Mental Health, 1981.

Nelson, E.C. Pornography and sexual aggression. In M. Yaffe & E. Nelson (Eds.), *The influence of pornography on behavior.* New York: Academic, 1982.

Orno, A.M. Social, psychological and surgical treatment for sexual and chronic criminals. *Canadian Journal of Corrections*, 1965, *7*, 414–422.

Ortmann, J. The treatment of sexual offenders: Castration and antihormone therapy. *International Journal of Law and Psychiatry*, 1980, *3*, 443–451.

Otterbein, K.F. A cross-cultural study of rape. *Aggressive Behavior*, 1979, *5*, 425–435.

Pacht, A.R. The rapist in treatment: professional myths and psychological realities. In M.J. Walker & S.L. Brodsky (Eds.), *Sexual assault: The victim and the rapist.* Toronto: Lexington, 1976.

Pacht, A.R., & Cowden, J.E. An exploratory study of five hundred sex offenders. *Criminal Justice and Behavior*, 1974, 13–20.

Pacht, A.R., Halleck, S.L., & Ehrmann, J.C. Diagnosis and treatment of the sexual offender: A nine-year study. *American Journal of Psychiatry*, 1962, *118*, 802–808.

Parks, R.D.M. Six men tell why "I am a rapist." *Sexology*, 1974, 12–15.

Perdue, W.C., & Lester, D. Personality characteristics of rapists. *Perceptual and Motor Skills*, 1972, *35*, 514.

Peters, J.J., & Roether, H.A. Group psychotherapy for probationed sex offenders. In H.L.P. Resnik & M.E. Wolfgang (Eds.), *Sexual behaviors: Social, clinical, and legal aspects.* Boston: Little, Brown, 1972.

Peters, J.J., & Sadoff, R.L. Psychiatric services for sex offenders on probation. *Federal Probation*, 1971, *35*, 33–37.

Peterson, M.A., Braiker, H.B., & Polich, S.M. *Doing crime: A survey of California prison inmates.* Santa Monica: Rand, 1980.

Pillard, R.C., Poumadere, J., & Carretta, R.A. Is homosexuality familial? A review, some data and a suggestion. *Archives of Sexual Behavior*, 1981, *10*, 465–475.

Pillard, R.C., Poumadere, J., & Carretta, R.A. A family study of sexual orientation. *Archives of Sexual Behavior*, 1982, *11*, 511–520.

Prentky, R.A. *Neurochemical prototypes for sexual aggression: Psychopathic and episodic offenders.* Paper presented at NATO symposium on "Biosocial bases of antisocial behavior," Skiathos, Greece, September 1982.

Prentky, R.A. The neurochemistry and endocrinology of sexual aggression: Review and methatheory. In J. Gunn & D. Farrington (Eds.), *Current research in forensic psychiatry and psychology.* Sussex, England: Wiley, 1984.

Quinsey, V.L. The assessment and treatment of child molesters: A review. *Canadian Psychological Review*, 1977, *18*, 204–220.

Quinsey, V.L. The baserate problem and the prediction of dangerousness: A reappraisal. *Journal of Psychiatry & Law*, 1980, *8*, 329–340.

Quinsey, V.L. Prediction of recidivism and the evaluation of treatment programs for sexual offenders. In S. Simon-Jones (Ed.), *Sexual aggression and the law.* Burnaby, British Columbia: Simon Fraser University Criminology Research Centre, 1983.

Quinsey, V.L., & Ambtman, R. Psychiatric assessments of the dangerousness of mentally ill offenders. *Crime and Justice*, 1978, *6*, 249–257.

Quinsey, V.L., & Ambtman, R. Variables affecting psychiatrists' and teachers' assessments of the dangerousness of mentally ill offenders. *Journal of Consulting & Clinical Psychology*, 1979, *47*, 353–362.

Quinsey, V.L., Arnold, L.S., & Pruesse, M.G. MMPI profiles of men referred for pre-trial psychiatric assessment as a function of offense type. *Journal of Clinical Psychology*, 1980, *36*, 410–417.

Quinsey, V.L., & Chaplin, T.C. Penile responses to non-sexual violence among rapists. *Criminal Justice and Behavior*, 1982, *9*, 372–384.

Quinsey, V.L., & Chaplin, T.C. Stimulus control of rapists' and non-sex-offenders' sexual arousal. *Behavioral Assessment*, 1984.

Quinsey, V.L., Chaplin, T.C., & Varney, G.W. A comparison of rapists' and non-sex-offenders' sexual preferences for mutually consenting sex, rape, and physical abuse of women. *Behavioral Assessment,* 1984, *3,* 127–135.

Quinsey, V.L., & Marshall, W.L. Procedures for reducing inappropriate sexual arousal: An evaluation review. In J.G. Greer & I.R. Stuart (Eds.), *The sexual aggressor: Current perspectives on treatment.* New York: Van Nostrand Reinhold, 1983.

Quinsey, V.L., Upfold, D., & Chaplin, T.C. *Sexual arousal to nonsexual violence and sadomasochistic themes among rapists and non-sex offenders.* In preparation.

Rachman, S. Sexual fetishism: an experimental analogue. *Psychological Record,* 1966, *16,* 293–296.

Rachman, S., & Hodgson, R.J. Experimentally induced "sexual fetishism:" A replication and development. *Psychological Record,* 1968, *18,* 25–27.

Rada, R.T. Alcoholism and forcible rape. *American Journal of Psychiatry,* 1975, *132,* 444–446.

Rada, R.T. Commonly asked questions about the rapist. *Medical Aspects of Sexuality,* 1977, *46,* 47–56.

Rada, R.T. (Ed.). *Clinical aspects of the rapist.* New York: Grune and Stratton, 1978.

Rada, R.T., Laws, D.R., & Kellner, R. Plasma testosterone levels in the rapist. *Psychosomatic Medicine,* 1976, *28,* 257–268.

Rader, C.M. MMPI profile types of exposers, rapists, and assaulters in a court services population. *Journal of Consulting and Clinical Psychology,* 1977, *45,* 61–69.

Radzinowicz, L. *Sexual offences: A report of the Cambridge Department of Criminal Science.* Toronto: MacMillan, 1957.

Rasmussen, D.R. Pair-bond strength and stability and reproductive success. *Psychological Review,* 1981, *88,* 274–290.

Revitch, E. Sex murder and the potential sex murderer. *Diseases of the Nervous System,* 1965, *26,* 640–646.

Riger, S., & Gordon, M.T. The structure of rape prevention beliefs. *Personality and Social Psychology Bulletin,* 1979, *5,* 186–190.

Riger, S., & Gordon, M.T. The fear of rape: A study in social control. *The Journal of Social Issues,* 1981, *37,* 71–92.

Riger, S., Gordon, M.T., & LeBailly, R.K. Coping with urban crime: Women's use of precautionary behaviors. *American Journal of Community Psychology,* 1982, *10,* 369–386.

Roberts, L.M., & Pacht, A.R. Termination of inpatient treatment of sex deviates: Psychiatric, social and legal factors. *American Journal of Psychiatry,* 1965, *121,* 873–880.

Rosenberg, R. *An empirical determination of sexual offender subtypes.* Paper presented at the meeting of the American Psychological Association in Los Angeles, August 1981.

Rubin, H.B., & Henson, D.E. Effects of drugs on male sexual function. In T. Thompson & P.B. Dews (Eds.), *Advances in behavioral pharmacology,* 1979, *2,* 65–86.

Ruff, C.F., Templer, D.I., & Ayers, J.L. The intelligence of rapists. *Archives of Sexual Behavior,* 1976, *5,* 327–329.

Sanday, P.R. The socio-cultural context of rape: A cross-cultural study. *The Journal of Social Issues,* 1981, *37,* 5–27.

Sarafian, R.A. Treatment of the criminally dangerous sex offender. *Federal Probation,* 1963, *27,* 52–59.

Scanlon, R.L. Canadian crime rates: Sources and trends. *Impact,* 1982, *1,* 1–10.

Schiff, A.F. A statistical evaluation of rape. *Forensic Science,* 1973, *2,* 339–349.

Schiff, A.F. Rape in foreign countries. *Medical Trial Techniques Quarterly,* 1974, *20,* 66–74.

Schwartz, B. The effect in Philadelphia of Pennsylvania's increased penalties for rape and attempted rape. *Journal of Criminal Law, Criminology and Police Science,* 1968, *59,* 509–515.

Schwartz, P. The scientific study of rape. In R. Green & J. Weiner (Eds.), *Methodology in sex research.* Rockville, MD: NIMH, 1980.

Silver, S.N. Outpatient treatment for sexual offenders. *Social Work,* 1976, 134–140.

Smith, C.E. Correctional treatment of the sexual deviate. *American Journal of Psychiatry,* 1968, *125,* 615–621.

Soothill, K.L., Jack, A., & Gibbens, T.C.N. Rape: a 22-year cohort study. *Medicine, Science, and the Law,* 1976, *16,* 62–69.

Spence, J.T., Helmreich, R., & Stapp, J. A short version of the Attitudes Towards Women Scale (ATW). *Bulletin of the Psychonomic Society,* 1973, *48,* 587–589.

Spodak, M.K., Falck, Z.A., & Rappeport, J.R. The hormonal treatment of paraphiliacs with depo-provera. *Criminal Justice and Behavior,* 1978, *5,* 304–314.

Statistics Canada. *Crime and traffic enforcement statistics.* Ottawa, Canada: Author, 1981.

Stermac, L., & Quinsey, V.L. *The social competence of incarcerated sexual assaulters.* Manuscript submitted for publication, 1984.

Sturup, G.K. Treatment of sexual offenders in Herstedvester Denmark: The rapists. *Acta Psychiatrica Scandanavica,* 1968, *44,* 1–62.

Sturup, G.K. Castration: The total treatment. In H.L.P. Resnik & M.E. Wolfgang (Eds.), *Sexual behaviors: Social, clinical and legal aspects.* Boston: Little, Brown, 1972.

Swigert, V.L., Farrell, R.A., & Yoels, W.C. Sexual homicide: Social, psychological, and legal aspects. *Archives of Sexual Behavior,* 1976, *5,* 391–401.

Symons, D. *The evolution of human sexuality.* New York: Oxford, 1979.

Taylor, S.P., & Smith, I. Aggression as a function of sex of victim and male subject's attitude toward women. *Psychological Reports,* 1974, *35,* 1095–1098.

Thornhill, R. Rape in Panorpa scorpionflies and a general rape hypothesis. *Animal Behavior,* 1980, *28,* 52–59.

Thornhill, R., & Thornhill, N.W. Human rape: An evolutionary analysis. *Ethology and Sociobiology,* in press.

Thornton, W.E., & Pray, B.J. The portrait of a murderer. *Diseases of the Nervous System,* 1975, 176–178.

Titman, R.D., & Lowther, J.K. The breeding behavior of a crowded population of mallards. *Canadian Journal of Zoology,* 1975, *53,* 1270–1283.

Toner, B. *The facts of rape.* London: Hutchinson, 1977.

Turnbull, C.M. *The forest people: A study of the pygmies of the Congo.* New York: Simon and Schuster, 1961.

Turnbull, C.M. *The mountain people*. New York: Simon and Schuster, 1972.

Turner, S.M., & VanHasselt, V.B. Multiple behavioral treatment in a sexually aggressive male. *Behavior Therapy and Experimental Psychiatry*, 1979, *10*, 343–348.

Vera, H., Barnard, G.W., & Holzer, C. The intelligence of rapists: New data. *Archives of Sexual Behavior*, 1979, *8*, 375–378.

Walker, P.A., & Meyer, W.J. Medroxyprogesterone acetate treatment for paraphiliac sex offenders. In J.R. Hays et al. (Eds.), *Violence and the violent individual*. New York: Spectrum, 1981.

West, D.J., Roy, C., & Nichols, F.L. *Understanding sexual attacks: A study based upon a group of rapists undergoing psychotherapy*. London: Heinemann, 1978.

Wheeler, S. Sex offenses: A sociological critique. *Law and Contemporary Problems*, 1960, *25*, 258–278.

Whitman, W.P., & Quinsey, V.L. Heterosocial skill training for institutionalized rapists and child molesters. *Canadian Journal of Behavioural Science*, 1981, *13*, 105–114.

Wile, I.S. Sex offenders and sex offenses. Classification and treatment. *Journal of Criminal Psychopathology*, 1941, *3*, 11–31.

Williams, A.H. The psychopathology and treatment of sexual murderers. In I. Rosen (Ed.), *The pathology and treatment of sexual deviation: A methodological approach*. London: Oxford University Press, 1964.

Williams, A.H. Rape-murder. In R. Slovenko (Ed.), *Sexual behavior and the law*. Springfield, IL: Thomas, 1965.

Wilson, G.T., & Lawson, D.M. Expectancies, alcohol, and sexual arousal in male social drinkers. *Journal of Abnormal Psychology*, 1976, *85*, 587–594.

Wright, R. Rape and physical violence. In D.J. West (Ed.), *Sex offenders in the criminal justice system*. Cambridge, England: Cropwood, 1980.

Wydra, A., Marshall, W.L., Earls, C.M., & Barbaree, H.E. Identification of cues and control of sexual arousal by rapists. *Behaviour Research and Therapy*, in press.

Yates, E., Barbaree, H.E., & Marshall, W.L. *Anger and deviant sexual arousal*. Unpublished manuscript.

4.
Behavioral Expertise in Jury Selection

Thomas L. Hafemeister
Bruce D. Sales
David L. Suggs

ABSTRACT. This chapter critically reviews the continuing efforts to develop and evaluate the validity and reliability of jury selection techniques. A definition and description of the voir dire process is provided, as well as the uses and limitations of it as traditionally conducted. To remedy these limitations, various standardized techniques, which rely heavily on the expertise of behavioral scientists, have been devised to enable attorneys to more effectively conduct the voir dire. The three major strategies described are: the demographic rating system (community surveys), juror investigation (information networks), and in-court observations of prospective jurors. A detailed description of the theoretical and empirical bases for these approaches, their uses during the voir dire, and some practical considerations for application are included. Finally, criticisms of these approaches to jury selection, an appraisal of their effectiveness, and the ethical, legal and international implications are presented.

SOMMAIRE. Ce chapitre fournit une analyse critique des efforts qui sont faits continuellement pour développer les techniques de sélection du jury et pour évaluer leur validité et leur fiabilité. Il contient une définition et une description de la procédure de voir dire et un exposé de ses applications et de ses limites lors de son déroulement traditionnel. Pour corriger ces limites, différentes techniques standardisées faisant appel, dans une large mesure, aux connaissances des behavioristes, ont été mises au point pour permettre aux avocats de mener le voir dire de façon plus efficace. Les trois principales stratégies présentées ici sont le système de classement démographique (enquêtes sur la collectivité), l'enquête sur les jurés (réseaux d'information) et l'observation des futurs jurés au sein même de la cour. L'étude comprend une description fouillée des données théoriques et empiriques relatives à ces stratégies, de leur utilisation dans le voir dire et quelques considérations pratiques pour leur application. Enfin, les auteurs se livrent à une critique de ces approches de la sélection des jurés, à une évaluation de leur efficacité et ils présentent leurs implications d'ordre moral, juridique et international.

Introduction

Some commentators assert that the selection of a jury is one of the most important parts of a jury trial and is often central to the final outcome (see Hawrish & Tate, 1974–75). Thus, it is not surprising that trial attorneys have sought the aid of behavioral and social science experts (hereinafter behavioral experts) to help them in this process in the hope of gaining an advantage over their opponents.

This manuscript integrates, develops and refines prior writings on this topic by Bruce D. Sales: Berman & Sales (1977); Herbsleb, Sales, & Berman (1979); Suggs & Sales (1978a, 1978b, 1980).

The entrance of social scientists into the arena of jury selection is generally considered to have occurred in the winter of 1971–1972. The trial was that of anti-war activists Philip Berrigan and seven others accused of conspiring to destroy draft board records, kidnap Henry Kissinger, and blow up heating tunnels in Washington, D.C. Harrisburg, Pennsylvania, the site for the trial, was a conservative area and one that many people believed to be prejudiced against anti-war activists. In view of this, several social scientists volunteered to assist in jury selection in order to counter these possible prejudices in the community. The trial resulted in a hung jury, with the government eventually dropping all charges. (Frederick, 1978, p. 578).

Other authors trace the beginnings of scientific jury selection back either to the early 1950s when well-known attorneys such as F. Lee Bailey or Melvin Belli utilized the service of a "hypnoanalyst" in a number of famous trials, or back to the 1968 trial of Black Panther Huey Newton when a more traditional panel of behavioral experts was called upon to develop sophisticated *voir dire* questions and tactics to uncover racism and prejudice (Hans & Vidmar, 1982). Nevertheless, it is since the Harrisburg Eight trial that behavioral experts have participated in numerous civil and criminal trials.

The case which perhaps drew the most attention to the use of behavioral expertise in jury selection involved the trial of John Mitchell and Maurice Stans in 1974 on charges of conspiracy and perjury. In this post-Watergate litigation, the defense team turned to a market research consultant. Following their acquittal, Etzioni (1974) advanced the argument that scientific jury selection

threatened the integrity of the jury system by insidiously tampering with it, and increased the advantages of the rich and celebrated over the poor and obscure. Etzioni concluded, "Man has taken a new bite from the apple of knowledge, and it is doubtful whether we will all be better for it" (p. 28).

A steadily expanding body of legal, behavioral and social science literature has been developing which attempts to formalize these jury selection techniques and probes the validity and reliability of such efforts. The purpose of this chapter is to critically review the *voir dire* techniques suggested and used by these experts.

Voir Dire

Definition and Description

The sixth amendment guarantees to each criminal defendant the right to trial by an impartial jury drawn from a cross-section of the community.[1] In the federal system, the seventh amendment extends the right to a jury trial to suits at common law (i.e., any suits that are not of equity or admiralty jurisdiction).[2] The states are not required by the federal Constitution to grant the right to a jury in civil suits based solely on state law, but all states make provisions for such a right in their own constitutions.

One of the means by which the right to trial by an impartial jury is protected is through the process of *voir dire*. This term has been translated to mean "to speak the truth" or "to see what he or she says," and refers to the early portion of the trial in which prospective jurors are questioned by the judge or the attorneys, or both, to determine whether any of them are biased, prejudiced, or in any other way unqualified to serve as jurors.[3]

---

[1]The right was made applicable to defendants in state courts by the decision in *Duncan* v. *Louisiana*, 391 U.S. 145 (1968), on the theory that such a right was necessary to secure the individual's right to due process of law as guaranteed under the 14th amendment.

[2]See *Ross* v. *Bernhard*, 396 U.S. 531 (1970); *Curtis* v. *Loether*, 415 U.S. 189 (1974); and *Pernell* v. *Southall Realty*, 416 U.S. 363 (1974).

[3]A prejudiced juror is one who has actually pre-judged the case, whereas a biased juror has an inclination to favor one side rather than the other. The prejudiced juror may be eliminated as a matter of law but in order to successfully challenge a prospective juror for cause on the ground of bias, it must be shown that the bias is of such a magnitude as to lead to the natural inference that the prospective juror will not *act* impartially. See *Flowers* v. *Flowers*, 397 S.W. 2d 121 (Tex. Ct. of Civil App., 1965).

Note that *voir dire* also refers to the questioning of a witness to determine competency, bias, etc. For purposes of this article, however, we will use it only to refer to the questioning of prospective jurors. For an in-depth discussion of the mechanics and techniques involved in the *voir dire*, both as it has been traditionally employed and in light of recent developments, see Ginger (1980).

The *voir dire* has frequently been referred to as jury selection. This phrase is inappropriate because suitable jurors are not selected to sit on the jury; rather, those jurors deemed unsuitable are prevented from sitting by the judge and the attorneys after the jurors have been questioned. This process is known as exercising challenges—the challenge for cause and the peremptory challenge.

The challenge for cause is exercised whenever it can be shown that the juror does not satisfy the statutory requirements for jury service (e.g., age, residency, and occupational requirements)[4] or when it can be shown that the prospective juror is so biased or prejudiced that he/she cannot render a fair and impartial verdict based on the law and evidence as presented at trial. An unlimited number of challenges for cause may be exercised during the *voir dire*. When the challenge is made by an attorney, the judge determines its validity; in addition, the judge may remove a juror for cause *sua sponte* (on his/her own volition).

Successful challenges for cause on the grounds of bias or prejudice are relatively difficult for attorneys to obtain. First, assuming that the juror is willing to admit to being biased or prejudiced, the judge may decide that the juror is not so biased or prejudiced as to be incompetent to serve on the jury as a matter of law. Second, if the juror admits that he/she has formed an opinion about the case, it is standard procedure to ask if he/she can set aside that opinion and decide the case on the basis of the evidence to be presented. Since all of us like to think we can be fair, it is the rare juror indeed who will admit to being unable to set aside an already-formed opinion. As a result, challenges for cause are rarely sustained when the juror maintains that he/she can be impartial. Third, the problem of using challenges for cause to eliminate jurors is further complicated by the fact that "jurors often, either consciously or unconsciously,

lie on *voir dire*" (Broeder, 1965b, p. 538).

Therefore, attorneys must usually rely on the peremptory challenge to secure for their client the least negatively biased jury possible. A peremptory challenge is one exercised by the attorney to excuse a juror where no reason need be given for its use; thus, the respective attorneys may generally use their allotted challenges for whatever tactical reasons they desire. The number of peremptory challenges available to each side is limited either by statute or by the presiding judge in a pretrial conference.[5] Theoretically, after the attorneys have exercised their challenges, those jurors who were most biased will have been eliminated, with the resulting jury being relatively impartial ("Limiting the Peremptory Challenge," 1977).

Purposes

There are three judicially recognized purposes of the *voir dire*. The first is to determine whether the prospective jurors meet the legal and statutory qualifications to sit as jurors (i.e., jurors are questioned to determine whether they satisfy the age, residence and other requirements of the jurisdiction) (Amsterdam, Segal, & Miller, 1967). The second purpose is to determine whether prospective jurors can impartially participate in the deliberation of the issues of the case based solely on the law and the evidence presented at trial (Hare, 1968).[6] Nevertheless, the extent of questioning allowed for this purpose is restricted to determining if the juror is biased or prejudiced as a matter of law. Often, when the judge conducts questioning of this type, it will simply take the form: " 'Can you be fair?' Once the juror has answered 'Yes,' everything else is considered irrelevant and the judge passes on to the next juror, even though Adolph Hitler himself would have answered that

---

[4]A person becomes eligible for jury duty at the age of majority as governed by state law. Nonresidents are excluded from jury duty and some states exclude various governmental officials and attorneys from serving as jurors. Other grounds for challenges for cause commonly provided for by statute are: conviction of a felony, indictment for a felony within a fixed time, having scruples against capital punishment, relation by blood or affinity to a party in interest, relation by blood or affinity to the prosecutor or defense attorney, director or stockholder of a corporate party, previous jury service within one year, solicitation of service as a juror, and having a relationship with a party via partnership, principal/agent, employer/employee, or guardian/ward.

[5]Peremptory challenges are regarded as a privilege granted by legislative authority, and a litigant may exercise them as a matter of right only to the extent authorized by the legislature (see *Kunk* v. *Howell*, 40 Tenn. App. 183, 289 S.W.2d 874 [1956]). The trial judge, however, is usually given the discretion to increase the number of peremptory challenges. For a statistical model for determining the appropriate number of peremptory challenges for each party to a jury trial to ensure fairness, see Kadane and Kairys (1979).

[6]This second purpose is mandated by the sixth amendment guarantee of the right to trial by an impartial jury. See *Witherspoon* v. *Illinois*, 391 U.S. 510, 518, 521, (1968); *Crawford* v. *Bounds*, 395 F.2d 297 (4th Cir., 1968).

question in the affirmative" (Ginger, 1969, p. xxii). Obviously, these first two purposes are associated with establishing a basis for a possible challenge for cause.

The third purpose of the *voir dire* is to provide attorneys with an opportunity to obtain information in order to make an intelligent exercise of their right to peremptory challenge of prospective jurors ("American Bar," 1968; "Court Control," 1965; Hare, 1968; MacGutman, 1972; Van Dyke, 1976).[7] The scope of questioning for this purpose is much broader than that associated with challenges for cause. For example, under this rubric, questioning is often allowed to probe such things as the juror's occupation, marital status, number of children, past jury service, residence, exposure to news coverage of the case, attitudes toward the death penalty, degree of belief in the concept that the defendant is innocent until proven guilty, and attitudes toward racial minorities:[8]

The broader scope of permissible questioning for this purpose results from the importance of peremptory challenges, and the courts have frequently recognized this importance. In *Swain* v. *Alabama*, 380 U.S. 202 (1965), for example, the United States Supreme Court stated: "The persistence of peremptories and their extensive use demonstrate the long and widely held belief that peremptory challenge is a necessary part of trial by jury" (p. 219). This use of the *voir dire* is based on the recognition by the law that:

the rules of evidence can only partly limit the extent to which a juror's bias affects his deliberation. The tests which the law furnishes to the jury for weighing evidence are crude and imperfect and provide few internal checks on jury prejudice. There is a critical area in every case, where a juror must rely on his own experience to reach a decision. If bias permeates a juror's thinking, it may distort the importance of evidence consistent with it. . . . Bias may, therefore, be a fact of singular importance in the case. (MacGutman, 1972, p. 303–04).

The notion that verdicts are frequently affected by the jurors' values and biases is supported by a report that "in about two-thirds of all cases the jurors are likely to differ over the significance of the evidence presented to them in the trial. In only about one-third of the trials is the jury unanimous on the first ballot; in two-thirds of the cases the jurors differ in their vote" (Zeisel & Diamond, 1976, p. 173). Thus, the attorneys' task during the *voir dire* is to obtain sufficient information from and about the prospective jurors to identify those individuals that the attorneys feel are prejudiced or biased against their client or who will not be receptive to the arguments they wish to raise in the trial.[9] The attorneys must then exercise their challenges for cause or peremptory challenges in order to remove these undesirable prospective jurors. As already noted, when this process of elimination is carried out by counsel for both sides of the lawsuit, ideally, a fair and impartial jury is secured.[10]

---

[7]See *Evans* v. *Mason*, 82 Ariz. 40, 308 P.2d 245 (1957). Some jurisdictions, however, do not sanction this purpose, and allow only questions which might uncover legal grounds for challenges for cause (Amsterdam, Segal & Miller, 1967, note 12, § 334). In these jurisdictions, "any enlightenment given by the answers which serves to inform counsel's judgment on the intelligent exercise of peremptory challenges is at best a by-product, and often one suspiciously regarded." (*Id.*) See also Van Dyke, 1976, pp. 89–90.

[8]For general discussions of the proper scope of *voir dire*, see Amsterdam, Segal, and Miller, 1967, §§ 334, 336; Bodin, 1976, p. 225–62; Busch, 1959.

[9]Hans and Vidmar (1982) list three sources of bias which might render one particular juror more susceptible to prejudice than another: (1) dispositions, resulting from personality or experience, that bias them one way or another, regardless of the particular case in question; (2) elements associated with the type of case, such as the defendant or type of crime, that render a juror susceptible to bias; or (3) particular attitudes or knowledge about the specific case in question that induce bias. They note that these biases can be manifested through a number of different modes: (1) encoding and storage of information during a trial; (2) assessments of witness credibility; (3) retrieval of information and reconciliation of inconsistent facts during decision-making; or (4) susceptibility to unwarranted influence by other jurors during jury deliberations. For a similar analysis and a discussion of means for reducing juror bias, see Kaplan and Scherching (1980).

[10]It is possible for an attorney to "pack the jury" where there is an overwhelming community sentiment against one side and the other side has enough peremptory challenges at its disposal to remove all of the prospective jurors who do not follow the community sentiment. Such a circumstance is likely to be rare, however, in light of the availability of motions for a change in venue and the generally limited number of peremptory challenges which are available to each side.

A number of commentators have criticized these information-gathering purposes of the *voir dire* on the grounds that attorneys may abuse these purposes to select a jury biased in favor of their client (Brody, 1957; Imlay, 1973; Maxwell, 1970; Okun, 1968). This criticism falls short, however, if it is remembered that jury selection is a negative process. Those individuals who are deemed unfavorable for whatever reason are rejected, and the first 12 who pass muster by both sides form the jury panel (see "Peremptory Challenges and the Meaning," 1980).

Another author has raised the issue that peremptory challenges are no longer necessary, since reforms in the selection of the jury panel guarantee that jury lists represent a community cross-section and a party's ability to challenge a juror for cause if prejudice is uncovered during the *voir dire* examination may be sufficient to achieve a fair jury without the delay resulting from the use of peremptory challenges (Imlay, 1973). However, studies conducted following the imposition of such reforms have shown that social biases in jury panel selection remain, effectively discriminating against the poor, the young, racial minorities, women, and persons with low and high educational attainment (Alker & Barnard, 1978; Alker, Hosticka, & Mitchell, 1976). Furthermore, as Bermant and Shepard (1981) point out, there are no strong reasons to believe that broad demographic representativeness in juries, by itself, facilitates unbiased findings of fact. Placing 12 unique perspectives on a jury will not negate variations in cognitive abilities, emotional traits, and social attitudes both in regard to the 12 members of the jury as individuals working together as a group, and as in regard to those jurors as representatives of their respective demographic groups. Mere demographic representativeness will not assure the elimination of bias, and a vigorous *voir dire* remains essential to refine the random draw reflected in the jury panel into a less biased group.

In addition to the three information-gathering purposes of the *voir dire* noted above, it is often used for reasons which are not judicially sanctioned. For example, it has been noted that jurors' *voir dire* answers can provide insight into the appropriate manner for conducting the trial proper and for constructing the attorney's closing argument to the jury (Ginger, 1980). In addition, some attorneys abuse the *voir dire* by using it as a means to ingratiate themselves with the jurors and to indoctrinate the jurors to their version of the case before the presentation of evidence (Bermant & Shepard, 1981; Blunk & Sales, 1977; Field, 1965). A minimum level of rapport between the person conducting the *voir dire* and the jurors is necessary for a productive dialogue. However, at the point at which the establishment of effective rapport becomes an attempt at ingratiation, the law deems it unacceptable and mandates that this should be guarded against. Likewise, while the jurors must be given some minimum level of introduction to the facts of the case during the *voir dire* since the questioning cannot take place in a vacuum, and may need to be sensitized about the need to set aside prejudices in order to participate in the trial with an impartial mind, this introduction and sensitization should not be allowed to become indoctrination. The concern of the judiciary over these two unacceptable purposes of *voir dire* may be justified. A study of a number of cases in a midwestern federal district court concludes that attorneys use about 80% of *voir dire* time attempting to indoctrinate the jury panel (Broeder, 1965b).

Effectiveness

Although the *voir dire* is intended to aid the attorneys in identifying and removing biased and prejudiced jurors, how effective are they in conducting it? In a study based on posttrial interviews of 225 people who actually served as jurors in a federal district court, Broeder (1965b) concluded that indoctrination by attorneys often did not appear to succeed. More importantly he concluded that "*voir dire* was grossly ineffective not only in eliminating out 'unfavorable' jurors but even in eliciting the data which would have shown particular jurors as very likely to prove 'unfavorable'" (p. 505). Although in an early study Diamond and Zeisel (Note 1) presented data which indicate that the *voir dire* is effective in eliminating jurors disposed toward conviction, their more recent work (Zeisel & Diamond, 1978) tends to support the harsh assessment of Broeder. Although they conclude that peremptory challenges could have a substantial role in altering the outcome of a trial,[11] they further state:

---

[11]For a criticism of this conclusion based upon an analysis of the underlying methodology and assumptions utilized in the Zeisel and Diamond (1978) experiment, see Bermant and Shepard (1981).

our experiment suggests that, on the whole, the voir dire, as conducted in these trials, did not provide sufficient information for attorneys to identify prejudiced jurors. The average performance score of the prosecution was near the zero point . . . , indicating an inability to distinguish potential bias; defense counsel performed only slightly better. . . . Perhaps most significant is the inconsistent performance of attorneys. Occasionally, one side performed well in a case in which the other side performed poorly, thereby frustrating the law's expectation that the adversary allocation of challenges will benefit both sides equally. (p. 528–529)

Thus, the research indicates that although some attorneys may use the voir dire quite effectively, their overall performance during the voir dire is poor.[12]

Hans and Vidmar (1982) in their review of research on the effectiveness of selection techniques traditionally used by lawyers reached the same conclusion—that is, that selection strategies may be only minimally effective and have minimal impact on the jury's verdict. They point out that especially in situations where there is only a small amount of information about individuals, it is difficult to predict behavior accurately, and that in jury trials, the voir dire may be effective in eliminating openly prejudiced persons, but much more should not be expected.

There is one study (Padawer-Singer, Singer, & Singer, 1974), however, that did conclude that voir dire examinations by counsel diminish the effects of pretrial prejudicial information. It compared mock juries impaneled through the voir dire process with mock juries composed of people selected merely at random. Both groups listened to a tape based on the transcript of a real trial concerned with the issue of free press vs. free trial. Ten juries were randomly selected without voir dire examinations, while 13 juries were selected with voir dire examinations by a lawyer from the district attorney's office and a lawyer from the Legal Aid Society. It was found that jurors selected with the voir dire tended to (a) be more sympathetic to mitigating factors, (b) be less influenced by prejudicial pretrial publicity, (c) display a greater tendency to follow the law as explained to them, and (d) display fewer shifts of opinion during deliberation. Thus, this study indicates that a jury impaneled through the use of the voir dire will be a much better jury than one selected completely at random. Besides the possibility that the two particular lawyers utilized may have been individually proficient at utilizing the voir dire process, two other factors dictate caution in weighing these results. First, there are problems inherent in generalizing from mock jury results to actual courtroom situations (Bridgeman & Marlowe, 1979).[13] Second, cases dealing with free press issues might be considered to be more "explosive" in nature with a greater polarization of attitudes among prospective jurors. As a result, in such a case counsel may find it easier to identify potentially biased and prejudiced jurors, thereby increasing the effectiveness of the voir dire in removing such individuals.

The conclusion that the voir dire as traditionally conducted may not be effective is supported by an analysis of the voir dire procedure. It is often structured such that the information-gathering process is hampered in a number of significant ways. First, the time allowed for the voir dire may be limited by the trial judge and also by the attorney's own concern over antagonizing prospective jurors with lengthy questioning. Second, the scope of the questioning may also be limited. There may well be questions that the attorney would like to ask and that would provide insight into the state of the juror's mind but that are objectionable as legally irrelevant. For example, an attorney defending a homosexual accused of sodomy might wish to ask prospective jurors what their reactions would be if they found out that their sons or daughters were gay. If objected to,

[12]Bermant and Shepard (1981), based upon a survey of the federal trial bench, determined that judges observe considerable variation among lawyers in jury selection skills. Despite this evidence and despite lawyers' belief in the importance of these skills, they conclude that in light of other data these differences in jury selection skills do not greatly affect the outcome of the trial.

[13]As pointed out by Hans and Vidmar (1982), reviews of jury simulation research have criticized the methodological features characteristic of the studies, including college student subject population, short trial summaries, absence of group deliberation, inappropriate dependent measures, and the hypothetical nature of decisions. To this list they add their own criticism: absence of a judicial admonishment to set aside biases and render a verdict based solely on the evidence.

this question might not be allowed by some judges on the grounds that it does not address itself to the juror's ability to render a fair and impartial decision in the case at hand. Appellate courts have been very reluctant to reverse trial judges' decisions to not allow a particular line of questioning aimed at obtaining information for exercising peremptory challenges (Bermant & Shepard, 1981). In addition, in the federal courts, and in an increasing number of state courts, the trial judge will usually conduct most of the *voir dire* questioning and may not probe into desired areas of information or may not probe deeply enough to satisfy the attorney (Ashby, 1978; "Attorney Participation," 1977; Bermant & Shepard, 1981; Massey & Travis, 1980).[14] Third, the method by which the jurors are challenged may limit the effectiveness of the *voir dire* procedure. The two approaches primarily used are (1) the struck jury method of exercising challenges, in which the judge rules on all challenges for cause before the parties claim any peremptories, thereby providing a pool of potential jurors equal in size to the number of jurors to be utilized plus the number of peremptory challenges allotted to both sides, and (2) various sequential methods, in which counsels exercise their challenges without knowing the characteristics of the next potential juror to be interviewed. Where the struck jury method is utilized, an attorney can rank order those jurors he/she finds objectionable, ensuring that the most objectionable jurors will be eliminated. Where a sequential method is utilized, however, a lawyer has no way of knowing whether ensuing prospective jurors will be more or less agreeable to him. Thus, when a party's peremptory challenges have been exhausted, the next juror to be called will be seated upon the jury regardless of the fact that that particular juror may be more objectionable than jurors which were struck earlier. Fourth, there are a number of social psychological forces

(e.g., peer pressure, social distance between the interviewer and prospective juror, and the authoritarian setting of the courtroom) that encourage conformity of responses by prospective jurors (Chandler, 1954; Deutsch & Gerard, 1956; Dohrenwend, Columbatos, & Dohrenwend, 1968; Hare, 1962; Jourard & Friedman, 1970; Kleck, 1970; Knecht, Lippman, & Swap, 1973; Lassen, 1970; Sherif, 1958; Weber, 1973; Williams, 1969).[15] This last group of factors may be responsible for Broeder's (1965b) conclusion that "jurors often either consciously or unconsciously lie on *voir dire*" (p. 528). As a result of these factors, the attorney is forced to make decisions about using peremptory challenges based on quite limited concrete information and inference.

Methods for Conducting the Voir Dire[16]

Given the problems in conducting an effective *voir dire*, it is not surprising that attorneys have sought the aid of standardized techniques developed by other lawyers and behavioral experts. This section reviews those approaches that have been developed for accomplishing the judicially acceptable purposes of the *voir dire*. Before doing so, however, it needs to be reiterated that the acceptable purposes are eliciting information to determine (a) the statutory qualifications of a juror, (b) whether the juror is prejudiced or biased as a matter of law, and (c) whether to exercise a peremptory challenge.

Determining the statutory qualifications of jurors simply entails asking straightforward biographical questions, which requires no special technique. In order to use the *voir dire* as a means to eliminate biased or prejudiced jurors on a challenge for cause, the attorney must direct the juror to respond to questioning in such a way as to

---

[14]For a discussion of the value of judge-conducted as opposed to attorney-conducted *voir dire*, as well as a series of practical suggestions for the attorney in conducting the *voir dire*, see Cleary (1980); Fahringer (1980); Mogil (1979); Suggs and Sales (1980). For a discussion of recommendations to structure the mechanics and content of the *voir dire* to maximize disclosure of juror bias as well as ensure juror privacy, see Fortune (1980–81). For a review of recent case law setting the limits of the scope of inquiry permitted during voir dire, see Gaba (1977); "Voir Dire Examination" (1980). For a series of suggestions on how to revise court rules for conducting the *voir dire* to minimize improper usages of the *voir dire* by counsel without leaving the conducting of the *voir dire* totally to the court, see Strawn (1979).

[15]The above research reveals that there is a considerable inducement of conformity responses whenever groups of people are questioned together and that social distance (i.e., difference in status) between the interviewer and interviewee hampers self-disclosure. It also indicates that a large physical distance between the interviewer and interviewee (as is the case in the *voir dire*) also significantly reduces self-disclosure (Suggs & Sales, 1980).

[16]For a review of methods used to accomplish the judicially unacceptable *voir dire* purposes of ingratiation and indoctrination, see Blunk and Sales (1977); Suggs and Sales (1978).

convince the judge that the juror should be excused. Such questioning involves many of the
same techniques of examination that the attorney
is accustomed to using when examining a witness
in court. Thus, the first acceptable purpose of the
voir dire requires no special technique, whereas
the second purpose may be accomplished by skills
that every attorney should possess.

The use of the *voir dire* to gather information
necessary to exercise peremptory challenges, however, poses a number of special problems for the
attorney. It is necessary to determine how the
prospective jurors regard (a) counsel for each side,
(b) the opposing litigants, and (c) the legal and
factual issues that are relevant to the case. The
standardized procedures have been offered to aid
the attorney in exercising these challenges.

Intuitive Notions Involving
Socioeconomic Factors

The legal literature is replete with strategies based
on intuitive notions which attempt to correlate
socioeconomic characteristics with particular intellectual and emotional inclinations. Noted
plaintiff's attorney Melvin Belli has said that he
prefers men to women jurors because women are
too brutal. He does not like accountants and engi-
neers because they are too stingy, does not mind
bankers because they understand big amounts of
money, and does not like rank-and-file union members because they are not used to dealing with large
sums of money (Totenberg, 1982). These correlations are generally based on the individual proponent's experiences both in life and in the
courtroom, with little, if any, empirical verification (Hawrish & Tate, 1974–75; Hayden, Senna, &
Siegal, 1978; Simon, 1980). In actuality, they are
nothing more than stereotypes based upon prejudice, guesswork, and hypothesis. Not only are
these strategies conjectural but they are also at
times contradictory.

For instance, wealth is a factor that has been
suggested as a criterion, with Darrow (1936),
White (1952), and Bodin (1954) recommending
poorer people as favorable jurors for criminal de-

fendants and civil plaintiffs. But Harrington and
Dempsey (1969) recommended the wealthiest
members of the jury panel to the civil plaintiff on
the assumption that they would award the greatest
amount in damages. The meager empirical research that has been performed in this area tends to
support Harrington and Dempsey's conclusion that
wealthier jurors are more favorable to the civil
plaintiff than less wealthy jurors (Mayer, Note 2).

The sex of prospective jurors has been mentioned in another criterion, but once again the
recommendations are mixed. Bodin (1954) disapproved of women jurors on the grounds that they
were unpredictable and likely to be influenced by
their husbands' experiences. White (1952) likewise advised against women jurors, but on the
grounds that the experience of the average house-
wife tended to be limited and disqualified her as a
peer of the defendant. Goldstein (1938), however,
came out in favor of women jurors; he felt that
they were emotional, sympathetic, and conscientious in their duty. There is some empirical research that has demonstrated that women are *less*
likely to side with a civil plaintiff and that they
tend to defer to male jurors in cases involving
predominantly male activities (Broeder, 1965a;
Mayer, Note 2). Thus, the meager empirical research suggests that, in general, women may not
be favorable to the civil plaintiff.[17]

Ethnicity is one criterion on which there is an
apparent consensus of opinion in the legal literature. Numerous commentators have recommended the Irish, Jewish, and southern
Europeans as favorable and rejected the British
and northern Europeans as unfavorable jurors for
criminal defendants and civil plaintiffs (Darrow,
1936; Goldstein, 1938; Harrington & Dempsey,
1969; Rothblatt, 1966). There is even some empirical support for these conclusions, yet it is
doubtful whether they represent a consensus of
the legal community. Kallen (1969) conducted a
survey of 88 trial lawyers in the Chicago area and
concluded the following:

> Even though the practicing lawyers base
> their peremptory challenges upon juror

---

[17]For an analysis of five frequently recurring stereotypical factors relied on to eliminate women during *voir dire* examinations, see Mahoney (1978). Empirical evidence concerning these factors is reviewed with the author conclud-ing: (1) there is little evidence that women are harder on female defendants; (2) there is some proof that they are more likely to convict if a child was victimized; (3) there is contradictory data regarding the assumption that women favor the plaintiff in civil cases; (4) there is some evidence that women consider rape a more serious crime than men, and (5) some indication that women are less influenced by the attractiveness of the defendant or plaintiff than lawyers believe. However, Mahoney also declares that more substantial research is needed on all of these factors.

background with great frequency, there are no truisms recognized by the group. In fact, the survey seems to uncover a high degree of disagreement concerning the importance and direction of the effect of background upon juryroom decision-making. (p. 156).

Even if broad characterizations are true, their applicability in a given case may well be doubtful. A leading example was provided in the Harrisburg trial where an expected finding that younger people would be more favorably disposed to the anti-war defendants involved in the trial was shown to be invalid by the demographic survey which was utilized (Christie, 1976). In other words, if selection is to be made on the basis of jurors' socioeconomic background, there should be empirical research performed to determine which socioeconomic backgrounds tend to be associated with favorable or unfavorable juror attitudes in the particular case at hand. People are not likely to act in an identical way in all situations.

The Systematic Approach to Jury Selection

In recent years, behavioral experts have become increasingly involved in the *voir dire* process and have attempted to remedy the illogic of stereotypes. As one lawyer recently noted, "At a recent symposium, this writer was treated to a vision of a whole new world as far as jury selection and trial is concerned. That vision was presented in a portion of the program pertaining to the use of psychologists in jury selection" (Penner, 1982). The most widely publicized behavioral science method of evaluating prospective jurors is the "systematic approach to jury selection," which has been developed by Jay Schulman and the National Jury Project (Kairys, Schulman, & Harring, 1975; Schulman, 1973; Schulman, Shaver, Colman, Emrich, & Christie, 1973). This technique employs four main components: (a) a demographic rating system, (b) juror investigation, (c) juror surveys, and (d) in-court observation of prospective jurors. We describe this system briefly; for a more comprehensive description and evaluation

see Berman and Sales (1977).[18]

DEMOGRAPHIC RATING SYSTEM (COMMUNITY SURVEY)

Part of the system employed by Schulman and others is based on the assumption that a person's demographic background denotes a particular kind of socializing history for that person which produces a certain set of perceptions, attitudes and values which in turn are crucial in determining the decision an individual will make as a juror (Saks & Hastie, 1978). Based upon this logic, a scientifically designed random sample survey[19] of the population from which the jury panel will be drawn is conducted. To conserve costs and time, the initial survey may be conducted by telephone, followed by in-depth interviews with a selected subsample to confirm the telephone results and explore other issues in greater detail (Hans & Vidmar, 1982). The out-of-the-courtroom survey consists of questions designed to ascertain the respondent's (a) demographic characteristics (i.e., age, race, sex, occupation, religion, area of residence, etc.), (b) attitudes and opinions on the litigants, fact patterns, and legal issues involved in the case, and (c) opinions relating to matters that may not be directly litigated but that may correlate with the central aspects of the case. The latter is derived by asking indirect questions which, while not directly related to the facts of the case, the litigants, or the legal issues, measure the respondent's attitudes toward other issues which might correlate with the direct questions. From the survey data, a multiple regression analysis is employed to determine which demographic characteristics and/or indirect questions best predict, or are significantly associated with, particular responses to the attitudinal questions (Silver, 1978). The statistical models used to analyze the survey data have recently been criticized by Berk, Hennessy, and Swan (1977).

The rating system is then used in the *voir dire* in the following manner. The attorney asks the prospective juror questions that will elicit a self-description on the demographic variables found to be significant in the original sample survey. The

---

[18]Two other strategies suggested for systematically selecting jurors based on pre-trial predictions of their dispositions in a particular case are handwriting analysis and voice analysis (Moore & Wood, 1980). Neither approach has been used extensively in actual practice, and they have received scant commentary or empirical analysis in either the legal or behavioral science literature.

[19]Berk (1976) discusses two different sampling strategies in light of the goal of the survey, the construction and revision of the questionnaire utilized, the statistical analysis of the results obtained, and practical problems encountered.

responses of the juror are then put into a formula that, based on the survey data, assigns a numerical value for the various demographic characteristics and the sum of which indicates whether the prospective juror is likely to be a favorable or at least an unprejudiced, juror. By following this procedure with each prospective juror, a demographic rating can be obtained for each member of the panel. The attorney can then decide how to best exercise peremptory challenges by making comparisons of the suitability ratings of the prospective jurors in the panel.[20]

The advantage of having demographic predictors is that as soon as a prospective juror states his/her age, occupation, income, and so on, the attorney has some idea of how most people who have this particular set of characteristics feel about the central issues in the case. Having predictors consisting of attitudes toward issues indirectly relevant to the case is advantageous in that the lawyer can ask about these issues without the prospective juror or opposing attorney knowing exactly what a particular response might mean about that juror's predisposition toward the central issues. In addition, sensitive beliefs can be estimated which tend to be misreported by jurors and/or information can be provided which is outside the scope of allowable *voir dire* questioning (Frederick, 1978). A less obvious advantage of this method is that by surveying the general attitudes of the community, it will be possible to get a preliminary estimate of what proportion of the jury pool will be predisposed to one side or the other. Thus, in the early part of the *voir dire* some promising jurors can be excused based on the knowledge that better jurors will appear later (Frederick, 1978; McConahay, Mullin, & Frederick, 1977). Furthermore, the survey data may help the attorneys in organizing their trial strategy, giving them an indication as to what issues and tactics the jurors are most likely to be amenable to (Hans & Vidmar, 1982). Finally, a secondary use of such data is that it can be used in a motion for a change in venue to argue that the entire jury pool has already made up their minds of the facts of the case (Berk, 1976).

This approach relies on two assumptions: (1) people predisposed to certain opinions, e.g., beliefs concerning the guilt or innocence of the defendant, can be identified by distinctive characteristics they possess; and (2) if critical characteristics can be isolated, these characteristics can be used to predict the behavior of potential jurors (Frederick, 1978). It has even been suggested that the court itself should send out an extensive background questionnaire for prospective jurors so there could be a more informed and shorter *voir dire* (Ashby, 1978; Fortune, 1980–81).

The main drawback of using this approach by itself is that although the survey may be able to determine quite accurately that certain demographic characteristics are typically associated with favorable or unfavorable attitudes toward the side that the attorney represents, it cannot determine whether the *particular* prospective juror being examined holds the same opinions and attitudes as his/her socioeconomic group (Ashby, 1978) or with which subgroup, of the several to which he/she belongs, the juror identifies.

It may be the case that the particular prospective juror holds views contrary to those commonly held by members of his/her socioeconomic group or holds contrary views on the particular case at hand. These possibilities are particularly likely to occur in situations in which the prospective juror belongs to a socioeconomic subgroup with differing tendencies from the main group. For example, in a given case the survey data may indicate that Irish Catholics are negatively biased toward the defendant, while conservative Republicans would feel the opposite. The prospective juror who is both Irish Catholic and a conservative Republican presents a problem in analysis. Does the juror identify more with Irish Catholicism or conservatism? In addition, since a series of demographic variables describe any particular individual (e.g., sex, race, age, socioeconomic status), the predictive effect of any single demographic variable may be counterbalanced by the other demographic variables which describe the individual. Berk (1976) suggests that a number of predictive variables will need to be taken into

---

[20]The practitioners of this method have conducted posttrial interviews of both actual jurors and those prospective jurors who were dismissed in a number of cases and have concluded that the demographic survey is accurate about 70% of the time in predicting individual jurors' attitudes and dispositions (see Kairys et al., 1975). Unfortunately, the methodology of the follow-up assessment was not presented, making it impossible to determine the validity of the reported 70% success rate. For a fundamental discussion of the generation and utilization of these prediction equations, as well as an alternative computer program which will generate profiles of favorable jurors, and their superiority to intuitive judgments, see Saks and Hastie (1978).

account, which raises difficult questions of weighting. Mills and Bohannon (1980b) in emphasizing the danger of considering the relationship between jury behavior and any variable in isolation, suggest that a chi-square analysis be utilized to keep more clearly in mind the modifying effects of the various demographic variables on each other. They found that little predictive ability was gained by a linear combination of the variables, but with the use of multivariate analysis, a particular demographic variable could be identified as a primary predictor, but the one which surfaced depended upon the type of case involved. In addition, it is possible that none of the potential predictors are strongly related to the respondent's dispositions toward the case. This is especially likely to happen if the population sampled is relatively homogeneous (Berman & Sales, 1977). Furthermore, social scientists have generally found a poor relationship existing between attitudes and behavior (Berman & Sales, 1977; "Defendant's Right to Impartial," 1979). Thus, even though a person may hold negative attitudes toward issues relevant to one side in the litigation, it does not mean that the person will also vote against that side. Finally, as Berk (1976) notes, the aggregate data supplied by a survey analysis will at best reveal where people fall on various continua, with arbitrary cut-off points constructed to transform this continuous data into the nominal categories of good vs. bad juror. However, there are no easily defined criteria to judge how good is good and how bad is bad. These factors may explain why Bridgeman and Marlowe (1979), after conducting a questionnaire-interview procedure with 65 actual jurors following the completion of 10 felony trials, found that demographic data was related neither to trial outcome nor first-ballot voting behavior.

Other disadvantages of utilizing this method include the overall expense of it, and the difficulty of: ensuring that the sample drawn from the community adequately represents the prospective jury pool; constructing a valid and reliable questionnaire; recruiting, training, supervising, and retaining the workers gathering the survey data; and trial scheduling which typically requires the compilation, integration, and interpretation of a great deal of information in a short amount of time. The availability and use of computers has helped to alleviate this latter problem. Nevertheless, Mullin (1980) reported that some firms engaged in civil suits paid as much as $125,000 for this service. The average cost has been placed at $12,000, with 1,000 satisfactory survey interviews required, each taking approximately 20 minutes, and requiring contacting as many as 20,000 people in the community (Penner, 1982).

Thus, it is clear that sole reliance on a demographic rating system to evaluate prospective jurors is logically inadequate, expensive, and time-consuming, and that there must be some method employed that evaluates the individual aspects of the prospective jurors in the context of the particular court-room settings. In addition, there are court opinions that suggest that the use of the peremptory challenge to exclude members of the venue solely on the basis of a cognizable characteristic of a group of persons (including, but not limited to, race, sex, religion, age, economic position, and political affiliation) may not be allowed. Thus, *People* v. *Wheeler*, 22 Cal. 3d 258, 583 P.2d 748, 148 Cal. Rptr. 890 (1978), in effect, ruled contrary to the rule set down by the United States Supreme court in *Swain* v. *Alabama*, 380 U.S. 202 (1965) and the rule in the majority of the states. *Swain* established an almost insurmountable presumption that prosecutors' peremptory challenges had been exercised fairly so as to secure an impartial jury, and no justification had to be provided for their use. The court in *Wheeler* found that the prosecution's systematic exclusion of certain groups, in this case blacks, from a jury violated the defendant's right to an impartial jury drawn from a representative cross section of the community. Thus, the court held that the peremptory challenge could not be used to exclude members of a cognizable group on the sole presumption that such persons will think alike when considering the issues of a case. Similar rulings have been made in Massachusetts in *Massachusetts* v. *Soares*, Mass., 387 N.E.2d 499 (1979); in Louisiana in *Louisiana* v. *Brown*, 371 S.2d 751 (1979); in New York in *People* v. *Payne*, 79-1013 (1982).

It has been suggested that such an analysis should also be applied to the more sophisticated approaches by behavioral experts who attempt to insure that the jurors retained will be favorably partial to particular litigants based on their demographic and personality profiles, possibly by limiting the number of challenges available or eliminating them altogether ("Impartial Jury," 1979; Van Dyke, 1977a). However, it has generally been agreed that the holding in *Wheeler* is a narrow one, that is, that it only addresses exclusion on the basis of group affiliation (*People v. Wheeler*, 1979) and that the burden of the party challenging the exercised peremptory challenge is a formidable one ("Curbing," 1980; "Defendant's Right to Object," 1979; "Peremptory Challenges," 1979). In addition, the California Supreme Court itself limited the scope of *Wheeler* in *Rubio* v. *Superior Court*, 24 Cal. 3d 93, 593 P.2d 595, 154 Cal. Rptr. 734 (1979) when it refused to designate ex-felons and resident aliens as legally cognizable groups and found that exclusion of these groups was permissible. One commentator concluded that the court in *Wheeler*,

> has not taken away the ability to exercise peremptory challenges on the basis of non-group-based, stereotypical and spurious reasons so long as they are related to the case at bar; the court merely forbade certain types of stereotypes from being the basis of a peremptory challenge. ("Prohibition," 1978–80, p. 360).

This author goes on to say,

> It cannot be emphasized enough that the Wheeler court did not limit in any way the ability of counsel to exercise peremptory challenges on the basis of personalities, lifestyles, and attitudes of jurors. . . . *Wheeler*, however, does lay the roots for changing the nature of the peremptory challenge since, in certain defined circumstances, it forces the litigant to explain the reasons for its exercise. (p. 362–3).

(In addition, see Brown, McGuire, & Winters, 1978, for their discussion of the adoption of the *Wheeler* doctrine in Massachusetts, and their argument that peremptory challenges by prosecutors are and have been exercised to systematically exclude minority groups from jury service, and thus should be abolished. See, "Exclusion," 1977, for a discussion of an aborted effort within the federal judicial system to restrict the unbridled use of peremptory challenges to similarly exclude minority groups. On the other hand, see "Defendant's Right to Object," 1979, and "Peremptory Challenges," 1980, for a discussion of why the attempts to apply the Supreme Court's cross-section of the community standard in compiling jury pools is inappropriate when applied to the use of the peremptory challenge to systematically exclude members of social groups from juries themselves.)

Another court ruling which may be waving a red flag at this jury selection approach is *United States* v. *Barnes*, 604 F.2d 121 (2d Cir. 1979), *cert. denied*, 446 U.S. 907 (1980). The announced rationale of the court in affirming the trial judge's decision not to allow *voir dire* questioning of potential jurors about their religion and ethnicity, was to preserve the jurors' rights to privacy. However, one commentator has pointed out that counsel sought this information in the belief that these factors correlate with general sympathies and values which, though not reaching the level of bias required for a challenge for cause, influence a juror's decision and thus might serve as the basis for a peremptory challenge ("Voir Dire Limitations," 1980). Yet the court implicitly rejected this conception of peremptory challenges, limiting them to removals for hidden prejudices which, if revealed, would justify challenges for cause. The author concludes:

> The court, of course, should be ready to screen out frivolous inquiries. But the interest in promoting peremptory challenges that protect against group-based bias suggests that inquiry into jurors' private thoughts should be allowed even when they are not directly related to issues in the case. Society's immediate concern with according criminal defendants a fair trial outweighs any speculative injury to the juror's privacy. (p. 792)

JUROR INVESTIGATION
(INFORMATION NETWORKS)

One traditional method of evaluating the individual aspects of the prospective juror is to gather personal information by conducting background investigations of the jury panel members themselves outside the courtroom. Government prosecutors have been known to rely on police reports,[21] FBI investigations,[22] and IRS reports[23]

---

[21]See *Losario* v. *Mavher*, 178 Colo. 184, 496 P.2d 1032 (1972).

[22]See *Best* v. *United States*, 184 F.2d 131, 141 (1st Cir., 1950); *cert. denied*, 340 U.S. 939 (1951).

[23]See *United States* v. *Costello*, 255 F.2d 876, 883 (2d Cir., 1958); *cert. denied*, 357 U.S. 939 (1958).

to obtain specific information about prospective jurors. Some private attorneys have relied on "jury services," which investigate jurors and which are available by subscription from private detective firms. Schulman and other practitioners of the systematic approach to jury selection incorporate a similar method of evaluation through the use of an investigation network. To use the network, for example, a defense team solicits assistance from people who have many community contacts, or alternatively, by contacting the defendants and the friends, families, and supporters of the defendants. Each of these in turn contacts several other people, who in turn contact several other people, and so on. When the identities of the prospective jurors are learned, members of the network are asked if they have any personal knowledge of the prospective jurors or if they know of someone who does. Mullin (1980) emphasizes that valuable information is not limited to personal descriptions of the relevant prospective jurors, but encompasses such items as the person's job, neighborhood, church, and political affiliation, for to a certain extent, people reflect the attitudes of the institutions to which they belong. In addition, she suggests contacting local planning boards; university geography or demography departments; the Board of Elections office; proprietors of local stores, bars, mortuaries, and insurance agencies; and attorneys, police officers, postal carriers, and precinct leaders. She also suggests viewing property tax lists and the jurors' homes; and visiting with their neighbors. Schulman (1973) has estimated that a network of about 400 people is sufficient to produce information on 70%–80% of the prospective jurors in most cases. Three points must be kept in mind in using this system: (a) the network must consist of trustworthy people from as many sectors of the community as possible from which jurors come; (b) all people in the network must be carefully instructed about the type of information desired, how and to whom to report it, and the laws concerning jury tampering (direct contact with members of the jury list would likely bring such charges); and (c) the network must be well organized and well staffed so that information is quickly and accurately processed (Schulman, 1973).

These are five main problems with using such an information network. First, the information that is obtained is often third- or fourth-hand and may contain considerable distortion. Second,

since the jurors on the panel are often drawn from a very large geographic area and a minimal staff may be all that is available to construct and supervise the network, it may be very difficult to establish the elaborate network required for this procedure (Berman & Sales, 1977). In addition, sometimes those individuals in the best position to provide valuable information as a result of their social position may not be willing to cooperate (Christie, 1976). Therefore, only rarely will the team have network information on all of the prospective jurors.

Third, the information gathered is often isolated; that is, we usually do not have sufficient comparable information about individual jurors so that we can confidently compare them to other potential jurors. Measurement of any type requires that we make comparisons among objects, persons, and so forth on some common dimension, using common procedures. To compare attitudes, the reasonable procedure is to ask the same questions or observe the same behavior of the people being compared. Yet this may often result in a comparing of apples and oranges as the behavioral experts attempt to compare the predispositions of jurors on the basis of information from such investigations. For example, the network may reveal fourth-hand that juror A attended an antibusing demonstration, that juror B moved within a year when a black family moved in next door, and nobody in our information network knows anything about juror C; he may have done both these activities, or neither, or something equally eye-catching. On what grounds can one say that one of these people is more or less prejudiced than the other two? Thus, even though we may think we have some information on A and B, it very well may be useless information for making comparisons among jurors.

Fourth, and maybe most importantly, the use of the information network can backfire on the attorneys using it if the network members are indiscrete about whom they contact. A typical reaction of many jurors upon discovering that they are being investigated is to become hostile toward the investigators. In one case, a member of the network contacted an acquaintance of the prospective jury panel who informed the prospective juror that he was being investigated. The panel of prospective jurors became so hostile upon learning this that the attorneys felt compelled to ask the jury selection team to withdraw from the case in an attempt to mollify the jury panel.

Fifth, in *United States* v. *Barnes*, 604 F.2d 121 (2d Cir. 1979), *cert. denied*, 446 U.S. 907 (1980), it was held that potential jurors' names and addresses can be withheld in the interest of protecting the safety of the potential jurors, raising the possibility of rendering the information network useless. In addition, in *United States* v. *Stokes*, 506 F.2d 771 (5th Cir. 1975), it was ruled that a jury list could be retained until the morning of the trial as long as there was no evidence that the discretion exercised by the court was arbitrary.

JUROR SURVEYS

A third method which would appear to probe the prospective jurors more directly than the demographic survey and/or the information network, capitalizes upon juror surveys sent out by the court itself, seeking background information from each of the jurors. As explained by Mullin (1980), these questionnaires cover basic areas such as employment, marital status, prior jury service, and other general topics and are often seen by judges as a helpful tool in conserving valuable court time. Litigants may be allowed to expedite and supplement this process by supplying the judge with their own carefully constructed, thoughtful questionnaire, including attitudinal questions. Mullin reports that many judges are cooperative in regard to such an endeavor, often finding the results interesting, and are not necessarily antagonistic to the idea of sending out a lengthy questionnaire.

Nevertheless, this approach is subject to many of the same drawbacks from which demographic surveys and information networks suffer. Besides the obvious problem arising when the judge either refuses to allow such a survey or insists on conducting it totally on his/her own, there exists the fact that: (1) knowing the individual juror's demographic characteristics doesn't provide data on whether or not this particular prospective juror holds the same opinions and attitudes as that particular socioeconomic group; (2) although attitudinal questions may be incorporated in an effort to provide more individual-specific data, answers to such questions are often apt to be highly evasive, general to the point of being meaningless, and slanted and distorted by prospective jurors in such a way as to allow them to respond to what they perceive as the demand characteristics inherent in the situation in order to provide the socially-acceptable response (e.g., that they are fair and impartial individuals holding views similar to what they believe a judge would profess).

IN-COURT OBSERVATION OF PROSPECTIVE JURORS

Fourth, and finally, are those techniques that have been proposed to evaluate prospective jurors while they are in the courtroom. Although each technique can be used as part of the systematic approach to jury selection, each is proposed in such a way that it can be used independently and as the sole technique for evaluating jurors.

These techniques have in common the fact that they all consist of the behavioral expert rating each prospective juror on some dimension during the *voir dire*. However, the aspects of dimensions of the jurors that have been rated have varied considerably, depending on the nature of the trial, and what seems to have been even more important, the area of professional expertise of the expert.

Body Type. The evaluation of jurors based on *body type* is an approach that has been proposed by Rothblatt (1966), who implicitly suggested the use of Sheldon's body-type theory (Sheldon & Stevens, 1942; Sheldon, Stevens, & Turner, 1940). According to this theory, people may be broadly classified into three types: endomorphic, mesomorphic, and ectomorphic. Endomorphs have a heavy, roundish build, a relatively small frame, and little muscular development. Mesomorphs have large bones and muscles and have a squarish build, whereas ectomorphs have long, slender extremities and a lack of muscular development.

According to the theory, the endomorphic build is associated with relaxation, love of comfort, slow reaction, sociability, amiability and complacency. The mesomorphic build is associated with assertiveness, love of physical adventure, dominating, risk and chance-taking, and directness of manner. The ectomorphs are supposedly anxious, secretive, inhibited, and introverted in thought. Rothblatt (1966) recommended endomorphs to the attorney defending a criminal case and advised against having ectomorphs on the jury. Mesomorphs are apparently difficult to categorize according to Rothblatt. Ironically, no behavioral explanation of these assertions is offered. It should be pointed out that Sheldon's somatotype theory has fallen out of favor in the last 30 years and that there are no empirical data by which to assess the efficacy of evaluating jurors by this method.

Legal Development. Tapp (Tapp & Kohlberg, 1971; Tapp & Levine, 1974) has proposed evaluating prospective jurors on the basis of their *legal development*, or on their attitudes toward rules and laws, by positing that there are three levels of such development: preconventional, conventional, and postconventional reasoning. People who are at the preconventional reasoning stage of legal development base their attitudes toward law on fear of punishment, apprehension of physical harm, or deference to power. Laws are rigid entities to the individuals at this level, and justice is seen as a retaliatory mechanism. People at the conventional level are concerned with personal and social conformity to role expectations. They believe very strongly in an orderly society and that everyone must bow to the group norms that have been established. Justice at the conventional level of legal development is synonymous with the majority vote and the even application and interpretation of rules. At the highest level of legal development, postconventional people are able to see the need for a structured and orderly social system, yet recognize the validity of a set of universal ethics that may differ from the rules established by a particular social system. Individuals at this level are able to distinguish the concept of justice from a set of concrete laws and are able to independently judge the ethical legality of the social system itself.

Tapp and Keniston (Note 3) have also specified a set of criteria for what is considered to be a fair juror.

A fair juror is someone who can (1) understand the rules of a court and laws (laws and criminal procedure); (2) apply these rules to a set of facts about a person's behavior (evidence) alleged to demonstrate that said person violated a law; (3) give judgment that reflects the outcome of (2). So far, probably almost anyone would agree with this description. The legal levels view adds "spice"; The fair juror (4) has a well developed system of ideas about how rules and laws function generally, independent of specific rule systems; (5) evaluates substantive issues of rules, laws, and evidence against this more abstract, principled system of his/her own, so that (6) a fair and just judgment is achieved by evaluation of both law and evidence. Finally, the fair juror covers (7) a flexible attitude toward specific rule systems and exhibits (8) a critical autonomy from the apparent wish of authority or authority systems to apply steps 1–3 and ignore 4–8. It may be the case that a fair juror ultimately will judge the law (and even the authority) to be guilty, rather than to condemn the defendant (or declare him/her innocent).

Obviously, Tapp and Keniston's (Note 3) conception of the fair juror is most completely satisfied by those people who function at the postconventional level of legal development. The strategy for conducting the *voir dire*, then, is to identify the legal development of prospective jurors, eliminate as many of the preconventional jurors as possible, and retain those prospective jurors at the postconventional stage of legal development.

The process of identifying the level of legal development in the prospective jurors requires the in-court observers to abstract the characteristics of the jurors' legal thinking from the responses given to questions asked during the *voir dire*. That is, the observers must assess how the prospective jurors conceive of the law, rules, individual rights, and the nature of individual compliance with laws and rules. Tapp and Keniston noted that the prospective jurors' behavioral responses to questioning from the judge may be especially helpful in this assessment. They have hypothesized that preconventional jurors will be timid and fearful when interacting with the judge and will eagerly respond in whatever way the judge seems to desire. Conventional types are expected to respond with propriety to the judge (i.e., addressing the judge as Sir or Your Honor), whereas postconventional types are expected to appear more relaxed, less deferential, and to willingly express unsolicited views.

Tapp and Keniston have conducted post-trial assessments of actual and challenged jurors in one trial and found that the in-court ratings of the jurors' level of legal development correlated .49 ($p < .025$) with a more formal and refined measurement instrument of legal development. Thus, the in-court method of assessment seems to have a measure of accuracy in identifying the level of legal development of jurors. What is needed is empirical research to validate the theoretical propositions concerning what constitutes a fair juror. Also, investigations should be made to determine whether and to what extent the hypothesized behavioral responses to questioning by the judge correlate with the typologies of legal development.

It should be noted that the technique proposed by Tapp and Keniston (Note 3) does not concur with the usual, practical conception of the *voir dire* as part of the adversary process. The fair juror as hypothesized by them should be one who is acceptable to both the prosecution and the defense. Recognizing this fact, they suggest that behavioral experts employing this technique might best be suited to a nonpartisan involvement in the *voir dire* as *amicus curiae* (see also, Redmount, 1957). Ironically, it would seem that if this technique were to be used as an adversarial tool, it would be best suited for a criminal prosecutor. This observation stems from the fact that preconventional and conventional types are more easily swayed by authority figures, whereas postconventional types are at best independent of others opposed to authority. A prosecutor using this technique might employ the strategy by eliminating the postconventional prospective jurors, thus leaving prospective jurors who are more likely to be conforming and responsive to authority.

Authoritarianism. The evaluation of jurors based on *authoritarianism* is an approach that seems to be somewhat similar to the Tapp legal development method. It has been employed by Richard Christie (Note 4) in a number of cases involving political defendants (e.g., Wounded Knee and Attica). In this type of trial, the defense seeks to obtain juries that are as civil libertarian as possible. Since the hallmark of the authoritarian personality is the combination of dominance over subordinates and submission to authority, the defense would want to eliminate those types of persons from serving on the jury. For example, the findings of experiments conducted to determine the characteristics of authoritarian jurors have generally indicated, although not always, that persons rated high on authoritarianism are more likely than low authoritarians to draw more direct inferences from incriminating evidence (Garcia & Griffitt, 1978) and to convict a defendant and punish him or her severely (Boehm, 1968; Bray & Noble, 1978; Centers, Shomer, & Rodrigues, 1970; Epstein, 1966; Jurow, 1971; Vidmar, 1974). Thus, Fried, Kaplan, & Klein (1978) argue that prosecutors will tend to favor authoritarian jurors because such jurors tend to approach the trial with a closed or rigid cognitive set, while the defense should favor egalitarian jurors because they are more willing to consider conflicting information.

Thus, Christie attempts to rate each prospective juror's degree of authoritarianism. Ideally, that rating should be based on one of the paper-and-pencil tests developed to assess authoritarianism in people. However, because of the unacceptability of that procedure to most, and possibly all, judges, Christie has had to rely on observations of the jurors during the *voir dire*. Like Tapp and Keniston (Note 3), Christie searches for indications of deference to and fear of the authority figures involved in the *voir dire*. Mullin (1980) asserts that individuals with highly pronounced authoritarian attitudes perceive themselves as staunch upholders of the established value system and thus as persons most qualified to serve as jurors. She therefore suggests looking for individuals who show an extreme respect for authority figures and an inability to see themselves as being anything except fair and impartial. She also contends authoritarians will "often express the rigidity of their personalities with a masklike face topping a ramrod straight body. . . . The militarism of their personality may also be expressed with the continual 'yes sir,'. . . . Because their minds think only in absolute terms, the language used contains few qualifying words. . . . Little time will be necessary to think out their answers to questions" (p. 151). She concludes that they should be eliminated from juries in cases involving minority persons, social non-conformists, and other controversial persons.

For an attempt to test the validity of a similar approach, see "Juror Bias" (1980). In that study, a 30-item Legal Attitudes Questionnaire, designed to probe for the existence of authoritarian and antiauthoritarian attitudes in order to predict which potential jurors are most likely to harbor certain biases, was distributed to individuals who had just completed jury duty. A follow-up interview was then conducted within two weeks with each respondent. The study compared groups predicted to hold biases on the basis of their questionnaire responses with those who gave actual indications of bias in the post-trial interviews. The study concluded that authoritarian jurors were more likely to exhibit the conviction-prone biases against defendants studied than other jurors. The author concludes that the attitudes tapped by the questionnaire are fundamental and highly verdict-relevant in nearly any type of criminal trial and have substantial predictive value for identifying jurors who hold extreme biases. A major drawback with this approach is that before it can be utilized the court must be willing to set aside the time for the completion of the questionnaire, as well as being willing to expose jurors to the survey. Ashby (1978) feels that both procedural difficulties and concerns for juror privacy can and should be worked out, and such tests should be administered at the beginning of jury service.

Yet, even if the difficulties are resolved, a careful look at the research literature suggests that this technique should be used with caution since authoritarians do not act unidimensionally. For example, Soder (1976) reported that authoritarian jurors, as identified by a jury selection scale, voted in favor of the first presentation they heard, the prosecution, unless they felt similarity to the defendant, wherein they voted for acquittal. Thus, there are cases where an authoritarian juror would tend to be less punitive. Frederick (1978) reports that the authoritarian also may be less punitive where he/she reacts negatively to the victim, e.g., the crime of rape where they tend to respond negatively to the plight of the rape victim. Thus, keen attention must be paid to the key issues of the case in determining which pole of the construct is likely to be most favorable to the party conducting the juror selection. In addition, the construct of authoritarianism may not be the most germane to the issues involved in a particular case.

Internal Responsibility. Stanley Brodsky (Note 5) has suggested some further avenues by which prospective jurors might be evaluated. For example, we would categorize prospective jurors' *beliefs in internal reponsibility for events in one's life* (Joe, 1971; Jones & Shrauger, 1968; Phares, Wilson, & Klyver, 1971; Rotter, 1966). Persons who are high on the internal pole of the internal-external dimension might not be as easily swayed by extenuating or mitigating circumstances, thus making them less favorable as jurors for the criminal and civil defendant.

In empirical applications of the theory it was found that internals attributed more responsibility for the crime to the defendant than did externals (Phares & Wilson, 1972), and that internals rendered harsher sentences than externals (Sosis, 1974). From this data, Frederick (1978) tentatively concluded that internals tend to be less lenient with defendants than externals, in terms of both responsibility attributions and punishment.

Another dimension on which it might be useful to categorize jurors is the degree to which they hold a *belief in a "just world"* (i.e., a world in which people get what they deserve; see Jones & Aronson, 1973; Lerner & Matthews, 1967; Lerner & Simmons, 1966; Rubin & Peplau, 1973, 1975; Lerner, Note 6). People who function according to this theory are not likely to be very sympathetic to the victim of a crime or to a civil plaintiff. Brodsky has also suggested examining prospective jurors' *fiscal prudence.* Prospective jurors who rate high on this dimension are not likely to award substantial damages to the civil plaintiff. Finally, Brodsky suggests examining the jurors' *sense of personal safety.* Prospective jurors who live in fear for their safety are likely to be sympathetic to a civil plaintiff and most probably unsympathetic toward a criminal defendant. All of these suggestions need to be explored empirically, however.

Dimensions of Character. In a vein similar to Brodsky's, Mills & Bohannon (1980a) have also focused upon personality variables and recently concluded a study of three dimensions of individual character structure which they found related to the personal and group decisions of jurors. These three dimensions, *socialization, empathy, and autonomy,* were measured by standardized psychological testing scales. These variables were conceptualized as dimensions of a person's orientation toward the social rules that govern behavior, those aspects of personality that organize one's responses to the ordinary rules and values of conventional society. They hypothesized that: (1) since highly socialized individuals are predisposed to follow social rules, values, and prohibitions, they should be predisposed to reach more guilty verdicts; (2) highly empathic individuals are inclined to consider the viewpoint of others, including the defendant's intentions in making decisions, and thus are more likely to reach not-guilty verdicts. In addition, they should be more effective in influencing the decisions of other jurors, since the high empathy scorer is described as charming, poised, and tactful; and (3) highly autonomous individuals, described as independent and decisive, should be able to withstand group influence, influence other jurors, and find the decision-making process relatively easy.

This approach suffers from handicaps akin to similar systems based on personality constructs as discussed earlier. In fact, Mills and Bohannon reported that the effects of these personality constructs were modified by the sex, race, education, and age of the particular juror involved. Further empirical support is needed to support this approach's reliability, practicality and generalizability.

Non-Specific Empirical Research. Another approach, similar in substance to Schulman's demographic rating system based on community surveys described earlier, relies instead upon a different procedure for securing the information utilized in formulating predictions. This approach omits the community survey and relies solely upon *non-specific empirical research* for disclosing correlations between various demographic characteristics of jurors and their attitudes toward particular legal issues. The studies rely on post-trial interviews of actual jurors or observations of and interview data taken from mock jurors.[24] No attempt is made to test the reliability of the studies in relation to the particular trial and community of interest.

For example, to mention just a few of the more recent studies, Feild (1978) found that older and more educated jurors tended to give more lenient sentences in rape cases than younger or less educated ones. In a follow-up study, Feild and Bienen (1980) reported findings separately for white and black jurors in rape trials. Of the simple correlations computed between seven juror demographic characteristics and white jurors' recommended length of prison sentence, the age and education variables continued to provide significant, although weak correlations. For black jurors, educational level remained statistically significant; however, juror age did not. Instead black juror

service at a previous trial was found to be associated with sentencing, with those having served previously on a jury giving harsher sentences than individuals who had not. The authors concluded that the specific predictors to be used for selecting jurors in rape trials should differ depending upon the race of the juror. Feild and Bienan also note, however, that the explanation of the variability in jurors' decisions was significantly improved when attitudinal variables (including woman's responsibility in rape prevention, sex as motivation for rape, severe punishment for rape, victim precipitation of rape, normality of rapists, power as motivation for rape, favorable perception of a woman after rape, resistance as woman's role during rape, and attitudes toward women) were added to the background characteristics.

Mills and Bohannon (1980b) found that age was the best predictor of verdicts for murder cases (older people less likely to convict); age and education for rape cases (older, less educated jurors less likely to convict); and sex for robbery cases (women more likely to convict). Winston and Winston (1980) found that individuals who had completed jury duty within the previous 12 months, who were younger, less educated, lower income, didn't watch news on television, were still working, and who rated their neighbors as "not good or bad" had the least favorable attitudes toward the death penalty and thus should be the most predisposed to the defense in a capital case. Interestingly, they found that sex, race, measures of morals or life satisfactions, military rank, newspaper reading, whether or not they had a friend who was a law enforcement officer were not sensitive indicators of attitudes on this issue (also see, Moran & Comfort, 1982; Nemeth, 1981; Simon, 1980).

---

[24]Mock juries should be distinguished from shadow juries. The former attempts by various means to simulate the conditions present in an actual trial without involving the mock juror in an actual trial. For example, the mock jurors may be seated in an actual courtroom within the jury box, watch a videotape of an actual trial, and then retire to the room used by actual juries in determining their verdict. However, the dynamics of an actual ongoing trial remain absent. The shadow jury is an approach designed to further simulate the conditions of an actual trial. The shadow jurors are brought into the courtroom throughout the course of an actual trial simultaneously with the actual jurors. They see everything the actual jury sees. When the actual jury is excused, the shadow jurors also leave the courtroom. When the actual jury retires to deliberate, the shadow jurors are taken to a separate room to reach their verdict. The shadow jury can serve at least five useful purposes: (1) it provides counsel with an opportunity to ascertain how successful their trial strategy is on an ongoing basis; (2) it may capture more of the "drama" of an actual trial by immersing the shadow jurors in the "charged" atmosphere of an actual trial; (3) as is true for mock juries, it allows the experimenter to conduct in-depth demographic and personality analyses of the individuals involved; (4) it allows the manipulation and control of key independent variables, a virtue also true of mock juries, and (5) it allows for the surreptitious observation of the shadow jurors as they deliberate, providing other measurable dependent variables to utilize in analysis, again as may occur with mock juries. Although the shadow jury technique is available, no reported empirical research is available documenting its dynamics or value in predicting real juror behavior.

Unlike the strategies based on intuitive, stereotypical notions concerning particular socioeconomic characteristics which were discussed earlier, this approach has the advantage of being based on empirical research. In addition, it avoids the extensive and expensive out-of-the courtroom survey required by Schulman's strategy. However, Moran and Comfort (1982) found four flaws with a great number of such studies: (1) their scarcity and small sample size; (2) the narrow range of demographic and personality variables that were considered; (3) their failure to take into account the increased heterogeneous composition of venires since 1970 resulting from changes in modes of selecting jury panels; and (4) their attempts to establish relationships between single predictors and juror behavioral criteria. In addition, these studies suffer from the danger of overgeneralization which the Schulman approach was designed to rectify. In other words, the Schulman approach is able to develop correlations drawn from the specific locale in which the trial was to be held, eliminating the concern over national and regional differences as well as allowing a specific matching with the case and prospective jurors of interest, thereby allowing the development of more reliable predictors.

Thus, it is not surprising that Simon (1980) noted after surveying this literature:

> What seems most striking about this review is its skimpiness, its tentativeness, and the absence of any strong support for many of the expected relationships and beliefs about how jurors of various backgrounds would in fact behave in criminal and civil trials. . . .
> The irony of all this is that these beliefs have so little basis in fact. The evidence as manifested by empirical studies shows that there is some relationship between verdicts and the jurors' personal and social characteristics, and that the relationship is in the expected direction; *but* the relationship is not strong. It is not nearly strong or consistent enough to merit as much attention and effort as the practice of challenging and selecting jurors has received from the bar. (pp. 40–41)

Nemeth (1981) reached similar conclusions.

Communicative Behavior. A number of legal commentators have advised the attorney to observe prospective jurors' dress, speech, and demeanor, but they have not sufficiently specified how these behaviors are to be used in evaluating jurors (Appleman, 1968; Davis & Wiley, 1965; Katz, 1968–1969; Shepherd, 1964–1965). Authors have suggested that observers be posted to watch the jurors' arrival at the beginning of the day, their behaviors during lunch breaks, and their departure at the end of the day, with instructions to note such items as whether jurors come or leave alone, with other jurors, with spouse, or with friends; with whom the jurors socialize; how they group themselves and interact with one another; whether these interactions occur with members of the same sex and/or race; what type of vehicles they arrive in, particularly their cost, state of repair, and any distinctive characteristics such as gun racks or bumper stickers; any changes in groupings as the trial progresses, both in and out of the courtroom; any distinctive modes of dress; any particular persons who stand out from the crowd, seeming to be in charge, asking questions, acting as leaders (Mullin, 1980). When specific behavioral criteria have been proposed, the recommendations have been somewhat curious. For example, one commentator noted, "The juror who is a little surly, a little careless, who is ignoring you, is not doing anything but reflecting a favorable sign" (Harrington, 1969, p. 173). However, a technique to appraise and evaluate the *communicative behaviors* of prospective jurors has been proposed by Suggs and Sales (1978b) which rests upon a sounder empirical basis.

Communicative behaviors can be classified in terms of three dimensions: verbal, paralinguistic, and kinesic. The verbal dimension consists of the words which are actually spoken and their syntactical arrangement. The paralinguistic dimension consists of aspects of speech—such as breathing, pauses and latencies, pitch and tone of voice, and speech disturbances—that are not actually concerned with words or sentences (Pittenger & Smith, 1957). In other words, when we look at paralinguistics, we are interested in *how* something is said rather than *what* is said. Kinesic behavior, or body language, consists of such behaviors as facial expressions, body movements, body orientation, eye contact, and hand movements.

The legal training of attorneys most probably enables them to be particularly astute at analyzing the verbal component of an individual's communicative behaviors. But it is doubtful that they consciously and systematically attend to the prospective juror's paralinguistic and kinesic behavior. This omission is unfortunate because, for the purposes of the *voir dire*, the nonverbal cues may be the most important part of a prospective juror's behaviors. This is so because psychological and communication research indicates that verbal behavior is used for communicating information about events external to the speaker (a function which is appropriate in the examination of witnesses), while nonverbal cues are used to establish and maintain interpersonal relationships, to communicate interpersonal attitudes, to express emotion, and to make a presentation of the self (Argyle, 1969; Hunt & Kan Lin, 1967; Mehrabian & Ferris, 1967; Mehrabian & Wiener, 1967).

It has been demonstrated that through their nonverbal behavior people "leak" their true feelings and provide clues that deception is taking place (Ekman & Friesen, 1969; Ekman & Friesen, 1974b). This latter point is particularly important in light of Broeder's conclusion referred to earlier that "jurors often, either consciously or unconsciously, lie on voir dire" (Broeder, 1965b, p. 528). Furthermore, Mullin (1980) contends that prospective jurors suffer a great deal of anxiety from entering the alien and foreign environment of the courtroom, being subjected to what they perceive as an interrogation by the attorneys during the *voir dire* process, and feeling pressured to live up to their own self-image of being a fair and impartial individual, able to understand courtroom procedure, and able to render a just and correct decision. As a result of this anxiety the prospective juror attempts to present the perfect image of a "good" citizen entirely capable of performing jury duty ably and well. As a result they "close-down" and attempt to carefully think out their answers during the *voir dire* questioning. However, since emotions, attitudes, and clues of deception are transmitted primarily through the nonverbal channels of communication, a systematic analysis of the nonverbal behaviors presented during the *voir dire* should be a fruitful method by which the attorney could determine a prospective juror's suitability to serve.

The analysis of nonverbal communicative behaviors discussed here is *not* of the type proposed by the popular literature. Much of those writings advance the notion that particular gestures and

movements have very specific meanings. This may be so within individuals, but the research literature indicates that different people will exhibit different communicative behaviors, and that the meaning of the various nonverbal behaviors exhibited is idiosyncratic rather than universal in nature (Krause, 1961). The literature also reveals, however, that there are some common nonverbal indicators of emotion and situational anxiety; it is these behaviors that are important to the attorney and on which we will focus our attention in the remainder of this section.

There are several assumptions which can be made in weighing whether a prospective juror is more favorably disposed toward one side than the other and whether that juror is making truthful responses to the questions posed. First, it is reasonable to assume that the prospective juror will feel relatively more anxiety when being questioned by an attorney whom the jury regards with disfavor or who represents a client toward whom the juror has a negative bias. Second, anxiety also should manifest itself when the juror is being questioned about sensitive issues on which he/she has strong feelings (e.g., racial prejudice, death penalty, "law and order"). Finally, it is reasonable to assume that a juror will feel anxiety, unless he/she is a pathological liar, when being deceptive in response to questioning. The anxiety which the juror feels in each of these cases is situational anxiety—that is to say, the anxiety is generated by the particular situation at hand rather than being a stable personality trait of the individual. Research indicates that it is precisely this situational-type anxiety that is made manifest in the individual's communicative behaviors. Thus, a careful and systematic analysis of these behaviors could yield valuable insights into the individual's feelings and dispositions toward the various sides of the lawsuit, the issues, and the litigants. The goal of these ratings, therefore, is less like the other in-court procedures, which attempt to measure jurors' stable personality traits, and more like the out-of-court procedures that attempt to measure jurors' attitudes and reactions to the sides and issues in a particular trial.[25]

PARALINGUISTIC CUES

Speech Disturbances. One of the manifestations of situational anxiety is in the area of speech

---

[25]For an anecdotal account of a team of psychologists' application of a similar approach to the juror selection in the Angela Davis trial, see Sage (1973).

disturbances. These phenomena have been studied by numerous investigators. Dibner (1956) found that the speech patterns of unfinished sentences, breaking in with new thoughts, self-interrupted sentences, repeating words or phrases, stuttering, saying "I don't know" not in answer to a question but as in resignation or disgust, sighing or taking deep breaths, inappropriate laughter, voice changes, questioning the interviewer, and blocking (unusual hesitation) are clearly related to situational anxiety and not to anxiety as an overall personality characteristic. This finding has been substantiated by many other investigators (Eldred & Price, 1958; Kasl & Mahl, 1965; Mahl, 1956; Pope & Siegman, 1967).

The increase in speech disturbances under anxious conditions for the interviewee is substantial. Mahl (1956) found that during anxious phases of interviews, the average increase in speech disturbances was 29%. Cook (1969) found that when the areas of interviews generating anxiety were identified and pursued by further questioning, the speech disturbances increased markedly even though the severity of questioning was mild.

Not only is there an increase in speech disturbances when the interviewee feels anxious, but the whole character of speech changes. For example, Eldred and Price (1958) found that when an interviewee feels anxious, his speech becomes more stilted and stereotyped with less differentiated word usage. Thus, if a prospective juror had been responding to questioning in an informal manner and switched to a more formalistic and pompous style when questioned about his/her attitudes toward racial minorities, it could well be that the juror feels some anxiety about the subject matter and is perhaps being deceptive in answering.

Amount of Speech. A number of investigators have found that people tend to talk longer with people toward whom they have positive emotions (Howeler & Vrolijk, 1970; Pope & Siegman, 1967; Wiens, Jackson, Manaugh, & Matarazzo, 1969; Worthy, Cary, & Kahn, 1969). By examining the amount of verbal output of the prospective jurors to questions posed by the attorneys, observers could determine with which side the prospec-

tive juror feels more comfortable.

Speed of Speech and Breath Rate. Goldman-Eisler (1955) found that people talk noticeably faster after they have been asked an anxiety-arousing question, and that the interviewee's breathing is inhibited when he/she feels anxious or fearful. This increase in the speed of speech and the inhibition of breathing could lead to noticeably labored breathing and indicate anxiety in reaction to the particular areas probed.

Pauses and Latencies. A pause refers to a prolonged silence within a spoken sentence or phrase. Latency refers to the time between a question and the beginning of the interviewee's response to the question. Cassotta (1966) found that pauses and long latency periods are positively correlated with induced state anxiety and not with a personality trait type of anxiety. This would be another fruitful approach for aiding in the analysis of a prospective juror's responses.

KINESIC CUES

Eye Contact. The variable of eye contact as it relates to state anxiety has been researched by a number of investigators. Day (1967) maintains that when an interviewee is anxious, there is a marked increase in the frequency of lateral eye movements. Kanfer (1960) felt that the average eyeblink increased when anxiety-arousing topics were discussed, although this increased rate declines with time. Even more impressive is the work done in three studies, where it was discovered that when individuals are being deceitful, there is a decrease in the amount of visual interaction with others (Ekman & Friesen, 1974b; Exline, Thibaut, Brannon, & Gumpert, 1961; Mehrabian, 1971a).[26]

The variable of eye contact, in addition to indicating anxiety and deceitful behavior, can also be used to define the type of relationship which exists between two people. A number of investigators have found that increased eye contact indicates a positive feeling toward an individual (Argyle & Dean, 1965; Mehrabian, 1969a; Mehrabian, 1970).[27] Closely related to this finding are the

---

[26]An exception to this general proposition is the finding by Exline et al. (1961) that people high in Machiavellianism maintain as much eye contact when they are lying as when they are telling the truth.

[27]A word of caution is in order here. Ellsworth and Ross (1975) have noted that a direct linear relationship between eye contact and intimacy appears to hold true only for women subjects. Males tend to view continuous eye contact from another (particularly from other males) as threatening.

results of Efran's (1968) work in which he found that individuals maintain more eye contact with people of whom they have a high expectancy of approval. Efran's work is particularly important because of the nature of the *voir dire*. The average prospective juror enters the *voir dire* knowing none of the parties concerned, and thus should not have either positive or negative feelings toward any of the participants. Thus, his relative eye contact with the different attorneys, will indicate from whom the juror *expects* approval and a positive relationship. It is reasonable to assume that such an expectation of approval from an attorney representing a particular side is indicative of bias in favor of that side.

Facial Cues. All of us, to some extent, attempt to read facial cues when we are trying to understand a person's true feelings. It is difficult to verbally specify exactly which expressions are indicative of which emotions, but there is considerable evidence to indicate that our common sense opinions of what constitutes negative or positive emotions in the face are indeed valid (Ekman, Friesen, & Ellsworth, 1972). A cross-cultural study found that people universally attribute similar facial expressions to the emotions of happiness, sadness, anger, surprise, disgust, and fear (Ekman & Friesen, 1971). These facial expressions arise spontaneously when people are involved in verbal behavior (Ekman, 1964).

The utility of using the facial cues of prospective jurors during the *voir dire* to analyze their responses is underscored by the work of Mehrabian (1971b); Mehrabian and Ferris (1974); and Zaidel and Mehrabian (1969). These investigators found that facial cues are much more effective in communicating a person's attitudes than either the verbal or paralinguistic portions (pitch, tone of voice, etc.) of the communication. Some investigators have pointed out that facial cues show *what* emotion the individual is feeling whereas body cues show the *intensity* of a felt emotion (Ekman, 1965; Ekman & Friesen, 1967).

A note of caution must be made, however, in regard to facial cues. Ekman and Friesen (1974b) have pointed out that while the face is the major site of affect displays, it is also the site which is under the most control of the individual. Thus, if a person wished to disguise true emotions, he/she could fairly easily display false emotions on the face. Body postures and movements are not as easily controlled, however, and also should be

watched for signs of emotion. Fortunately, researchers have found that when the use of facial cues is precluded, body cues can be used effectively in perceiving emotional cues (Dittmann, Parloff, & Boomer, 1965; Ekman & Friesen, 1974a, 1974b). If the body cues contradict those given by the face, one must suspect deception by the prospective juror.

Body Postures and Movements. Body postures and movements are used by everyone whenever they interact with other individuals. Mehrabian has demonstrated that the concepts of immediacy and relaxation of body posture indicate an individual's attitude towards another person (Mehrabian, 1967c; Mehrabian, 1968; Mehrabian, 1969b; Mehrabian & Friar, 1969; Scheflen, 1964). His concept of immediacy refers to the distance between individuals, forward lean, eye contact and whether or not an individual squarely faces the person with whom he is interacting. The more immediate a person's body orientation to another the more positive is the regard shown. A person's postural relaxation is indicated by arm position asymmetry (such as one hand in the lap and the other draped over the back of a chair), side-ways lean, leg position asymmetry, hand relaxation, neck relaxation, and a slight reclining angle. The more relaxed a person's body posture when interacting with another, the more positive is the regard shown. One exception to this description must be made, however. A slight reclining angle indicates a hostile or more negative attitude.

Investigators have found that body movements are indicative of emotional arousal (Ekman, 1965; Ekman & Friesen, 1967). Still body positions occur either when there are low levels of arousal or when an act is inhibited and a tense position results. It could be safely assumed that if a prospective juror was trying to be deceptive, he/she would be emotionally aroused and this emotional arousal would become manifest either in an observable increase in body movements or in a tense, still body posture.

Hand Movements. Hand movement is another variable which could be used to detect deception on the part of prospective jurors during the *voir dire*. Freedman and Hoffman (1967) felt that body-focused activities such as finger-tapping, wringing of the hands, and manipulating various parts of the body with the hands function to modify sensory experience and may effect the state of body tension by relieving or intensifying it. Ekman and Friesen (1972) examined the same type of hand movements and concluded that body-focused hand activities occur when an individual is in psychological discomfort or anxiety. An increase in the frequency of body-focused hand movements by a prospective juror could indicate that the juror feels uncomfortable with a particular attorney or feels anxious because he/she is being deceitful.

VERBAL CUES

Immediacy of Language. Mehrabian's (1966) concept of immediacy in interaction was first introduced in regard to body posture. He also used the concept in regard to language as a measure of the directness and intensity of interaction between the communicator and the object of the communication. Examples of the concept of non-immediacy in language are such things as: the speaker referring to the object of communication by using demonstrative pronouns such as "that" and "those"; referring to the object in past or future tense instead of the present tense; indicating that the relationship between the communicator and the object is imposed; referring to the relationship as possible rather than actual; indicating that only one aspect of the communicator is involved with the object; indicating that a group of people, including the communicator, is related to the object; and indicating that a group of objects, including the object, is related to the communicator.

Mehrabian and others have concluded that communications about affectively or evaluatively negative people or events contain more nonimmediacy than communication about positive events or people (Mehrabian, 1967a, 1967b; Mehrabian & Wiener, 1966). The essential point which Mehrabian is making is that a style of language which places distance between the speaker and the topic of conversation indicates that the speaker feels negatively toward the topic of conversation. As an example of non-immediacy in language, consider the situation where two prospective jurors are questioned about any bias they

may have against blacks. Juror 1 responds, "No, I don't think I'm prejudiced against blacks," while Juror 2 responds, "No, I don't think I'm prejudiced against those people." Mehrabian would assert that Juror 2 is exhibiting more non-immediacy (and thus, probably more negative emotions towards blacks) than Juror 1.[28]

UTILIZING COMMUNICATIVE CUES

If it is observed that a prospective juror's communicative behavior indicates that he/she is feeling situational anxiety, such a result may be because of: anxiousness about being questioned by anyone in such a public forum; anxiousness and a negative emotional response to the interviewer at the time; strong emotional feelings related to the particular subject matter being discussed at the time; or deceptiveness in responding and anxiousness about being found out.

By isolating the cause of the juror's anxiety (or lack of it), a better impression of his/her suitability can be formed. One method for accomplishing this is as follows. During the initial questioning by the judge and the attorneys, the interviewers invariably start out by asking the prospective juror questions to elicit background information about such things as occupation, marital status, and address. These questions are unlikely to evoke emotional and deceptive responses, and thus, this phase of the questioning may be used to obtain a baseline of the juror's repertoire of kinesic, paralinguistic, and verbal behaviors in response to questioning by the particular interviewer. The observers then rate these communicative behaviors in terms of their positiveness or negativeness toward each interviewer. Table 1 is an example of how the juror's responses may be coded.

Suggs and Sales (1978) have found it most convenient to use the 3-point (i.e., negative, neutral and positive) scaling of communicative responses illustrated below. The ratings are guided by the criteria outlined in the previous sections, but a certain degree of subjectivity is invariably introduced in assigning a particular rating. To reduce

---

[28]Sage (1973) notes that the psychologists involved in selecting the jury for the Angela Davis trial determined that the way a juror distorted the questions while phrasing his replies indicated how that particular juror was shaping information to fit his conceptions of the world at large. In addition, they felt that if a juror consistently distorted or misunderstood the questions of one side's counsel, but seemed to comprehend immediately what the other side was asking, that juror was suspected of having emotional conflict, making it difficult for that juror to relate to one side as opposed to the other. This slant in attitude was felt to be emphasized if he could be brought to qualify his replies to one side but stuck with those he made to the other. Also it was felt that those fragments of the conversations which tended to recur in a juror's answers gave an indication of the types of facts he would be likely to remember.

this bias, it is best to have at least two observers independently rate each juror.

Table 1. The Coding of Juror Responses

Name	J	P	D
Eye contact	+	+	+
Facial cues	0	+	-
Body orientation	+	+	0
Body movements	0	0	-
Body posture	0	+	-
Hand movements	+	+	+
Speech disturbances	0	0	0
Pauses & latencies	0	0	0
Speech output	0	+	0
Style of language	0	+	+

Column J = Juror's responses to baseline phase of questioning by the Judge.
Column P = Juror's responses to baseline phase of questioning by the Prosecuting or Plaintiff's Attorney.
Column D = Juror's responses to baseline phase of questioning by the Defense Attorney.

The juror's responses on these same dimensions are again rated when the interviewer asks attitudinal questions which are relevant to the case.[29] These questions will vary from case to case, but, in general, will deal with the prospective juror's dispositions toward the attorneys, litigants, and the legal and factual issues of the case.

The observers compare the juror's responses *within* each interview in an attempt to determine whether the juror has positive or negative feelings toward the attitudinal issues which were discussed. In other words, the observers attempt to determine whether and at what point in the interview the juror becomes positively or negatively aroused in communicative behaviors by comparing baseline responses with later responses. As an example, suppose that a prospective male juror had emitted favorable responses toward the interviewer (the prosecuting attorney) during the baseline phase (i.e., direct eye contact, direct body orientation, relaxed body posture, an absence of body-focused hand activities, etc.), but when the interviewer asked him if he had formed an opinion about the guilt or innocence of the defendant, the juror said, "no" and averted his eyes, oriented his body away from the interviewer, became more tense in his body posture, and began to play with his ring. Given this large discrepancy between the juror's baseline response and his later response, it would seem fairly safe to conclude that the juror may well have an opinion as to the defendant's guilt or innocence, and that he was being deceptive in his response to the latter question. Further questioning would then be needed to probe the reason for this deception.[30]

The observers also compare the juror's kinesic, paralinguistic, and verbal behaviors *across* interviewers in an attempt to determine the juror's affective responses to the respective sides of the case. This determination merely involves a comparison of the juror's baseline behavior in response to questioning by each interviewer. Since the content of the baseline phase of questioning by each

---

[29]Although the observers attend to the same behavioral dimensions during questioning relating to attitudes, the authors have found that it is impractical to employ a separate grid for the coding of responses to each line of questioning. The impracticality arises from the speed with which the *voir dire* is conducted and because attorneys frequently do not address the same questions to each juror. Our procedure during the attitudinal phase of questioning has been to note on a separate sheet of paper only the particularly-revealing responses of jurors in regard to important attitudinal questions.

[30]A slight variation of this approach in a slightly different context has been suggested by Watson (1978), albeit without an expansive delineation of the procedure to be utilized. He notes the need to discover during the *voir dire* process whether a particular juror can comfortably listen and pay attention to the material which will be presented during the upcoming trial. For example, in a brutal homicide case, counsel will need to question a juror as to his/her ability to deal with photographs of a bloody corpse. Watson states,

When this question is asked, the crucial aspect of the examination is for counsel to observe the juror's *behavioral* manifestations, from which his anticipated feelings about seeing such evidence can be deduced. He might squirm, blanch, blush, develop sweaty palms, swallow hard, or his voice might croak when he answers. But the next question is the crucial one for determining the juror's desirability. "How did you feel when I asked you that question?" . . . If you have observed squirming or any of the other signs listed above and the juror says, "Oh, it didn't bother me at all," that is a juror to be avoided if possible. You will have just observed psychological denial, and that kind of listening will be detrimental to the fact-finding process. On the other hand, if he says, "I guess that made me kind of uncomfortable, but I think I could handle it all right," he is the kind of juror one wants. He will be able to stand right in with the evidence and perhaps empathize and understand the bloody event. (p. 235).

interviewer is usually very similar, differences in the juror's baseline behavior between interviewers is most probably reflective of the juror's affective response to the interviewer on an interpersonal level or as a representative of a particular viewpoint in the case.[31] From the observations within and across interviewers, the observers can rate the juror's suitability for either side.

PRACTICAL CONSIDERATIONS

Since the attorney who is actually conducting the *voir dire* must attend to his/her own performance, it will be next to impossible for that individual to make a systematic evaluation of the jurors' nonverbal behavior. Therefore, it will be necessary for the lead attorney to use other observers. These people should be seated as closely as possible to the prospective jurors and positioned so that they may have a head-on view of them. If the observers are seated too far away or at an angle, it will be difficult for them to distinguish between a smile and a grimace or to determine with whom the prospective juror is making eye contact. Typically, the best place from which to make the observations is at the counsel table. If the observers are attorneys, their placement presents no problem. If the attorney chooses to employ psychologists or psychiatrists to make the observations, a frequently-raised question is whether and how the behavioral experts should be introduced; the fear being that the jurors will react negatively toward them. It is our position that the presence of these observers should be fully disclosed and explained to the jurors. In post-trial interviews conducted with numerous jurors in both civil and criminal cases, we have never encountered a juror who objected to or resented the presence of behavioral experts during the *voir dire*. Furthermore, it is possible that their announced presence may have tactical advantages. One set of researchers has speculated that the visible use of such experts during the *voir dire* may give the side using them a psychological boost and demoralize the opponents (McConahay, Mullin, & Frederick, 1977).

They also note that it is possible that the use of an unusual technique to pick a fair jury may create a bond between the jurors and the side which has used the technique to "certify" them as fair jurors.

If the observers elect to use the rating form which was presented in Table 1, 12 to 14 rating boxes should be placed on a single legal size page. Given the usual rapid pace of *voir dire* and the number of ratings to be made on each juror, it is easier to make the ratings on four to five large pages than to be shuffling 50 or more single rating forms.

Finally, it should always be remembered that the use of this technique involves the evaluation of communication cues, and will be most effective when jurors are questioned with a view toward eliciting as much communication as possible from them (Sage, 1973). The attorney should also remain aware that he/she also is relaying communication signals to the prospective juror. Rapport should be established with the juror whenever possible, and it has been suggested that the attorney conducting the *voir dire* (1) eliminate everything that physically separates them from the juror, including tables, podiums, and legal pads; (2) that when an attorney chooses to move closer to a juror, this should be done slowly and carefully with an awareness that the individual juror not be made to feel anxious because their sense of personal space has been invaded; and (3) that the *voir dire* questioning be conducted in a conversational tone (Mullin, 1980). Open-ended questioning should be used whenever possible—i.e., "What are your feelings about the death penalty?" rather than "Do you have any negative feelings about the death penalty?" Silence on the part of the attorney should not be overlooked as a means to elicit additional communication cues. After a juror has answered a probing open-ended question, the attorney's silence may cause the juror to feel that the answer was incomplete and more information may be communicated (Mullin, 1980). Moreover, as the *voir dire* becomes more extensive, the ability to make accurate assessments of the jurors increases. Deeply-held value systems will be subject to greater exposure, and more clearly defined nonverbal communication interaction between attorney and prospective juror will

---

[31]As an example, the figure reproduced earlier indicates that the juror is most responsive to the prosecuting attorney and least responsive to the defense attorney. By comparing the P and D columns it is easily seen that the juror's responses to the defense attorney were less favorable on the dimensions of facial cues, body orientation, body movements, body posture and speech output. On none of the dimensions were the juror's responses more favorable to the defense attorney than to the prosecuting attorney.

be established.[32] If a juror expresses an opinion which is antagonistic toward the position to be taken by the attorney, the attorney should refrain from using the juror's statement as a springboard to "educate" the jury until after the remaining jurors have been questioned on the same subject. If the jurors are "educated" too early, the remaining jurors may not disclose their true opinions out of fear of giving the "wrong" answer.

As would be the case with the other juror selection methods discussed earlier, it has been suggested that if the initial questioning leads the observers to conclude that a particular juror be rejected, a line of questioning should be pursued which might get the potential juror excused for cause (e.g., that they would be unable to set their prior opinions aside) rather than exhausting a valuable peremptory challenge (McConahay, Mullin, & Frederick, 1977).[33]

In addition, where permitted, it has been suggested that at the conclusion of the trial, an in-depth questionnaire be administered to the jurors in order to determine which trial strategies worked and which did not (Mullin, 1980). Thereby a valuable data-bank may be compiled for future use and reference.

USING IN-COURT OBSERVATIONS

There are *limitations and drawbacks to using in-court observations.* As mentioned earlier, the trial judge has considerable latitude in determining how the *voir dire* will be conducted,[34] with the format chosen having great influence on the success of the in-court ratings. The time given for *voir dire* may be too short to allow the lawyers to ask each venire person all the questions they want and thus prevent an adequate assessment. On the other hand, the judge may decide to do all the questioning. In which case, he/she may choose not to ask the predictor questions or may ask them in such a manner as dictates the response. A third *voir dire* format which limits the success of these techniques is the group *voir dire*. With this approach, after the first few jurors are questioned, the remaining jurors are able to anticipate forthcoming questions, what type of answer produces what type of response by the attorneys, judge, and audience, and are able to prepare their responses so as to present themselves in certain ways. This format, as opposed to individual sequestration of venire persons during *voir dire*, has been shown to hinder attempts to discover bias in potential jurors regardless of the type of jury selection methods employed (Nietzel & Dillehay, 1982; Suggs & Sales, 1981).

COMBINING THE INFORMATION

Although each of these systematic approaches to jury selection can be and has been used by itself, a common approach has been to use some or all of the methods in conjunction with each other. Thus, sometime between the conclusion of the *voir dire* and the peremptory challenges, a meeting is held in which all the information on each juror is pooled for the purpose of rank-ordering the prospective jurors from least- to most-desirable. Representatives from the survey team, from the investigation team, each of the people who rated jurors during the *voir dire*, the attorneys,[35] and the litigants typically attend the meeting. As each prospective juror's name comes up, every person at the meeting gives an assessment of that person. Those jurors who everyone agrees are very good or very bad for one side are quickly

---

[32]In the Angela Davis case, as the result of an unusual happenchance in the conducting of the *voir dire*, the behavioral experts responsible for analyzing the nonverbal behavior of prospective jurors were provided an opportunity to conduct a more in-depth appraisal of those jurors. Both defense attorneys were black, but one was obviously so in terms of physical features, while the other defense attorney was assumed to be white for some time by many courtroom participants. By studying the way each juror responded to questioning by the two attorneys, the experts responsible for helping to select the jury hoped to spot hidden antipathies and racial characteristics, which might reflect concsious or subconscious prejudicial attitudes to blacks, diminishing the opportunity of Davis, a black individual, to secure a fair hearing (Sage, 1973).

[33]For a discussion of mathematical models on how to optimize the utilization of the peremptory challenges when striking jurors, see Bermant and Shepard (1981).

[34]As the Second Circuit concluded in *United States* v. *Taylor,* 562 F.2d 1345 (2d Cir. 1977), the only restriction on the trial judge's discretion is that questioning be fair to the parties, enabling them to exercise challenges intelligently. Thus, questions need not cover specific points requested by a particular party. See "Defendant's Rights to Impartial" (1979).

[35]The value of an experienced trial lawyer's "hunches" should not be overlooked. Their past experience with jurors' reactions to trial procedures, witnesses and other types of evidence can provide a highly useful adjunct for predicting how the particular jurors will react in response to the highly unique unfolding sequence of events which is the hallmark of the litigation process.

identified, and the remainder of the meeting is spent discussing the pros and cons of the venire persons who are rated in the middle or about whom there is disagreement.

At this stage, time is spent on predicting certain juror characteristics that were implicitly, but not explicitly, evaluated in the juror selection process. For example, how persuasive versus persuadable each juror might be during jury deliberations is one such factor. There are several "rules of thumb" that have typically been employed. First, it is considered dangerous to allow on a jury a person who has been rated as persuasive and whose predisposition toward the case is unfavorable or unknown, since that person may persuade others toward the opposing side during deliberations. Conversely, leaving on the jury one persuasive individual who is favorable to your side is desirable, in hopes that he/she will be the jury foreman and influence the others. Finally, it is felt that it is usually better to include in the jury a person who is unfavorably disposed but a persuadable follower, rather than a person whose dispositions are in doubt but who is considered persuasive (Sage, 1973).

In addition to considering the persuasability dimension when combining information, it has also been the practice to attempt to anticipate coalition formation within the prospective jury and which jurors will assume roles of leadership in the deliberations. There is a great deal of behavioral science evidence showing that similar people are attracted to each other. Thus, it is considered safe to assume that those jurors who share similar background and personality characteristics will form a subgroup within the jury. Also, attention has been given to selecting "bridge" persons who can relate to more than one of the subgroups (Mullin, 1980). In making these determinations, attention should be given to how jurors react to statements directed to other jurors, and the effects their answers are having on them. It can be noted which jurors consistently sit near each other or converse with one another frequently before and after recesses. Lineups at water coolers, groupings at lunch breaks, and couples in the halls leading to and from the courtroom have been suggested as worthy of note (Sage, 1973). Other tip-offs on the imminent formation of juror coalitions which have been listed include: meaning-laden eye contact and matching gestures between the waiting potential jurors (e.g., jurors folding their arms at the same time) (Cohn & Udolf, 1979).

Group coalition will interact with the considerations of persuasiveness considered above. For example, it has been the practice to include in the jury a person whose predisposition may be unfavorable, but who will very likely be part of a subgroup which contains a more persuasive and favorably disposed person. Similarly, it has been shown that a minority opinion is less likely to be disclosed and listened to if the individual holding that opinion stands alone (Hans & Vidmar, 1982). For reviews of those studies which attempt to determine which jurors will be the most influential in determining the group's decisions see Simon (1980) and Nemeth (1981).

After considering this information, the group must make a series of contingency plans as to when to strike in what order so that responses can be made to whatever the opposition does. This is essential since each side obviously is unaware of which venire persons the other side will strike. This means that these meetings can last quite a long time; it is not uncommon for them to continue for 7 or 8 hours. See DeGroot and Kadane (1980) for a study of optimal strategies to be followed by lawyers in their use of the peremptory challenges that are available to them.

There are several problems which may arise during this stage of jury selection. Lack of time poses one difficulty. Combining of the information requires a large amount of time between the end of the *voir dire* questioning and the exchange of peremptory challenges. Unfortunately, judges do not always feel that they can delay proceedings to allow for this process since the court calendar is generally overloaded with cases that must be moved along as quickly as possible.

Another practical problem lies in the "looseness" of the methods typically used to integrate the information. Given that each expert gives an assessment of each juror, it might be inferred that the information is somehow systematically combined. Although techniques have been outlined for combining the data into a mathematical prediction equation (Christie, 1976; McConahay, et al., 1977), unfortunately a systematic synthesis of the information is the exception rather than the rule. The effectiveness of the group sessions have depended heavily upon who emerged as the leader, the personalities of the people involved, and how successful the people working on each component of the selection process were at collecting "good" and persuasive data. The leader has been important because he/she structures the meeting by determining who speaks first, how long discussion lasts, and so on. The other personalities involved, however, have also made a difference. For example, if the person representing the survey was more argumentative and articulate than the person representing the juror investigations, then the former type of information tends to determine close decisions more often than the latter. Thus, potentially valuable information from less vocal and less assertive group members is often disregarded. And the fact that the various sources of data are of uneven quality can be lost in the course of the discussion. In order to reduce distortion and contamination, it has been suggested that evaluation be made in written form prior to this pooling process (Hans & Vidmar, 1982). However, even assuming that sufficient time is available for this additional step, this may do little to reduce the forcefulness of a particular individual's presentation, and the tendency of less dominant group members to submit to the formulations of the more dominant members.

Another crucial factor relating to the effective utilization of these techniques, which Christie (1976) points out, is the working relationship between the behavioral experts and lawyers involved in a particular case. He contends that these techniques are not a radical departure from more traditional legal practice, but, rather, an outgrowth and systematization of trial lawyers' informal techniques. Nevertheless, differences in education, training, and emphasis lead to different conceptual approaches to jury selection, and can make cooperation between the two groups difficult, if not impossible.

CRITICISMS OF
THE SYSTEMATIC APPROACH

Despite all of the foregoing, it should be noted that some experts feel that attempts to influence the composition of the jury do not have a significant impact on the outcome of a trial (e.g., Saks, 1976b). They feel that the evidence,[36] the argument, and the courtroom style are of much major importance in determining verdicts that the composition of the jury is, in comparison, rather insignificant. In addition, Christie (1976) points out that two constraints must be satisfied before systematic jury selection can even hope to be worthwhile: (1) there must be enough ambiguity in the evidence of the case to give a reasonable juror cause for thought and (2) the initial composition of the jury pool must be heterogeneous enough to permit discrimination among potential jurors. Berk (1976) warns that only very pronounced variables and only those which can be translated into factors assessable in court can be taken seriously. Others argue that jury selection is important, but that the current system of causal and peremptory challenges and of admonitions to the jurors about being fair—from both judges and lawyers—is sufficient in many cases to produce a favorable, or at least reasonably fair, jury (Berman & Sales, 1977). There also is controversy around whether or not behavioral experts are actually doing any better at selecting favorable or neutral juries than was done before by lawyers acting alone or in concert with the advice of the clients (Berman & Sales, 1977; Saks & Hastie, 1978). And it has been pointed out that both lawyers and behavioral experts vary tremendously in their ability to make appropriate discriminations between potential jury members (Christie, 1976; Parker, 1980).

Nevertheless, the behavioral science techniques for jury selection continue to have strong advocates. As one author concluded, these techniques can remove much of the guessing (Mullin, 1980). Another author concluded that "jury selection techniques as offered by social scientists appear to have some real value in cases where the evidence is ambiguous and where the potential pool of jurors is sufficiently heterogeneous to allow for discrimination in the selection of individuals" (Parker, 1980, p. 179).

Some of the methods' proponents argue for their effectiveness by pointing to the number of trials where they have been used by one side who went on to attain a favorable verdict. The fact that a high proportion of verdicts have favored the behavioral experts is indisputable. It is not at all clear, however, that the method of jury selection made any difference in these cases. There are a host of other factors that may have been the important determinants of the verdicts. First, the bulk of these trials have been highly publicized affairs where the defendant has been portrayed as

---

[36]Hepburn (1980) found that jurors' attitudes toward those issues constituting the basis for the case and toward those social groups which testify during the trial do contribute to the jurors' verdict, but only indirectly. Verdict was found to be directly affected by the perceived strength of evidence, which in turn was related to the jurors' case-relevant attitudes. Thus it was suggested that strength-of-evidence variables be included in systematic jury selection procedures.

"fighting an oppressive system."[37] Second, well-known and very competent lawyers have generally represented the defendants. Third, frequently the major charge has been conspiracy—apparently a very difficult charge to prove. Fourth, besides the extraordinary efforts at jury selection, there have been extraordinary efforts at other aspects of these trials, such as legal research, expert testimony, and the collection of evidence.[38] Berk (1976) notes that in most previous trials where behavioral science data has been utilized it was the defense that sought assistance. Thus even if only one sympathetic and stubborn juror could be found, a hung jury was assured. However, if a plaintiff or prosecutor was involved, an entire jury has to be convinced with a much smaller margin for error.

Other authors suggest that the selection process had side effects, and that it is these side effects which produced the success rate. The lawyers utilizing the system believed it to be effective, raising their morale and causing them to work harder, with a reverse effect operating upon the opposing litigation team. Further, it was speculated that the process made the jurors feel special because they had been chosen by "experts," resulting in a favorable attitude toward the side which utilized those "experts." In addition, the exceptionally detailed *voir dire* may have indoctrinated the jurors to an unusual degree about being impartial (McConahay et al., 1977; Hans & Vidmar, 1982). The amassing of such data may raise issues that otherwise would have been ignored or relieve attorneys of anxiety so that they can more easily move on to other issues (Berk, 1976).

Since the favorable verdicts in trials where the method has been used are not *convincing* evidence for its effectiveness, we might ask whether there is convincing data elsewhere. The answer at this time is a tentative no (see Saks, 1976b). There have been cases where a behavioral science method was used and the jurors were interviewed after the trial in an attempt to determine their disposition toward the defendant before the trial began, at the first balloting, during jury deliberation, and at the last balloting. Unfortunately, reports have been scarce and have not included a comparison between the behavioral expert's correlations and the lawyer-client correlations. That is, as already noted, the lawyers and clients may be as good or even better than the experts at judging jurors' predispositions.

Some authors go so far as to suggest that the variables involved in trials are so numerous that rigorous and systematic evaluation of the approach is virtually impossible (Parker, 1980). Bermant and Shepard (1981) point out that there are factors inherent in the legal system itself which make it difficult to secure an accurate assessment of the validity of behavioral science techniques for jury selection. They point out that the cooperation of both attorneys and judges is essential for the employment of the best research designs. However, the attorney's overriding responsibility is to see to it that the client wins, leaving no room for a disinterested variation in the trial practice that would be necessary to insure the required controlled observations. Furthermore, advocates are unlikely to expose their own ignorance and/or inability in conducting the *voir dire* process to scrutiny, since such public exposure might deflate their value and ability to earn a living from trial work, even though they may be quite amenable to suggestions from behavioral experts as to *voir dire* tactics to apply on particular cases. Bermant and Shepard also note that judges may not be supportive because their primary interest may be in maximizing the speed and efficiency of the judicial process; thus, they may find the expert's goals in conflict with this interest. They also contend that the experts may find it difficult to maintain their disinterestedness in testing these tactics. They suggest that it is possible that the expert will be caught up by the advocacy nature of the judicial system, tending to identify with and develop a commitment to the particular tactic.

Yet, there have been some studies of effectiveness that do provide relevant data. In one, it was

---

[37]This factor may in part be lessening in importance as the number of practitioners of scientific jury selection and the acceptance and utilization of it by the legal profession grows. Increasingly, scientific jury selection is being incorporated into a wide gamut of cases.

[38]For example, Hans Zeisel, a well-known University of Chicago sociologist, was hired by the Ford Motor Company to aid in jury selection. Ford was successful in its defense of a case in which the company was charged with criminal homicide in connection with the deaths in Indiana of three young women in a Pinto automobile (Totenberg, 1982). Also note, however, that this remained a highly-publicized case, with well-known and very competent attorneys representing Ford, with extraordinary efforts expended in other portions of the trial. In addition, the trial involved highly volatile issues which may have tended to polarize potential jurors, making the discrimination between "good" and "bad" jurors an easier task.

concluded that no more than 16% of verdict preferences could be predicted from the juror's personal characteristics and attitudes about the justice system and crime. Although admitting that a more explosive case, with deeper-seated biases held by jurors, may lend itself more to behavioral science techniques of jury selection, in the relatively mundane cases the author studied he concluded that these techniques would do little to help a lawyer predict how an individual juror will vote (Winter, 1980). Relatedly, Saks (1976a) studied 27 predictor variables and found they accounted for only 13% of the variance in the verdicts, and concluded that the degree to which the evidence was incriminating was the most potent predictor of the verdict (also see Horowitz, 1980).

In the most recent study in this vein, Moran and Comfort (1982) attempted to correct flaws found in prior research (see p. 41) by greatly expanding both the sample size and the number of demographic and personality variables which were taken into account. But they too were unable to generate convincing support for the contention that particular demographic and personality variables could be used to universally predict juror behavior. After analyzing completed questionnaires from jurors who had randomly served on felony juries in the state courts in Miami during 1975–1976, they found that for male jurors only 3 of 23 predictor variables significantly contributed to the regression equation. For female jurors only one variable was statistically significant in the regression analysis used.

In addition, their study suffered from problems recurrent in such probes. First, their questionnaire contained excerpts from full personality scales, which casts doubt on the reliability and validity of any conclusions about the respondents' personality. Second, when such a large number of predictor variables are examined, a certain number of them can be expected to be statistically significant by chance alone. Third, there is the likelihood of a nonrepresentational response by those jurors to whom the questionnaire is sent (e.g., only 21.3% of the sample of 1,500 jurors to whom the questionnaires were sent returned them. Only 4% of the respondents were black, while a previous study had shown that 16% of the venire from which the sample was drawn were black. Fourth, the predictor variables for male jurors explained only 10.7% of the variance, and an associated discriminant analysis indicated that verdict prediction was only 66.5% correct. The single significant predictor variable for the female jurors accounted for but 5.9% of the variance,

and discriminant analysis indicated that 67.7% of female jurors' verdicts were predicted accurately. Obviously for both male and female jurors other far more powerful variables were being overlooked. Also, since the conviction rate in this jurisdiction was 65%, an attorney could very nearly match the accuracy provided by the predictor variables by merely assuming the juror voted guilty. Without providing the analyses, Moran and Comfort do note that by calculating predictor-criterion correlations for each income subclassification, the median accuracy for both males and females increased to 87%, a substantial improvement. However, such extensive and complex posthoc analyses suggests the possibility that these results may be idiosyncratic, specific to the Miami area, of little value predictively, and that a more case-specific analysis might be more appropriate. Fifth, the important comparison is not included, namely, how accurately could lawyers, relying on their own intuition, predict jurors' verdicts. Finally, it should be kept in mind that Moran and Comfort were only testing the efficacy of one mode of jury selection, that based upon non-specific empirical research.

Moreover, in a survey of juror selection studies, Saks and Hastie (1978) concluded that the evidence is the most important, and a substantially more potent, determinant of jurors' verdicts than the individual characteristics of jurors. They ground their determination in small-group research which shows that individual difference variables account for little of the variation in group performance. However, they qualify this by noting that while situational variables (e.g., the evidence in the case) are more determinative of behavior than individual difference variables, it is the interaction between the two which is the best predictor of all.

Hans and Vidmar (1982) agree, noting that the literature is plagued with the faulty assumption that if personality- or demographically-based dispositions exist, they will override the evidentiary and situational factors associated with the type of case. They assert this assumption fails to take into account the currently prevailing view that personality dispositions interact with situations in complex ways. They conclude that a theory of case-characteristic dimensions needs to be developed and then integrated with a theory of personality dimensions before clear-cut predictions can be drawn about juror behavior. They further suggest that where and how juror bias manifests itself may be an important element for consideration. Pre-trial dispositions, interpreting or recalling evidence, following jury instructions, and susceptibility to persuasion from other jurors during the deliberation process are all possible occasions where they see personality dispositions exerting an influence, but the nature and extent of that influence will vary with the particular situation involved.

Our emphasis on the difficulties with the behavioral science techniques is not intended to imply that the methods are in fact ineffective. The point is that there are some reasons why they might be ineffective and that sufficient evaluation data are not available. Even if an evaluation of a technique were conducted, and it did not demonstrate the efficacy of the technique, it would still be a serious scientific error to assume the truth of the null hypothesis; the failure to find an effect can be due to any number of deficiencies in methods, measurement, or design. Given the great difficulty of doing this type of research, it would not be surprising if a rather powerful effect were to go undetected.[39]

If, on the other hand, effectiveness is convincingly found, the next task would be to pinpoint exactly what aspects of these methods produce their results. One possibility is that its value lies not in any specific component of the techniques or specific dimensions which are measured, but rather in the fact that the number of assessors has been increased. Psychometricians have demonstrated that the more items there are on a psychological scale, the closer the sum of those items is to a person's true score on that scale. The reason is that the errors of measurement on individual items cancel each other when the items are summed. Thus, should a technique prove to be effective, it could be because it brings so many more assessors to the task that the measurement errors of any one group or person are cancelled by the errors of the others.

ETHICAL AND LEGAL IMPLICATIONS

Etzioni (1974) and Van Dyke (1977b) take another tack in criticizing the use of behavioral science techniques to scrutinize prospective jurors. They find that such practices, while perhaps effective, oftentimes lead to public doubt about the impartiality of the verdict of an apparently hand-picked jury. They urge that if the outcome of a trial can be manipulated simply by impaneling jurors designated acceptable by behavioral experts, the purpose of a trial by a cross-representational jury has been destroyed. They conclude that the interests of justice would be better served if the lists used to impanel jurors were more complete, if fewer excuses and challenges were allowed, if all out-of-courtroom investigations were forbidden, if the questioning and removal of prospective jurors were left exclusively to the judge, and if, as a result, the resulting jury more accurately reflected the diversity of the community.

In rebuttal, however, Saks (1976), points out that for centuries it has been considered proper for lawyers to impanel the most favorable juries possible for their clients, and just because they now have the means to do so should not make this goal suspect. In addition, Saks points out that if both sides have access to these techniques, the final jury panel will consist, as it is supposed to, of neutral jurors. If one side has greater access to these techniques it is a result of the inequity of the judicial system, not the inherent evil of a method which, if effective, promotes the pursuit of justice by eliminating the extremes of partiality.

Yet, there are inherent ethical implications for both the lawyer[40] and the behavioral expert in

---

[39]However, it should be noted that at least one individual, Berk (1976), has gone on record as saying that in light of the conceptual, methodological, and operational problems, at least with the community survey approach, it is doubtful that any striking benefits are likely to result from that approach.

[40]Three provisions of the American Bar Association's (ABA) *Code of Professional Responsibility* (which has both a binding effect and a directive effect on lawyers in those states where the respective state bar association has adopted the code, with all 50 states having adopted some form of the code) has application in regard to jury selection. Disciplinary Rule 7-108(A) reads, "Before the trial of a case a lawyer connected therewith shall not communicate with or cause another to communicate with anyone he knows to be a member of the venire from which the jury will be selected for the trial of the case." Disciplinary Rule 7-108(E) states, "A lawyer shall not conduct or cause, by financial support or otherwise, another to conduct a vexation or harassing investigation of either a venireman or a juror." Disciplinary Rule 7-108(F) extends this position to members of the family of a venireman or juror. These provisions have not been interpreted as of yet to foreclose any of the jury selection techniques which have been discussed. However, it should be noted that more restrictive guidelines were provided in the ABA *Standards Relating to the Administration of Criminal Justice*, 2nd Edition (tentative draft approved, February 12, 1979), in which virtually identical directives are provided for the prospective and defense lawyers in a criminal case:

In those cases where it appears necessary to conduct a pretrial investigation of the background of jurors, investigatory methods of the prosecution (lawyer) should neither harass nor unduly embarrass potential jurors or invade their privacy and, whenever possible, should be restricted to an investigation of records and sources of information already in existence. (Standards 3-5.3[6] and 4-7.2[6]).

attempting to procure a jury which is more than "fair"—that is, a jury which is likely to be partial to one side over the other. This question may be magnified when the aid of these experts is available to one side and not the other, or to one class of litigants and not to others (Sage, 1973).

Furthermore, should there be a requirement that the information gathered be shared with all concerned parties? Currently such requests are frequently refused based upon the "work product" privilege (Penner, 1982). Issues concerning invasion of the privacy of prospective jurors by both out-of-court investigations and the nature of in-court *voir dire* questioning might also be raised ("Defendant's Right to Impartial," 1979),[41] as well as the confidentiality of the material gathered. Concern has been raised over the lack of regulation of this crucial aspect of the trial process, and over the possiblity that wide-spread interviewing outside the courtroom may insidiously prejudice the population from which the jury is drawn (Penner, 1982). For a detailed discussion of these matters see Berman and Sales (1977) and Herbsleb, Sales, and Berman (1979).

INTERNATIONAL IMPLICATIONS

Finally, given the composition of our readership, we need to ask if the approaches reviewed in this paper will be of value to behavioral experts in other countries. In fact, jury trials are not a universal phenomenon. The number of countries that utilize them are limited, with many countries having discontinued their use. For example, between 1812 and 1936 Spain enacted and then abolished eight different laws involving the use of jury trials. One law provided that jurors be selected according to the amount of taxes they paid. The more they paid, the greater the likelihood the individual would become a juror, with each party having the right to challenge up to 30 jurors. Most of the laws were terminated following government dissatisfaction with the high rate of acquittals which resulted. The new Spanish Constitution again permits jury trials but awaits the passage of enabling legislation by the Spanish legislature (Burros, 1982).

Many countries introduced jury trials as the result of English influence and/or colonization, only later to abandon them.[42] Such was the case in Singapore, which found jury trials inefficacious and abolished them in 1969. Discussing the possible reintroduction of jury trials in Singapore, Cheang (1973) noted the exclusion of certain classes of people from panels of prospective jurors and the lack of trial by peers in Singapore under the prior system. A requirement that the juror understand English excluded a fair percentage of the population, with trial by the English-educated resulting. A similar pattern occurred in South Africa following the introduction of British rule. Again the jury system was not considered a great success, with civil trial juries abolished in 1927 and criminal trial juries eliminated in 1969 (Mittlebeeler, 1968; Strauss, 1973).

The jury system continues in force in other countries greatly influenced by the British, but there too has drawn fire for the unrepresentativeness of the modes of jury selection. For a discussion of the Irish jury, see Robinson (1973); for New Zealand, see Burns (1973); for Australia, see Brown (1973), Hale (1973), Hayes (1973); for Nigeria, see Mittlebeeler (1973).

However, along with the United States, it is Great Britain that is looked to as the primary proponent of the jury trial, although the purpose behind jury selection there is somewhat different than in the United States. Their goal is to assemble a jury which reflects a cross-section of the community from which it is drawn. The concept that a jury be without bias or prejudice is of secondary importance. But there too the jury system is under attack. The use of a jury trial in civil litigation is practically non-existent and is rare in criminal cases. There are a number of possible reasons that could account for this phenomenon. On the civil side, dissatisfaction with jury trials is largely traceable to demands for a cheaper and speedier procedure, claims that jury trials were less predictable and the quality of jurors was deteriorating, and a desire to have damage awards controlled by the judiciary (Driscoll, 1979). On the criminal side, demands for a quicker method of prosecution have led to an increasing number

---

[41]In *United States* v. *Barnes*, 604 F.2d 121 (2d Cir. 1979), *cert. denied*, 446 U.S. 907 (1980), it was held that *voir dire* questioning of potential jurors about their religion and ethnicity can be prohibited to preserve the jurors' rights to privacy.

[42]Despite the pervasive influence of the English system, jury trials are not an English invention. The first general purpose courts involving jurors drawn from all segments of the citizenry were found in Athens about 590 B.C. (Bertoch, 1971).

of crimes being reclassified as not entitling the defendant to opt for a jury trial. But even where one is permitted, defendants have decreasingly requested jury trials perhaps because of the gradual curtailment in their ability to challenge its composition. Until 1948, a defendant had a right to peremptorarily challenge up to 15 jurors. In 1948 this was reduced to seven, and dropped to three in 1977. Even this right is rarely exercised since the Lord Chief Justice's practice direction now prevents defendant's counsel from questioning potential jurors and since occupations, a common basis for such challenges, have been deleted from the jury list.[43] Further compounding the disadvantage the defense works at is that the prosecution's right to challenge jurors is unlimited and they have the ability to ask the police to investigate prospective jurors (Driscoll, 1979). This disparity, until very recently, was most likely to be effected where serious offenses with strong political overtones were involved (Nicol, 1979). However, new guidelines promulgated by the Attorney-General circumscribe the circumstances in which police checks on prospective jurors may take place, and except in terrorist cases, bans them in cases with political implications ("Jury Checks," 1980).

At least one commentator has noted with displeasure the unfairness to the accused of this imbalance. He conjectures that excluding certain categories of jurors from jury panels by the prosecution may be the crucial factor in determining the guilt or innocence of the accused. And since the appearance of justice can be just as important as its actual implementation, this same commentator recommends that the Crown be limited in the number of challenges without cause it is allowed, putting it on a par with the defense, mirroring the American courts. He also cautions, however, that the effects of jury challenges upon jury verdicts are unclear and require further research to ascertain their impact (McEldowney, 1979).

As mentioned, there has been little empirical data gathered in Great Britain on the effect of jury selection on jury composition and jury verdicts, and coincidentally, "scientific" methods of jury selection have not been introduced into the country. Baldwin and McConville (1980) provide the leading English study on the subject. In the largest analysis of jury trials undertaken in England, they collected background information on 3,912 jurors, including their sex, age, occupation, race and number of prior jury sittings. They then attempted to correlate these characteristics to the pattern of verdicts returned. They found that English juries were reasonably representative of the wider community in certain important respects (age and occupational structure), but less so in others (sex and race). Nevertheless they felt that English juries were more representative of the general community than their American counterparts, although they do not provide data to substantiate their claim. The *voir dire* also had substantially less impact than it does in the United States. They found only 101 challenges in the 370 criminal trials examined, with only 13 jurors being rejected by the Crown. Of those defendants making challenges, three-quarters were found guilty. However, this latter item would have carried more weight had they reported what the conviction rate was for those jurors not raising challenges concerning individual jurors.

In addition, Baldwin and McConville found that imbalances in the composition of the jury had little impact on the verdicts reached. For sex, age, and social class, imbalances of jury composition did not produce any significant change in the pattern of verdicts. They thus conclude that there was no support from their study for the effectiveness of selection procedures based upon these particular characteristics. It should be noted, however, that their study only investigated one city (Birmingham) in England, creating the possibility that a homogeneous group was being examined, thereby obscuring distinctions prevalent in a more heterogeneous sample; lumped all types of criminal trials together, eliminating another possible distinguishing variable; and investigated a limited number of demographic variables, thereby overlooking other variables which may have contributed to the verdict patterns.

Moreover, based upon this brief review of jury usage in other countries, it appears that the techniques discussed in this chapter will have mixed applicability elsewhere. In those countries that only provide for bench trials, these techniques will be useless. But even where jury trials function, the value of scientific selection is speculative since baseline data on juror and jury behavior in

---

[43]This latter change occurred after a number of building workers were acquitted of conspiracy charges allegedly connected with a national building workers strike. The defense had managed to secure a predominantly working class jury (Driscoll, 1979).

these countries is apparently sparse or nonexistent. The collection of such data is necessary both to choose an appropriate technique or set of techniques and to understand how to best use these techniques. For instance, the research that supports the communicative behavior technique was gathered on United States subjects. There is every reason to assume that these behaviors will vary in other countries, which in turn may necessitate revising the scale that is used to evaluate prospective jurors on this dimension or the type and direction of ratings that are made when the scale is used. Once such data is available, however, it is likely that the other countries will start experimenting with scientific jury selection similarly to what is happening in the United States today.

Conclusion

The *voir dire* can serve a variety of purposes. It may be used as a method for eliminating from the panel prospective jurors who are unsuitable either as a matter of law or because of an unspecified predilection of the attorneys trying the case. The *voir dire* may also be used as a means for attorneys to ingratiate themselves with the jury or to plant the seeds of an argument before the presentation of evidence.

This article has sought to review and critique the legal and behavioral science literature that has offered suggestions concerning methods that can be used to accomplish the judicially sanctioned purposes of the *voir dire*. The review demonstrated that the suggestions from the legal literature for the most part are based on hypothesis and folklore. Very little, if any, empirical work has been performed to substantiate the reliability and validity of the techniques proposed by the legal writers. The recent entrance of behavioral experts into this field is encouraging since they have the expertise to empirically evaluate the efficacy of current legal practices and of offering alternatives based on research.

Reference Notes

1. Diamond, S., & Zeisel, H. *A courtroom experiment on juror selection and decision-making.* Paper presented at the meeting of the American Psychological Association, New Orleans, September 1972.
2. Mayer, J. *An experimental evaluation of the lawyer's folklore for jury selection.* Unpublished manuscript, Hofstra University 1955.
3. Tapp, J.L., & Keniston, A., Jr. *Wounded Knee— Advocate or expert: Recipe for a fair juror?* Paper presented at the meeting of the American Psychological Association, Washington, DC, September 1976.
4. Christie, R. *A psychohistory of conspiracy trials.* Paper presented at the meeting of the American Psychological Association, Washington, DC, September 1976.
5. Brodsky, S. *The Holiday Inn caper: A psychological porthole in jury selection.* Unpublished manuscript, University of Alabama, 1977. (Available from author, Department of Psychology, Box 2968, University of Alabama, University, Alabama 35468.)
6. Lerner, M. *The unjust consequences of the need to believe in a just world.* Paper presented at the meeting of the American Psychological Association, New York, September 1966.

References

Alker, H.R., & Barnard, J.J. Procedural and social biases in the jury selection process. *Justice System Journal,* 1978, *3,* 220–241.

Alker, H.R., Hosticka, C., & Mitchell, M. Jury selection as a biased social process. *Law and Society Review,* 1976, *11,* 9–41.

American Bar Association. *Project on minimum standards for criminal justice: Standards relating to trial by jury.* New York: Institute of Judicial Administration, 1968.

Amsterdam, A.G., Segal, B.L., & Miller, M.K. *Trial manual for the defense of criminal cases.* Philadelphia: American Law Institute, 1967.

Appleman, J.A. Selection of the jury. *Trial Lawyer's Guide,* 1968, *12,* 207–239.

Argyle, M. *Social interaction.* New York: Atherton Press, 1969.

Argyle, M., & Dean, J. Eye contact, distance and affiliation. *Sociometry,* 1965, *28,* 289–304.

Ashby, J.B. Juror selection and the sixth amendment right to an impartial jury. *Creighton Law Review,* 1978, *11,* 1137–1168.

Attorney participation in voir dire examination in Illinois. *University of Illinois Law Forum,* 1977, 1145–1166.

Baldwin, J., & McConville, M. Does the composition of an English jury affect its verdict? *Judicature,* 1980, *64,* 133–139.

Berk, R.A. Social science and jury selection: A case study of a civil suit. In G. Bermant, C. Nemeth, & N. Vidmar (Eds.), *Psychology and the law.* Lexington, MA: Lexington Books, 1976.

Berk, R.A., Hennessy, M., & Swan, J. The vagaries and vulgarities of scientific jury selection: A methodological evaluation. *Evaluation Quarterly,* 1977, *1,* 143–158.

Berman, J., & Sales, B.D. A critical evaluation of the systematic approach to jury selection. *Criminal Justice and Behavior,* 1977, *4,* 219–240.

Bermant, G., & Shepard, J. The voir dire examination, juror challenges and adversary advocacy. In B.D. Sales (Ed.), *The trial process.* New York: Plenum, 1981.

Bertoch, M.J. The Greeks had a jury for it. *American Bar Association Journal*, 1971, *57*, 1012–1014.

Blunk, R., & Sales, B.D. Persuasion during the voir dire. In B.D. Sales (Ed.), *Psychology in the legal process*. New York: Spectrum, 1977.

Bodin, H.S. *Selecting a jury*. New York: Practicing Law Institute, 1954.

Bodin, H.S. Selecting a jury in civil litigation and trial techniques. In H.S. Bodin (Ed.), *Civil litigation and trial techniques*. New York: Practicing Law Institute, 1976.

Boehm, V.R. Mr. Prejudice, Miss Sympathy, and the authoritarian personality. *Wisconsin Law Review*, 1968, 734–750.

Bray, R.M., & Noble, A.M. Authoritarianism and decisions of mock juries: Evidence of jury bias and group polarization. *Journal of Personality and Social Psychology*, 1978, *36*, 1424–1430.

Bridgeman, D.L., & Marlowe, D. Jury decision making: An empirical study based on actual felony trials. *Journal of Applied Psychology*, 1979, *64*, 91–98.

Brody, A. Selecting a jury—Art or blind man's bluff. *Criminal Law Review*, 1957, *4*, 67–78.

Broeder, D.W. Occupational expertise and bias as affecting juror behavior: A preliminary look. *New York University Law Review*, 1965, *40*, 1079–1100. (a)

Broeder, D.W. Voir dire examinations: An empirical study. *Southern California Law Review*, 1965, *38*, 503–528. (b)

Brown, D. Some recent criticisms and problems of trial by jury. *Western Australian Law Review*, 1973, *11*, 256–263.

Brown, F.L., McGuire, F.T., & Winters, M.S. The peremptory challenge as a manipulative device in criminal trials: Traditional use or abuse. *New England Law Review*, 1978, *14*, 192–235.

Burns, P.T. A profile of the jury system in New Zealand. *Western Australian Law Review*, 1973, *11*, 105–110.

Burros, M.G. The Spanish jury: 1888–1923. *Case Western Reserve Journal of International Law*, 1982, *14*, 177–246.

Busch, F.X. *Law and tactics in jury trials* (Vol. 1, encyc. ed.). Indianapolis: Bobbs-Merrill, 1959.

Cassotta, L. The stability and modification of the vocal behavior of individuals in stress and nonstress interviews. *Dissertation Abstracts International*, 1966, *27*, 2867B. (University Microfilms No. 67-587)

Centers, R., Shomer, R.W., & Rodrigues, A. A field experiment in interpersonal persuasion using authoritative influence. *Journal of Personality*, 1970, *38*, 392–403.

Chandler, M. An evaluation of group interview. *Human Organization*, 1954, *13*, 26–28.

Cheang, M. Jury trial: The Singapore experience. *Western Australian Law Review*, 1973, *11*, 120–132.

Christie, R. Probability v. precedence: The social psychology of jury selection. In G. Bermant, C. Nemeth, & N. Vidmar (Eds.), *Psychology and the law*. Lexington, MA: Lexington Books, 1976.

Cleary, J.J. Jury selection in a federal criminal case (with form). *The Practical Lawyer*, 1980, *26*, 37–52.

Cohn, A., & Udolf, R. *The criminal justice system and its psychology*. New York: Van Nostrand Reinhold, 1979.

Cook, M. Anxiety, speech disturbances and speech rate.

British Journal of Social and Clinical Psychology, 1969, *8*, 13–21.

Court control over the voir dire examination of prospective jurors. *De Paul Law Review*, 1965, *15*, 107–117.

Curbing prosecutorial abuse of peremptory challenges—The available alternatives. *Western New England Law Review*, 1980, *3*, 223–247.

Darrow, L. Attorney for the defense. *Esquire Magazine*, May 1936, 36–37, 211–213.

Davis, B.E., & Wiley, R.E. Forty-nine thoughts on jury selection. *Trial Lawyer's Guide*, 1965, *9*, 351–356.

Day, M.E. An eye-movement indicator of type and level of anxiety: Some clinical observations. *Journal of Clinical Psychology*, 1967, *23*, 438–441.

The defendant's right to an impartial jury and the rights of prospective jurors. *University of Cincinnati Law Review*, 1979, *48*, 985–998.

The defendant's right to object to prosecutorial misuse of the peremptory challenge. *Harvard Law Review*, 1979, *92*, 1770–1789.

DeGroot, M.H., & Kadane, J.B. Optimal challenges for selection. *Operations Research*, 1980, *28*, 952–968.

Deutsch, M., & Gerard, H. A study of normative and informational social influences upon individual judgements. *Journal of Abnormal and Social Psychology*, 1956, *51*, 629–636.

Dibner, A.S. Cue-counting: A measure of anxiety in interviews. *Journal of Consulting Psychology*, 1956, *20*, 475–478.

Dittmann, A.T., Parloff, M.B., & Boomer, D.S. Facial and bodily expression: A study of receptivity of emotional cues. *Psychiatry*, 1965, *28*, 239–244.

Dohrenwend, B.S., Columbatos, J., & Dohrenwend, B.P. Social distance and interviewer effects. *Public Opinion Quarterly*, 1968, *32*, 410–422.

Driscoll, J. The decline of the English jury. *American Business Law Journal*, 1979, *17*, 99–112.

Efran, J.S. Looking for approval: Effects on visual behavior of approbation from persons differing in importance. *Journal of Personality and Social Psychology*, 1968, *10*, 21–25.

Ekman, P. Body position, facial expression, and verbal behavior during interviews. *Journal of Abnormal and Social Psychology*, 1964, *68*, 295–301.

Ekman, P. Differential communication of affect by head and body cues. *Journal of Personality and Social Psychology*, 1965, *2*, 726–735.

Ekman, P., & Friesen, W.V. Head and body cues in the judgment of emotion: A reformulation. *Perceptual and Motor Skills*, 1967, *24*, 711–724.

Ekman, P., & Friesen, W.V. Nonverbal leakage and uses to deception. *Psychiatry*, 1969, *32*, 88–106.

Ekman, P., & Friesen, W.V. Constants across cultures in the face and emotion. *Journal of Personality and Social Psychology*, 1971, *17*, 124–129.

Ekman, P., & Friesen, W.V. Hand movements. *Journal of Communication*, 1972, *22*, 353–374.

Ekman, P., & Friesen, W.V. Detecting deception from the body or face. *Journal of Personality and Social Psychology*, 1974, *29*, 288–298. (a)

Ekman, P., & Friesen, W.V. Nonverbal leakage and clues to deception. In S. Weitz (Ed.), *Nonverbal communication*. New York: Oxford University, 1974. (b)

Ekman, P., Friesen, W.V., & Ellsworth, P. *Emotion in the human face*. New York: Pergamon, 1972.

Eldred, S.H., & Price, D.B. A linguistic evaluation of feeling states in psychotherapy. *Psychiatry*, 1958, *21*, 115–121.

Ellsworth, P., & Ross, L. Intimacy in response to direct gaze. *Journal of Experimental Social Psychology*, 1975, *11*, 592–613.

Epstein, R. Aggression toward outgroups as a function of authoritarianism and imitation of aggressive models. *Journal of Personality and Social Psychology*, 1966, *3*, 574–579.

Etzioni, A. Creating an imbalance. *Trial*, 1974, *10*(6), 28 + .

Exclusion of black veniremen through use of prosecution's peremptory challenges held to be in violation of Equal Protection Clause. *Cumberland Law Review*, 1977, *8*, 307–320.

Exline, R., Thibaut, J., Brannon, C., & Gumpert, P. Visual interaction in relationship to Machiavellianism and an unethical act. *American Psychologist*, 1961, *16*, 396.

Fahringer, H.P. "In the valley of the blind"—Jury selection in a criminal case. *New York State Bar Journal*, 1980, *52*, 197–199, 233–244.

Feild, H.S. Juror background characteristics and attitudes toward rape—Correlates of jurors' decisions in rape trials. *Law and Human Behavior*, 1978, *2*, 73–93.

Feild, H.S., & Bienen, L.B. *Jurors and rape—A study in psychology and law*. Lexington, MA: Heath Lexington, 1980.

Field, L. Voir dire examination—A neglected art. *University of Missouri at Kansas City Law Review*, 1965, *33*, 171–187.

Fortune, W.H. Voir dire in Kentucky: An empirical study of voir dire in Kentucky circuit courts. *Kentucky Law Journal*, 1980–81, *69*, 273–326.

Frederick, J.T. Jury behavior: A psychologist examines jury selection. *Ohio Northern University Law Review*, 1978, *5*, 571–585.

Freedman, N., & Hoffman, S.P. Kinetic behavior in altered clinical states: Approach to objective analysis of motor behavior during clinical interviews. *Perceptual and Motor Skills*, 1967, *24*, 527–539.

Fried, M., Kaplan, K.J., & Klein, K.W. Juror selection. In N. Johnston & L.D. Davis (Eds.), *Justice and corrections*. New York: Wiley, 1978.

Gaba, J.M. Voir dire of jurors: Constitutional limits to the right of inquiry into prejudice. *University of Colorado Law Review*, 1977, *48*, 525–545.

Garcia, L., & Griffitt, W. Evaluation and recall of evidence: Authoritarianism and the Patty Hearst case. *Journal of Research in Personality*, 1978, *12*, 57–67.

Ginger, A.F. (Ed.). *Minimizing racism in jury trials: The voir dire conducted by Charles R. Garry in People of California v. Huey P. Newton*. Berkeley: The National Lawyers Guild, 1969.

Ginger, A.F. *Jury selection in criminal trials: New techniques & concepts*. Tiburon, CA: Lawpress, 1980.

Goldman-Eisler, F. Speech-breathing activity—A measure of tension and affect during interviews. *British Journal of Psychology*, 1955, *46*, 53–63.

Goldstein, I. *Trial technique*. Chicago: Callaghan, 1938.

Hale, J. Juries: The West Australian experience. *Western Australian Law Review*, 1973, *11*, 99–104.

Hans, V.P., & Vidmar, N. Jury selection. In N.L. Kerr & R.M. Bray (Eds.), *The psychology of the courtroom*. New York: Academic Press, 1982.

Hare, A.P. *Handbook of small group research*. New York: Free Press of Glencoe, 1962.

Hare, F.H., Jr. Voir dire and jury selection. *Alabama Lawyer*, 1968, *29*, 160–175.

Harrington, D.C., & Dempsey, J. Psychological factors in jury selection. *Tennessee Law Review*, 1969, *37*, 173–184.

Hawrish, E., & Tate, E. Determinants of jury selection. *Saskatchewan Law Review*, 1974–75, *39*, 285–292.

Hayden, G., Senna, J., & Siegel, L. Prosecutorial discretion in peremptory challenges: An empirical investigation of information use in the Massachusetts jury selection process. *New England Law Review*, 1978, *13*, 768–791.

Hayes, R. The jury verdict in defamation: Common-sense or conniption? *Western Australian Law Review*, 1973, *11*, 140–168.

Hepburn, J.R. Objective reality of evidence and the utility of systematic jury selection. *Law and Human Behavior*, 1980, *4*, 89–101.

Herbsleb, J.D., Sales, B.D., & Berman, J.J. When psychologists aid in the voir dire: Legal and ethical considerations. In L.E. Abt and I.R. Stuart (Eds.), *Social psychology and discretionary law*. New York: Van Nostrand Reinhold, 1979.

Horowitz, I.A. Juror selection—A comparison of two methods in several criminal cases. *Journal of Applied Social Psychology*, 1980, *10*, 86–99.

Howeler, M., & Vrolijk, A. Verbal communication as an index of interpersonal attraction. *Acta Psychologica*, 1970, *34*, 511–515.

Hunt, R.G., & Kan Lin, T. Accuracy of judgments of personal attributes from speech. *Journal of Personality and Social Psychology*, 1967, *6*, 450–453.

Imlay, C.H. Federal jury reformation: Saving a democratic institution. *Loyola University of Los Angeles Law Review*, 1973, *6*, 247–273.

Impartial jury—Restricting the peremptory challenge—*People* v. *Wheeler*. *Suffolk University Law Review*, 1979, *13*, 1082–1100.

Joe, V.C. Review of the internal-external control construct as a personality variable. *Psychological Reports*, 1971, *28*, 619–640.

Jones, C., & Aronson, E. Attribution of fault to a rape victim as a function of respectability of the victim. *Journal of Personality and Social Psychology*, 1973, *26*, 415–419.

Jones, S.C., & Shrauger, J.S. Locus of control and interpersonal evaluations. *Journal of Consulting and Clinical Psychology*, 1968, *32*, 664–668.

Jourard, S.M., & Friedman, R. Experimenter-subject "distance" and self-disclosure. *Journal of Personality and Social Psychology*, 1970, *15*, 278–282.

Juror bias—A practical screening device and the case for permitting its use. *Minnesota Law Review*, 1980, *64*, 987–1020.

Jurow, G.L. New data on the effects of a death qualified jury on the guilt determination process. *Harvard Law Review*, 1971, *84*, 567–611.

Jury checks. *New Law Journal*, August 7, 1980, *130*, 694.

Kadane, J.B., & Kairys, D. Fair numbers of peremptory challenges in jury trials. *Journal of the American Statistical Association*, 1979, *74*, 747–753.

Kairys, D., Schulman, J., & Harring, S. *The jury system: New methods for reducing prejudice*. Philadelphia, PA: National Jury Project and National Lawyers Guild, 1975.

Kallen, L. Peremptory challenges based upon juror background: A rational use? *Trial Lawyer's Guide*, 1969, *13*, 143–165.

Kanfer, F.H. Verbal rate, eye blink, and content in structured psychiatric interviews. *Journal of Abnormal and Social Psychology*, 1960, *61*, 341–347.

Kaplan, M.F., & Schersching, C. Reducing juror bias: An experimental approach. In P.D. Lipsitt & B.D. Sales (Eds.), *New directions in psycholegal research*. New York: Van Nostrand Reinhold, 1980.

Kasl, S.V., & Mahl, G.F. The relationship of disturbances and hesitations in spontaneous speech to anxiety. *Journal of Personality and Social Psychology*, 1965, *1*, 425–433.

Katz, L.S. The twelve man jury. *Trial*, December 1968-January 1969, 39–40; 42.

Kleck, R.E. Interaction distance and nonverbal agreeing responses. *British Journal of Social and Clinical Psychology*, 1970, *9*, 180–182.

Knecht, L., Lippman, D., & Swap, W. Similarity, attraction, and self-disclosure. *Proceedings of the 81st Annual Convention of the American Psychological Association*, 1973, *8*, 205–208.

Krause, M.S. Anxiety in verbal behavior: An intercorrelational study. *Journal of Consulting Psychology*, 1961, *25*, 272.

Lassen, C.L. Interaction distance and the initial interview: A study in proxemics. *Dissertation Abstracts International*, 1970, *31*, 1542B. (University Microfilms No. 70-16, 292)

Lerner, M., & Matthews, G. Reactions to suffering of others under conditions of indirect responsibility. *Journal of Personality and Social Psychology*, 1967, *5*, 319–325.

Lerner, M., & Simmons, C. Observer's reaction to the "innocent victim": Compassion or rejection? *Journal of Personality and Social Psychology*, 1966, *4*, 203–210.

Limiting the peremptory challenge: Representations of groups on petit juries. *Yale Law Journal*, 1977, *86*, 1715–1741.

MacGutman, S. The attorney-conducted voir dire of jurors: A constitutional right. *Brooklyn Law Review*, 1972, *39*, 290–329.

Mahl, G.F. Disturbances and silences in the patient's speech in psychotherapy. *Journal of Abnormal and Social Psychology*, 1956, *53*, 1–15.

Mahoney, A.R. Sexism in voir dire—The use of sex stereotypes in jury selection. In W.L. Hepperle & L. Crites (Eds.), *Women in the courts*. Williamsburg Virginia: National Centre for State Courts, 1978.

Massey, R.L., & Travis, J.S. Voir dire. *Chicago Bar Record*, 1980, *62*, 103–110.

Maxwell, R.F. The case of the rebellious juror. *American Bar Association Journal*, 1970, *56*, 838–843.

McConahay, J.B., Mullin, C.J., & Frederick, J. The uses of social science in trials with political and racial overtones: The trial of Joan Little. *Law and Contemporary Problems*, 1977, *41*, 205–229.

McEldowney, J.F. "Stand by for the Crown": An historical analysis. *The Criminal Law Review*, 1979, *41*, 272–283.

Mehrabian, A. Immediacy: An indicator of attitudes in linguistic communication. *Journal of Personality*, 1966, *34*, 26–34.

Mehrabian, A. Attitudes inferred from neutral verbal communications. *Journal of Consulting Psychology*, 1967, *31*, 414–417. (a)

Mehrabian, A. Attitudes inferred from non-immediacy of verbal communications. *Journal of Verbal Learning and Verbal Behavior*, 1967, *6*, 294–295. (b)

Mehrabian, A. Orientation behaviors and nonverbal attitude communication. *Journal of Communication*, 1967, *17*, 324–332. (c)

Mehrabian, A. Relationship of attitude to seated posture, orientation, and distance. *Journal of Personality and Social Psychology*, 1968, *10*, 26–30.

Mehrabian, A. Significance of posture and position in the communication of attitude and status relationships. *Psychological Bulletin*, 1969, *71*, 359–371. (a)

Mehrabian, A. Some referents and measures of nonverbal behavior. *Behavior Research Methods and Instrumentation*, 1969, *1*, 203–207. (b)

Mehrabian, A. A semantic space for nonverbal behavior. *Journal of Consulting and Clinical Psychology*, 1970, *35*, 248–257.

Mehrabian, A. Nonverbal betrayal of feeling. *Journal of Experimental Research in Personality*, 1971, *5*, 64–73. (a)

Mehrabian, A. Nonverbal communication. *Nebraska Symposium on Motivation*, 1971, *19*, 107–161. (b)

Mehrabian, A., & Ferris, S.R. Inference of attitudes from nonverbal communication in two channels. *Journal of Consulting Psychology*, 1967, *31*, 248–252.

Mehrabian, A., & Ferris, S.R. Inference of attitudes from nonverbal communication in two channels. In S. Weitz (Ed.), *Nonverbal communication*. New York: Oxford University, 1974.

Mehrabian, A., & Friar, J.T. Encoding of attitude by a seated communicator via posture and position cues. *Journal of Consulting and Clinical Psychology*, 1969, *33*, 330–336.

Mehrabian, A., & Wiener, M. Non-immediacy between communicator and object of communication in a verbal message: Application to the inference of attitudes. *Journal of Consulting Psychology*, 1966, *30*, 420–425.

Mehrabian, A., & Wiener, M. Decoding of inconsistent communications. *Journal of Personality and Social Psychology*, 1967, *6*, 109–114.

Mills, C.J., & Bohannon, W.E. Character structure and juror behavior—Conceptual and applied implications. *Journal of Personality and Social Psychology*, 1980, *38*, 662–667. (a)

Mills, C.J., & Bohannon, W.E. Juror characteristics: To what extent are they related to jury verdicts? *Judicature*, 1980, *64*, 22–31. (b)

Mittlebeeler, E.V. Race and jury in South Africa. *Howard Law Journal*, 1968, *14*, 90–104.

Mittlebeeler, E.V. Race and jury in Nigeria. *Howard Law Journal*, 1973, *18*, 88–106.

Mogil, M. Voir dire and jury psychology. *New York State Bar Journal*, 1979, *51*, 382–383 + .

Moore, M., & Wood, J. The use of handwriting analysis in jury selection. *Case and Comment*, 1980, *85*, 38–41.

Moran, G., & Comfort, J.C. Scientific juror selection: Sex as a moderator of demographic and personality predictors of impaneled felony juror behavior. *Journal of Personality and Social Psychology*, 1982, *43*, 1052–1063.

Mullin, C.J. Jury selection techniques: Improving the odds of winning. In G. Cooke (Ed.), *The role of the forensic psychologist*. Springfield, IL: Charles C. Thomas, 1980.

Nemeth, C. Jury trials: Psychology and law. *Advances in Experimental Social Psychology*, 1981, *14*, 309–367.

Nicol, A. Official secrets and jury vetting. *The Criminal Law Review*, 1979, *6*, 284–291.

Nietzel, M.T., & Dillehay, R.C. The effects of variations in voir dire procedures in capital murder trials. *Law and Human Behavior*, 1982, *6*, 1–14.

Okun, J. Investigation of jurors by counsel: Its impact on the decisional process. *Georgetown Law Journal*, 1968, *56*, 839–879.

Padawer-Singer, A.M., Singer, A., & Singer, R. Voir dire by two lawyers: An essential safeguard. *Judicature*, 1974, *57*, 386–391.

Parker, L.C. *Legal psychology*. Springfield, IL: Charles C. Thomas, 1980.

Penner, R.W. Jury selection: Madison Avenue/horserace style. *For The Defense*, June, 1982, 2–3.

People v. *Wheeler*: California's answer to misuse of the peremptory challenge. *San Diego Law Review*, 1979, *16*, 897–920.

Peremptory challenges and the meaning of jury representation. *Yale Law Journal*, 1980, *89*, 1177–1198.

Peremptory challenges of a cognizable group—Denial of fair trial. *Missouri Law Review*, 1979, *44*, 559–566.

Phares, E.J., & Wilson, K.G. Responsibility attribution: Role of outcome severity, situational ambiguity, and internal-external control. *Journal of Personality*, 1972, *40*, 392–406.

Phares, E.J., Wilson, K.G., & Klyver, N.W. Internal-external control and the attribution of blame under neutral and distractive conditions. *Journal of Personality and Social Psychology*, 1971, *18*, 285–288.

Pittenger, R.E., & Smith, H.L. A basis for some contributions of linguistics to psychiatry. *Psychiatry*, 1957, *20*, 61–78.

Pope, B., & Siegman, A.W. Interviewer warmth and verbal communication in the initial interview. *Proceedings of the 75th Annual Convention of the APA*, 1967, *75*, 245–246.

The prohibition of group-based stereotypes in jury selection procedures. *Villanova Law Review*, 1979–80, *25*, 339–363.

Redmount, R.S. Psychological tests for selecting jurors. *University of Kansas Law Review*, 1957, *5*, 391–403.

Robinson, M.T.W. The jury system in Ireland. *Western Australian Law Review*, 1973, *11*, 111–119.

Rothblatt, H.B. Techniques for jury selection. *Criminal Law Bulletin*, 1966, *2*, 14–29.

Rotter, J.B. Generalized expectancies for internal versus external control of reinforcement. *Psychological Monographs*, 1966, *80*(1, Whole No. 609).

Rubin, Z., & Peplau, L.A. Belief in a just world and reactions to another's lot: A study of participants in the national draft lottery. *Journal of Social Issues*, 1973, *29*, 73–93.

Rubin, Z., & Peplau, L.A. Who believes in a just world? *Journal of Social Issues*, 1975, *31*, 65–89.

Sage, W. Psychology and the Angela Davis jury. *Human Behavior*, 1973, *2*, 56–61.

Saks, M.J. Social scientists can't rig juries. *Psychology Today*, 1976, *9*, 48. (a)

Saks, M.J. The limits of scientific jury selection: Ethical and empirical. *Jurimetrics Journal*, 1976, *17*, 3–22. (b)

Saks, M.J., & Hastie, R. *Social psychology in court*. New York: Van Nostrand Reinhold, 1978.

Scheflen, A.E. The significance of posture in communication systems. *Psychiatry*, 1964, *27*, 316–331.

Schulman, J. A systematic approach to successful jury selection. *Guild Notes*, 1973, *2*, 13–20.

Schulman, J., Shaver, P., Colman, R., Emrich, B., & Christie, R. Recipe for a fair jury. *Psychology Today*, May, 1973, 37.

Sheldon, W.H., & Stevens, S.S. *The varieties of temperament*. New York: Harper, 1942.

Sheldon, W.H., Stevens, S.S., & Turner, W.B. *The varieties of human physique*. New York: Harper, 1940.

Sheperd, J.C. Techniques of jury selection from the defendant's point of view. *Proceedings of the American Bar Association Section of Insurance, Negligence and Compensation Law*, 1964–1965, 359–362.

Sherif, M. Group influence upon the formation of norms and attitudes. In E.E. Maccoby, T.M. Newcomb, & E.L. Hartley (Eds.), *Readings in social psychology* (3rd ed.). New York: Holt, Rinehart & Winston, 1958.

Silver, D. A case against the use of public opinion polls as an aid in jury selection. *Rutgers Journal of Computers and the Law*, 1978, *6*, 177–195.

Simon, R.J. *The jury: Its role in American society*. Lexington, MA: Lexington Books, 1980.

Soder, D.A. Testing a jury selection scale and theory in court. *Dissertation Abstracts International*, 1976. (University Microfilms No. 77-1829, 104)

Sosis, R.H. Internal-external control and the perception of responsibility of another for an accident. *Journal of Personality and Social Psychology*, 1974, *30*, 393–399.

Strauss, S.A. The jury in South Africa. *Western Australian Law Review*, 1973, *11*, 133–139.

Strawn, D.U. Juror perceptions—Ending the voir dire wars. *Judges Journal*, 1979, *45*, 44–48.

Suggs, D., & Sales, B.D. The art and science of conducting the voir dire. *Professional Psychology*, 1978, *9*, 367–388. (a)

Suggs, D., & Sales, B.D. Using communication cues to evaluate prospective jurors during the voir dire. *Arizona Law Review*, 1978, *20*, 629–642. (b)

Suggs, D., & Sales, B.D. Juror self-disclosure in the voir dire: A social science analysis. *Indiana Law Journal*, 1981, *56*, 245–271.

Tapp, J.L., & Kohlberg, L. Developing senses of law and legal justice. *Journal of Social Issues*, 1971, *27*, 65–69.

Tapp, J.L., & Levine, F.J. Legal socialization: Strategies for an ethical legality. *Stanford Law Review*, 1974, *27*, 1–72.

Totenberg, N. The jury pickers: How the experts *really* decide who'll sit in judgment. *Parade*, May 9, 1982, 12.

Van Dyke, J. Voir dire: How should it be conducted to ensure that our juries are representative and impartial? *Hastings Constitutional Law Quarterly*, 1976, *3*, 65–97.

Van Dyke, J. *Jury selection procedures: Our uncertain commitment to representative panels*. Cambridge, MA: Ballinger, 1977. (a)

Van Dyke, J. Selecting a jury in political trials. *Case Western Reserve Law Review*, 1977, 27, 609–622. (b)

Vidmar, N. Retributive and utilitarian motives and other correlates of Canadian attitudes toward the death penalty. *The Canadian Psychologist*, 1974, *15*, 337–356.

Voir dire examination—Scope of inquiry. *Defense Law Journal*, 1980, *29*, 469–487.

Voir dire limitations as a means of protecting jurors' safety and privacy: *United States* v. *Barnes*. *Harvard Law Review*, 1980, *93*, 782–792.

Watson, A.S. On the preparation and use of psychiatric expert testimony: Some suggestions in an ongoing controversy. *Bulletin of the American Academy of Psychiatry and the Law*, 1978, *6*, 226–246.

Weber, J.W. The effects of physical proximity and body boundary size on the self-disclosure interview. *Dissertation Abstracts International*, 1973, *33*, 3327B. (University Microfilms No. 73-789)

White, A.J. Selecting the jury. In J.A. Appleman (Ed.), *Successful jury trials: A symposium*. Indianapolis, IN: Bobbs-Merrill, 1952.

Wiens, A.R., Jackson, R.H., Manaugh, T.S., & Matarazzo, J.D. Communication length as an index of communicator attitude: A replication. *Journal of Applied Psychology*, 1969, *53*, 264–266.

Williams, J.A., Jr. Interviewer role performance: A further note on bias in the information interview. *Public Opinion Quarterly*, 1969, *32*, 287–294.

Winston, N.A., & Winston, W.E. The use of sociological techniques in the jury selection process. *National Journal of Criminal Defense*, 1980, *6*, 79–97.

Winter, B. 'Scientific' juror selection debunked. *American Bar Association Journal*, 1980, *66*, 1197.

Worthy, M., Gary, A.L., & Kahn, G.M. Self-disclosure as an exchange process. *Journal of Personality and Social Psychology*, 1969, *13*, 59–63.

Zaidel, S.F., & Mehrabian, A. The ability to communicate and infer positive and negative attitudes facially and vocally. *Journal of Experimental Research in Personality*, 1969, *3*, 233–241.

Zeisel, H., & Diamond. S. The jury in the Mitchell-Stans conspiracy trial. *American Bar Foundation Research Journal*, 1976, 151–174.

Zeisel, H., & Diamond, S. The effect of peremptory challenges on the jury and verdict. *Stanford Law Review*, 1978, *30*, 491–531.

5.
Forensic Assessment

Thomas G. Gutheil

ABSTRACT. This chapter will focus on the special forms of assessment unique to forensic psychiatric work in the civil and criminal areas. Forensic psychiatric matters lie at the interface between law and psychiatry, two disciplines with widely differing theoretical, procedural and empirical bases. We would expect that assessments taking place in the shadow of both systems would pose special challenges for the assessor: Indeed, this is the case.

The chapter begins with an early forensic topic, a review of assessment of individuals suspected of being witches in the Middle Ages. From this historical background, the chapter moves on to consider the theory of assessment in forensic practice, particularly as it differs from clinical work. The issue of agency is explored—who "employs" the assessor—as well as the differing data bases for clinical and forensic work and their differing perceptions of data in the two spheres; ethical tensions that surface in forensic work are delineated.

Subsequent sections explore direct assessments (such as examination of offenders, witnesses and other litigants) and indirect assessments (such as determinations of standards of care in malpractice).

Forensic assessment of various capacities is the subject of the next portion of the chapter. After a review of historical tests of competence to stand trial, current assessment techniques and instruments are delineated and critically reviewed. Other forms of competence, such as competence to consent to treatment or to hospital admission are described. The final segments of the chapter review criminal responsibility, testamentary capacity, competence to contract, competence to marry and questions of fitness as competence.

The author concludes by lamenting the paucity of empirical data, and notes the centrality of concern for the patient in all forensic work.

SOMMAIRE. Le présent chapitre porte sur les formes d'évaluation qui sont particulières aux travaux de psychiatrie légale dans les domaines du droit civil et du droit criminel. La psychiatrie légale se situe au carrefour du droit et de la psychiatrie, deux disciplines aux fondements théoriques, méthodes et sources empiriques très différents. On peut s'attendre donc à ce que les évaluations faites dans l'ombre des deux systèmes posent des problèmes particuliers pour l'évaluateur et c'est, en fait, le cas.

L'auteur commence par traiter de l'histoire de la médecine légale, et de la façon dont était évalué l'état des personnes accusées de sorcellerie au Moyen-âge, et sur cette toile de fond, il fait ensuite la théorie de l'évaluation en médecine légale; il montre, en particulier, comment elle diffère du travail clinique. Abordant ensuite la question du mandat, autrement dit pour qui travaille l'évaluateur, il présente les bases de données différentes qui servent aux travaux cliniques et aux travaux de médecine légale et souligne la variation des perceptions des données dans les deux cas ainsi que les tensions d'ordre éthique.

Dans les sections suivantes, il analyse les évaluations directes (l'examen des délinquants, des témoins et des autres intervenants au litige) et les évaluations indirectes (la fixation des normes de soins dans les cas d'action en responsabilité médicale).

L'évaluation légale des différentes capacités fait l'objet de la suite du chapitre. Après l'analyse des critères historiques de l'aptitude à subir le procès suit une présentation des techniques et instruments d'évaluation actuelle, accompagnée d'une étude critique. L'auteur expose d'autres formes de capacité, notamment pour le consentement au traitement et à l'hospitalisation. La fin du chapitre renferme une étude de la responsabilité criminelle, de la capacité testamentaire, de l'aptitude à contracter, en particulier pour se marier, ainsi que d'autres questions d'aptitude.

En conclusion, l'auteur déplore le manque de données empiriques, et il met en évidence le caractère essentiel du bien-être du patient en médecine légale.

Introduction

This chapter will focus on the special forms of assessment unique to forensic psychiatric work in the civil and criminal areas. Forensic psychiatric matters lie at the interface between law and psychiatry, two disciplines with widely differing theoretical, procedural and empirical bases. We would expect that assessments taking place in the shadow of both systems would pose special challenges for the assessor: indeed, this is the case.

We will review the questions of agency and of the different issues in legal and clinical determinations, criminal and civil competencies, criminal responsibility, and malpractice issues. Theoretical, clinical and empirical aspects will be presented, following an historical review.

The question might possibly be raised as to whether "assessment" as here employed is similar or identical to "diagnosis." In fact, assessment often aims at defining a clinical state in terms of a legal standard that may owe no allegiance to any clinical considerations. Additionally, environmental issues that may quite transcend the condition of the individual patient may play central roles in a particular forensic determination. Thus, the voluminous literature on diagnostic reliability and validity is not germane to the topic at hand.

Historical background

In 20th-century forensic psychiatry the question, "Which criminals are insane?" has tremendous social impact; this is true despite the fact that the number of criminals *found* insane is extremely small (Stone, 1982). In the 15th century, no question had a more staggering social impact than, "Who is a witch?" From the record, their numbers must have been legion.

Few forensic assessments in human history were as charged with meaning and intensity as witch detection; hence, an instructive starting point for our discussion of forensic assessment might be the witch-hunter's guidebook, a text whose ubiquity was matched only by its authoritativeness at the time of its publication. The text, of course, is *Malleus Maleficarum*, which may be translated as "The hammer of evildoers (witches)" (Kramer & Sprenger, 1486/1971).

This work was written in 1486 by two German Dominican monks, Heinrich Kramer and James Sprenger, and rested at the right hand of almost every member of the Inquisition during the subsequent bloody years, surely in part because it offered such detailed guidelines on witch diagnosis and assessment, conduct of trial, examination of witnesses, evidence, and so on. Because—like many subsequent forensic issues—witch-detection and trial involves legal, psychological, criminal, social and moral elements, we may begin our historical survey by examining those facets of a forensic assessment that were considered essential 500 years ago.

In the third part of the book there is a chapter that describes how witnesses who might ordinarily be excluded from giving evidence are not so excluded here:

> Note that persons under a sentence of excommunication, associates and accomplices in the crime, notorious evildoers and criminals, or servants giving evidence against their masters, are admitted as witnesses in a case concerning the Faith.

However, blind acceptance of just anyone's raw evidence was not the rule:

> If it manifestly appears that they do not speak in a spirit of levity, or from motives of enmity, or by reason of a bribe, but purely out of zeal for the orthodox faith . . . their testimony shall be as valid as that of anyone else, provided there is no other objection to it. (p. 439)

Note that the specific motivation of a witness was a legitimate subject of inquiry and consideration, despite the widening of the witness pool occasioned because of the weight of the matter.

The witnesses so produced were to be scrupulously examined as to the significance of their evidence, *even in context*, as it might pertain to the question:

Asked concerning the manner and reason of the accused's alleged words, [the witness] answered, [they were uttered] for such a reason and in such a manner. Asked whether he thought that the prisoner had used those words carelessly, unmeaningly and thoughtlessly, or rather with deliberate intention, he answered that he had used them jokingly or in temper, or without meaning or believing what he said, or else with deliberate intention.

Asked further how he could distinguish the accused's motive, he answered that he knew it because he had spoken with a laugh.

This is a matter which must be inquired into very diligently for very often people use words quoting someone else, or merely in temper, or as a test of the opinions of other people, although sometimes they are used assertively with definite intention. (p. 443)

Note here that the authors show a realistic appraisal of common social patterns of speech and specifically allow for their weighing in the assessment.

The text goes on to address matters of the burden of proof and the gathering of physical evidence:

And after [examining witnesses] the Judge shall decide whether the fact is fully proven; and if not fully, whether there are great indications and strong suspicions of its truth. Observe that we do not speak of a light suspicion, arising from slight conjectures, but of a persistent report that the accused has worked witchcraft upon children or animals, etc. . . . he shall first cause his house to be searched unexpectedly, and all chests to be opened and all boxes in the corners, and all implements of witchcraft which are found to be taken away (p. 444).

The subsequent material treats of the examination of the suspected witch him or herself. This involves not only an oath on the four Gospels but a family history.

Asked who were his parents, and whether they were alive or dead, he answered that they were alive in such a place or dead in such a place.

Asked whether they died a natural death, or were burned, he answered in such a way. (Here note that this question is put because as was shown [earlier], witches generally offer or devote their own children to devils, and commonly their whole progeny is infected; and when the informer has deposed to this effect, and the witch himself has denied it, it lays her open to suspicion.) (p. 445)

As in the good forensic examination, the family history is explored, since it may throw light on hereditary or environmental pathogenic influences that may buttress the diagnosis of disease.

One of the most interesting trick questions is the inquiry as to whether the accused believes in witches. The text urges caution when the accused denies this, as, it notes, witches are wont to do:

So if they deny it they must be questioned as follows: Then are they innocently condemned when they are burned? And he or she must answer.

The double-bind created here is this: the accused, speaking to a member of the Inquisition, must either acknowledge the existence of witches, thus perhaps seeming to reveal the inside knowledge that only a witch would have, or deny it, in which case he implicitly accuses his interrogator of burning innocent victims! (p. 445–6)

The text recommends care in assignment of counsel to the accused:

It should be noted that an Advocate is not to be appointed at the desire of the accused, as if he may choose which Advocate he will have; but the Judge must take great care to appoint neither a litigious nor an evil-minded man, nor yet one who is easily bribed (as many are), but rather an honorable man to whom no sort of suspicion attaches. (p. 456)

It is not clear from the text but the last section may be not only an exhortation to find an honest lawyer, no matter how vast the effort involved to do so, but also, perhaps, an adjuration to avoid men of paranoid inclinations—surely good advice, given the paranoia-generating qualities inherent in the subject matter.

Even the attorney himself is given guidelines that would not be out of place in a modern bar association code:

In his pleading he should conduct himself properly in three respects. First, his behavior must be modest and free from prolixity or pretentious oratory. Secondly, he must abide by the truth, not bringing forward any fallacious arguments or reasoning, or calling false witnesses, or introducing legal quirks and quibbles if he be a skilled lawyer, or bringing counter-accusations; especially in cases of this sort, which must be conducted as simply and summarily as possible. Thirdly, his fee must be regulated by the usual practice of the district. (pp. 456–7)

Unfortunately for the apparent fairness of these rules, the lawyer, too, is doubly bound in that if he actively (or perhaps, successfully) defends heresy, he is threatened with excommunication!

The next segment of the text describes the central and most notorious aspect of the assessment, the interrogation under and with torture. It is clear by inference that the silence of the putative witch (we might now say, catatonia or hysterical mutism or other psychologic entity) posed the most frustrating barrier to the seekers of truth, and many of their approaches are detailed whose specific object was breach of this silence. The times of the examination were to be frequently postponed to weaken resistance, the friends of the accused were to be recruited to the task of persuading the witch to confess, and the witch might be promised her life if she confessed, though the manual gives many means of breaking this promise by various duplicities.

It was recommended that tortures move from mild to severe since the manual cautions appropriately that evidence obtained under torture is not entirely reliable; it is recommended that the victim after torture-inspired confession be moved elsewhere and questioned again, to verify the data. The Judges were cautioned against allowing the accused to be alone lest they commit suicide.

In terms of the useful signs of witchhood, the manual is fairly narrow in its description. Great store is set by the test of whether a witch can cry, though the possibility of malingering cannot be excluded:

For we are taught both by the words of worthy men of old and by our own experience that this is a most certain sign, and it has been found that even if she be urged and exhorted by solemn conjurations to shed tears, if she be a witch she will not be able to weep: although she will assume a tearful aspect and smear her cheeks and eyes with spittle to make it appear that she is weeping; wherefore she must be closely watched by the attendants. (p. 474)

This ancient work, then, written half a millennium ago, echoes like the overture to an opera: all the major themes and motifs resound within it in the detailed instructions and cautions that have been reviewed in brief above: the gathering and winnowing of a wide range of selected data; exploration of the past; the assessor's consideration of his position in relation to both the Church and the accused; the role of counsel; and the number of ethical tensions surrounding the process. The remainder of this chapter will now elaborate the evolution of these elements into their modern forms and practices. While many related issues, such as the question of disposition of individuals following assessment, may seem to cry out for exploration, we must refrain from their discussion in this chapter. A later chapter will address the role of psychological testing in forensic matters.

Despite the emergence by the 19th century in English case law of an interesting variety of judicial conceptualizations of the interrelationship between mental state and the law, particularly in relation to the exculpatory effect on a defendant of "insane states," the field of forensic psychiatry as a specific discipline with a body of knowledge essentially did not exist until 1838. At that date the publication of a single work practically created the field, almost *de novo*, a quantum jump of sophistication virtually unprecedented in the history of forensic science.

The work, of course, was the *Treatise on Medical Jurisprudence of Insanity* (1838), by the American psychiatrist, Isaac Ray. Among the many original and seminal contributions of this work, we might single out a few for consideration. First, Dr. Ray was a clinician who actually worked with large numbers of the mentally ill. His occasionally scathing criticism of various authorities for their ignorance about the actual mental state of "lunatics" was, if not the quintessence of tact, at least based upon an unimpeachable data base of clinical experience.

Over the subsequent decades a number of other figures made dramatic contributions to the field in diverse arenas; the names of Weihofen, Guttmacher, Karpman, Menninger, Cleckley, Aichhorn, Bromberg, and others are justly famous. In the contemporary era, a host of serious scholars and clinicians, too many to note, swell the ranks of the forensic specialists, and a separate specialty board, the American Board of Forensic Psychiatry, is entering its 11th year of existence; an American Board of Forensic Psychology has also been formed. Most hearteningly, empirical work in this field is beginning to buttress with reliable clinical data the impressionistic, anecdotal and shadowy constructs on earlier practitioners.

In our review of the topic of forensic assessment we will consider both criminal and non-criminal topics, including competence to stand trial, criminal responsibility, negligence and malpractice, and testamentary capacity, as well as clinical correlates related to capacity of witnesses, areas of ethical conflict or ambiguity, adequacy of records and the like.

Theory of Assessment in Forensic Practice

This section will address the way in which forensic assessments differ from their counterparts in the treatment situation and the manner in which ethical considerations enter into the process in a different way, creating atypical pitfalls for the clinician. The section will also review direct and indirect assessment approaches and the types of data encountered.

Special Nature of Forensic Assessments

THE ISSUE OF AGENCY

A grasp of the concept of agency is central to an understanding of the forensic assessment process itself and its ethical problems. The term *agency* addresses the question of what party is functioning as an agent of what employer; thus an agent is someone who is an employee of another and who thus owes that other some service, allegiance or duty.

In the typical outpatient psychiatric setting in private office practice, the clinician works as the employee of the patient, as a "hired co-investigator" (Gutheil, 1982), and owes allegiance and duty directly to that patient. The primacy of this allegiance makes the relationship a fiduciary one, one based on trust. Exceptions, such as the putative duty to breach confidentiality and protect third parties from the patient, are rare (Gutheil & Appelbaum, 1982).

When agency is multiple or divided (that is, when more than one employer or an employer other than the subject patient exists) the issue becomes more complex.

For Example: A dangerous, psychotic patient is remanded to a hospital for confinement for 40 days to permit assessment of his criminal responsibility for a murder. Looking at the total situation we can see that a physician doing the assessment owes allegiance to the patient, expressed as helping the patient recover from his mental illness; allegiance to the court, expressed in performance of an evaluation that is intended to allow the court to go about its business; allegiance to the institution, expressed by care that the patient be kept from being a risk to staff or other inmates; and allegiance to society in minimizing the risk to the community, expressed, for example, by taking care to prevent the patient's escape.

Possible conflicts may arise as to these potentially competing allegiances. An example is the tension between liberal and conservative practice in the patient's management. When a pass to home is being considered, the pass may be in the interest of the patient's recovery but, should the patient escape and delay trial, it places the institution at somewhat greater liability risk, the community at greater injury risk, and the court at risk for thwarting of its purposes.

The fact that these tensions exist does not vitiate the possibility of successful resolution of the dilemma involved, despite the claims of some authorities (e.g., Stone, 1982) that the matter is irresolvable. Even when the evaluator is an agent of an employer other than the patient, moreover, the patient's treatment, care and wellbeing are not abandoned (Gutheil, 1980a). A later section will discuss the approaches to this problem.

CRITICAL ELEMENTS
IN THERAPEUTIC APPROACHES

Of the several central elements of the therapeutic relationship, two of the most important are the therapeutic alliance (Gutheil & Appelbaum, 1982; Gutheil & Havens, 1979) and the empathic bond (Greenson, 1960). I have elsewhere indicated with Havens (Gutheil & Havens, 1979) the varieties of alliance that may be formed; one important variety is the existential alliance, the essence of which is the therapist's willing total submergence in the patient's world view. Even in other forms of therapeutic relatedness and other schools of practice, the attempt to "see the world through the patient's eyes" is a cornerstone of successful engagement with the patient in the therapeutic task (to make the point explicit, I note that I am using the designation "therapy" to refer to the exploratory rather than supportive modes).

The existential therapist, then, takes deliberate aim at the goal of total vicarious subjectivity of perception of the world. As one might predict, the human faculty most useful to the therapist in this attempt is empathy. By the empathic approach, the therapist places himself or herself amid the patient's experience. Once there, the therapist works from within, first by accepting as valid the patient's subjective experience, *no matter how distorted*, and then attempting to expand the horizon of understanding together with the patient.

Thus, the patient's perception, veracity and skill as a *witness* are irrelevant to the therapeutic work. In the treatment situation it is taken for granted that the usual human tendency to distort will operate as it does everywhere (compare the disagreements of eyewitnesses in streetcorner incidents); therapy, however—at least, the exploratory, dynamically-oriented kind—owes no allegiance to the reality of the outside world since the work goes on from within the individual. In a closely related manner, the material that the therapist calls "history"—the self-reported chronology of the patient's life—would qualify as only "hearsay" in legal settings, since the patient is describing events and facts which the therapist cannot validate by experience or direct observation.

CRITICAL DIFFERENCES
IN FORENSIC APPROACHES

The foregoing customary elements in therapy become problematic when the setting is the forensic arena precisely because the latter places emphasis on *objectivity* above other considerations. While the therapist may comfortably assume that the patient's self-descriptions are "self-serving," in that they are invoked in protection of his or her own self-esteem, this form of bias does not impede (and may even advance) the goals of treatment. When a legal issue, particularly a serious or even capital one, hangs over the evaluation, however, the question of whether the data are "self-serving" becomes more critical.

For Example: A therapist is treating a patient whose complaints of pain after an injury may be dramatically exaggerated. The possibility that the patient is feigning or malingering is not the central question, since the crucial treatment issue is, what internal psychological goals would these practices serve? What relationships is the patient attempting to manipulate? What internal objects are being retained?

If, however, the question is one of psychic damages for pain and suffering resulting from that same injury, the possibility of artifice acquires a very different coloration. Under the latter circumstances, feigned injury may represent, not an interpersonal stratagem, but an attempt to defraud—a matter of pivotal significance in a forensic assessment, and one which might well cost the patient the decision in question.

Of several inferences that might be drawn from the foregoing, one is that the forensic evaluator must go beyond, or outside, the individual patient in search of secondary sources of information, external validation, disinterested reportage and consensus among other observers of a situation in question.

For Example: A therapist is working with a patient in understanding the patient's probably excessive guilt feelings around a juvenile shoplifting experience. What actually occurred is of secondary importance; in fact, the patient may have fantasized or dreamed the entire experience. Nevertheless, the patient's story "is" what happened. The idea of, for example, calling the owner of the candy store to verify the incident would be not only inappropriate, but also a probable breach of confidentiality.

The same therapist later evaluates a defendant in a robbery case as to the issue of criminal responsibility. He interviews the patient-defendant, the victims, the witnesses, the arresting officers and the attorneys. The information from these external validators, together with the patient's self-report, constitutes the appropriate data base for the assessment.

Note how the question of confidentiality is altered in the second example as a direct function of the alteration of agency. Since the clinician in the second part of the example is now working for the court to make an objective determination, a number of third parties are included in the process whose presence would be intrusive and even forbidden in a treatment context.

OBSERVATIONS, ALLEGATIONS AND HEARSAY

The forensic evaluator must distinguish explicitly among the variety of elements that make up the total data base of the assessment in question. Courts make sharp distinctions among the types of evidence brought before them, and assign different weights to evidence depending on how remote the reporting witness was from the important events. "Observations" are what the evaluator witnesses directly; an example might be speech blocking during an interview. When parties report their observations without validation by the evaluator, these reports are "allegations"; an example might be, "The arresting officer alleged that he called out to the perpetrator to stop." To use a clinical analogy, observations are to allegations as signs are to symptoms. All material that is reported by an individual who was not an eyewitness is considered "hearsay," although in the clinical setting this distinction is far less significant; many clinically important and valid decisions are made on what courts would consider hearsay evidence.

For Example: A forensic evaluator is asked to determine whether an incident that occurred on an inpatient ward represents malpractice. She interviews a nurse and a mental health worker who witnessed the incident, reviews the chart which contains a record of an end-of-shift report delivered orally to that same nurse and worker, and speaks with a staff member of the next shift on

duty who received an oral report on the incident and to whom was delegated the task of writing up an incident report. In writing up her summary of the case, the evaluator indicates that only the reports of the original nurse and mental health worker are direct observation; all other data is allegation (labeled "alleges" in the report), even though the incident report (and, presumably, other clinical decisions) were made on the basis of just such "hearsay."

DIFFERING CLINICAL AND LEGAL PERCEPTIONS OF DATA

Psychiatry and the law often use different data, or weigh similar data differently. For example, unconscious motivation and countertransference, are often ignored by the law, although they are clinically important. The psychodynamically-oriented psychiatrist, especially when working with seriously ill, psychotic patients, must be aware of the impact on the clinical state of the operation of the unconscious. Since the unconscious, by definition, is not known to the patient, the usual clinical pathway of access to this material is through inference from the patient's speech, slips, dreams, and other productions. Attention to the unconscious is standard in the therapeutic sphere, but the forensic evaluator must exercise caution in attempting to make inferences about the unconscious in the forensic arena, because they are inherently subjective. The evaluator must seek out objective material on which to base the conclusions of the forensic evaluation.

The use of countertransference presents similar difficulties. The experienced clinician routinely attends to his own reactions to the patient as part of the diagnostic and therapeutic process of reading clinically meaningful data. This approach draws from such familiar human elements as the contagiousness of emotions, the capacity of people to evoke feelings in others that relate to their own feeling states, and similar phenomena. Regardless of such therapeutic utility, the legal system finds little room for the clinician's "subjective" response as valid data. Once again, more defensible data emerge from discovering objective findings to support the conclusions drawn.

ETHICAL ISSUES

The clinician must consider an ethical tension created by the divided agency of the forensic assessor. When a person is in a stressful situation (e.g., charged before a court) and encounters someone who introduces herself as a physician and starts to ask questions, the logical assumption for the person to make is that, like other physicians, this individual is here to be of help. As earlier noted, however, this is a partly true, but insufficiently complete, description: The clinician also owes some allegiance to the court. This dual allegiance may have specific implications for what the patient tells the interviewer, and the effect these revelations may have on the case at hand. The ethical tension lies between the physician's healing mandate (expressed in sympathetic listening) and the requirement that he or she gather data that at some point may be directly detrimental to the patient.

In the criminal setting the arrested subject must be given the *Miranda* warning, an immediate statement of the arrested individual's rights, particularly the right to remain silent. In the clinical setting in Massachusetts, at least, an analogous ruling applies, derived from *Commonwealth* v. *Lamb* (1973), which mandates that a person must be told about the altered confidentiality that applies in court-connected assessments. The goal of these warnings, clearly, is to attempt to protect the accused from unwitting self-incrimination that might be rendered more likely because of the above-noted assumption, namely, that the physician is present in a purely therapeutic, rather than evaluative role.

Some propose (Gutheil & Appelbaum, 1982) that the ideal model to resolve the ethical complexity of the matter is that of "informed consent." The crux of this approach is to inform the patient-defendant of the agency issue in explicit terms before undertaking the examination. If—as quite often happens—the patient appears to be losing sight of the forensic nature of the interview and appears to be lapsing into a degree of therapy-like candor without cognizance of the potentially damaging results, the examiner should remind the patient about the novel situation that applies. In those cases where the patient appears unable to comprehend the matter at hand, because of the underlying illness or problem, the examiner should stop the examination and recommend that attempts be made to restore the patient to understanding, by treatment if possible. In dubious cases the patient's attorney should be consulted.

For Example: A patient charged with an assault

on his mother is referred for examination for competence to stand trial. The patient presents as intermittently hallucinating and suspicious but seems able to attend to the examiner. The examiner states: "Hello, Mr. Jones. I am Dr. Smith and I am a psychiatrist working for the court. I am here to see if you are clear enough in your mind to go to trial. What you tell me will not be kept secret from the court—this is different from when you talk to your own doctor—so don't tell me anything that you don't want the court to know about. Outside that, I'll try to be as helpful as I can."

The patient responds relatively freely to the inquiries but, at a certain point, begins to go into some spontaneous detail around the assault itself. The examiner halts the interview, repeats the warning, and resumes inquiries directed to the patient's understanding of court procedures.

Direct Assessments

Forensic assessments are divisible into direct and indirect. In direct assessments, the examiner has direct access to the subject or subject matter of the assessment and can make a diagnostic or other evaluative determination based specifically on the data that emerge. In indirect assessments, the examiner must make some abstract, comparative or multivariate determination by drawing inferences or conclusions based upon the direct source of the data involved. I shall first address direct assessments.

WRITTEN RECORDS

Written records are an important data source for the forensic examiner. They may play central roles in malpractice cases, in assessments of criminal responsibility, and in similar determinations. Examples of relevant records include progress notes of office outpatient practice, hospital charts, reports of previous evaluations for various agencies, and the like.

The fundamental principle in chart reviewing is to remember the specific purpose for which the examination is being conducted. Since the usual focus of a patient chart is preservation of many kinds of data with broad clinical utility, much extraneous, but often fascinating, information will almost certainly be included. The reviewer must read selectively, attending to that portion of the material that relates to the question before him or her.

A component of skilled review that is often omitted is cross-checking or cross-validation of information. When a chart is arranged, as many are, with separate sections for the various disciplines, it is likely that critical incidents may be found in different places within the record, even though the entries describe the same or simultaneous events.

For Example: An inpatient on a hospital ward started a fight in the occupational therapy room that resulted in an injury which led to litigation. Separate records of the event were found in: the main progress notes section of the chart, written by the patient's physician; the physician's private office notes; the occupational therapist's notes on the patient's O.T. performance; the nursing notes section of the chart; and an incident report separately describing the nursing department's standard investigation of the reported incident.

The skilled reviewer will examine all these recordings of the event with an eye to their areas of agreement and disagreement. Since nursing notes are usually written by those closest in time and space to the events on an inpatient ward, they are exceptionally important sources. Usually, they have the added advantage of being recorded with a time notation that permits more precise identification of the exact time of an incident than is possible from progress notes, which are often identified only by date.

There are certain common pitfalls in records assessment. Consistency in date and time notations, as suggested above, is often overlooked. Laboratory results and their implications, the outcomes of repeated consultations, and examinations may also fail to be given due significance. The observational bases for conclusions drawn may be assumed by the recorders without the clear presence of these elements in the chart.

EVALUATION OF OFFENDERS

The clinical evaluation of a suspected offender is a form of direct forensic assessment. The forensic evaluator may be asked to examine individuals suspected of crimes as part of the pre-trial or post-trial process, or in relation to a planned legal defense. Certain important principles that influence clinical evaluation will now be reviewed.

The setting in which a given offender is examined can exert a complex but essentially con-taminating effect on the evaluation of the central questions. It may be imagined that the average non-mentally ill offender whose competency, say, has been challenged and who thus finds himself in a mental hospital surrounded by actively hallucinating psychotics, may experience this as somewhat stressful and thus manifest to an examiner a range of anxiety-related symptomatology that does not represent his usual mental state. This same individual, restored to the familiar setting of jail, might well find it a far less stressful environment. Conversely, the chronic mental patient accused of a crime who is being evaluated inappropriately in prison, may well decompensate because of sensory deprivation and the indifference of staff.

By contrast, the structure and inherent protections supplied by both prison and mental hospital may exert powerful organizing effects on some disturbed offenders, especially those whose illnesses manifest themselves as sensory hyperesthesias and vulnerability to overstimulation in the various sensory modalities (Gutheil, 1978). Thus, even a jail cell may actually function like a seclusion room in a mental hospital and create a healing environment for the offender bombarded by sensory overload (as may occur in schizophrenia, mania, and PCP toxicity). Speciously benign clinical pictures may result. The patient's claimed insanity, for example, which was supposedly present shortly before the evaluation in prison may have cleared inside the "four walls," thereby muting or covering the original pathology. Similarly, the individual who tests out as competent within the reassuring hospital structure may decompensate utterly when seen in the bustling, unpredictable environment of open court. The practiced examiner will remain alert to these potential contaminants of a reliable examination and will attempt to make compensatory allowances for possible sources of error.

SELF-SERVING MOTIVATIONS

The examiner must be aware of the powerful incentives to duplicity that are inherent in the context of offender evaluation. While no forensic assessor, no matter how experienced, can function as a human lie detector, he can eschew naive acceptance of everything reported as veridical fact. Attention to factual inconsistencies at differing times during the evaluation, awareness of implausible constructions placed on events, and similar methods are obligatory safeguards against being too easily deceived. It is important to remember that it is not only the habitual criminal or the "flaming psychopath" that may yield to the temptation to fabricate. Even upright citizens, faced with the stresses of criminal process, may distort or slant the information they give. Suspected offenders may also falsify clinical entities to avoid guilt or to gain some secondary end, such as to obtain transfer from a harsh prison environment to the presumably (but not always actually) more supportive state hospital, or, more commonly, to promote eligibility for the insanity defense. While the average simulation of mental illness is quite transparent and unconvincing to the experienced clinician, there are a few offenders whose gift for mimicry can succeed in persuading an evaluator of the genuineness of their illness. While there is no absolute safeguard against this eventuality, the evaluator does well to maintain a suitable humility as to the infallibility of his perceptions.

LITIGANTS AND THE PROBLEM OF INTEREST

The forensic examiner may have to examine litigants in a case. A typical civil example might be a plaintiff who is examined to determine the degree of pain and suffering allegedly caused by the defendant.

For Example: A doctor in a hospital, in the process of obtaining informed consent for the use of an antipsychotic medication, informs the patient that she has schizophrenia, for which this particular drug is a standard and efficacious remedy. The patient later sues, claiming intense pain and suffering for being told this diagnosis which allegedly cost her the will to live, broke up her marriage, and caused a number of untoward and undesired effects. The patient is suing for emotional damages or emotional harms, another name by which pain and suffering are often described. The forensic examiner may be asked by the attorney of either side to assess this claim, either from plaintiff's side to document its validity or from defendant physician's side to invalidate or challenge it.

For Example: A patient with conversion symptomatology actually convinces a surgeon to operate. Subsequently, the accusation of negligence is leveled at the surgeon, and the forensic examiner is asked to assess the degree of pain and suffering caused by the outcome. In this case evaluating the psychogenic origin of the original symptoms, the complexity of determining the present problem and how much of it is due to the operation, and the formidable secondary gain elements that predate the actual surgery, but probably continue into the present, pose considerable difficulties.

These examples convey some of the flavor of the challenges for the assessor. The first takes place in a psychiatric setting and concerns an alleged psychiatric "cause"; the second demonstrates the psychiatric elements in general medical settings. Both reveal the enormous subjectivity of the data base on which the examiner must work.

WITNESSES

On occasion the forensic examiner will be asked to interview witnesses to determine their competence to serve as a witness. This usually hinges on whether the witness can give testimony with no greater distortion than that seen in witnesses generally. The question may arise when the witness suffers from an identifiable mental illness or when certain bizarre features of the testimony or the witness's behavior give reason to challenge the material. On occasion an attorney will ask for evaluation of a witness in an attempt at discreditation of the latter's possibly damaging testimony.

At worst the evaluator is being asked to serve an almost impossible function, that of human lie detector, a role which is always considered desirable by the legal profession. These subversions of the forensic examiner's role should be managed in a highly circumspect manner, to prevent misuse of the profession and the setting of goals impossible to achieve.

The evaluation method here is not generally different from the evaluation of competence to stand trial, although the competence being assessed is different. The witness's capacity should be no more perfectionistically assessed than that of the average citizen-observer. The witness need not be a human television camera attached to a videotape recorder; rather, the witness should be free of gross distorting influences, such as psychosis, paranoid trends, or hallucinations, that affect the testimony given. If the testimony is unaffected, the witness is competent despite the presence of mental illness.

Indirect Assessments

The present section will address the forensic areas in which the assessment hews more closely to abstractions, rather than individuals; that is, the assessor must move from observations and clinical data to inferences and principles. An example of this type of issue is the malpractice case. For mnemonic purposes, malpractice is usually identified according to the "four Ds": Dereliction of a Duty, Directly causing Damages.

Standards of Practice

The question of dereliction depends on the duty the physician owes to his or her patient. The law seeks to distinguish bad practice, aberrant practice and unusual practice from malpractice. The legal system has developed two standards.

THE COMMUNITY STANDARD

The community standard of care compares an individual to his actual peer group. The question asked is, How does the practice of this individual on this case compare to the practice of the average practitioner of that specialty with that degree of training (and/or specialization) in that community at that time? Note that this standard does not measure the subject against the yardstick of the best, finest or most reputable practitioners, but of the average ones.

Some time ago, when the average community was a more insular environment, the community was literally that: this particular small town or village, or one close by and similarly situated. With the present information explosion and the appearance of nationally-distributed professional journals, the standard is wider. Through continuing education and professional readership, the average practitioner has access to current *national* viewpoints and standards in the field. The practitioner is expected to keep up with these reported new developments.

THE REASONABLE PERSON STANDARD

This standard asks simply whether the practitioner acted unreasonably in the subject case. Note that the language of this rule is couched in retrospect, and therein lies the problem. Hindsight contaminates assessment under this standard. The high cliff that has gone unfenced for 200 years today serves as the method that a despondent person uses to kill himself; from this view the absence of the fence may suddenly seem quite unreasonable, history being forgotten. In any case, the matter hinges on whether the reasonable precautions were taken in a given instance.

Level of Care

The assessment of the standard of care requires an evaluation of each of the multiple elements of the care of an individual patient in the clinical setting.

To focus our discussion let us first consider that there is a difference between psychiatry and law in the definition of what would constitute conservative practice. For example, because of the ever-narrowing legal commitment standards, it becomes harder and harder for persons to be committed. In some jurisdictions (e.g., Massachusetts) the burden of persuasion has become identical with the criminal standard, "beyond a reasonable doubt." That is, conservative legal practice demands that the patient be *outside* the hospital unless he passes highly demanding criteria for commitment. By contrast, for the psychiatrist, the conservative approach is to hospitalize when in doubt about the patient's safety. Thus, the conservative practitioner wants the patient *inside* the hospital for close observation and monitoring. This difference in the two modalities can lead to both theoretical and practical tensions, as the torts of negligent release and false imprisonment war with each other.

Another consideration that affects the "outpatient vs. inpatient" status question is the legal concept of least restrictive alternatives, articulated in a number of legal decisions. This principle, reviewed elsewhere (Gutheil, Appelbaum, & Wexler, in press), holds that when a state must intervene in an individual's liberty, the least restrictive intervention is always preferable. Courts are quite content with this yardstick, although there is growing evidence that its heyday is waning. The problem from the clinical perspective is that the concept has highly ambiguous clinical meaning; that is, clinicians are trained and practiced in thinking in terms of utility for the patient, rather than restrictiveness. Restrictiveness considerations thus ill suit the actual work with patients (Gutheil et al., in press).

The importance of restrictiveness bears not only on the indirect assessment of whether or not a patient meets criteria for hospitalization. Even for patients already hospitalized, there is a spectrum of privileges and restrictions which must be individually prescribed. Consequently there is a necessary balance that must be struck between two considerations: close monitoring and pathogenic intrusiveness.

As earlier implied, one of the purposes of hospitalizing a patient may be to permit close observation that is impossible with outpatient treatment. There is, however, a trade-off at stake. The inpatient is necessarily placed in juxtaposition with numbers of other patients. The greater degree of visibility and control of movement thus gained by the clinician occurs at the cost of the relative decrease in the patient's ability defensively to put distance between self and others, as would be possible outside. This point gains clinical significance when we consider that some patients are in states of overstimulation, even hyperesthesia, in which the sensory input of even the average environment becomes sensory bombardment or overload (Gutheil, 1978). Thus, the inpatient environment may exert some countertherapeutic effects. The value of hospitalization, thus, must always be weighed against these possibilities: The need for monitoring is balanced against the toxicity of intrusiveness.

The forensic relevance of these considerations is obvious. When the assessor is attempting to determine the level of care devoted to a particular patient (a necessarily retrospective evaluation), he must attempt to see the case as seen by the treating personnel in terms of the above trade-off. Only then will the picture formed be a realistic one.

A complication is that the law is "client-centered," viewing the plaintiff in a vacuum, whereas the clinician sees the entire ward considering different parties' rights in tension. If a patient injures another patient, the latter's attorney may claim that his client should have been protected from the attacker by appropriate restraints. What is commonly ignored is that the civil rights of the *attacker* may have been at stake. Treating staff may have had to refrain from applying any sanctions or restraints until there was evidence of clear danger. Thus, before the fact, the attacking patient is given "the benefit of a doubt," while after the fact this same benefit may be characterized as negligent. The fact finder ultimately settles this question, but the example reveals the differences between clinical and legal viewpoints.

Closely allied to these questions is the problem of the foreseeability of human behavior. A vast number of suits are based on the following *post hoc* fallacy: "Mr. X committed suicide; ergo, he was suicidal; ergo, his suicidality should have been foreseen." This reason from hindsight may be invoked even when the patient has demonstrated no sign of suicidality or even, in some cases, depression.

A problem of current public concern is the ability of psychiatry to predict future dangerousness in individuals in general. This matter has profound implications, not only for the liability assessment now being considered, but for commitment, retention in regular or locked facilities, involuntary hospitalization after findings of "not guilty by reason of insanity," death penalty proceedings, and so on.

Foreseeability depends on reasonable anticipatory determinations that good care might require. All psychiatric patients, for example, should be asked on first encounter about suicidal (and many about homicidal) intent. Patients who deny these and give no contradictory messages by other means (communications to others than the examiner, body language, actions such as revising a will, etc.) should be taken at their word. Absent these indicators, it simply makes no sense and is not feasible to employ maximum precautions for all patients, despite the alleged decreased likelihood of liability that might result.

JUDGMENT, ERROR AND NEGLIGENCE

Summing up the foregoing review, we might note that the issue in these assessments is to distinguish legitimate errors in judgment from negligence, the latter defined as failure to provide due care so that harm resulted. Liability depends on the degree of care exercised in the situation. A wrong decision, as shown by outcome, is not negligent and no liability ensues if the standard of care was met; the same decision made without due care may well be negligent.

For Example: A patient, admitted after a suicide attempt, was diligently monitored and treated and gave every evidence of a steady and linear improvement. The day after discharge she committed suicide. Review of the case indicated that she had apparently "malingered health" so as to get out of the hospital and thus be able to accomplish her suicidal purpose. Since staff cannot act as lie detectors, and detect skilled, conscious fabrication, there was no finding of negligence; the patient had given every indication of being able to be discharged, and the staff had observed, inquired and carefully planned the discharge and aftercare.

In contrast, consider this example.

For Example: A similar patient was admitted and followed a similar course. Howver, there was no evidence from the chart during subsequent review (in connection with litigation) that the patient's state of mind around discharge had been specifically assessed as to whether the strong suicidal ideation that had marked admission was still present. Staff had apparently assumed that the patient had been in hospital long enough almost entirely because the patient had behaved himself on the ward. This failure to show that careful assessment had taken place led to a finding of negligence.

Implicit in the foregoing example is the absolutely central point that documentation is almost as crucial as good performance and, in the retrospective setting of the *post facto* review, perhaps even more so. This situation has been described as, "If you didn't write it, it didn't happen" (Gutheil, 1980b). For the assessor, it is even more important to search out documentation of the clinician's thought and planning. Without this proof of care, the entire issue rests on the unaided memory of the participants, often long after the fact and with the added likelihood of self-serving contamination of recollection, even if unconscious.

A second prophylactic against the charge of negligence coequal in importance with documentation, is the use of appropriate consultation. In practical terms, if the practitioner or care-giver of whatever discipline has conferred with even one peer about the wisdom or advisability of taking a given action, the fact that this step was taken clearly conveys care in the treatment of the patient. In addition, the consultation itself affords an opportunity for a current assessment of the community standard in regard to the action in question: At least one other member of the particular peer community has given sanction to the measure.

We should not leave this topic without noting that the average psychiatric practitioner's anxiety is far ahead of the realities in this area. Psychiatric liability has generally remained far below that of other disciplines in medicine, with the possible exception of a few procedures still considered special in risk, such as psychosurgery. A recent study of the Massachusetts experience (Dorof & Gutheil, unpublished data) showed a total liability outlay over a seven year period statewide of only ca. $100,000.

The same social shift to a more conservative position, earlier described in relation to offenders found NGI, applies here. While civil rights activism pressed clinicians to loosen their grip, as it were, on patients under their care, the social community, through judges' and juries' decisions about negligence, was pressing to have the patients held tighter. Failures to do this were held as litigable, because negligent, omissions.

These social currents make the approach to malpractice assessment for the examiner (or, for the clinician, malpractice prevention) far more difficult. A conservative posture is now maximally in keeping with the climate in this area. The clinician-examiner must retain what has regrettably become an anachronistic, patient-centered view in performing the assessment, using the earlier-described standards founded on care for the patient.

We will now turn to the use of tests to determine important forensic capacities, beginning with the history of this approach.

Review of Historical Tests

The impact of historical legal developments has been felt particularly in the areas of competency and responsibility. These historical precedents will be reviewed here in brief for their heuristic value.

Competence to Stand Trial

Historically, the question of competence to stand trial rests on a subtle but essential aspect of the judicial system: the perception of fairness. This principle relates to the fact that, in order to serve a society, a judicial system requires credibility, a quality that would be subverted if defendants were tried who were clearly incompetent (that is, defendants who, even to a layman's eyes, would be clearly incapable of coping with, or defending themselves against, the system within which they were functioning). Thus, by its careful focus on the elements of "due process" in the competency determination, the credibility of the judicial system is supported.

The original "test" for incompetency was the notorious *peine forte et dure*, loosely, "suffering fierce and hard." In this method of competency assessment, an accused individual in England prior to the 1770s who refused to enter a plea for any one of a variety of reasons, including, probably, mental illness or retardation, was subjected to having successively heavier boulders placed on top of him until either he pled something or "the necessity for the trial disappeared" (Gutheil & Appelbaum, 1982). The crudity of this method was gradually replaced by a confusion of criteria (as will later be described) particularly in American forensics, where for many years the distinctions between presence of mental illness (particularly psychosis), committability, competence and criminal responsibility were poorly understood. The problem was perhaps accentuated by the heavy emphasis of those standards on cognitive faculties to the exclusion of affective influences, a bias no doubt deriving from the neuropsychology of the 18th and 19th centuries. While later tests found room for the impact of affect on competence, the most recent proposal of the American Psychiatric Association appears to propose a shift back to giving more determinative weight to the more cognitive capacities.

An important event occurred in 1959 with the trial of Melton Dusky on charges of illegal interstate transport of a kidnapped teenager. The essential import of the case was the statement by the appellate court of the test for competence to stand trial, namely that the defendant "has sufficient present ability to consult with his lawyer with a reasonable degree of rational understanding and whether he has a rational as well as factual understanding of the proceedings against him" (*Dusky v. U.S.*, 1960).

The seasoned clinician will realize immediately that, since all the terms (reasonable, rational, factual, etc.) are not precisely defined, or perhaps even definable, the application of this ostensibly clear standard to actual human beings in various states of mental disorder will be challenging, to say the least. Indeed, a wide range of cases after *Dusky* showed an equally wide range of conditions in which the standard was or was not met. Nevertheless, these two elements—some kind of grasp of the proceedings and some kind of capacity to collaborate with counsel—have been the durable pillars on which rest the criterion of competence to stand trial since that case.

A subsequent case, *Pate v. Robinson* (1966), established the right of an accused individual to have a competency hearing on a constitutionally-protected basis, even if defendant's counsel failed to raise the question. This case also addressed the question of what level of doubt was required to raise the question, a point also brought out in *Drope v. Missouri*, 1975, where a detailed list of indicators was identified, and any of which items might provide adequate evidence that the matter of competence was in doubt; these indicators included courtroom demeanor, medical evidence and the like.

These important cases speak to various facets of the assessment process as viewed from the judicial perspective on competence. The clinical side has been the subject of active investigation as well.

Modern Attempts at Assessment Guidelines

Until just after mid-century, an apparently vast amount of confusion governed the role of psychiatrists in forensic proceedings. Forensic psychiatry as a discipline did not exist; consequently, individuals were left to formulate, in essence, their own idiosyncratic ideas about the forensic application of their clinical training. In the late 1960s, McGarry, Curran, Lipsitt, Lelos, Schwitz-Gebel, and Rosenberg (1973) lamented:

> Thus, when a court takes the trouble (which it usually doesn't) to articulate the tripartite common law criteria for competency and gets back the answer, "Schizophrenia," we are witnessing the interdisciplinary lack of rational communication which has governed the handling of the competency issues in this country with rare exceptions. (p. 1)

Prior to this sobering opinion, McGarry had obtained, in 1964, empirical evidence of its validity (McGarry, 1965) in Massachusetts. He surveyed the 13 state hospitals as to their forensic processing of 1,437 patients of all ages, genders, diagnoses and crimes. His conclusion:

> The observations cited . . . support the hypothesis that one judgment is made, a medical judgment with regard to diagnosis. The legal questions of criminal responsibility and competence for trial presumably are subsumed, in the eyes of the psychiatrist, under the medical diagnosis and follow uniformly under the psychosis-nonpsychosis

criterion. It is not at all clear that the psychiatrists involved were aware of the distinction between the two quite separate issues of criminal responsibility and competence to stand trial. (p. 625)

McGarry also discovered that the courts of that time tended to ignore the question that they themselves were asking and would treat the doctor's clinically-based recommendations for hospitalization as an implied declaration of the patient's incompetence. The misunderstandings, therefore, afflicted both clinicians and the legal process.

It was in the spirit of rectification of these misunderstandings, or perhaps, even, abuses, that McGarry and others attempted to develop a systematic approach to the determination of competence to stand trial. The results are outlined in a monograph (McGarry et al., 1973) entitled "Competency to Stand Trial and Mental Illness." In the study therein reported, McGarry developed instruments for screening for competency early in the judicial process as well as a means to test competence in a reliable and replicable way.

The competency screening test (CST) consists of a list of 22 sentence completion questions. Examples are:

(2) When I go to court the lawyer will. . .
(20) When Phil thinks of what he is accused of, he. . .
(13) When the witnesses testifying against Harry gave incorrect evidence, he. . .

The individual being screened is instructed that these questions relate to the law and to going to court, and that there are no right or wrong answers. The answers themselves may be scored 0, 1, or 2, with higher totals implying higher competency. Scores lower than 20 are felt to raise a question about the individual's competency.

To convey in brief the method of scoring, we may note that each question is rated as to its adherence to "legal criteria" (embracing such elements as ability to cooperate with the attorney and awareness of court proceedings) and "psychological criteria" (including ability to relate or trust, and capacities of coping, realism, acceptance of the situation and the like). For example, on question (2) above, "When I go to court the lawyer will," an answer of "defend me" or "represent me" would receive full 2 points, an answer of "be there" would receive 1, and an answer of "put me away" would receive 0.

McGarry and his co-workers also developed an actual assessment instrument for competency that forms the core of their monograph (McGarry et al., 1973). The competency assessment instrument (CAI) is a model for examination based on 13 determinations, listed below. Each category is scored on a scale of 1 to 5, with 1 representing "total incapacity" and 5 representing "no incapacity." The categories are:

(1) Appraisal of available legal defenses.
(2) Unmanageable behavior.
(3) Quality of relating to attorney.
(4) Planning of legal strategy, including guilty plea to lesser charges where pertinent.
(5) Appraisal of role of: (a) Defense counsel; (b) Prosecuting attorney; (c) Judge; (d) Jury; (e) Defendant; (f) Witnesses.
(6) Understanding of court procedure.
(7) Appreciation of charges.
(8) Appreciation of range and nature of possible penalties.
(9) Appraisal of likely outcome.
(10) Capacity to disclose to attorney available pertinent facts surrounding the offense including the defendant's movements, timing, mental state, actions at the time of the offense.
(11) Capacity to realistically challenge prosecution witnesses.
(12) Capacity to testify relevantly.
(13) Self-defeating vs. self-serving motivation (legal sense).

While these are fairly self-explanatory, a brief example will be given as provided in the monograph for the last category, since that one contains a possible ambiguity for clinicians.

(13) Self-defeating v. self-serving motivation (legal sense). This item calls for an assessment of the accused's motivation to adequately protect himself and appropriately use legal safeguards to this end. It is recognized that accused persons may appropriately be motivated to seek expiation and appropriate punishment in their trials. Of concern here is the pathological seeking of punishment and the deliberate failure by the accused to avail himself of appropriate legal protections. Passivity or indifference does not justify low scores on this item. Actively self-destructive manipulation of the legal process arising from mental pathology does justify low scores.

In this item the issue turns on the willingness of the accused to take advantage of appropriate *legal* protections even though he may feel that he should be punished. Will he, in other words, play the game; taking advantage of the rules built into the system for his protection. Relevant questions:

We know how badly you feel about what happened—suppose your lawyer is successful in getting you off—would you accept that? Suppose that the District Attorney made some legal errors and your lawyer wants to appeal a guilty finding in your case—would you accept that? We know that you want to plead guilty to your charge—but what if your lawyer could get the District Attorney to agree to a plea of guilty to a lesser charge—would you accept that?

Clinical examples: A 33-year-old paranoid schizophrenic is accused of murder. He is convinced that he will and should be executed since his is the "second messianic crucifixion." He declines a negotiated plea of manslaughter and attempts to intruct his attorney not to call any defense witnesses. He intends to address the court to request the death sentence since "he owes this to sinning mankind." He received a score of 2, indicating severely impaired functioning and a substantial question of adequacy for this item. (pp. 113–114)

This somewhat protracted example from the monograph conveys the flavor of the material, as well as an insight into the approach as presented to the reader-student: The category is supplied, together with its definition, relevant questions that serve as models for elicitation of the information required, and some clinical vignettes to demonstrate the system in actual use. A later section of this chapter will critically review this model.

We now turn to another checklist approach devised by Ames Robey in 1965, when he was Medical Director of the Massachusetts Correctional Institution in Bridgewater. He called attention to problems with the court's failure to define the questions asked of its psychiatric consultants and to the complementary problem of the psychiatrists' ignorance of the tests or criteria. To remedy this problem, Robey devised a checklist for determination of competence to stand trial; the list evolved "out of the experience" at a high-security setting for the "criminally insane," but has not been independently validated.

The Robey Checklist

The Robey checklist (Robey, 1965) is divided into three major categories of subjects which not only relate to the substantive criteria of the competency determination—comprehension of court proceedings and ability to advise counsel—but also include a crucial yet rarely addressed element of the process, namely, a separate assessment of whether the individual is likely to be susceptible to decompensation either while awaiting or standing trial.

Each category contains a listing of items designed to guide the examiner in interviewing the patient. The text of Robey's article gives the essential rationale for each listing, together with more detailed instructions as to the specific determination. Each listing is marked in three columns, headed "OK," "mental illness," and "mental deficiency." We will now review the listings as grouped within the categories.

Under the first heading, comprehension of court proceedings, Robey lists seven component abilities. These are: recognition of the reality surroundings; understanding of the procedures taking place; correct identification of the principals (i.e., courtroom and trial personnel); awareness of the charges pending; understanding of the possible verdicts that may eventuate; knowledge of the possible penalties that may follow a guilty finding; and knowledge of the pertinent legal rights.

Under the second heading, ability to advise counsel, Robey subsumes the defendant's ability to provide counsel with the facts of the alleged crime, the ability to formulate, in negotiation with the attorney, a feasible plea and legal strategy, the capacity to maintain the relationship with the lawyer through the trial, the capacity to maintain a consistent defense without impulsive or paranoid reshufflings, an appreciation of the issues when certain rights are to be waived, the capacity to assess critically the testimony of witnesses, and—if necessary—the ability to testify from the stand in a constructive manner, this last option depending on whether the attorney believes that it should be utilized with this particular client.

The third category is in some respects the most original and critical, since much of the misunderstandings and ill will that may arise between court and hospital in the competence area derives from those occasions when a patient, found competent in the hospital, decompensates into an unpleasantly disruptive state under the stresses of court. This leads the court (inappropriately) to lose faith in the hospital's credibility and leads the hospital to feel that the court is mistreating the patient when the latter is sent back for a repeat of an evaluation thought to have been already adequately performed. Robey recommends that the evaluator assess the patient's potentials for developing, during the proceedings, "signs of violence, acute psychosis, suicidal depression or regressive withdrawal under the stress of trial" (Robey, 1965). Robey also counsels alertness to the problem of progressive organic deterioration which might well not be detected. Though Robey does not specifically so state, this caveat would presumably apply to the possibility of a patient's "sundowning" (becoming disoriented and agitated in conditions of lowered illumination) if the trial day extends past sunset. Once again, a critique of this approach will await a later section of this review.

Roesch's and Golding's Contributions

We turn now to a recent and fairly innovative approach to assessment research in the area of competence to stand trial. The issues in this study are presented in the book, *Competency to Stand Trial*, by Roesch and Golding (1980).

The book reports on four studies which the authors performed to examine various aspects of competency determinations, and the legal-judicial process. Two of these are of particular relevance to our consideration of assessment.

The first, "designed to provide information about the mental health system's procedures for evaluating competency to stand trial," was a study of evaluation procedures in an institutional setting. From a total discharged population over the study time period of 2,055 patients (including the NGI patients) sent out of the forensic unit at Dorothea Dix Hospital in North Carolina, the authors extracted a sample of 642 patients by eliminating short-stay patients (all believed to be competent by the authors' assumption), and repeatedly-evaluated defendants (seen more than once in the same fiscal year) under the reasoning that the repetition might indicate court disagreement with the recommendations from the hospital. The 642 records were then examined and 130 defendants were discovered who had been found incompetent by the hospital staff to stand trial. A control group of 140 competent defendants were selected from a 10-year admission pool and were matched with the subject group by year of admission and county of referral to control for possible differences in either the clinical or judicial environment. The authors note that they specifically refrained from matching other variables (e.g., offense, age, etc.) because of the possibility that these items would capture real differences between competent and incompetent populations.

After coding specific data of a demographic type, staff attempted to obtain copies of the initial mental status examination, as well as a diagnostic conference report and discharge summary (DCDS), a form representing the hospital's definitive report to the court. In addition to this document, which was usually employed for defendants sent immediately back to court, a separate diagnostic conference report (DCR) was utilized for those defendants who stayed in the hospital beyond a 60-day limit; this report would thus not include the post-hospital recommendations of the DCDS. In addition, a simple discharge summary (DS) was used when a defendant was being returned to court as competent or released because the charges had been dismissed.

The authors then devised a coding system for these essentially narrative reports, the details of which will be omitted here; the process generated a 77-item listing divisible into 12 major behavioral categories. Raters were trained and tested on the use of scales of behavioral descriptors and the scales were refined during this process; then the raters were assigned the records in pairs. Court outcomes were finally obtained for the subject population.

In attempting to summarize and generalize from the results of a highly elaborate study, we must regretfully do even further violence thru condensation than has already been perpetrated. The relevant portion of the results relates to the question of what predictors in the data contained in various hospital reports indicated differences between competent and incompetent populations; a principal component analysis was employed, with elaborations omitted here, for the mental status exam, the DCDS, the DCR and the DS (see above).

The striking conclusion of their analyses was that for most of the axes, "the information available from the initial psychiatric interview alone is sufficient for making a decision about competency. . . In other words the data collected from a variety of other sources which necessitate a lengthy and institutional evaluation, such as ward evaluations, psychological tests, and social histories, do not seem to be of critical importance in reaching a decision about competency" (p. 160).

The authors also reached the following conclusions:

Incompetent defendants were described as being delusional, hallucinating, confused, uncooperative and having impaired judgement and insight. Competent defendants were described as having no major symptoms, with the frequent exception of histories of alcohol and/or drug abuse. The most interesting finding with respect to the psychiatric reports was that the prediction of group membership (competent or incompetent) based on information contained in the Mental Status Exam was about as accurate as the prediction based on information contained in the Diagnostic Conference Report. (p. 172)

This finding is important because the MSE is done by one psychiatrist shortly after admission while the DCR presumably picks up data deriving from 4 to 6 weeks of assessment time plus a variety of tests, interviews and utilization of ancillary sources of information. The authors caution that the inappropriateness of many referrals (where patients are sent from court for purely dispositional reasons) must play a part in this finding; yet they feel relatively confident in questioning the operational necessity of the extended periods required for the evaluation in hospitals. The authors appropriately point to the implied suitability of court clinics or other types of community-based settings. If courts use the competency determination period for largely dispositional goals or, at worst, as a means of attaining detention without bail for certain defendants, however, then the possibility that the duration of the evaluation might be excessive is not a significant consideration in the judge's or prosecutor's actual intention, and may even be desired.

Another study reported by Roesch and Golding (1980), a pilot study of the "utility of a brief, immediate competency screening interview," is germane to our topic. In this study, 30 defendants referred in a 2½ month period for competency evaluation were given, in essence, a modification of the McGarry Competency Assessment Instrument (CAI) earlier described. The modifications

consisted of additional questions drawn from a number of the empirical studies and instruments described above. In addition the raters participated in a multi-modality training session.

In highly condensed form, the results of this admittedly small sample pointed to the conclusion that the "brief interview has the potential for screening competent defendants prior to a lengthier evaluation. The high rate of agreement between the interviewers' and the hospitals' determination of competency points to the fact that most decisions about competency are straightforward and that hospitalization is not necessary."

The authors further infer that an interview solidly based on the legal issues may yield a sufficient data base for the assessment. For the specific purpose of guiding the interview, the CAI appears to offer valuable direction, a point we have made elsewhere (Gutheil & Appelbaum, 1982).

Assessment of Other Forms of Competence: Roth, Appelbaum and the Pittsburgh Group

In the civil area, an important competency is the competence to consent to treatment, a determination with both empirical and normative components. The criteria for this competence include the ability to assimilate relevant information, weigh risks and benefits, manipulate information rationally, and evince a choice (Roth, Meisel, & Lidz, 1971). Any or all of these components may be affected by mental illness. Despite the importance of this issue, little systematic empirical effort has been made to determine how psychiatric patients actually perform on these tests.

Several studies, many in research settings, however, have at least illuminated the complexity of this area. A major focus of these reviews has been on the process of obtaining consent—a process which aims to assess the patient's reception of information and voluntary as well as competence. Some authorities have been highly pessimistic, referring to informed consent as a "myth" (Fellner & Marshall, 1970) or "fiction" (Chayet, 1976; Lafoot, 1976). Others have noted the problems of information transmission in regard to distortion (Golden & Johnston, 1970), recall (Kennedy & Lillehaugen, 1979; Robinson & Merav, 1979), and the capacity of certain patients with schizophrenia to give consent (Grossman & Summers, 1980). Of particular interest in this last category is the work of Soskis (1978), who found *inter alia* that schizophrenic patients with paranoid symptomatology tended to remember medication or procedural side effects with disproportionately better recall than benefits, a finding highly relevant to the matter of weighing risks and benefits as a component of competence.

In an important review of the assessment of competency as it may be influenced by clinical realities, Roth, Meisel and Lidz (1971) pointed out the many impingements on the psychiatric patient's competency to consent to treatment. In their review they enumerated five components of the assessment that affect the determination.

The first was the patient's personality, particularly its psychodynamic elements. This insufficiently-considered factor addresses the point that decisions, no matter how ostensibly rational, are not made in an "affective vacuum." Careful attention must be given to the potentially highly emotionally charged meaning of the treatment issue to the patient, a meaning that may be quite idiosyncratic. They note, "the recommendation for the procedure itself [by inspiring anxiety and fear] may force the patient into an apparently incompetent state and may preclude the obtaining of competent consent" (p. 1463).

The second factor described is the importance of external validation of the historical material provided by the patient, since many patients, especially paranoid individuals with relatively circumscribed delusions and a clear sensorium, may present as calm and apparently competent on too cursory an examination of the patient alone. Next of kin may provide corroborating information, or the opposite, when the historical material is in doubt.

The third factor is the importance of the examiner's awareness of what information has been presented to the patient, and how it has been presented. Simple misinformation may masquerade as incompetency based on mental illness or deficiency. The authors warn: "In the modern general hospital, in which many professionals share responsibility for each patient's care, it becomes increasingly likely that no one person will consider it his or her unique duty to sit down with the patient to provide the necessary information" (p. 1464). The authors also underscore the point that inadequacy of information may obscure the patient's actual *incompetency* as well.

The fourth factor concerns the stability of the patient's mental status over time. The authors point out that competency may fluctuate, influenced by many variables including the nature of the illness, treatment, effects of medications and the like. An obvious remedy is repeated examinations over time to attempt to control for this variation; the authors suggest at least two evaluations on two different days.

Finally, the authors point out that the setting is not neutral in the assessment process. They offer as example: "That a patient is unwilling or unable to attend to presentation of information from a physician he or she dislikes or in a hospital at which he or she is furious does not warrant the conclusion that the patient is necessarily unable or unwilling to hear the information from another person or in another place" (p. 1465).

Appelbaum, together with Mirkin and Bateman (1981), performed an important study, empirically assessing newly-admitted psychiatric patients to determine whether they were competent to consent to their voluntary admission. This study was all the more important because the District Court judge in an important right-to-refuse-treatment case, *Rogers* v. *Okin* (1981), later named *Mills* v. *Rogers*, had ruled that patients in a hospital were competent until proven otherwise.

The authors employed an interview questionnaire on 50 new admissions, representing that portion of the 75 actual admissions during the study period who would consent to fill out the questionnaire. Some typical questions were:

Do you think you have psychiatric problems? Why do you think that the doctor who saw you recommended that you go into a hospital? Are there any disadvantages to your being in a hospital?

Other queries dealt with knowledge of rights and issues related to competency to consent to treatment as well.

Only about "half of the patients, all of whom had voluntarily entered a psychiatric hospital a day or two previously, could clearly acknowledge that they had psychiatric problems and that these problems required treatment." The authors point out the obvious conclusion: a large percentage of the voluntary patients surveyed were incompetent to consent to their own admission, using fairly broad criteria for competence. The authors also note some methodological problems, including the fact that patients were usually interviewed after some early treatment interventions had taken place (e.g., medication), so that the patients may have been even *more* incompetent at the actual time of admission processing. The selection of subjects, the authors note, "again [probably] underestimate the overall degree of incapacity," since it is likely that still sicker patients might be more likely to refuse participation.

The authors thoughtfully include a caveat that, because competency to consent to admission, like most other competencies, is inadequately defined in any manner capable of evoking agreement, the instrument employed may have failed to pick up other criteria somehow essential for this determination. They aver, however, that the poor showing made by the patients was evident in all tested areas, a finding so forceful that, "however we ultimately decide to define competency, these patients were not engaging in the rational manipulation of information that is a desirable element of any definition." The authors conclude with the response to the judge in *Rogers* (noted above): "Whatever the outcome of [future] such studies, it seems likely that at least the presumption of competency to consent to psychiatric hospitalization will have to fall" (p. 1175).

Competency to Marry

A reader who performs the thought experiment of making a quick mental survey of his or her married friends would probably conclude that the institution of marriage owes nothing to competence considerations, and perhaps owes nothing to considerations of reality, reason or wisdom. Nowhere else but in matrimonial decision-making is there so trenchant a demonstration of the proverb, "The heart has reasons which the reason does not understand."

For the forensic examiner, however, this whimsical-seeming matter can take on serious and challenging features for the assessment process. Formally stated, competence to marry requires an understanding of the nature of the marriage relationship and its attendant obligations. As with other broadly defined competencies, this definition clearly leaves a wide margin for variation in interpretation in relation to a specific individual. But, as with testamentary capacity, the complexity of the issue derives, not from a grasp of the standards against which this matter is measured, but from the circumstances in which this test is most often invoked. The best way to grasp the matter is through the following example which,

though caricatured for heuristic reasons, often bears significant contiguities with real-life situations that come to forensic attention (needless to add, in the overwhelming majority of cases, the competence of either the marrying parties may be privately impugned by friends and associates but is usually not brought forward for assessment in a formal way):

For Example: An elderly rich man suddenly informs his family and heirs that he is planning to marry his teen-aged practical nurse who has been so helpful to him during his dotage. He cheerfully announces as well that he plans to change his will to name her his principal heir.

Or:

A rich elderly woman similarly announces her wish to marry her 20-year-old groundskeeper who, she says, "loves her passionately and wants to make her final years happy ones."

In either case the heirs, fearing exclusion from the estate of the older person, raise immediate question about the subject's competency to marry and demand a forensic examination.

Though dramatic, these examples are actually easier to analyze than an equally common assessment problem, the *retrospective* determination of whether an individual was competent at the time of a marriage which took place earlier. This determination, often also clouded by the cries and laments of displaced heirs, bears the difficulties earlier enumerated for all retrospective assessments such as testmentary capacity assessed post mortem.

Further complicating the matter is the well-known reluctance of courts to tamper with marriages, especially to void them. If a person was manifestly "insane" in the popular sense at the time of marriage, a court would have little problem with the decision, as with a fully intoxicated bride or groom. An annulment would reasonably follow. With borderline or ambiguous cases, however, the matter may be far less certain, even given the broad definition of the competency involved.

An additional complexity involves the question of which party may bring an action after the fact. This issue is variable in many jurisdictions and also in some degree of flux.

The presumptively incompetent party may bring suit for annulment based on having been incompetent to participate knowingly in the transaction of marriage. The presumably competent party is most commonly restricted to initiating action only if he or she were unaware of the grounds for incompetency (e.g., the existence of incapacitating mental illness or retardation) in the spouse. With drunkenness as the putative grounds for incompetence, it is almost always the intoxicated spouse only who may so petition; again, the intoxication must be shown to have impaired the requisite capacities noted above.

Some common entities that emerge in assessments of competency to marry include, besides alcoholism and mental illness, senior retardation (again, severe enough to affect the requisite capacity) and psychogenic impotence, which—if not made known to and accepted by the spouse— is considered an impediment to fulfillment of one of the "obligations" earlier mentioned, i.e., intercourse, though it does not, of course, affect mental capacity.

Critiques of assessment instruments

One of the most searching and systematic critiques of empirical assessment studies was performed by Roesch and Golding (1980). Their main points are as follows:

Roesch and Golding note that the Competency Screening Instrument (CSI) of McGarry and others (1973) is designed about the hypothesis that "lower total scores would suggest significant behavioral or cognitive deficits which might interfere with participation in the defense" (p. 59). The authors assume that the high inter-rater reliability achieved (coefficient of .93 means that each rater's judgement was standardized relative to his or her mean scale usage and variation). They continue:

Such a procedure is highly questionable, since it would result in a spuriously high reliability coefficient by eliminating rater differences in scale usage from the reliability analysis. In the real world of its intended usage, such a removal of rater "biases" (tendency to be too hard or too lenient, to see more or less pathology) would not be possible. (p. 60)

The authors recommend use of a "generalizability estimate" which would theoretically compensate for rater effects, and they speculate that

this reliability index would be markedly lower than that described by McGarry et al. (1973).

Roesch and Golding make a second major point concerning an alternative explanation (rather than actual incompetence) for a low score on the CST. Low scores may reflect feelings of powerlessness, helplessness and futility in dealing with the legal system—feelings based on actual previous experience, for example. (The authors allude to notions of locus of control and game playing theory that cannot here be elaborated; interested readers are referred to the work in question.)

The next major point, based on the putative "sample-specific" nature of the CST, is that "its items may have different meanings to competent and incompetent defendants, and suggests that it may not discriminate the populations on the basis of incompetency to stand trial."

Commenting on a reported validation study of the CST on seriously ill patients in a maximum security setting, where CST scores were dichotomized into low and high (centering on the score of 20), Roesch and Golding note that 23% of the hypothetical decisions would be in error when gauged against the final recommendations of the hospital staff. This study also demonstrates another serious statistical problem. In reality, the CST was designed for use with populations whose base rate of incompetency is relatively low (they estimate a rate of 10 to 20%). Thus, attempts to validate the instrument in a sample whose rate is demonstrated by the actual study to be markedly high (44%) risks "serious misrepresentation of its validity." An additional confounding element is the close relationship between the subjects' CST scores and simple intelligence itself.

Roesch and Golding point out that the assumption in some of the validational studies that the staff's recommendation to the court is "correct" or "true" produces the situation in which "we only have a measure of the validity of the measure in relation to another unvalidated measure." This is the case even though the psychiatric recommendations were found to exert a powerful, even controlling, effect on court outcome. The authors conclude with other critical comments that complain that the CST is cumbersome, biased toward defendants with a positive attitude toward the judicial system, and fails to substitute effectively for clinical judgment. While lauding the CST's intention of placing this important assessment on a sound legal basis, they concluded that the major current use for the CST was experimentation in the area of competency determination, not pragmatic decision-making.

Roesch and Golding similarly offer a critique of the Competency Assessment Instrument (CAI), also devised by McGarry et al. (1973), described earlier in this chapter. Again they comment that this instrument addresses itself to legal, rather than strictly clinical dimensions of competency. They also lament the paucity of reliability and validity data, the small sample size, and the probable inutility of the instrument in real arenas.

Roesch and Golding then address other instruments, some of which we have reviewed above. They note the absence of any confirmatory studies for the Robey checklist. They comment that the structured interview devised by Bukatman, Roy, and Degrazia (1971), while also intended "to promote a legal focus of the competency evaluations," may be useful as a "guide for interviewers." But neither this method nor the Robey checklist has been validated, and thus their use at this time in the actual arenas of decision-making is unjustified.

To these criticisms we might add that a fundamental problem nowhere comprehensively addressed is the probable underlying motives behind the trial competency assessment as earlier suggested, namely, the wish to preserve the perceived fairness of the judicial system and the wish to achieve rapid dispositional temporizations in both knotty cases and those with a clear "mental health" coloration. Neither of these highly pragmatic goals is addressed by the complex assessments earlier described; thus, the latter operate in something of a teleologic vacuum. We would certainly agree that a *skilled*, on-the-spot assessment can almost always supplant a longer in-hospital evaluation at the level of discrimination required; yet this misses the "actual" intent of the process.

The most significant development in the assessment of competence is, in one sense, the recognition of the obvious; namely, that incompetence can be quite specific and focal in its effects (Gutheil & Appelbaum, 1982). This had led to a trend away from declarations by courts that individuals are globally incompetent, to the designation of limited incompetence and the concomitant use of limited guardianships over those specific areas. The inherent problem has been alluded to elsewhere (Gutheil & Appelbaum, 1982), namely, that the vagueness of criteria that has constantly plagued assessors of general competence will not abate merely because the assessment has become focal rather than global.

Competence to stand trial has not altered to any great degree from the underlying concept proposed in the *Dusky* standards or the others earlier described. The majority of cases can be evaluated by attention to the "twin pillars" of the determination, the grasp of the proceedings and the ability to work with the lawyer.

Two difficulties emerge from attempts to perform this measurement. The first is that the only accurate way to determine capacity to work with an attorney is to see the dyad in action. The second is that if the patient is not to be put on the witness stand (a legitimate courtroom tactic for the attorney) the level of competence pragmatically required may be considerably less than if the witness is expected to testify.

Caution must also be exercised in applying the standards involved with a degree of reasonableness. The problem in this regard is that the average lawyer feels that the ideally competent defendant would be another lawyer, sensitive to every nuance of the issue. Clinicians working in this area, on the other hand, feel that a day in court is so essential that they tend to accept the competence of the average citizen as adequate competence, a view that militates in favor of return to trial for the greater number.

Yet another area of difficulty with the competency assessment approaches above delineated is the fact that nowhere is an allowance made for three aspects of the process, at least, that exert an extremely powerful influence on the end result.

The first is the problem of fluctuating or state-dependent competence earlier described. While this author has alluded to the problem above, it must be noted that none of the measures described attempt to address this issue quite commonly encountered in clinical practice. It is also difficult to determine whether the patient's rights and society's requirements are best served by the viewpoint that any irregularity of competence should count as incompetence (allowing due process and substitute decision-making) or as competence (under the principle that a person is competent unless firmly proven otherwise).

The second problem area relates to the inherent difficulty of determining the role of affective impairment in the competency assessment. In contrast, cognitive impairments are relatively easy to define and to pick up on appropriately designed testing. Affective impairments, however, appear to strike more at the semanticity of language and decision-making. For example, a patient in a hypomanic state may be able to grasp the concept that the death penalty could be an outcome of the trial at hand for which his competence is being assessed. He may be unable to accord this threat its proper weight and seriousness because of his illness itself, thus to some extent affecting his competence to weigh the outcome in the decision. Similarly, the depressed individual may be able to recite verbatim the content of a decision, yet be unable—because of the guilt and pessimism inherent in his disease—to look with any reasonable objectivity at positive features of the outcome: to feel, for example, that there is any hope of helping the attorney to defend his hopeless-seeming case. Clinical experience can provide countless other examples on this theme.

The third problem area concerns the relatively underinvestigated issue of the interactive nature of these assessments. The central issue here is easily grasped when we replace the concept, "able to cooperate with his or her attorney," with the probably more accurate: "able to cooperate with *some* attorneys." This rephrasing highlights the common clinical observation that different people make differing impacts upon mentally ill individuals. Familiar examples include homosexual panic, feeling threatened by physically imposing or attractive individuals, becoming paranoid about certain physical or vocal peculiarities of the attorney, and the like. These problems can arise *regardless* of the interpersonal interviewing and communicating skills of the attorney in question.

For completeness, of course, we must include the problem at the assessor's end of the relationship. Though trained to handle transference distortions of his or her role, function and goals, the clinician may be unable to perform a suitably objective assessment because of the factors noted above, or because of other elements such as racial differences and language barriers between assessor and patient. Thus the problem might be stated by the catchphrase: "competent to the assessment by some clinicians."

The above areas constitute the "unknown territory" of the competency assessment—areas requiring future empirical investigation. We turn now to another critical forensic assessment.

Criminal Responsibility and the Insanity Defense

Historically, the fundamental social question of criminal responsibility has produced a number of legal tests which are of importance to us in studying the evolution of the assessment process in forensic matters; current sensationalism in reporting of insanity trials has heightened public interest in this matter as well.

Interest, however, is not coterminous with knowledge. Pasewark (1981) has commented:

It is claimed that the insanity plea is the most written about topic in the literature of English jurisprudence. Yet, ironically, there is observed an extreme dearth of empirical data relating to the plea. (p. 357)

This author and others have investigated the perceptions of the defense by jurors, legislators, patients, the public and attorneys (Pasewark & Craig, 1980; Pasewark & Pantle, 1979).

Clinical authorities have referred to the insanity defense as a "fiction" (Halpern, 1980), a "judicial anachronism" (Halpern, 1977), and as a potentially "unconscionable" practice (Perr, 1975).

In this author's view, the social and psychological underpinnings of the responsibility issue and the related insanity defense stem from the issue of "perception and fairness"; the credibility of the judicial system is at stake. The spectacle of the "drooling idiot or raving lunatic" being held as strictly accountable as a normal person for his crimes is as distasteful to the judiciary, and the public whose faith supports it, as the equivalent situation during the trial process, where the manifest incompetency of the defendant assaults the onlooker's faith in the inherent justness of the procedure.

Consideration of this topic must begin with the case of Daniel M'Naghten, a man with an elaborate history of a delusional system involving important historical figures of his day. Apparently motivated by these psychotic misperceptions, he shot at a person he believed to be Sir Robert Peel, but who was actually his secretary. The critical matter, from the viewpoint of assessment, was M'Naghten's responsibility for the crime and the question of insanity as a defense.

Previous incarnations of the insanity defense had been notably crude, going back to the so-called "wild beast test" of the 18th century, in which the accused was held to be not responsible if he "doth not know what he is doing, no more than . . . a wild beast." After M'Naghten was acquitted, the public outcry forced reexamination of the matter of insanity, in a striking parallel with modern widespread calls for reform after the Hinckley trial in America. Just as the Hinckley jury was called to answer to a Senate investigation, so the House of Lords called the judges to answer five questions, briefly summarized here.

The first question was, fittingly enough, about assessment in relation to the insanity defense, e.g., "whether at the time of the commission of the alleged crime, the accused knew he was acting contrary to law . . . ?" The second question addresses the problem of jury instructions. The third question asks, "In what terms ought the question be left to the jury, as to the prisoner's state of mind at the time when the act was committed?" This query, of course, appears to betray a distrust of the jury's decision-making role, a striking parallel to that revealed by the aforementioned Senate inquiry. As in the contemporary furor, so in the past one, the public appears, in sensational criminal cases, to lose faith in the system that it otherwise values when it perceives the outcome as "wrong;" this ubiquitous finding appears to this author to confirm the view that the issue of public perception of fairness is central to this entire question.

The fourth crucial question was, "If a person under an insane delusion as to existing facts, commits an offense in consequence thereof, is he thereby excused?" This question, of course, addresses the ultimate issue before the courts then and now.

The last question, here given in its entirety, most specifically addresses the matter of assessment:

> Can a medical man conversant with the disease of insanity who never saw the prisoner previously to the trial, but who was present during the whole trial and the examination of all the witnesses, be asked his opinion as to the state of the prisoner's mind at the time of the commission of the alleged crime, or his opinion whether the prisoner was conscious at the time of doing the act, that he was acting contrary to the law, or whether he was labouring under any and what delusion at the time? (Clark & Marshall, 1958)

The noteworthy features of this crucial question include: (1) the question of whether a medi-

cal opinion is germane or reliable; (2) the description of insanity as a *disease*; (3) the inevitably retrospective nature of the examination, requiring use of present-time data such as testimony of witnesses; (4) the accused person's awareness of the law at the time of the act; and (5) the materiality of delusional content to the question at hand.

The core of the judicial answer to this probing series of inquiries has come to be the *M'Naghten* test, which avers:

> That to establish the defense on the ground of insanity, it must be clearly proved that at the time of the committing of the act, the party accused was labouring under such a defect of reason, from disease of the mind, as not to know the nature and quality of the act he was doing, or if he did know it, that he did not know he was doing what was wrong. (p. 342)

With Appelbaum I have commented elsewhere (Gutheil & Appelbaum, 1982) that "A literal reading of *M'Naghten* would seem to leave little room for applying it to most mentally ill individuals." This comment focuses on three components of the test that have drawn often-intense criticism, almost from the moment of the statement of the test itself! These areas are the matter of "knowing," the meaning of "wrong," and the absence of consideration of impulsivity in the test.

The *M'Naghten* test has been most aggressively criticized for its ostensible adherence to a question of "knowing" defined in such a way as to seem to fix upon cognition only, at the expense of consideration of the essential role of affect as it may bear on an individual's perception of what he was doing. This fixation is claimed to derive from 19th-century "faculty" psychology, with its image of the mind as made up of discrete and separated compartments. Courts appear to have, if only covertly, expanded the "know" question in actual practice to include emotional shadings of the cognitive core, so that this objection may not carry as much weight as may be imagined. One of the best comments on the problem is that of Hall (1947) who stated:

> Moral judgment (knowledge of right and wrong) is not reified as an outside, icy spectator of a moving self. On the contrary, the corollary is that value-judgments are permeated with the color and warmth of

emotion—as is evidenced by the usual attitudes of approval that coalesce with right decisions. Indeed, all action, especially that relevant to the penal law, involves a unified operation of the personality. (p. 499)

Critics have observed that the *M'Naghten* decision left the term, "wrong," ambiguous. Does "wrong" mean an act seen as illegal or socially disapproved, or morally wrong in a more profound sense? As we have noted elsewhere (Gutheil & Appelbaum, 1982),

A schizophrenic . . . convinced that her landlord was an agent of the devil bent on turning her mind to thoughts of sex, and who therefore had to be killed, could be held not to "know" the wrongness of her act of murder, though she might respond in the abstract that to murder was wrong [meaning, for the purposes of this example, morally wrong]. (p. 280)

The third element of criticism faults the test for its silence on the matter of the role of impulse, often termed "irresistible impulse" in such discussions. To raise this point is to reveal a deeper question. Professor Alan Stone has noted (Stone, 1982) that an absolutely central assessment problem in the area is distinguishing truly irresistible impulses from those simply not resisted on the particular occasion in question—a distinction that might well tax the abilities of the ablest clinician (though, of course, this is ultimately a decision for the fact-finder in the case). At the time of *M'Naghten*, however, perhaps the most energetic criticism appeared to come from the American, Isaac Ray (1838), who commented at one point:

Without mentioning all the objections to which this test of responsibility is liable, it is enough to say that it furnishes no protection to that large class of the insane who entertain no specific delusion, but act from momentary irresistible impulses. (p. 48)

A brief digression is called for here. This excerpt, through Ray's choice of words, "this test . . . furnishes no protection, etc. . .", reveals an extremely common tension in forensic work. For the clinician, whose main and constant focus is the welfare of the patient, this conceptualization of the test as *protecting* the patients, ostensibly

from the unmitigated force and strictness of the law, is a natural concomitant of clinical work. In a forensic assessment, however, the clinician is to some degree an agent of the court, an agent who is indirectly serving the system's underlying goal, as earlier noted: promotion of the perception of fairness of the system. Thus "protection" of the patient in the clinical sense does not precisely capture the social-judicial purpose of the insanity defense. Moreover, the protective impulse is one to which forensically-inexperienced clinicians are peculiarly prone: They may see the insanity defense, not as an inherent mechanism of the law with moral overtones, but as a means of protecting or even exonerating the patient only. This response resembles the so-called "rescue fantasies" seen in psychotherapeutic work, where the tyro singlehandedly attempts to save the patient without attending to vital issues of the patient's autonomous contribution to both the disease and the cure. Regrettably, public perception of the psychiatrist in insanity trials often echoes this view that "the psychiatrist wants to get the patient off without due punishment"; this view, however, ignores the adversary process and the central decision-making role of jury or judge. In any case the temptation to protect (rather than to assess objectively) the patient must remain a pitfall into which the unsophisticated expert witness may fall.

The so-called "irresistible impulse" test plays a part in some jurisdictions in the definition of exculpatory insanity, and it is also used in conjunction with the *M'Naghten* test, which is still the rule in a number of American states. As the name suggests, the issue for the fact-finder is whether the defendant was in the grip of an irresistible impulse at the time of the alleged crime; if so found, this condition is exonerating.

The *Durham* test (*Durham* v. *U.S.*, 1954), which lasted almost 20 years in the District of Columbia, is another historically important test. This rule states: "An accused is not criminally reponsible if his unlawful act was the product of mental disease or defect." This rule, also nicknamed the "product test," was intended by its author, Judge David Bazelon, to permit maximum scope to the expert witnesses, who could thus provide all possible relevant information concerning all facets of the accused's psychiatric diagnosis, formulations, symptoms, and personality structure to the fact-finder to aid the decision.

From the viewpoint of the dynamically-trained

clinician, the problem with the actual application of this test may be obvious: The principle of multiple function or the concept of overdetermination in psychic process (Waelder, 1936) suggests that any single event or act may be traced into connection with the entire associative web of the patient's mental experience. Thus, the most remote psychic phenomena may impinge on a given act and thus be acceptable for consideration as causal in determining the act as product.

The principal reason for disillusionment with the test, however, was that the expert witnesses were felt to undermine the fact-finding function of the jury by being drawn into offering conclusory opinions on the ultimate issue of "productivity." In *U.S.* v. *Brawner* (1972) Bazelon himself complained that the expert witnesses had a "stranglehold" on the jury's opinions. The *Durham* test is rarely employed today.

The next major event in the evolution of the insanity test was the test adopted by the American Law Institute (ALI [1955]) in its Model Penal Code. The test states:

(1) A person is not responsible for criminal conduct if at the time of such conduct as a result of mental disease or defect he lacks substantial capacity either to appreciate the wrongfulness of his conduct or to conform his conduct to the requirements of the law. (2) As used in this Article, the terms, "mental disease or defect" do not include an abnormality manifested only by repeated criminal or otherwise anti-social conduct. (p. 170)

There are four important points about the significance of the specific choice of wording here. First, the term "appreciate" is intended to broaden application beyond the merely cognitive to areas of mentation influenced by pathological affects. Second, the test adds a behavioral or volitional component to the cognitive one, in the words: "conform his conduct." Third, and perhaps most important, by supplying the criterion "substantial capacity," the ALI permits some attention to gradations of clinical conditions and their resulting impairment, a nod to psychiatric reality that was significantly lacking in the older, "all-or-none" formulations of test criteria.

Finally, section (2) is clearly intended to deal with the problem of the psychopath, an entity with which neither the criminal justice nor the

mental health systems has been able to contend successfully. The intent of the phrasing is to exclude psychopaths from employing the defense, but an interesting secondary difficulty has unexpectedly presented itself, relating to the evolution of nosology. I have described it with Appelbaum thus:

At the time that the Model Penal Code was published, many psychiatrists argued and many judges accepted that, "as the majority of experts use the term, a psychopath is very distinguishable from one who merely demonstrates recurrent criminal behavior [DSM-II, the second edition of the APA's diagnostic and statistical manual, echoed this view, excluding the mere repeater from the diagnosis of psychopath]." The DSM-III diagnostic criteria, on the other hand, refer only to a history of legal and social infractions [thus theoretically excluding DSM-III-diagnosed psychopaths from the insanity defense] . . . one wonders still if some of the psychological factors mentioned in DSM-II are not concomitants of the syndrome. The danger here is that the law will focus on a set of criteria that may represent the most reliably diagnosed features of the condition and assume that the set is completely descriptive of the syndrome. (Gutheil & Appelbaum, 1982)

I shall now describe some recently evolving developments. In its position paper on the insanity defense, the American Psychiatric Association has proposed, *inter alia*, that the defense be reserved for severe mental illnesses only. The paper has candidly addressed the limitations of the psychiatric profession in providing legally relevant information. Perhaps most importantly, the proposal recommends deletion of the volitional component of the test, leaving the question to turn solely on the defendant's capacity to understand the reality of his or her actions.

The American Bar Association (ABA), updating its Criminal Justice Standards, also supports deleting the volitional component as it wrestles with the tensions between individual protections and the safeguarding of society. The new standard, as with the APA proposal, represents almost a return to the cognitive dimension in *M'Naghten*, without inclusion of a volitional component. That is, the ABA standard omits any formulation similar to the ALI's test component, "substantial capacity to conform his conduct to the requirements of the law."

The ABA also resisted replacing the insanity defense with alternatives such as "guilty but mentally ill." This last term appears to offer greater control over the defendant post-trial by finding him or her "guilty" (and thus subject to judicial, rather than medical, monitoring). Critics of this concept point out that such a finding, however, allows juries an "easy out" that avoids their coming to grips with the thorny moral questions at issue, questions which should be the focus of the fact-finder's attention.

At this time, despite the host of often ill-conceived legislative proposals for insanity defense reform which followed the Hinckley trial, the legislative fate of the APA and ABA proposals remains uncertain.

Professor Alan Stone (personal communication, May 11, 1980) suggests that the current furor in part derives some of its force from the activities in earlier decades by legal advocacy groups whose civil libertarian reforms have simply made it harder to keep patients of any kind in hospitals. As commitment criteria grew ever narrower, with the patients perceived as in danger of being victimized by the "psychiatric establishment," which was seen in turn as "wanting to put people away," more patients were released. With a current societal swing to a more conservative position, the society itself is seen as the victim who is endangered by the promiscuous release of the dangerous mentally ill person. As a result, psychiatrists in the forensic arenas are now vilified for *not* keeping people in hospitals with sufficiently high thresholds for release. The effects of this pendulum swing often catch the patient and psychiatrist, as it were, stranded on the cusp. From the clinician's standpoint, these social trends place perhaps an even greater burden on the care with which the assessment process is performed.

As noted above, the potential impetus given to careful study of this issue by the attempted assassination of the President and the resulting trial of the would-be assassin has had, in all probability, a deleterious, rather than salutary, effect. Opportunities for sober research have been clouded by hasty, vengeful and ill-considered proposals in many areas for reforms of statutes and regulations, fueled by gross distortions in the public mind of the actual scope of the problem.

In this as in other forensic areas the lack of availability of reliable follow-up data is the largest barrier to articulation of an intelligent perspective on the matter of what actually happens to those found not responsible. It is absolutely certain, however, that the public's perception of the insanity defense as a cavernous loophole through which hordes of dangerous criminals pour out of the justice system into society is massively exaggerated.

Perhaps the most interesting approach to the problem of what to do with the offender found NGI comes from a system employed in Oregon, which uses a board of multidisciplinary membership to monitor and assess these individuals after the trial (Rogers, Bloom, & Manson, 1982). This Psychiatric Security Review Board, founded in 1977, is composed of a private psychiatrist, a private psychologist, a lawyer, a parole or probation expert, and a lay citizen; the Board retains jurisdiction over the individuals and retains certain powers (e.g., to issue subpoenas) to enforce its function. Many protections are provided for the individual as well. Besides diffusing liability for release (thus making responsible release to the community possible) and employing varied informational input, this approach appears to have a reasonable degree of success and effectiveness in minimizing rates of recidivism in released offenders. It remains to be seen if this approach can be employed in other, more urban areas, with public acceptance, without which it cannot succeed anywhere.

The perceptive reader of the foregoing can surely grasp the issues here: enormous public concern; historical conflict within law, within psychiatry and between law and psychiatry; and vast challenges to the assessor—all illumined against a backdrop of total darkness as to the empirical data concerning *what actually happens* to the defense, to the defendants, to the process, and to the outcomes in a social sense.

Even more regrettably, this subject may defeat certain fundamental empirical goals. While it may be possible to design research to track cohorts of individuals through the tangled thickets of the criminal justice system and while we may then be able to state with some confidence what the critical legal and clinical determinants are for the various outcomes, the issue is so contaminated with questions of attorneys' tactical decision-making strategy, political impingements and influences from the particular degree of public outcry concerning a notorious case and the like, that simple data-based investigation may fail to produce the answers valuable for their practical utility, for example, to guide rational reforms of abuses and harms. Only the size of the lacuna in our knowledge about the facts in this area can compel us to make the effort to obtain whatever data we can about this disproportionately troublesome subject.

Comments on Other Current Assessment Issues

Testamentary Capacity

Another highly complex subject in actuality shares elements of both direct and indirect assessments: competency to make a will. This examination may be quite straightforward when performed on the still-living individual who, because, say, of a history of illness or even frank incompetence, wishes to make his testament sound against future challenge.

Competence to make a will remains defined by the classic three parameters: knowledge of one's presumptive heirs, knowledge of one's actual estate (i.e., property or assets), and comprehension of the meaning of a bequest. It might be said that there is an upswing of sentiment in at least the forensic psychiatric community that this assessment should be among the most circumspectly undertaken, for the following reasons.

The problem arises both clinically and ethically, when heirs seek to challenge in retrospect the will of an already-deceased person on the basis that he was incompetent at the time of writing it. Although this kind of retrospective assessment may be seen fairly frequently in some jurisdictions, it poses a problem resembling that seen in criminal responsibility when the examination occurs far after the event; the central difference, of course, is that the deceased cannot be interrogated to determine certain relevant details. Experienced forensic assessors often comment that the next of kin, seeking to overturn the last wishes of the loved one, are among the least disinterested parties ever encountered in clinical work!

To this problem of bias is added the central dilemma of providing an opinion about someone that the examiner has never directly interviewed. This is an ethically sensitive issue since, on the one hand, a clearly bizarre outcome—the wealthy eccentric, ignoring the children's needs for education, bequeaths the entire corporation to his pet guppy—does harm to the socially desirable goal of ensuring continuity of property within a family of legitimate heirs; yet on the other hand, a person in our society maintains the right to dispose of legitimately-held property in any way desired, even to make a dramatic point, including ways that might be considered foolish by others.

In defense of the former position, it must be acknowledged that in some situations a convincing case can, indeed, be made for the fact that a person was clearly incompetent to make a will, on the basis of reliable albeit indirect clinical evidence. The burden of proof that must prevail in the minds of judge or, occasionally, jury, is no more or less attainable than in any other kind of forensic assessment brought into the judicial arena. Obviously, caution in statement and humility in knowledge are crucial features for the examiner in such a matter. The examiner who refuses on ethical grounds to participate in such determinations in which he cannot see the patient must be acknowledged as proposing a valid standard of practice.

The counterposed viewpoint proposes that this determination resembles another clinical process, the psychological autopsy, which—although serving a clinical rather than forensic purpose—is nevertheless embarked upon with the same potentially daunting retrospective view.

Competency to Contract

Competency to contract is another area that may involve a further retrospective evaluation, since the assessment may follow the actual signing of a contract, though on occasion, as with a negotiation planned with an individual of clearly potentially impaired competence (mentally ill or retarded), the examination may occur in advance.

The essential role of contracts in the social fabric affects this determination to a great degree. The presumption is made that individuals contract in good faith. If someone wishes to void a contract he has already signed on the basis of his own past incompetence to understand the issue, the questions must be raised as to whether the matter involved so-called "necessaries," i.e., food clothing and shelter; the presumption is that these would have to be obtained in any case, so that a contract used to obtain these items is considered binding.

If the "other party" wishes to void a contract because of his partner's supposed incompetence, this is looked on askance since that individual had, in the first place, the choice of whether to sign or not with someone of suspect competence on the other side.

Management of Funds

Another competency whose assessment may lie with the forensic psychiatrist is competence to manage or receive funds, a situation that may often occur for the indigent ill or retarded person who is receiving public funds as support, pensions, or insurance payments. It is important to note that if an individual, when examined, displays incapacity to manage funds, a rush to adjudicate incompetence with guardianship or conservatorship should be avoided; it may well prove possible to involve others in the community around the person to aid in management either of the funds or of the goods and services at issue. For example, a halfway house director might be made the payee, with suitable accountability, for the person if the majority of that individual's expenses relate to that house.

This caveat aside, the assessment of capacity to manage funds requires both imaginative testing (meaning of worth and value, making change, basic calculations, hypothetical situations) and, more importantly, historical evidence from reliable sources and observers of this ability in action in the real world.

Fitness as Competence

A number of other competencies are better described under the rubric, "fitness," which has, unfortunately, a judgmental or moralistic cast; these determinations are occasionally put forth for forensic psychiatric assessment. The most common include competence to drive an automobile (occasionally this question is related to driving while under psychoactive medication which, while necessary, may pose a problem of driver alertness or other effects); competence to work or work at a particular skill level; and competence to own certain articles like drugs, toxins and firearms.

With all these assessments the abstract issue of competence is deeply imbued with matters of public safety; thus, "competent to drive" is often more accurately understood as meaning (at least in terms of the referral source) "safe to drive."

Since the psychiatric profession has had as little success with the prediction of safety as with its converse, the prediction of dangerousness, these determinations are quite difficult to perform and guidelines are, for the most part, unreliable, the more so since the only valid way of assessing many of these capacities is to see how the person actually performs the task, e.g., driving; evaluators seldom have or even take the chance for this observation. A "catch-22" situation may arise wherein the person cannot be tested for the task since the basic fitness is what is at issue, and that can only be determined from a trial of the task itself!

Partly because of these difficulties and partly to insure that only a modest degree of magical promising prevails in an area where the future is nearly unknowable, I have elsewhere (Gutheil & Appelbaum, 1982) recommended an austere method of reportage of this material, utilizing a "double-negative" grammatical construction. That is, a statement of a person's present fitness for some task may seem to the referrer to be tantamount to a psychiatric promise of success or safety at that task, the failure of which forecast may result in liability. To minimize this specious "promise" dimension, some verbal construction like the following may be suitable:

> As a result of my evaluation of Mr. Jones on 7/8/63 I find that at this time there are no psychiatric contraindications to his (task at issue).

This mode of expression makes it clearer that no promise of future success is being vouchsafed, but rather a present-time determination of freedom from disqualifying factors has occurred.

The subject of determination of fitness for parenting, as in issues of alleged child abuse or questions of parental custody in divorce are too extensive to be undertaken here. I might note only that such determinations are increasingly being performed by child psychiatrists who develop special expertise in these matters. One of the thorniest questions to arise in this sub-specialty field is whether a single examiner should assess the child and the parental situation, seeing as many parties as necessary, or whether the adversary model, strictly construed, should mandate experts to perform evaluations on both sides on an explicit partisan basis. The answer to this question tends to differ with different judges and jurisdictions.

Pain, Suffering and Psychic Damages

The forensic examiner may be called upon to make this determination in relation to a suit where the damages are not to be calculated in actual costs of repairs or medical expenses, but in terms of those imponderables, pain and suffering. In some jurisdictions, an efflorescence of this aspect of litigation has produced unexpected assessments, such as determination of psychic injury from constant water damage, damaging permanent waves, insect infestation and discrimination on several bases.

One of the most ethically complex determinations is that of no less than the value of human life, as in this case example taken from actual practice.

For Example: A man brought a wrongful death action against a company for negligence in the death of his wife. A new state statute had articulated the explicit issues to be addressed in making the determination of the damages in such a case. The losses to be identified included the wife's: "care, comfort, support, advice, companionship, etc." Each of these matters was to be given a value and the total would represent the monetary total of damages from the wrongful death.

For the clinician this quantification is, and should be, outside his or her ken. The task of the evaluator in such a case is to define what impacts in terms of recognizable psychic entities the alleged injury has caused, and to describe its presentations. Particular attention must be paid to physical symptoms (e.g., weight loss, ulcers, sleep cycle changes, tics, and so on) since courts appear to be giving these precedence over other more subjective signs and symptoms, perhaps inappropriately.

Conclusion

This survey has been an attempt to provide a critical review of an inordinately diverse and complex subject, forensic assessment. In attempting to bridge the gap between two probably irreconcilable disciplines, psychiatry and law, the forensic area requires shifting of cognitive gears, or, to use another metaphor, a kind of intellectual diplomacy to reconcile and smooth the differences between two alien states.

It may prove valuable to reflect at this point on the limitations of such a review. Law and psychiatry certainly operate from differing worldviews and differing perceptions of the human condition. Moreover, the law evolves slowly through the reflection of social trends in case law, as libertarian and conservative philosophies in turn dominate the thinking of the judiciary. Similarly, psychiatry evolves as new discoveries and reassessments are joined by new empirical data to alter both the scientific data base and the basic assumptions that may pervade the field at a certain moment in time.

Even more problematically for the assessor, psychiatry depends to a significant degree on subjective and thus non-replicable data-gathering through empathic rapport, intuitive leaps of understanding, introspective self-observation and mastery of countertransference responses, which —though forming the human basis for sound clinical work—represent profound incongruities when superimposed upon the legal reference frame.

This perspective may aid us in avoiding the simplistic view that either discipline has at present reached the final truth about humanity and its behavior in the social system.

One clear lesson must be that this area is urgently in need of an expanded empirical data base. A second lesson is that each area of the subject, no matter how precisely or explicitly described in statute or case law, requires some skill and art in its application and offers pitfalls for the unwary. We have attempted to convey in this review some of the range of the subject (though much has had to be omitted for reasons of space); most of all, we have tried to convey the manner in which the fundamentals of clinical wisdom—the care of the patient—must stand as the cornerstone to any efforts in this area.

References

American Law Institute. *Model Penal Code.* Philadelphia: Author, 1955.

Appelbaum, P.S., & Roth, L.H. Clinical issues in the assessment of competency. *American Journal of Psychiatry,* 1981, *138*(9), 1462–1467.

Brawner v. *U.S.*, 471 F. 2d 969 (D.C. Cir. 1972).

Bukatman, B.A., Roy, J.L., & Degrazia, E. What is competency to stand trial? *American Journal of Psychiatry,* 1971, *127*, 1225–1229.

Chayet, N.L. Informed consent of the mentally disturbed: A failing fiction. *Psychiatric Annals,* 1976, *6*, 295–299.

Clark, W.L., & Marshall, W.L. *A treatise on the law of crimes* (6th ed.). Chicago: Callaghan & Co., 1958.

Commonwealth v. *Lamb*, 303 N.E. 2d 122, 1 Mass. App., Aff'd 311 N.E. 2d 47, 365 Mass. 265 (1973).

Dorof, E., & Gutheil, T.G. *A study of the Massachusetts experience*. Unpublished manuscript.

Drope v. *Missouri*. 420 VS162 (1975).

Durham v. *U.S.*, 214 F. 2d 862 (D.C. Cir. 1954).

Dusky v. *U.S.*, 362 U.S. 402; 80 S.Ct. 788 (1960).

Fellner, C., & Marshall, J. Kidney donors—The myth of informed consent. *American Journal of Psychiatry*, 1970, *126*, 1245–1251.

Golden, J., & Johnston, G. Problems of distortion in doctor-patient communication. *Psychiatric Medicine*, 1970, *1*, 127–148.

Greenson, R.R. Empathy and its vicissitudes. *International Journal of Psycho-Analysis*, 1960, *41*, 418–424.

Grossman, L., & Summers, T. A study of the capacity of schizophrenic patients to give informed consent. *Hospital & Community Psychiatry*, 1980, *31*(3), 205–207.

Gutheil, T.G. Observations on the theoretical bases for seclusion of the psychiatric inpatient. *American Journal of Psychiatry*, 1978, *135*, 325–328.

Gutheil, T.G. The judge, the adversary posture, and the rhetoric of generalization. *Man & Medicine*, 1980, 5, 92–96.(a)

Gutheil, T.G. Paranoia and progress notes: A guide to forensically informed psychiatric record keeping. *Hospital & Community Psychiatry*, 1980, *31*, 479–482.(b)

Gutheil, T.G. On the therapy in clinical administration, part II. *Psychiatric Quarterly*, 1982, *54*, 11–17.

Gutheil, T.G., & Appelbaum, P.S. *Clinical handbook of psychiatry and the law*. New York: McGraw-Hill, 1982.

Gutheil, T.G., Appelbaum, P.S., & Wexler, D. The inappropriateness of least restrictive alternative analysis for involuntary interventions with the mentally ill. *Journal of Law and Psychiatry*, in press.

Gutheil, T.G., & Havens, L.L. The therapeutic alliance: Contemporary meanings and confusions. *International Review of Psycho-Analysis*, 1979, *6*, 467–481.

Hall, J. *General principles of criminal law*. Indianapolis: Bobbs-Merrill Co., 1947.

Halpern, A.L. The insanity defense: A judicial anachronism. *Psychiatric Annals*, 1977, 7, 41–63.

Halpern, A.L. The fiction of legal insanity and the misuse of psychiatry. *Journal of Legal Medicine*, 1980, 2, 18–74.

Kennedy, B.J., & Lillehaugen, A. Patient recall of informed consent. *Medical and Pediatric Oncology*, 1979, 7(2), 173–178.

Kramer, H., & Sprenger, J. *Malleus maleficarum*. (M. Summers, trans.) London: Arrow Books, Ltd., 1971. (Originally published, 1486.)

Lafoot, E.G. The fiction of informed consent. *Journal of the American Medical Association*, 1976, *235*, 1579–1585.

McGarry, A.L. Competency for trial and due process via the state hospital. *American Journal of Psychiatry*, 1965, *122*, 623–631.

McGarry, A.L., Curran, W.J., Lipsitt, P.D., Lelos, D., Schwitzgebel, R., & Rosenberg, A.H. *Competency to stand trial and mental illness*. Rockville, MD: National Institute of Mental Health, 1973.

Pasewark, R.A. Insanity plea: A review of the research literature. *Journal of Psychiatry and Law*, 1981, winter, 357–401.

Pasewark, R.A., & Craig, P.L. Insanity plea: Defense attorneys' views. *Journal of Psychiatry and Law*, 1980, winter, 413–441.

Pasewark, R.A., & Pantle, M.L. Insanity plea: Legislators' views. *American Journal of Psychiatry*, 1979, *136*, 222–223.

Pate v. *Robinson*, 383 U.S. 375; 86 S.Ct. 836 (1966).

Perr, I.N. Is the insanity defense "unconscionable?" *Journal of Forensic Science*, 1975, *20*, 173.

Ray, I. *Treatise on medical jurisprudence of insanity*. Boston: Charles Little & James Brown, 1838.

Robey, A. Criteria for competency to stand trial: A checklist for psychiatrists. *American Journal of Psychiatry*, 1965, *122*, 616–623.

Robinson, C., & Merav, A. Informed consent: Recall of patients tested postoperatively. *The Annals of Thoracic Surgery*, 1979, *22*, 209.

Roesch, R., & Golding, S.C. *Competency to stand trial*. Urbana, IL: University of Illinois, 1980.

Rogers, J.L., Bloom, J.D., & Manson, S. Oregon's innovative system for supervising offenders found NGI. *Hospital & Community Psychiatry*, 1982, *33*, 1022–1023.

Rogers v. *Okin*, 478 F. Supp. 1342 (D. Mass. 1979), 634 F. 2d 650 (1st cir. 1980), cert. granted 49 USLW 3788 (April 20, 1981).

Roth, L.H., Meisel, A., & Lidz, L. Tests of competency to consent to treatment. *American Journal of Psychiatry*, 1977, *134*(3), 279–284.

Soskis, D.A. Schizophrenic and medical inpatients as informed drug consumers. *Archives of General Psychiatry*, 1978, *35*(5), 645–647.

Stone, A.A. The insanity defense on trial. *Hospital & Community Psychiatry*, 1982, *33*, 636–640.

Stone, A.A. Personal communication, May 11, 1980.

Waelder, R. The principle of multiple function: Observations on overdetermination. *Psychoanalysis Quarterly*, 1936, 5, 45–62.

6.
The Assessment of Responsibility in Criminal Law and Psychiatric Practice

Seymour L. Halleck

ABSTRACT. *The manner in which psychiatrists go about assessing the responsibility of patients for their conduct has never been reviewed in a systematic manner. When psychiatrists do concern themselves with the issue of blaming or excusing patients that process is usually initiated by the criminal justice system and the specific issue is the sanity or insanity of the defendant. This paper reviews the issue of responsibility in much broader perspective. Psychiatric assessments of responsibility are much more than a forensic issue and are an everyday aspect of psychiatric practice.*

The basic issues involved in the assessment of responsibility and the manner in which psychiatrists go about making such assessments tends to be obscured by the criminal justice process. In dealing with issues of criminal liability, the law sets certain thresholds and considers the influence of psychological variables as significant excusing factors only when the degree of disability which can be found in offenders exceeds such thresholds. While this practice is perhaps necessary to preserve the stability of the criminal justice system the creation of an "all or none" model of imposing liability obscures the actual nature of the assessment process. Once the issue of assessment is viewed in terms of how various types of mental disorder influence an individual's capacity to behave in a variety of ways, it is simplified. It is then possible to conceptualize a method for assessing responsibility based on detailed examination of an individual's psychological, social, and physical capacities. In effect, the degree of responsibility can be quantified and related directly to the degree of incapacity.

There has been little discussion in the literature as to how assessments of responsibility are made in every day or ordinary psychiatric clinical practice. In non-forensic practice, psychiatrists deal with the issue of responsibility by either excusing or failing to excuse certain forms of conduct. Whatever stance the psychiatrist takes with regard to excuse-giving has a direct influence upon the patient's emotional state and the manner in which the patient responds to various therapeutic interventions. The manner in which this process works will be reviewed in detail.

The same principles which govern the assessment of responsibility in the forensic setting are applicable to ordinary clinical settings. In both situations such assessment should be based on an evaluation of the patient's capacities. In both situations assessment can be quantified by considering the manner in which various impairments influence an individual's capacity to adhere to a particular pattern of conduct.

As a general rule society seeks to maximize the extent to which people are held accountable for their actions. In examining both the forensic and ordinary clinical situation it will become apparent that there are utilitarian as well as moral reasons for doing so.

SOMMAIRE. On n'a jamais étudié de façon systématique comment les psychiatres procèdent pour évaluer si les patients sont responsables de leur propre conduite. Lorsque les psychiatres s'intéressent à la question de l'imputation de la responsabilité aux patients, ou de leur exonération, ce processus est habituellement lancé par le système de justice criminelle et le problème alors en cause consiste à dire si le défendeur est sain d'esprit ou non. Dans le présent article, l'auteur place la question de la responsabilité dans une perspective beaucoup plus vaste. Les évaluations psychiatriques de la responsabilité sont bien au-delà de l'aspect légal, et elles constituent un élément quotidien de la pratique en psychiatrie.

Les principaux problèmes posés par l'évaluation de la responsabilité et la façon dont les psychiatres procèdent pour la faire tendent à être occultés par le processus de la justice criminelle. En matière de responsabilité criminelle, la loi fixe certains seuils et ne tient l'influence des variables psychologiques comme un facteur d'excuse significatif que dans la mesure où le degré d'incapacité qui peut se trouver chez les délinquants dépasse ces seuils. Tandis que cette pratique est peut-être nécessaire pour préserver la stabilité du système de justice criminelle, la création d'un modèle du "tout ou rien" pour l'imputation de la responsabilité a pour effet de cacher la véritable nature du processus d'évaluation. Une fois que la question de l'évaluation apparaît comme l'étude du mode d'influence des différents types de désordre mental sur la capacité de l'individu de se comporter d'un certain nombre de façons, elle est simplifiée d'autant, et il est alors possible de conceptualiser une méthode d'évaluation de la responsabilité d'après un examen détaillé des capacités psychologiques, sociales et physiques d'un individu. En effet, le degré de responsabilité est quantifiable, et il est directement proportionnel au degré d'incapacité.

Il n'y a eu que peu de discussions dans les ouvrages et articles sur les modes d'évaluation de la responsabilité dans la pratique clinique quotidienne ou ordinaire en psychiatrie. En dehors de la pratique légale, les psychiatres traitent la question de la responsabilité soit en excusant certaines formes de conduite, soit en ne les excusant pas. Quelle que soit la position prise par le psychiatre à l'égard des excuses fournies, elle a une influence directe sur l'état émotif du patient et sur la façon dont il répond à différentes interventions thérapeutiques. Nous étudierons dans le détail la façon dont se déroule le processus.

Les mêmes principes qui régissent l'établissement de la responsabilité dans le cadre de la psychiatrie légale s'appliquent aussi dans le cadre clinique courant. Dans les deux cas, cette évaluation devrait être fondée sur l'appréciation des capacités du patient. Dans les deux cas, l'évaluation peut être quantifiée si l'on étudie le manière dont les différents handicaps influent sur la capacité de l'individu d'adhérer à un modèle de comportement particulier.

En règle générale, la société tend à donner un degré de responsabilité de plus en plus grand aux individus pour leurs actes. L'étude, à la fois, du cadre de la psychiatrie légale et du milieu clinique ordinaire va mettre en évidence de raisons tant utilitaires que morales pour qu'il en soit ainsi.

Introduction

Psychiatrists have traditionally been concerned with assessing the extent to which mentally disabled individuals should be held responsible for their conduct. Much of this concern has developed as a result of psychiatric participation in the trials of those who plead insanity. The efforts of psychiatrists and jurists to conceptualize the manner in which mental illness may mitigate criminal responsibility has produced a great deal of useful commentary. Psychiatrists, however, have paid much less attention to conceptualizing how responsibility for conduct should be assessed in the evaluation and treatment of mentally handicapped individuals who have not committed crimes.

My purpose in this essay is to develop a conceptual framework for evaluating the manner in which patients who are encountered in clinical as well as forensic settings should be held responsible for their conduct. The concepts which will be considered are derived from a re-examination of the more familiar problem of the assessment of criminal responsibility. I will argue that the assessment of every patient's responsibility for his or her conduct is an integral aspect of psychiatric practice, and that psychiatric treatment is most effective when such assessment is based on consistent adherence to logical principles.

Definition of Terms

It will be useful to briefly consider the meaning of the term responsibility and the meaning of other terms which are frequently used in this type of discussion such as will, choice, and capacity.

In this essay the term *responsibility* will in most instances refer to the ascription of moral accountability or blameworthiness to individuals because they have taken or have failed to take certain actions. Many human behaviors can be evaluated as blameworthy. Those who are blamed and who are held responsible for their conduct are then viewed as appropriate objects for some form of punishment (Hermann, 1983). In most social situations, punishment is a benign-to-moderate aversive consequence, such as verbal condemnation or withdrawal of reinforcement. In criminal law, punishment is likely to be severe and usually involves loss of freedom.

There is some relationship between the above described use of the term responsibility and the use of the term to denote obligation. Sometimes individuals are said to be responsible for accomplishing a given task. In this context the term responsible is a description of an obligation and not an ascription of blame. Blame may be ascribed, however, if the obligation is unfulfilled. This can happen when individuals fail to perform a certain behavior, or when they fail to live up to an obligation to refrain from performing a prohibited act. As a general rule, when the term responsibility is used to denote obligation the user is referring to a future or anticipated act. The conduct which is to be judged has not yet taken place. When the term responsibility is used to denote accountability or blame the user is generally referring to past conduct.

The term responsible may also imply causality (Heidel, 1958). A statement that a husband is responsible for having blackened his wife's eye by hitting her, for example, implies that his actions are the cause of her injury. The causes of most events are likely to be multiple. Often some minor action, or lack of action, initiates a chain of events which results in an undesirable consequence. When this is the case, only partial responsibility may be ascribed to the person who committed the original misdeed, depending on the importance of other causal factors.

The term *will* refers to the human faculty of conscious and deliberate action. It designates conduct that is judged to be under the governance of control of the mind. Willful behavior is voluntary behavior. In medical practice most muscular activity which is regulated by the voluntary nervous system is viewed as willful. This designation is also used to describe voluntary muscular actions which satisfy cravings for food, sex, or other pleasures such as temporary alteration of consciousness through the use of alcohol or other mind-altering drugs. Physicians are somewhat reticent, however, to consider behavior which appears to have powerful instinctual urges as entirely under the control of the will. Excesses or deficiencies of eating or sexuality or drug abuse are sometimes assumed to be influenced by forces the individual cannot control (Halmi, 1980).

The activities of the autonomic or vegetative nervous system such as heart rate, respiration or temperature, are generally viewed as beyond the control of the will. As evidence mounts that people can be trained to alter their blood pressures, heart rate or skin temperatures through techniques of biofeedback, however, physicians acknowledge that autonomic functions are not completely independent of voluntary control (Shapiro & Surwit, 1979).

Physicians and most other people tend to view disease as outside of the control of the will as long as what is being called disease is associated with a significant biological impairment. If there is a structural or functional defect in some organ system, much of the behavior associated with that defect will not be seen as willful. Once a physician discovers the existence of a peptic ulcer, for example, the patient will not be held responsible for epigastric pain. Behavior which cannot be related to a structural or functional deficit will, however, be viewed as willful. The patient who persistently complains of pain in the absence of any biological deficit which could be causing the pain is likely to be suspected of having willfully created his or her symptoms.

In the law the term will denotes intent or purpose. It implies self-determined conduct which is beyond the influence of biological, psychosocial, or even divine forces. Will is believed to be a special gift possessed only by human beings which leaves them free to create their own destiny. In referring to conduct governed by the will, the legal system often uses the expression free-will. Since willful conduct is assumed to be free of external restraint this usage is redundant.

As used in this essay, the term *choice* implies the existence of alternatives and the selection of one aspect of conduct over another. (The terms choice and will are closely related. If an act is considered to be chosen it is also viewed as willful.) An act is not considered chosen unless it can be assumed that the actor could have behaved differently either by not perpetrating the act or performing a more socially acceptable act. The range of choices available to people are determined by their social situations and their biological and psychological capacities.

Physicians are most likely to view conduct as chosen when it is need-gratifying and when it is not influenced by biological impairment. Like all other citizens, physicians assume that behavior which gratifies needs such as hunger or sex are, at least, partially under control of the will and are chosen. Behavior that is influenced by biological impairment is less likely to be viewed as chosen. Physicians are also uncertain as to whether they should view irrational behavior as chosen. If people engage in actions which seem to gratify no needs or are potentially injurious to themselves, physicians will often begin to question whether such acts are uncontrollable (Halleck, 1967).

In law there is a general assumption that just as almost all conduct is willful, almost all conduct is chosen. The legal system generally takes an "all or none" view of choice. With rare exceptions, it does not deal with the reality that making socially desirable choices is harder for some people than others. Unless conduct is viewed as the result of a mistake of fact, or of duress, or as determined by a severe mental malady, it is viewed as chosen (Hall, 1947).

As used here, the term *capacity* refers to an individual's ability to perform or complete a given task. The kinds of capacities required for any task vary with the nature of that task. To play football, for example, one must have a relatively sturdy body, must be able to understand the rules of the game, and must be able to cooperate with others. To stand trial for a crime, defendants must be able to understand the proceedings against them and to cooperate with their attorneys (*Dusky* v. *United States*, 1960). To be held accountable for an obligation such as taking medicine, patients must be able to identify the medicine, appreciate that it is needed, and remember when it is to be taken. People are excused or absolved of the responsibility to perform some task on the basis of their lack of capacity. A football player with a broken leg is excused from the game. A defendant who lacks the intellectual capacity to grasp the

meaning of the criminal trial is excused from proceeding further in the criminal justice process. Children or mentally defective adults whose intellectual capacities are limited are not expected to regulate their own intake of medicine.

Capacities are always relative rather than absolute. Individuals vary significantly in their ability to perform a given task. No two football players have exactly the same skills. No two defendants have exactly the same capacities to defend themselves. In fact, no two individuals have exactly the same capacity to obey the law. There are a variety of forms of conduct which allow individuals to gratify their perceived needs. The capacities of individuals to find gratification in these various forms of conduct will be a powerful factor influencing how they eventually behave. Those who can find gratification in the greatest variety of behaviors have the greatest number of choices. Because they have more alternatives they have greater capacity to refrain from engaging in socially undesirable acts.

Psychiatry and the Assessment of Criminal Liability

The criminal justice system must determine who is blameworthy and who is not. This is a moral as well as a fact-finding exercise. Even those who may have committed an illegal act may not be punished if blame or responsibility cannot be justly attributed. This has been put most succinctly by Judge David Bazelon when he noted that "Our collective conscience does not allow punishment where it cannot impose blame" (*Durham* v. *United States*. 1954). For almost 1,000 years our society has recognized that some who commit illegal acts are so disabled, by virtue of having a disability of mind, that they cannot justly be held responsible or blameworthy (Pollock & Mattland, 1952). Those whose disability reaches the threshold of excusability are called insane. The mechanism by which they are excused is the insanity defense.

While the insanity defense involves only a few individuals and has little direct influence on our society, it nevertheless raises questions which fascinate most thoughtful citizens. The consequences of being excused or blamed in this situation are very powerful. Here, society must deal with the issue of responsibility and how it is affected by disability against a background of high drama. One of the most important actors in this drama is the psychiatrist who tries to assist the court in determining when mental illness should excuse a defendant from criminal liability.

There are many who doubt the value of utilizing psychiatric knowledge in this critical process of blaming or excusing. As a rule, psychiatric testimony is viewed as a necessary part of the insanity defense proceedings but it may also be viewed as lacking in true value or authenticity (Brooks, 1974; Gaylin, 1965). Sometimes psychiatric testimony is denounced as fraudulent. More often, it is tolerated as a necessary part of the insanity proceedings. The most common view is that psychiatric testimony is based on an "infant science" which has not yet developed sufficient maturity to assist society in resolving questions of fact or law.

Even when viewed most charitably, psychiatric testimony is regularly subjected to the following two critiques. First, psychiatrists as physicians are not trained in dealing with matters of morality and have little expertise to offer the courts in making moral decisions. Second, psychiatrists are incapable of developing a conceptual framework which might allow them to relate their knowledge to the court in a manner which would assist the judge or jury in dealing with the moral issues involved.

With regard to the first critique, I will note in the second half of this chapter that whether they are trained in dealing with moral issues or not, physicians must make decisions on a daily basis regarding the ascription of responsibility. In the process of so doing, it is conceivable that they gain more experience in dealing with the problem than the average person.

The first part of this essay is an effort to refute the second critique. I will try to describe how even with its limited scientific base modern psychiatry is capable of conceptualizing the manner in which mental disability is related to criminal liability. This will require some review of how the criminal justice system has traditionally dealt with this issue.

The Historical Basis of Liability Assessment in Criminal Law

Unfortunately, criminal law has developed in a manner which discourages utilization of psychiatric or other scientific concepts in assessing criminal liability. Criminal law considers the mental state of the defendant, but it deals with this issue only in a carefully circumscribed manner. Because most students of the insanity defense have considered the relevance of scientific data only within the confines of established legal structures, they have been distracted from freely conceptualizing how mental disability influences criminal liability. This argument will be clarified by briefly considering the historical development of criminal law and the insanity defense.

Our legal system was not developed with the intention of relating punishment to the criminal but, rather, to the crime. Prior to the 19th century little attention was paid to the causes of crime and there was, therefore, little need to look at the differences in social, biological, or psychological characteristics of offenders which may have played a role in their committing crimes. The primary problem for society with regard to crime has always been to determine what to do about it, and this purpose was largely achieved without considering its causes. If asked why people commit crimes, most legal theorists of the 18th century, and perhaps most now, would probably say that they do it out of greed, weakness, or evil. All of these "reasons" assume the presence of will or choice and are more appropriately viewed as judgments of blameworthiness than as explanations of criminal conduct. Viewed in this light, crime is not determined, it is chosen, and the "reasons" for choosing it are much the same for all offenders. The exclusion of concern with causation or individual differences from the criminal justice process supports a retributive approach to crime in which punishment is simply related to the degree of harm the offender has inflicted on society. According to this view, society is morally obligated to inflict an appropriate degree of punishment upon those who have perpetrated such harm. This is the basis of the "just deserts" model of criminal justice which has dominated the field of criminal jurisprudence since the 17th century.

In the latter part of the 18th century the process of justice also began to be influenced by more utilitarian goals. This was the "age of reason" in which liberal scholars such as Cesare Beccaria and Jeremy Bentham developed a view of punishment which was largely based on the principle of deterrence. According to the historian Rennie, "To 18th-century thinkers, the criminal was a rational being who could precisely calculate his chances of detection and the quantum of punishment and decide that this crime is worth committing, that crime is not. If this were indeed the fact, then the calculus of hedonism could be as precisely plotted as the trajectory of the planets, making possible, for the first time, a rational system of criminal justice" (Rennie, 1978). In practice, this school of jurisprudence placed more emphasis on certainty than severity of punishment. Its proponents believed that to deter the offender from committing a new crime and to deter others from committing a similar crime it was only necessary to impose a penalty severe enough to outweigh the probable benefits the defendant might perceive in the criminal act. Rennie (1978) notes that the following principles derived from 18th-century liberalism have continued to exert critical influence in European and American criminal law:

That man is a rational being; that he avoids pain and pursues pleasure; that the criminal law should impose such sanctions as will outweigh the rewards of crime; that sanctions should be announced in advance; that they should be proportional to the offense; that everyone should enjoy equal justice; and that what a man does, not what he thinks, is the proper ambit of the criminal law.

As with the "just deserts" principle, the deterrence principle described here provides a guide for dealing with crime without having to deal with issues of causality or with differences between offenders. Neither principle requires us to be concerned with the offender's mental processes. These are assumed to be rational and essentially the same for all offenders. Both principles complement one another and provide relatively uncomplicated guidelines for inflicting varying degrees of punishment on offenders.

At the time it was advocated there were important advantages to a justice-deterrence model of criminal jurisprudence (Practices based on combined use of desert and deterrence approaches are sometimes referred to as the classical school of criminology.) Dealing with the crime rather than the criminal increased the likelihood of a fair approach to retribution in a society which was often characterized by unequal treatment before the law. Justice in the 18th century was not the same for the nobleman, the tradesman, or the peasant. The classical approach to criminology was in large part associated with a movement to break down the oppression of class rule and to provide equal justice to all elements of the society

(Bentham, 1948). To an arguable extent, it succeeded in that goal and in many ways it is still the most equitable approach to the problem of criminal behavior.

The development of the classical approach to criminology was followed by the emergence of many sociological, psychological and biological theories of crime causation (see, for example, Lombroso, 1918). These theories suggested that criminals differed from law-abiding individuals in dimensions other than morality and that their illegal behavior was related to measurable causes. Some of these theories were supported by a great deal of scientific data. Others were based on mere speculation. In total, however, they have had surprisingly little influence on the criminal justice system. In assessing liability the criminal justice system continues to stress the crime rather than the criminal. Even at those times when a substantial number of criminologists have believed that a particular social, biological or psychological factor was a major cause of crime, the presence of that factor has rarely been considered in assessing criminal liability. While our criminal justice system has evolved so that it puts little emphasis on the biological, social, and psychological differences between offenders, it has, nevertheless, left some room for judges and juries to consider certain aspects of psychological differences in assessing guilt. As early as the 12th century, English common law was structured so as to impose liability only if there was evidence of fault or evil intent on the part of the defendant. Moral blameworthiness rather than the simple commission of injurious acts became the foundation of legal guilt (Lefave & Scott, 1972). In our current system of justice, illegal conduct does not in itself constitute a crime. To be found "guilty" an offender must also have a guilty state of mind. For most crimes there can be no conviction unless there is a mental element (*mens rea*) as well as voluntary illegal conduct (*actus reus*) (Perkins, 1969). Concern with the offender's state of mind gives rise to a series of defenses which are invoked when the offender cannot be justly blamed. Our criminal justice system allows for the excusing of those who have committed a crime because of mistake of fact, duress, or insanity. Of these excusing conditions, the insanity defense is the only one which directs the court's attention to the psychological differences between offenders.

Depending on the jurisdiction in which the plea is raised, the insanity defense may be viewed as a *mens rea* defense (the presence of mental illness prevents the defendant from having the evil intent) or as an affirmative defense (the *actus reus* and *mens rea* are acknowledged but the defendant is too mentally incapacitated to be held responsible) (*Mullaney* v. *Wilbur*, 1975). Irrespective of how the defense is viewed, however, the courts have been consistent in excusing only those whose mental disorders make them conspicuously different from other criminals. Ordinarily, the defendant must have a major cognitive or volitional defect to be found non-responsible. Past experiences, motivations for committing the crime, social circumstances, physical health, or even the presence of most types of psychiatric disorders are largely irrelevant for the purpose of determining guilt. Nor is the determination of guilt influenced by evidence that the behavior of the defendant in the course of the crime was of such a nature that most people would have adjudged it irrational.

In restricting consideration of mental disability to the insanity defense, the criminal justice system tends to treat the issue of the responsibility of the mentally disordered in an "all or none" manner. A few are excused and all others are fully responsible. Punishment which is associated with the ascription of responsibility is determined by the seriousness of the offense, not the characteristics of the actor. As will be noted later, this approach deviated significantly from the manner in which responsibility is assessed in most other social situations or in the practice of medicine.

The unusual manner in which our criminal justice system deals with the issue of responsibility is related to the needs of the system to retain a certain degree of stability. A system which is based on just deserts and deterrence must focus on the act and not the actor. The excusing of an occasional severely deranged defendant may be as much as our criminal justice system can do to acknowledge differences between offenders without destroying itself.

The need of our criminal justice system to retain its stability by rejecting too much consideration of individual differences is apparent in the concerns of those who fear expanded use of psychiatric testimony in the criminal law. Some of the most frequently voiced concerns are the following:

(1) Scientific explanations of criminality can in themselves be viewed as exculpatory. Conduct which is understood is often excused. If too much is excused, not enough is deemed blameworthy, and the assumption of choice or free will is challenged (Judge Weintraub's Opinion in *State* v. *Lucas*, 1959). The system of criminal justice could not function efficiently if even a substantial minority of those whose conduct could be explained in scientific terms were excused (Kadish & Paulsen, 1975).

(2) Consideration of scientific variables in assessing the liability of every offender might force the courts to assess degrees of disability in every case. This would be an extremely expensive and time-consuming task (Goldstein, 1967).

(3) If the degree of liability of each offender were to be evaluated it would be difficult to develop standards of judgments. Absent standards for deciding guilt or degrees of guilt, there would be too many arbitrary punishments (Fingarette & Hasse, 1979).

(4) If liability were viewed in terms of individual variation, it is possible that an increased number of offenders would receive shorter sentences or perhaps no sentence. Some of those excused might be the most dangerous (Szasz, 1963). This would jeopardize public safety.

Given a societal commitment to a retributive-deterrent model of justice, these arguments are powerful. They have, for the most part, been persuasive in keeping consideration of psychology and other sciences out of most of the guilt assessment process.

It has also been argued that the current use of the insanity defense as an "all or none" approach to assessing liability serves to promote the stability of the criminal justice system by providing a loophole for dealing with the worst possible cases (Stone, 1976). The excusing of severely deranged offenders allows society to acknowledge the scientific reality that some offenders are severely incapacitated. At the same time, it also allows society to preserve the belief that all other offenders are without significant impairment. In this sense, the insanity defense is the exception that proves the rule. By excusing the few who violate the law, society confirms the responsibility of the many.

The problem with this restrictive but system-stabilizing approach to relating mental disorder to criminal liability is that it forces society to ignore a great deal of data about the realities of crime and criminals. Many offenders who are not found insane are severely incapacitated and can be described as having severe mental illnesses. It is reasonable to ask whether this group has the same capacity to choose law-abiding behavior, or to not choose criminal behavior, as more psychologi-cally-stable offenders. If they do not, perhaps they are less responsible. It is also reasonable to ask how different members of this group are from those found insane. If they are not too different, perhaps they should be treated more like the in-sane and less like ordinary offenders. These con-siderations have not escaped the attention of some legislators, mental health professionals, and jurists. They have provided impetus to a variety of efforts which have been made to offer a broader basis of exculpation based on mental disorder.

One method of increasing the number of of-fenders excused from punishment on the basis of a mental disorder is to liberalize the standards for determining insanity. Throughout this century ef-forts have been made to move away from the *M'Naghten* standard which negates guilt only if the defendant did not "know" the nature and quality of wrongfulness of his act (*M'Naghten's Case*, 1843). The American Law Institute stan-dard, which is now used in almost half of the jurisdictions in the United States, allows exculpa-tion if the defendant lacks "substantial" (as op-posed to total) capacity to "appreciate" instead of "know" the criminality of his conduct (American Law Institute, 1962). It also calls for the excusing of those who lack "substantial capacity" to con-form their behavior to the requirements of the law. In so doing, it invokes a volitional as well as a cognitive exculpatory factor. The *Durham* stan-dard, which was utilized in the District of Colum-bia for several years until it was replaced by the American Law Institute standard, was in many ways even more liberal and allowed for the ex-culpation of those whose crimes were judged to be a product of a mental illness (*Durham* v. *U.S.*, 1954).

Another approach to broadening the base of exculpation has been to allow the courts to con-sider other mental disabilities which do not rise to the standard of insanity in assessing criminal liability. These are disabilities which are believed to diminish the defendant's capacity to be fully responsible for a given crime. They are severe enough to justify less punishment than would usually be imposed for that crime but not so severe as to excuse the defendant altogether. This particular rationale for using knowledge of psy-chological incapacity to attenuate the harshness of punishment is referred to as the doctrine of dimin-ished capacity (Morse, 1979).

There are two variants to this doctrine. Under

the so-called *mens rea* variant, defendants can introduce psychological evidence which demon-strates that they were disturbed enough at the time of the crime to have lacked one of the ele-ments of the charged offense. This approach is used primarily when the law grades the degree of punishment for certain types of conduct and re-quires that different mental elements be proven at each gradation. Mentally disordered offenders charged with first degree murder, for example, might contend that they lacked the capacity to premeditate or deliberate. This would reduce their liability to second degree murder which re-quires killing with intent, but without premedita-tion and deliberation.

Under the so-called partial responsibility vari-ant, defendants can introduce evidence of their disability as formal mitigating factors which by statute remove their offense into a separate cate-gory carrying a lower maximum penalty. In England, for example, evidence of a mental im-pairment at the time a homicide is committed may be utilized to reduce liability for murder to liability for manslaughter (Byrne, 1968).

A third way in which evidence of psychological differences between offenders is considered in assessing punishment is by modifying the length of the sentence after guilt has been determined. Many jurisdictions are quite liberal in allowing evidence of a defendant's psychological impair-ments to be heard at a sentencing hearing. The judge or jury may be swayed by such evidence to impose a lesser sentence. There is also a possibility here that psychological data will be used to im-pose harsher penalties upon offenders if that data suggests that they are dangerous. (When psycho-logical factors are considered in determining length of sentence, it is not entirely clear if the decisions of the courts are based on utilitarian or moral considerations. The court may be interested in considering how the defendant's mental condi-tion at the time of the crime might relate to his responsibility. But, it is also interested in issues such as dangerousness and treatability which re-late to the more utilitarian issues of the need for restraint or the possibility of rehabilitation.)

In our current political and judicial climate the use of psychiatric data in the sentencing process is expanding. At the same time the use of psychiatric testimony in determining insanity or diminished capacity is contracting. There is no way of know-ing whether we will eventually see more or less consideration of psychological variables in the assessment of liability. What is clear is that the current method of relating mental disorder to criminal liability continues to be an "all or none" approach, and it is unlikely to change unless the entire system of criminal justice switches to more of an individualized approach. This situation has discouraged serious efforts to conceptualize how the existence of various types and degrees of mental disability in offenders might be logically related to an assessment of their responsibility for criminal acts.

What Guidelines Should Be Considered in Grading the Responsibility of Offenders?

The task of conceptualizing the relationship of mental disorder to criminal liability can be simplified by temporarily putting aside consideration of the needs of the current criminal justice system and asking "What guidelines would psychiatrists and the courts utilize if they were required to grade the degree of liability or blameworthiness of every defendant who is suspected of having a mental disorder?" By framing this type of question, the issue of ascribing responsibility can be approached free of the artificial restraints imposed by the criminal justice system. Responsibility can be evaluated as it is in all other aspects of human existence, by considering the actor as well as the act. Among a group of individuals who had committed the same act, some would be viewed as less responsible than others because of mental disability. Many degrees of punishment would be possible.

The guidelines psychiatrists and the courts would turn to in grading the criminal responsibility of all offenders would be based on a detailed examination of the biological, psychological, and social capacities of each defendant. In most situations in life when we say individuals are responsible for having acted in a given way, we are making a statement as to their capacities. We are saying that they had the capacity not to have behaved in that way or were capable of acting differently. When we excuse a behavior we assume that its perpetrator is in some way disabled (or in law is mistaken as to the fact of the situation or is under duress) and lacks the capacity to have restrained that behavior or to have behaved differently. The American Law Institute test is explicit about viewing insanity in terms of incapacity. It excuses those who, because of mental disease or defect, lack *substantial capacity* to

appreciate the criminality of their conduct or to conform their conduct to the requirements of law.

It is possible to evaluate most human responses to various events and situations in terms of individual capacities. Human behavior is determined by who a person is (genetic makeup, physical strengths and weaknesses, and past learning experiences) and by where he or she is (the nature of all the interpersonal and social factors or events in that person's environment). Another way of putting this is that behavior is determined by how an individual interacts with the environment. Psychiatrists and psychologists study human behavior by observing how individuals with varying characteristics respond to a variety of events which characterize their environment. The quality of an individual's response to these events is determined by the nature of the events and by the individual's capacity to deal with them. Biological characteristics and previous learning experiences define and limit each person's capacities (Halleck, 1978).

For the purpose of ascribing responsibility, the most important environmental events to be considered are those that either reinforce behavior (that increase the probability or the rate of the recurrence of the behavior) or punish behavior (usually aversive consequences which diminish the likelihood of a behavior recurring). Society creates reinforcements which are available to those who engage in socially-conforming behavior. It creates punishments for those who engage in deviant conduct. These positive and negative sanctions allow for a considerable degree of societal control. People differ, however, in their innate and learned capacities to respond to these sanctions and some are severely handicapped. In seeking to judge the responsibility of a person for a given act, it is necessary to determine how various incapacities limited that person's ability to respond to the multiple reinforcements and punishments (both those that reinforce conforming behavior and those that punish deviant behavior) presented by the environment at a given point in time. To the extent that one person has less capacity to respond to societal sanctions than another, that person may be considered less responsible for the same conduct.

The limits of an individual's capacity to respond to societal sanctions are determined by that person's learning experiences prior to the criminal act and by his or her psychophysiological status at the time of the act. The nature of an individual's learning experiences are in large part determined by the nature of the environment in which an individual is raised. But innate and acquired biological variations also influence individual responsivity to similar environments. Individuals who have certain biological characteristics may experience a kind of learning that makes them less responsive to social sanctions than others. Those born with limited intelligence or those who experience prolonged physical or mental illness in early life will have a difficult time learning to develop the kind of behavioral patterns society expects of them. Even small biological differences may profoundly influence the manner in which children respond to social conditioning. Children with minor deficits of perception may not be fully responsive to reinforcements and punishments as adults (Mednick & Volavka, 1980).

An individual's past learning experiences may exert a critical influence on his or her conduct in the present. There are also a large number of biological conditions which will modify an individual's responsiveness to societal sanctions at the time he or she performs an act. These include psychophysiological states associated with impaired emotionality and cognition. People who are experiencing a severe organic brain syndrome or psychosis cannot be fully responsive to society's reinforcements and punishments. Those experiencing states of severe anxiety, tension or depression will to a lesser extent have similar problems. All of these emotional disorders produce varying degrees of impairments of the individual's capacity to perceive, understand, and respond appropriately to societal sanctions.

One way of conceptualizing how past and present conditions and events limit an individual's responsivity to social sanctions is to hypothesize that the offender makes a benefit-risk analysis of all of the possible rewards or punishments society provides for legal or non-legal behavior and then makes the most self-serving response. (It is necessary to emphasize that I am simply proposing a hypothetical construct. It is unlikely that ordinary offenders go through a systematic analysis of the risks and benefits of their conduct. I also do not wish to imply that most offenders go through a rational process of weighing risks and benefits. Commonly, offenders misperceive risks and benefits and have difficulty in judging what course of action serves them best.)

The benefits of a criminal act can be described as follows:

(1) Gratification of some perceived need. Sometimes the need is a simple one such as money, power, or sex. Sometimes the need is more complex. A significant number of crimes are preceded by periods of psychological tension, which may in part be alleviated by the performance of the criminal act. The nature of that tension or its relationship to the criminal act may be created by motivations which are unconscious or outside of the offender's awareness.

(2) The possibility of peer group support. Certain types of criminal actions will bring offenders a certain degree of positive reinforcement from individuals whom they depend upon or admire. This is particularly true when offenders are part of a cultural group whose code of moral conduct supports values at variance with that of the greater society (Wolfgang & Ferracuti, 1967).

(3) An increase in self-esteem. Some offenders have had learning experiences which favor their praising or reinforcing themselves when they behave in an antisocial manner. As with the second benefit, there is a social factor involved. Individuals raised in subcultures which condone criminal activities may feel a greater sense of self-esteem and self-approval when they successfully violate the law (Glaser, 1980).

The risks of committing a criminal act are:

(1) The possibility of societally-imposed punishment, usually in the form of imprisonment. The creation of this risk is a major preoccupation of our entire system of correctional justice.

(2) Peer disapproval. Even if society did not seek to punish offenders, many would consider the possible anger or rejection of other citizens as a major aversive consequence of crime. Even when not accompanied by imprisonment or fine, the moral condemnation of others is a substantial punishment, especially when those who condemn are closely related to the offender.

(3) Self-punishment. To the extent that we are trained to believe that criminal actions are wrongful or bad, and to the extent that we are responsive to such training, the mere anticipation of antisociality elicits an internalized aversive response in most of us. When we think "bad" thoughts or do bad deeds we inflict a certain degree of punishment on ourselves or our self-esteem diminishes (Beck, 1967). It is this particular risk of criminal activity which society hopes will maximize law-abiding behavior, and thereby make the other risks of socially-imposed punishment or condemnation unnecessary.

By considering the risks and benefits of criminal versus conforming acts, it is possible to examine how various incapacities influence the offender's ultimate "choice." In evaluating an offender's liability for a criminal act, it is useful to make the following three assessments:

(1) The degree to which non-criminal and gratifying alternative behaviors were available and were perceived at the time of the crime. Often the perceived needs, conscious or unconscious, which are gratified by committing a crime could also have been gratified in a law-abiding manner. The availability of legal alternatives, however, is often limited by factors such as biological deficits, inadequate learning experiences, or social oppression. The offender may also fail to perceive the availability of alternatives in states of mental impairment characterized by a clouded sensorium, severe anxiety, and defective reality testing. Those who do not have or do not perceive as many non-criminal alternatives as others will of necessity develop an exaggerated view of the benefits of crime. They will be less influenced by social sanctions than others and might be judged less blameworthy than others.

(2) The extent of the offender's awareness of the benefits and risks of crime. It is unlikely that offenders are ever completely aware of all these factors. Offenders will differ in their capacity to perceive, understand, and integrate information related to the criminal act and its consequences. Those who are confused as to their purpose in committing an illegal act, or of how they and others will respond to that act, will be less responsive to societal sanctions, and therefore, less blameworthy than those who have more accurate cognitive and perceptual capacities. This assessment requires an examination of the offender's cognitive and perceptual processes. The presence of any of the psychiatric disorders which impair cognition or perception should automatically raise the issue of diminished blameworthiness.

(3) The offender's capacity to rationally balance the risks and benefits of criminal conduct. This capacity is influenced by many mental disorders which are characterized by a tendency to exaggerate or devalue the degree of risk or benefit associated with an act. In some disorders such as the manic phase of bipolar disorder, individuals may perceive their needs to take certain types of actions as uncontrollable. For them, the benefits of an action which may subsequently be defined as illegal are exaggerated. Individuals who have

anxiety or personality disorders who sometimes feel driven to commit illegal acts to reduce states of painful tension may also exaggerate the benefits of illegal action. In most psychotic disturbances, the benefits of perceived need, peer group support, or self-approval are likely to be miscalculated. Psychotic illness will also increase the likelihood of failure to assess the probable high severity of the risks of external punishment, social condemnation, or self-condemnation. Depressed offenders may already be subjecting themselves to massive self-punishment. They may not fear societally-imposed punishment and may even welcome it. The miscalculation of risk in these individuals is related to their inability to comprehend that their depression is not likely to be permanent and that the punishment which will be imposed on them is something they will not welcome when they are well. Any organic brain syndrome will impair offenders' capacities to balance risks and benefits. Alcohol intoxication, the commonest organic dysfunction at the time of a crime, may be associated with an exaggeration of the benefits of crime. It is almost always associated with a miscalculation of the risk of crime. Intoxicated offenders tend to minimize the possibility of externally imposed punishment and to ignore the likelihood of self-imposed punishment.

Which Incapacities Should Receive Greatest Exculpatory Weight?

The assessment of the availability of alternatives, the degree or awareness of alternatives, risks and benefits, and the capacity to weigh risks and benefits provide a rough but quantitative means of judging how individuals may be impaired in their capacity to respond to social sanctions. Utilizing these criteria, many gradations of responsibility can be ascribed. At the extreme, there are psychologically-intact individuals who are aware of and capable of utilizing many legal alternatives available to them, who are fully capable of weighing risks and benefits, and who commit a crime on the basis of a rational conviction that the benefits outweigh the risks. These individuals are fully responsible. At the other extreme are those who have few alternatives or who perceive them inaccurately, and who are so deranged that they are unaware of risks or benefits or alternatives and, therefore, lacking in ability to balance them. They should be completely relieved of liability. All of those falling in between these extremes by virtue of having reduced access to legal alternatives, or impairment of capacity to perceive alternatives, or to perceive and weigh risks and benefits, can be judged partially responsible.

If the degree of partial responsibility is to be determined on the basis of incapacity, it would be useful for those who make moral judgments to have some criteria for deciding what type or what extent of incapacity should be considered exculpatory. Which type of incapacity is most practically viewed as compromising choice? How severe should a disorder be before it is given a great deal of exculpatory weight?

One critical issue is whether some type of excuse should be provided for the socially incapacitated. Poverty-stricken individuals surely have less capacity to respond to social sanctions than those who are wealthier. On the other hand, a society which wishes to sustain its stability will be wary of excusing individuals because of conditions it has itself created. When legal scholars on occasion call for exculpation for sociological reasons, their suggestions are not, as a rule, taken seriously (Bazelon, Morse). Another practical issue is whether those who have non-psychotic disorders should be excused as liberally as those who are more severely impaired.

One way of developing a principle for dealing with these problems is to examine more carefully the manner in which various incapacities impair an individual's responsivity to reinforcement and punishment. Some disorders which impair an individual's responsivity to ordinary social sanctions are more easily influenced by increasing the power of societal reinforcements and punishments, or by increasing the availability of alternative responses than are others. The frequency of a behavior can be diminished by teaching and then reinforcing alternative behaviors or by decreasing the benefits and increasing the risks of the undesired behavior. As a rule, we do this by providing a greater number of desirable alternatives and by escalating the risk of punishment, and reducing the degree of reinforcement for that specific behavior. There are practical and ethical limits to these interventions. Alternative behaviors are not always available and there is a limit to how much money society is willing to spend to create them. It is extremely difficult to decrease the benefits of many forms of antisocial conduct without making major changes in the social structure. It is much more practical to escalate punishment but there are also limits to this strategy. If risks are increased

by escalating punishment, the severity of punishment must be such that it does not offend the sensibilities of the community. (Physical punishment, for example, is used only in certain forms of behavior modification and is carefully scrutinized by ethical therapists and the courts.)

The usefulness of societal efforts to control antisocial behavior by providing more socially acceptable alternatives or by escalating punishment will ultimately be determined by the offender's capacity to be influenced by such changes. The impairments of some individuals are such that neither the presentation of desirable new alternatives nor the escalation of non-physical punishment will have significant influence in diminishing the frequency of their behavior. These individuals are not fully responsive to escalations of the ordinary reinforcements and punishments which shape behavior.

The above considerations would translate into the following principle for ascribing responsibility for criminal acts. If we believe that a given behavior cannot be diminished by providing a reasonable number of more desirable alternative behaviors or by a socially-acceptable escalation of punishment, the individual should be held less responsible for that behavior. Conversely, if we believe that a given behavior can be controlled by escalating sanctions, the perpetrator can be held more responsible. This principle would allow society to ascribe responsibility to economically-deprived but rational criminals who could, in theory, be controlled by either increasing their opportunities or escalating the risks of their crimes. It might also provide the courts with greater direction in deciding how to deal with non-psychotic offenders who allegedly commit crimes to relieve some type of stress. If we believe that their acts could have been controlled by efforts to provide more alternatives or by escalating the risk of punishment, we may be more justified in holding them responsible. The question as to which mental disorders are most responsive to escalating sanctions is, however, complex and must be considered in some detail.

In general, those incapacities which are primarily related to biological dysfunction are most likely to be unresponsive to escalation of environmental sanctions. A person who is deeply confused as a result of an organic brain disease or other psychotic process will not be greatly influenced by the presentation of desirable alternatives or the threat of greater punishment. Nor will the patient who is in a state of acute mania or in a morbid state of depression be greatly influenced. It should be noted that these individuals are not completely refractory to changes and sanctions. Over a long period of time even highly deteriorated psychotic patients can be made more conforming by taking total control of their environment and creating a token economy in which reinforcements are provided in a strict and sophisticated manner (Ayllon & Azrin, 1968). As a rule, however, biologically impaired patients, including psychotic and extremely depressed individuals, are not very susceptible to an escalation of sanctions.

It is also probable that learned responses which are associated with, but not necessarily caused by, significant biological dysfunction are more refractory to escalating environmental contingencies than those that are not. Most of the responses which fall into this category are unlikely to be associated with criminal conduct, but they are noted here because they have some general relevance to the problem of excuse-giving. Phobias which are associated with states of extreme anxiety are minimally influenced by escalating sanctions. Punishment might have to be escalated to a level of cruelty in order to keep a person with a snake phobia from trying to escape a close encounter with a snake. Somatiform disorders or disorders of sexual performance or sleep are especially difficult to influence by simply escalating sanctions. Sleep and sexual performance are paradoxically made worse by setting up sanctions which appeal to the will. The harder one tries to sleep or to perform sexually, the less likely will he or she succeed. The behavioral treatment of these disorders requires that individuals learn to exert less rather than more control (Friedman, Weler, LoPiccolo, & Hogan, 1982).

Mental disorders which are characterized by a deviation in the aim or object of a sexual drive may, if acted upon, lead to criminal behavior. The extent to which these kinds of behavior can be influenced by escalating sanctions is difficult to determine. Sexual deviants are unlikely to be greatly influenced in the short run by the availability of alternative forms of gratifications. Providing a homosexual pedophile with mature female partners may have little influence on his sexual behavior. Such an individual has limited choices and must either refrain from overt sexuality or gratify his sexuality through a criminal act. On the other hand, he may be significantly influenced by increased risk of punishment. The choice of sexual abstention may be a difficult one, but it is probably made easier if there is a high risk of severe punishment for sexual expression. The unusual plight of those also cannot satisfy biological needs without breaking the law lends to their being treated ambivalently by society. Sex offenders are not usually excused unless they have other disorders as well. At the same time, they also tend to be viewed as sick persons who are often given psychiatric treatment at the same time that they are being punished.

The most difficult problem for psychiatrists and the courts is determining the extent of liability which should be imposed on those whose disorders are believed to be related to maladaptive learning experiences and which are associated with only minor or insignificant biological variations. This group includes offenders diagnosed as personality disorders, particularly of the antisocial, borderline, narcissistic, or histrionic type, as impulse disorders, as dissociative disorders, or occasionally, as anxiety disorders. The behavior of these patients is often explained in psychoanalytic terms as heavily influenced by unconscious forces. While there is limited evidence that these patients are, on a biological basis, different from ordinary individuals, these patients are not ordinarily viewed as biologically-impaired (Monroe, 1978). Sometimes their crimes seem to be irrational and when that irrationality is especially evident they may be excused by the courts. Such excuses are usually based on psychodynamic rather than biological explanations. It will be useful to consider the exculpatory weight of various psychodynamic explanations of crime in the light of principles of escalating sanctions which have been elaborated above. The following psychoanalytic or psychodynamic explanations will be briefly reviewed.

(1) Crime as adaptation.
(2) Crime as symbolism.
(3) Crime related to dissociation.
(4) Crime related to guilt.

CRIME AS ADAPTATION

In 1967 I proposed that various psychoanalytic theories of crime could be synthesized into an adaptional model (Halleck, 1967). I hypothesized that an individual under a variety of psychological and social stresses could either conform to them, try to overcome them through legal means, develop a mental illness, or try to deal with them by illegal means, i.e., committing a crime. In this adaptional framework, any characteristic or event which reinforces conformity, legal activism, or even mental illness, diminishes crime. Removal of these alternatives tends to increase crime. Anything which makes crime attractive increases its likelihood. And anything which makes it less attractive diminishes its frequency. I am, of course, describing a fairly complicated model in just a few sentences but, for the purpose of this essay, it should be noted that any explanation which views a crime as the best adaptional alternative for a given individual must rely on a general systems approach which puts considerable emphasis on environmental reinforcements and punishments. Under this model there is always less likelihood of crime if there are more and better non-criminal alternatives and greater punitive sanctions. Since general adaptional explanations are based on the assumption that people are likely to be responsive to escalating sanctions and to the presentation of new alternatives, there is nothing about them that provides a unique basis for exculpation of criminal activities.

CRIME AS SYMBOLISM OR DISPLACEMENT

Some crimes have been viewed as satisfying unconscious wishes (Guttmacher, 1960). The person who steals may be seeking affection. The stolen object may symbolize the affection of a loved one. This type of crime, if repeated, is often viewed as a compulsive crime. People may also commit crimes to increase self-esteem or to gain the attention or recognition of others. They may not be aware that these are their true motivations. Still other individuals may inflict harm on people who symbolize persons in their past or present life towards whom they have felt intense but repressed rage. There is an awareness of motivation to harm in this situation but the wrong person is attacked.

In each of the above type of explanations offenders have blocked out awareness of the original drive and may be compromised in their capacity to be aware of or find alternatives to the criminal act. The presentation of desirable alternatives will have an inconsistent affect on their behavior. Those who allegedly commit crimes because of wishes for love, attention, or recognition would be less likely to commit such acts if they received more positive reinforcement for performing more socially-acceptable behavior. This might occur even if they remained unaware of their true wishes. Offenders who wish to inflict harm on others and select the wrong person, however,

would be less influenced by the presentation of the desirable alternatives until they became aware of their true motivations. Even then they might still be likely to commit a criminal act.

It is conceivable that all individuals whose crimes are based on motivations of which they are unaware might overestimate the psychological benefit of the crime. These individuals often experience a painful sense of tension shortly before the crime which is likely to be relieved once the act is committed. At the same time, however, this group may be less influenced by the monetary benefits or peer group acceptance of crime than other offenders. It should be noted that there is nothing in this class of psychoanalytic explanations of crime which suggests that individuals who can be described by these patterns have any problem in perceiving and weighing the risk of crime. No matter how powerful the unconscious drive and no matter how great the exaggeration of benefits of the crime might be, the escalation of sanctions to socially-acceptable limits is still likely to influence their behavior. Since behavior based on this type of unconscious motivation is, in theory, deterrable by escalating punitive sanctions (although not always deterrable by providing desirable alternatives), it is questionable whether evidence of unconscious motivation should be given a great deal of exculpatory weight.

Behavior which can be explained in psychodynamic terms as a form of displacement rarely occurs as an isolated psychiatric finding. Often it is associated with other psychological deficiencies such as a personality disorder. It may also be associated with more serious handicaps such as depression. To the extent that unconsciously determined behavior occurs concurrently with a more clearly defined biological impairment, it may have greater exculpatory weight. The mere existence of a dynamic pattern in which crime can be understood as an expression of an unconscious drive, however, does not in itself constitute reason for exculpation. There is no reason to believe that unconscious processes are immune to conditioning associated with the escalation of ordinary social sanctions.

CRIME RELATED TO DISSOCIATION

People can forget many aspects of their past behavior, can lose their sense of reality, or can behave as if they are different people when exposed to certain types of stress. The dissociative disorders, including psychogenic amnesia, depersonalization disorder, psychogenic fugue, and multiple-personality disorders are frequently invoked to excuse criminal conduct (Watkins, 1976). In the case of professed amnesia for a crime, there is, of course, no way of knowing much about the defendant's responsivity to social sanctions at the time of the crime. The presence of other dissociative disorders, however, does not provide significant grounds for exculpation. The phenomenon of depersonalization is relatively common in offenders at the time of the crime and may simply be a function of the anxiety associated with the risks of the criminal act (Justice Burke's opinion in *People* v. *Goedecke*, 1967). Unless extreme, it is not likely to cloud awareness of alternatives, risks or benefits, nor to make the individual non-responsive to social sanctions.

The existence of the phenomenon of multiple-personality also fails to provide a strong rationale for excusing crime. Presumably each personality of those who have this disorder shares the same learning experiences and the same biological potentials for the other. (Minor variations in physiological states have been noted as people "change" personalities, but these variations could not occur unless the organism in which the personalities reside had the potential for making them.) While separate personalities may repress awareness of one another's experiences, the potential for full awareness and complete integration of all personalities is always present. Unless the personality which committed the crime can be shown to be in a psychotic state associated with biological impairment (an unlikely finding in persons diagnosed as multiple-personality), it should be responsive to the same sanctions which control others. Similar considerations apply to psychogenic fugue states. Patients who experience this type of disorder are usually capable of quite appropriate responses to social sanctions even if selected aspects of their awareness are repressed.

The use of dissociative phenomena to justify exculpation is obviously fraught with dangers of abuse. They are often invoked as a basis for excusing someone the society may have reason for excusing for social reasons, such as a police officer, or someone whose crime may elicit public sympathy, such as a mother who kills her child. The evidence for pre-existing illness or severe disability at the time of the crime in these cases is generally weak (Orne, Dinges, & Orne, in press). It is also important to note that dissociative phenomena including multiple-personality are relatively easy to simulate by people who wish to use the diagnosis to be excused from socially-unacceptable conduct

(Orne, 1972).

CRIME RELATED TO GUILT

In an early publication Freud described the case of a man who committed a crime in order to be punished for forbidden Oedipal wishes (Freud, 1974). The guilt this patient experienced over his repressed Oedipal longings could only be dealt with by doing something illegal that society would then punish. Freud argued that the patient committed a lesser crime in order to avoid self-punishment for what he considered a greater crime. The patient, of course, was unaware of his wish for punishment and could not rationally explain the reasons for his behavior. This paradigm is rarely seen in clinical work with ordinary mental patients or criminals. On the other hand, there are offenders who seem to consciously wish to be punished. Some may even be seeking to have the state take their lives. The extent or the origin of guilt in these individuals is not entirely ascertainable. It is likely, however, that most of them are seriously depressed. There would appear to be formidable limits to the extent that the criminal activity of those who seek punishment can be diminished by increasing their punishment. When it can be demonstrated that an individual actually sought punishment to deal with unconscious feelings of guilt or the ravages of depression, these factors should have exculpatory weight.

Closely related to psychoanalytic explanation of crime as a response to guilt is a paradigm sometimes noted in the practice of family therapy in which one member of a family may act in an antisocial manner in order to help others. It is sometimes argued that the delinquency of a child may be an effort to draw the family's attention to him or her and to hold the family together by virtue of its concern over the child's conduct (Minuchin, 1974). The child, in effect, sacrifices him or herself to preserve family stability. Presumably, all members of the family are unaware of this mechanism and the dynamics of the situation can be explained in terms of unconscious motivation. This is another situation in which the antisocial behavior would be difficult to influence by escalation of sanctions. If a child is motivated towards self-sacrifice for benevolent reasons, it might require a severely cruel degree of punishment to alter his or her behavior.

In summary, those psychiatric disorders which are not associated with significant biological impairments are, with a few exceptions, responsive to escalation of social sanctions. This does not mean that people who have these disorders have the same capacities to behave in a socially acceptable manner as those who do not. (Those who have severe personality disorders, for example, may at times be severely handicapped.) It simply means that their behavior can be shaped by socially-acceptable modification of environmental contingencies. As long as society has the power to influence the individuals by blaming them, it may have reason to be grudging in excusing them.

I have argued in the first section that there is a relatively straightforward way of relating mental illness to criminal liability. This involves a systematic approach to evaluating the defendant's incapacities and then considering the extent to which conduct related to these incapacities can be modified by imposing blame. Such an approach has limited practical value for a system of criminal justice which does not wish to deal with individual differences and which tends to blame or excuse on an "all or none" basis. I believe, however, that this conceptualization of criminal responsibility can be useful to those who work in the criminal justice system.

First, it may guide psychiatrists who become involved in assessing the responsibility of offenders. The legal standards which define insanity do not provide specific instructions to psychiatrists as to which of the defendant's mental facilities should be evaluated. The concepts presented here guide the psychiatrist to evaluate the defendant's capacity to perceive alternative behaviors and to perceive and evaluate the risks and benefits of the criminal act. These are clinical assessments well within the expertise of the psychiatrist.

Second, it may provide to all persons who deal with the issue of criminal liability a new perspective from which to consider the two main factors that are generally viewed as exculpatory, deficits of understanding and deficits of volition. Defects of understanding are created when the defendant lacks full awareness of the nature of alternatives to a criminal act or to its possible benefits and risks. If there is no understanding of risks, benefits, and alternatives, they cannot be accurately weighed. The earliest jurists who considered the insanity defense were aware of this logic and argued that where there is no understanding there can be no free will (Hale, 1736). Defects of volition exist when the defendant cannot adequately evaluate risks and benefits. It is conceiv-

able that the defendant may understand the risks and benefits of a criminal act but may, because of some incapacity, exaggerate the benefits and minimize the risks. That individual will be more likely to engage in conduct that is ordinarily controlled. Note that in this conceptualization the almost mystical idea that behavior is determined by an irresistible impulse is put in operational terms. Volitional deficits can be, at least, crudely measured rather than simply assumed to exist and a certain amount of circular thinking can be avoided. This issue will be elaborated in a later section of this chapter which deals with the concept of control in psychotherapy.

Responsibility in Psychiatric Practice

Although physicians are generally hesitant to view themselves as moralistic they cannot avoid dealing with issues of blame and responsibility in their day-to-day practice. Like the judge or jury who must decide who will be excused because of insanity, the physician must judge who is to be excused because of illness. Physicians excuse people both for acting and for failing to act.

A child who is cranky will not be punished if he or she is taken to a physician and is diagnosed as ill. Here, the child's past undesirable conduct is excused. The process of excusing in medicine, however, may relate to future as well as past conduct. The child who is excused for crankiness may also be relieved of the obligation of having to go to school the next day. There are two ways of looking at what happens in this process. We can view the child as being excused from the obligation of performing a socially desirable act, i.e., going to school, or we can view the child as being excused from being accountable for that conduct involved in staying home.

Being excused from future obligations or from blameworthiness for past actions is part of the learning experience of every individual growing up in Western society. Beginning in childhood and continuing throughout adult life people learn to view illness as the most powerful excuse for undesirable conduct. In a society highly committed to health values rather than spiritual values, physicians have become society's main providers of excuses (Robitscher, 1980). As long as physicians have the power to excuse they also have the power to hold patients responsible for conduct which is believed to be chosen or under control of the will.

The critical factor which leaves the patient open to blame is the physician's unwillingness to provide an excuse.

The Consequences of the Physician's Failure to Excuse

When doctors refuse to excuse patients for past behavior or future obligations they put these patients in jeopardy of experiencing the punitive response of blame. Such blame can come from three sources: the patient, those who are intimately related to the patient, or the physician.

In most cultures people are trained from childhood to blame themselves when they behave poorly or fail to meet obligations. In the process of maturation external punishments become internalized. We learn to punish ourselves for behavior which falls below our moral standards by feeling guilt or shame. The punitive power of these emotions is variable depending on the situation and the past learning of the individual, but self-punishment can be extremely powerful. At the same time as we learn to develop internal punitive responses, however, we also learn that there are events and conditions which partially or fully excuse us from blameworthiness.

A personal example may illustrate this process of self blame and excuse. A number of years ago, I was experiencing a sense of conflict as to whether I should drive to the local airport during an ice storm to catch a plane which would enable me to get to a meeting I was supposed to chair. I had a strong sense of obligation to be at the meeting on time. At the same time I knew that road conditions were treacherous and I had no wish to undertake what would probably be a hazardous ride to the airport. As I weighed the risks and benefits of the situation and considered my options, I realized that if I did not attempt to get to the airport I would feel very badly. The issue would not only have been what my colleagues thought about my not being present. The main problem would have been my shame over a failure to meet an obligation I had assumed. I decided to undertake the trip to the airport and just as I pulled out of my driveway the car radio announced that because of ice conditions the airport had been closed. At this point I knew I would have to miss the meeting and yet I was immediately free of shame or guilt. Getting to the meeting was no longer within my control. I was completely excused.

Most of the excuses we learn to give ourselves in

early life are related to illness, not to acts of God. Let us assume that if I had been in the above situation and if the conditions that made me hesitant as to whether I could make the trip were that I was feeling weak, dizzy and nauseous, rather than that the roads were icy, I might very well have undergone a similar process of self-blaming and excuse-seeking. I would have wondered if I had a case of flu and whether I was too sick to be able to manage the trip without risking my health in a serious way. If I had taken my temperature and had noted that it was elevated, this would certainly have made it easier to stay home. But if my temperature had been only mildly elevated, my own inclination and that of many other people would have been to have undertaken the trip. The only way in which I could have decided to stay home without punishing myself would have been if I had seen a doctor who had said to me, "You are a sick man. You must go to bed. You cannot travel in your condition."

The medical excuse rescues us from an endless variety of situations in which we might otherwise blame ourselves. Unpleasant behaviors such as withdrawal, moroseness, irritability, incompetence and even belligerence can often be at least partially excused if we can relate them to some aspect of illness. When we go to the physician, in addition to seeking relief of symptoms we are also, in part, looking for an excuse for past behavior or perhaps an excuse for not meeting some future obligation. If that excuse is not forthcoming, we are likely to blame ourselves for what we have done, and if we continue to feel so poorly that we think we may try to avoid future obligations, we will feel guilty over that as well.

The patient who is not excused is also in jeopardy of experiencing the aversive responses of others. This is particularly true of psychiatric patients, whose illness is often defined in terms of behavior which is unpleasant and troublesome to others. The depressed patient, for example, may withdraw from loved ones, complain constantly, demand the attention of others and fail to meet daily obligations. Patients who have personality disorders may engage in a variety of antisocial, selfish, and socially-offensive behaviors. The chronic pain patient may refuse to meet customary obligations, may demand extra help from others and may complain constantly. Loved ones, friends or work associates who must deal with such patients on a day-to-day basis are always puzzled as to the extent to which they should tolerate such troubling conduct. Their tolerance is increased to the extent that evidence is available that those who are behaving in a troubling manner are sick. In the case of most psychiatric syndromes, that evidence is not immediately apparent. Psychotic individuals, of course, may behave so bizarrely and so self-destructively that others have little problem in hypothesizing that they are ill. But patients who are depressed, who complain of pain, and particularly those patients whom we define as character disorders, who seem to have no apparent illness and who seem to be no different from the rest of us cannot always anticipate a benevolent response.

A critical factor which protects psychiatric patients from the blame of a friend or loved one is the excuse of the doctor. When doctors step in and say that depression is an illness, the patient is treated more solicitously by loved ones. Similar considerations apply to the character disorder and the pain patient. It is even possible, at times, to excuse behaviors such as drug abuse or gambling by referring to such activity as an illness. The doctor's excuse is both a protective mantle for the patient and a stimulus for compassionate responses of those who disapprove of his or her actions. At the same time that it shields the patient from blame it may elicit responses of concern, sympathy and even tenderness from those involved with the patient. To the extent that those involved with the patient accept the doctor's excuse they must suppress their anger and behave compassionately.

One way of emphasizing the power of the medical excuse on those involved with the patient is to consider material which has been presented in the news media regarding how the parents of the attempted presidential assassin John Hinckley responded to his behavior. It appears from the newspaper accounts that some time prior to the assassination attempt when this young man was behaving strangely the psychiatrist to whom he was sent for treatment concluded that some of his behavior was not excusable. The parents were advised that they should not treat Mr. Hinckley as though he were ill, but should be firm with him and demand that he behave "responsibly." The parents now claim that in response to this advice they cut Mr. Hinckley off from their financial support and affection, a rather formidable aversive consequence. After he shot the President, Hinckley's parents seem to have viewed the successful pursuit of an insanity defense as a way of proving that a mistake had been made, that their son should have been viewed as a sick person and that the doctor who had failed to appreciate his sickness and provide him with an excuse was medically negligent. When their son was found insane they felt some degree of vindication. They were able to view their own aversive response to him as unjustified just as the finding of guilt would have been unjustified. They seem to have concluded that their own conduct was excusable, however, because they had simply followed the advice of their son's doctor who had erred in failing to excuse his behavior.

Any psychiatrist who has observed family members, friends, employers or hospital staff interact with a psychiatric patient soon learns that these individuals have both angry and compassionate feelings towards that patient. They are also troubled by their ambivalence and usually seek help from the patient's doctor in determining which set of feelings is most appropriate. Hospital staff who deal with a patient who has a personality disorder are often quite forthright in asking attending physicians "Can this patient control his behavior or is he too sick to do so?" In asking such a question they are looking for guidance on whether to be firm or indulgent. Psychiatrists can manipulate the punitive or indulgent responses of hospital staff (or family, friends or employers) by judicious application of excuses. There are, of course, limits to the psychiatrists' powers. If psychiatrists continue to excuse noxious behavior which continues to get worse, people will not take the excuses seriously and will return to blaming the patient. If the psychiatrist fails to excuse and the patient shows signs of deep mental anguish or pain, the psychiatrist's failure to excuse will be seen as an error. Loved ones may continue to be indulgent towards the patient in spite of the psychiatrist's recommendation of firmness.

Physicians for all of their search for objectivity are also ambivalent as to whether they should use their powers to excuse certain patients from blame or obligation. Sometimes physicians feel anger for patients whom they view as blameworthy. When doctors talk about such patients informally they may use pejorative labels such as "crock" or "turkey." These terms are applied to patients whose symptoms are viewed as being largely controllable. In psychiatry certain character disorders are described by appellations such as "psychopath" or "sociopath" which have invidious connotations. Even the terms narcissistic or borderline personality, currently acceptable in DMS-III nomenclature, are often used in a pejorative sense. Sometimes psychiatrists as well as other physicians even acknowledge that certain patients are "hateful" (Groves, 1978).

It would require a kind of saintliness for physicians to keep all of their negative emotions out of their work. At their worst, some physicians can be quite crude in telling patients, "There is nothing wrong with you, it's all in your head." Such a communication is a direct and powerful aversive response. Physicians can be aversive even when they are less abrasive. A hasty explanation, a tendency to interrupt, an unwillingness to listen, or a failure to be empathic or compassionate can all leave patients feeling that they are to blame for their symptoms. Even when physicians are abrupt or crisp for reasons which they perceive as being in the patient's interest, they may still leave the patient feeling badly. Physicians can also communicate their sense of exasperation with patients by ordering too many tests, asking for too many consultations, or hospitalizing patients who don't really need to be treated in an inpatient setting. Conversely, they may communicate the same message by minimizing their interventions, not taking the patient seriously or ordering treatment that seems designed to placate the patient. Patients can sense the physician's exasperation. They wonder, "Why doesn't the doctor talk to me about this? Does the doctor think it is all in my head? Does the doctor know how much I am suffering?"

Excusing Behavior in Psychotherapy: Theoretical Issues

Most psychiatric disorders are diagnosed on the basis of observable patterns of behavior. To the extent that psychiatrists view their therapeutic tasks as that of changing behavior, they are more likely to be concerned with the issue of the patient's responsibility than other physicians. Efforts to change behavior will usually call for much more than simply doing something to the patient such as initiating a procedure or providing a medication. Patients must be active participants in the treatment process. Psychiatrists expect that patients will take some role in helping to change their own behavior. All of this implies that patients have some capacity to cooperate with their therapists and to exercise will in the therapeutic process.

The therapeutic task of changing behavior requires psychiatrists to make repeated judgments as to the extent to which their patients' day-to-day behavior is willful. With few tests available to determine when biological incapacities directly influence the patient's repertoire of behaviors, psychiatrists tend to make such judgments largely on the basis of their personal view of the human condition. All of this lends itself to a situation where the manner in which the therapist should deal with the issue of responsibility so as to provide maximum benefit to the patient is not conceptualized in a meaningful way. Too often the issue of responsibility is either dealt with on an intuitive basis or handled inconsistently.

Some schools of psychotherapy insist that efforts should be made to hold patients responsible for as much of their conduct as is possible (Fromm, 1941; Kaiser, 1965; Perls, 1969). The limits of responsibility or the points at which an excuse might be given, however, are not defined. Other schools are more flexible in demanding that therapists hold patients responsible (Eysenck, 1977). Again, however, they have not developed guidelines for determining excusability.

It is also possible to note a splitting in the approach psychiatrists take to responsibility as it involves theory versus practice. Most theories of psychopathology upon which treatment is based are deterministic. They provide explanation of all aspects of the patient's behavior and the process of explanation makes it easier to excuse it. At the same time, most psychotherapists in actual practice tell their patients that they will make therapeutic progress only if they view themselves as responsible individuals who have the capacity to exercise will and to play a role in determining their future. This inconsistency in dealing with the free-will/determinism controversy is rarely acknowledged but it is characteristic of most schools of psychotherapy. Psychoanalysis, for example, is firmly grounded in psychic determinism. Yet, Freud (1961) at one time stated:

Obviously, one must hold himself responsible for the evil impulses of one's dreams. What else is one to do with them? Unless the content of the dream (rightly understood) is inspired by alien spirits, it is part of my own being. If I seek to classify the impulses that are present in me according to social standards into good and bad, I must assume responsibility for both sorts; and if in defense I say that what is unknown, un-conscious and repressed in me is not my 'ego,' then I shall not be basing my position upon psychoanalysis.

One way of viewing Freud's statement is to note that like most other psychotherapists, he re-lies on deterministic theory to explain past behav-ior, but invokes the concept of free will to treat patients in the present. In practice, many psy-chotherapists have a rather simple formula for dealing with excuses and responsibility. They ex-cuse all behavior which occurred prior to the time patients enter treatment. Once patients enter treatment, however, they are told that their be-havior is under control of their will and that they are responsible for how they behave in the present and future. It appears that these psychiatrists are invoking the concept of free will in order to help change behavior. The belief in the patient's capac-ity to choose, shared by both the patient and the doctor, functions as a major determinant which allows for new, and hopefully more adaptive, patterns of behavior to develop.

The most interesting efforts to conceptualize the problem of responsibility in psychotherapy have been made by psychologists concerned with the issue of causal attribution. A number of psy-chologists have studied the manner in which peo-ple attribute causation of their own behavior. People generally view their behavior as caused by a variety of events in their lives. Some events are perceived as being under the control of the indi-vidual; others are not. Attribution theorists con-sider psychotherapy to be a process in which patients learn that there are causes of their prob-lems which may be under their own control (Weiner & Kikla, 1970). These causes include the way they perceive events, and the way they think, believe, feel, or act about events. The task of the psychotherapist is to help patients learn to seek personal causes of their behavior which they also perceive as capable of being influenced by their will or effort. In successful therapy patients re-define and increase the extent of their behavior for which they view themselves as responsible. Attri-bution theory is consistent with the teachings of all schools of psychotherapy which seek to help patients gain greater self-control and greater re-sponsibility for their own existences.

Attribution theorists note that there are a va-riety of views of responsibility which people use in assessing their own or others' conduct. These describe various degrees of leniency people invoke to justify excusing their behavior. The most le-nient view of responsibility which is referred to as "justified commission" holds that people are re-sponsible for their actions and the effects of their actions only if there are no compelling external reasons for them to have committed the acts (Strong, 1970). Under this view if people are un-der sufficient pressure to perform an act they should not be held responsible for that act. Suf-ficient pressures, here, are events and circum-stances that ordinarily favor committing a given act. The rule of thumb is that if most people would carry out the action given the circum-stances, either situation or historical, then the person is not responsible but is justified in that action and is excused from aversive responses which might ordinarily follow such action. More stringent concepts of responsibility hold persons responsible for anything they intended to do and even for consequences of actions they may not have intended but which they could have fore-seen. The latter view of responsibility does not exculpate carelessness or negligence. It advocates judging people by what they do, not by the rea-sons why they do them. The theory is harsh and unrelenting in that what one does is what one is. This latter theory is referred to as the "careless commission" view. According to attribution theorists the process of psychotherapy can be described as one in which the therapist seeks to discredit the "justified commission" view of re-sponsibility and replace it with the "careless com-mission" view (Strong, 1978).

Patients in most forms of psychotherapy are taught to impose a stringent model of responsibil-ity upon themselves. Perhaps the easiest way to illustrate how the "careless" or "negligent" model of responsibility is used in psychotherapy is to consider the behavior of psychoanalysts in dealing with parapraxes, and other types of behavior which are undesirable and are determined by un-conscious motivation. The patient is held account-able for a slip of the tongue and is directed to investigate the meaning of the slip. Once the motivation behind the slip is brought to conscious-ness the patient assumes responsibility for it. In most schools of therapy the patient who forgets about a treatment hour or who comes later is generally subjected to a rigorous effort on the part of the therapist to investigate the reasons for such absence or tardiness. Patients are usually charged for the full hour whether they are simply late or fail to appear at all. Hardly any reason other than physical incapacity will excuse. Once the true meaning or motivation for absence or tardiness is discovered, the patient is expected to acknowledge it. In most schools of psychotherapy, therapists also try to reinforce attitudes or actions on the part of patients which indicate that they are adopting a more stringent personal view of responsibility and are perceiving more of their behavior as within their control.

Excusing Behavior in Psychotherapy: Practical Issues

In the process of psychiatric treatment some behavior is excused and some is not. Excuses are usually granted by acknowledging the patient's limits. A patient who is trying to continue at a job while plagued with overwhelming anxiety may simply be told, "You are really too anxious to work. You would be better off to stay home for a few days." A patient who is about to undertake a task that the therapist believes is too stressful may be told, "You have been very sick in the last few months. Perhaps you should not take on too much right now." The patient who is lamenting a past indiscretion may be told, "At the time you committed that indiscretion you were under enormous pressure. You really didn't hurt others nearly as much as you think. Right now you are mainly hurting yourself and it would help you if you simply forgave yourself." Or, the patient who is severely depressed and who tries to deal with depression by "willing" it away or insisting on "fighting" it may be told, "You are very sick and there is very little you can do about your symptoms by yourself at this time. You are under our care and all we ask of you is to follow our instructions and cooperate in the administration of our treatment. We don't hold you accountable for doing anything else."

Limits are also acknowledged in a non-verbal way when patients are given medications or other biological treatments. When we give the patient medication we are delivering an indirect message that there are aspects of the patient's behavior that the patient cannot influence by will alone. When we prescribe antidepressants for depressed patients, for example, we are telling them that it is unlikely that they could simply choose not to be depressed. We deliver similar kinds of messages when we hospitalize patients. Here, in effect, we are telling them that they lack the capacity to make rational or self-serving choices in daily living and that they will function better when others are given the power to make these choices for them. Actions such as prescribing medicine or recommending hospitalization may simply, by virtue of being taken, provide the patients with a powerful form of relief.

Many patients become anxious or depressed by their symptoms. They blame themselves for being sick and in the process they make themselves worse. If patients perceive their plight as one they cannot influence by their own actions but which can only be influenced by a chemical agent or the actions of others, they often are able to stop berating themselves for having failed to have willed the condition away. They are no longer responsible for feeling badly. Such limiting of responsibility may have powerful and immediate therapeutic effects.

The failure to excuse behavior is best conceptualized in terms of demands that are made upon the patient to behave in certain ways. These demands may be as benign as simply asking for cooperation in treatment or they may require the patient to experiment with new forms of behavior. Even the simple directive of "Say whatever comes to your mind" implies that the patient can choose what is to be communicated during the therapeutic hour. More forceful demands are made when patients are advised to try being more assertive, more open in communication or more willing to express feelings. These directives imply that the patient can choose to do what the therapist suggests. Psychiatrists have other ways of communicating to patients that there is a whole range of behavior for which they are fully accountable. In reviewing a past situation they may tell patients that they could have dealt with it differently. Or they will point out that a variety of choices exist in a future situation and that the patient will be held accountable for choosing poorly. Some therapists have developed techniques which emphasize forgiveness of the past and accountability in the future. Through a process of imagery, patients who are dealing with a painful memory are asked to try to imagine themselves back in the same situation, not as the person they once were but as the person they now are. This emphasizes the patient's current maturity and helps the patient to re-experience and master the painful moment. It also, however, implies forgiveness of the past and reminds patients that they can now do better (Lazarus, 1981).

Psychiatrists often frame directives in the form of a question. Consider the following questions that are often posed by therapists:

"I wonder why you didn't tell your wife you were angry." This implies that the patient could have been more open with his spouse and is being held responsible for not having done so.

"What else might you have done in that situation?" Here the therapist implies that there were other choices available. The patient is not excused for failing to act on them.

"Did you think of simply walking away from that situation rather than getting into an argument?" Here the therapist describes an alternative behavior and implies to the patient that it was a more suitable choice.

"That's an interesting situation you've gotten yourself into. I wonder what you're going to do about it?" This statement and question hold the patient responsible for both past and future conduct. It is an especially powerful reminder that future conduct will be carefully scrutinized and if found wanting will not be excused.

The aversive consequences of the psychiatrist's failing to excuse poor behavior are the same in psychotherapy as they are in any other medical treatment. Patients who behave poorly and are not excused are left to the mercy of their internal aversive responses, and the potentially aversive responses of others. They also risk at least the mild disapproval of the therapist which in the context of an intimate interpersonal relationship might be a powerful aversive stimulus.

Similarities and Differences
in Ascribing Responsibility
in Psychotherapy and
in the Forensic Setting

The problem for the therapist in determining which behaviors are to be excused and which should not bears many resemblances to the problem posed by the legal system in determining who will be held liable for criminal behavior. As is the case in determining criminal liability, the decision to excuse or hold people responsible can most efficiently be based on an assessment of their capacities. Capacities to meet obligations (either obeying the law or behaving appropriately) are compromised when alternatives are not available, when they are not perceived, or when the patient is unable to make appropriate risk-benefit evaluations of the proper course of action.

In practicing psychotherapy, psychiatrists tend to emphasize biological incapacity as a major reason for excusing. When they do this they are following the principle described in an earlier section and are recognizing that behavior associated with biological dysfunction is less amenable to escalation of ordinary sanctions such as reinforcement or punishment. Therapists do not put major demands on those who are psychotic or severely depressed. They are usually (but not always) gentle in pushing phobic patients to expand their activity. They are most demanding of patients who are felt to have a good deal of psychological strength.

Psychiatrists are uncertain as to how demanding they should be in dealing with disorders that appear to be related to the will such as eating disorders and drug abuse. Here, there is always some question as to how these patients will respond to an escalation of demands and the provision of new alternatives. The most common approach is to tell these patients that they have the capacity to control their behavior. Sometimes this is backed up by an escalation of external punitive sanctions, for example, loss of privileges for anorectics or the threat of arrest for drug abusers. In the treatment of obesity or bulimia, external sanctions are not as a rule increased but it is anticipated that the patient will be influenced by the internal punishment of shame and guilt.

Psychiatrists probably have the most difficulty in deciding whether patients with personality disorders should be held responsible for their often socially-noxious conduct. This area is of sufficient complexity to warrant separate discussion in a later section.

There are also important differences in the way responsibility is judged in the clinical as opposed to the legal setting. One major difference is that the therapist must evaluate dozens or even hundreds of past or future acts and the legal system is usually concerned with a single act. In psychotherapy, assessments of capacity must be made swiftly and often intuitively. The therapist can also modify assessments over short periods of time as the patient's situation or state of health changes. Such flexibility is obviously not possible in evaluating a single past act.

Therapists also have control over the degree of responsibility they demand from patients. By their verbal and motoric behavior they can regulate the degree of blame or punishment the patient receives. A patient, for example, may be told,

"For a person with your problems you were in a very difficult situation but I still think you could have handled it a little better." Here the therapist invokes a form of diminished capacity. The patient is not fully excused nor is he or she fully blamed. In most situations in medical practice, punishment is utilized in a "graded" manner and rarely on an "all or none" basis.

It is also important to note that the process of ascribing responsibility in the treatment of patients is characterized by more of a concern with utilitarian issues than the process of determining the liability of defendants. In medical practice patients are blamed or excused for the clearly defined purpose of changing their behavior. In the criminal justice system there is much more of a moral component to the blaming or excusing process. It must be recognized of course that physicians can also be moralistic when they blame. And it must also be acknowledged that most of the moral precepts of criminal law, such as punishing to educate the public, punishing to affirm the innocence of those who have done no wrong, or punishing to preserve the stability of the community, might on closer scrutiny easily be translated into utilitarian terms. Still, there is a substantially greater commitment to practical goals in the process of blaming or excusing those who are defined as patients. Though physicians who blame or excuse patients may appear to be moralizing, and may even perceive themselves as moralizing, the major purpose of this intervention is to shape behavior. They are using the process of ascribing responsibility in a manner similar to the way in which parents use it to raise children or the society uses it to govern its citizens.

When responsibility is ascribed for utilitarian purposes such purposes are most likely to be achieved when those who are blamed or excused have a belief in their own capacity to choose. It is the belief in free will that makes people responsive to demands which imply blame (Guidano & Liotti, 1983). People could not respond to demands for behavioral change unless they perceived themselves as having substantial control over their own behavior.

All patients come to the physician in a state of high susceptibility to demands which imply that they have the ability to control much of their behavior. Society perpetuates a belief in free will by providing its children with methods of learning which insure that they develop internal mechanisms which direct and set limits on their conduct.

We raise our children by setting up reinforcements and punishments and communicating to them when they will receive them. We interpret their behaviors as good or bad and we try to convince them from an early age that they can choose when they are good or bad. Eventually, children internalize the belief systems we wish to impose upon them. To do this they must perceive themselves as choosing individuals. They reward themselves for being good and punish themselves for being bad. This pattern of internalized control based on a belief in free will continues into adulthood.

In adults, internalized rewards or punishments retain power to influence behavior in direct proportion to the extent that people believe they choose it. People experience emotions such as guilt when they believe they have chosen to do wrong. Such guilt may play a major role in shaping their subsequent conduct. It is also true that people feel little or no guilt when they believe that their behavior has been shaped by powers beyond their control. When people have this view of their behavior there is less likelihood that they will change it. All of this means that patients are likely to respond best to any form of treatment when the degree of responsibility they assume for their own actions is maximized. The physician's demand that patients hold themselves maximally responsible for their conduct is much more than a moral imperative; it is a technique which serves the utilitarian purpose of bringing about behavioral change.

Two Clinical Uses of a Systematic Approach to Ascribing Responsibility

It may be useful to conclude this section by pointing out clinical situations in which awareness of the problems of ascribing responsibility can lead to useful changes in psychotherapeutic techniques. Two examples which are relevant here involve the treatment of character disorders and the use of language in psychotherapy.

THE TREATMENT OF CHARACTER DISORDERS

In many ways the art of psychotherapy can be characterized in terms of the therapist's skill in demanding maximum responsibility from patients while at the same time finding a rational and humane way of excusing them. Errors can be made by overemphasizing or underemphasizing responsibility. Patients who are told that they are responsible for actions or events they are incapable of influencing will obviously be distressed. On the other hand, patients who are merely told that they have a disease which must be treated with a drug may miss out on many opportunities for therapeutic change.

It is extremely difficult for the therapist to provide the most therapeutically useful degree of blaming or excusing of each patient's conduct over a period of time. Some therapists will be consistently too demanding or consistently too permissive. Either error diminishes therapeutic progress. Most commonly, however, therapists are inconsistent. They hold patients accountable for a behavior on some occasions but excuse them from the same or similar behavior on others. Such inconsistency may lead to an escalation rather than an amelioration of the patient's symptomatology. Just as inconsistent messages from political leaders cause social turmoil and just as inconsistent childrearing practices create disturbed adults, inconsistent communications around the issue of responsibility will impede the process of psychotherapy. The problems of inconsistent ascription of responsibility is most commonly encountered in the treatment of personality or character disorders particularly those listed in DSM-III as antisocial personality disorder, histrionic personality disorder, narcissistic personality disorder, and borderline personality disorder.

In addition to experiencing some suffering themselves, people diagnosed as personality or character disorders may also behave in ways which disturb others. These are the individuals who make suicide attempts, who are impulsive, who throw temper tantrums, who make unrelenting and melodramatic demands for medical relief, and who frequently violate community norms of acceptable conduct. They have little difficulty adopting the sick role and once they do, they seem to have an unlimited capacity to exaggerate and utilize their symptomatology in order to influence the environment. In entering a helping relationship, they are very likely to insist that they are unable to control the less desirable aspects of their behaviors. This is particularly true when they relate to physicians. In medical contacts, particularly with non-psychiatric physicians, these patients are often presented with the message that they are not responsible for their symptoms. They readily accept this message and justify their behavior by refusing to acknowledge that they have control over it.

Psychotherapists have ambivalent feelings towards patients with character disorders. On the one hand, they feel compassion for their patients' suffering. On the other hand, the unconventional and sometimes obnoxious behavior of these individuals often irritates or angers psychiatrists who then vacillate between wanting to nurture them and to make demands that they do something to improve their behavior. Often patients are aware of their therapists' ambivalence. Such patients may then learn that the easiest way to elicit compassionate responses from therapists and to avoid punitive or demanding responses is to escalate symptomatology. Beginning therapists especially have difficulties in dealing with this type of situation. They are prone to experience their angry or demanding feelings towards patients as antitherapeutic and may, through a process of reaction formation, be especially nurturant to those towards whom they feel angry. This process is not consistent, however, and there will be times where the therapist's anger will be expressed in demands that the patient change. The patient, in the meantime, becomes more fervently committed to the sick role and to persuading the therapist to accept the message "I cannot help myself."

Patients with character disorders are especially likely to have a negative response to treatment in the university hospital setting where they are seen by inexperienced therapists who are heavily committed to the medical model. These settings offer emergency-room or walk-in services provided for the most part by a group of doctors assigned to the patient on a rotating basis. Some doctors will be annoyed by these patients; others will be quite attracted to them. The attitudes of the individual doctor will also change as it becomes clear that the patient really is suffering or really can be very obnoxious. Younger doctors are never sure as to the extent to which these patients can "control" their behavior. Even when the patient is treated by the same doctor, that doctor's attitudes may shift between demandingness and nurturance.

The psychiatric treatment of character disorders requires an experienced therapist who is available to his or her patients for a relatively long period of time. These patients do best when the therapist acknowledges that it may be very difficult for them to behave more appropriately but repeatedly and gently reminds them that they can do better. An escalation of symptoms should be greeted with a certain amount of concern but within reasonable limits should never be allowed to disrupt the structure of therapy. These patients do best if they receive maximum reinforcement for responsible behavior and as little reinforcement as possible for their symptoms.

LANGUAGE AND RESPONSIBILITY
IN PSYCHIATRIC TREATMENT

One of the most useful ways in which the therapist can maximize the patient's capacity to assume responsibility for his or her behavior is to observe the patient's language and to urge the patient to substitute language which implies responsibility for language which implies non-responsibility. Patients, for example, will frequently use the word "need." "I need love." "I need to be understood." "I need more material possessions." It is useful to gently remind the patient that human beings have relatively few basic needs and the patient should more accurately use the words "wish for" or "want," rather than "need." Talking about wishes or wants implies a certain degree of autonomy. Talking about needs does not. Similar considerations apply to the use of the word "can't." "I can't bring myself to break off the relationship." "I can't get angry at people who are rude to me." It is better to urge patients to acknowledge that they fear taking certain actions or are ambivalent about them than to proclaim they are incapable of taking them. Again, the effort should be to encourage the use of language which implies responsibility.

The therapist must also be sensitive to any statements the patient uses implying lack of control such as "I cannot help myself." "I always lose control of my emotions in those situations." "I lost control and took the pills." Actually, the concept of controlling one's behavior is at best metaphorical and at worst tautological. When we say a person cannot control himself, we cannot describe a mechanism by which a behavior is either expressed or not expressed. We are saying nothing more than that we have decided not to blame that person for that action. This is a moral judgment. The circular nature of this kind of thinking is perhaps a little easier to appreciate if we consider how we judge an impulse to be irresistible. We sometimes say that a certain person had an "irresistible" impulse to be violent. How do we know that it was irresistible? Because the person did not resist it.

If control is a mystical concept, it has unfortunately gained a powerful foothold in our language and particularly in the language of psychiatric theory and psychotherapy. I believe that psychotherapy would be more rational and perhaps more successful if therapists would learn to use a different concept in assessing behavior. Rather than speaking of certain undesirable behaviors as resulting from loss of control, it would be better to think of these behaviors in terms of the factors which go into the patient's evaluation of their risks and benefits.

Let us suppose that the patient comes into a therapy hour and states, "I don't know what happened to me last night; I completely lost control of myself. I had a fight with my wife and I hit her again." The therapist who accepts this statement is well on the way to encouraging the patient to assume a stance of non-responsibility towards that action. To the extent that both therapist and patient agree that there is some type of "control" mechanism that in this instance failed to function, they will both be in pursuit of defining and remedying a process that does not exist. It is more useful to conceptualize the patient's actions in the form of risks and benefits and point out to the patient:

> You obviously gained something from hitting your wife, and one good hypothesis is that it helped you express some of your feelings and relieve some of your tension. One way of dealing with your problem then is to help you find other, non-violent ways of expressing these feelings and relieving tension. You also would have probably been less likely to have hit your wife if you had feared that she would hit you back or would call the police. There is probably not much we can do right now about the way in which your wife responds to your violence. One of the risks of violence we can do something about involves your own response to your violence. Perhaps, you do not anticipate sufficient self-condemnation after a violent act. It may be that you should become more aware of your self-condemning propensities or it may even be desirable that you increase them.

Note, that by looking at the concept of risk-benefit appraisal rather than at the elusive concept of control, it is possible to put into operation therapeutic strategies. There is no mystification and the patient cannot abdicate responsibility.

Some Concluding Comments

Our legal system has long feared that a deterministic model of behavior might serve to negate society's belief in free will and thereby have a deleterious effect upon the social order. It has vigorously resisted the expansion of medical excuses for criminal liability, not only to preserve its own structure but to provide a message to society that people must continue to think of themselves as responsible beings. Yet, society's fears that the law will become psychiatricized or medicalized have proven to be unfounded.

The real danger of an unreflecting approach to determinism in dealing with troubled people is in medical and psychiatric practice. Over a decade ago, Karl Menninger described a trend in our society towards an individual and collective sense of non-responsibility (Menninger, 1983). He pointed out that criminal law has held fast in limiting excuses for conduct, but noted that in the rest of our society much behavior previously viewed as sinful was being redefined as symptomatic of illness. The tendency to label many forms of undesirable behavior as diseases and to put them in the province of excusable conduct has, in my opinion, drastically increased in the last decade. (Again, criminal behavior remains exempt.) One reason for the increased emphasis on excuse-giving in medicine is our expanded awareness of the biology of behavior. As we discover more about the biological variations associated with various behavioral patterns we are often tempted to conclude that such variations are the necessary and sufficient cause of these behaviors. We forget that even if aberrant behavior is biologically caused it is still responsive to environmental variables and one of the most important of these variables is that the behavior can be viewed by those who deal with it, as chosen.

In psychiatry, there is an especially distressing tendency these days to label behaviors which were formerly thought of as problems of will as diseases which negate personal responsibility. Alcohol abuse and drug abuse (which, paradoxically, are treated by methods based on the assumption that abusers have some control over their behavior) have long been defined as diseases. Psychiatrists are increasingly fascinated with the phenomenon of multiple personality and are "discovering" a large number of new cases of individuals who deny responsibility for conduct undertaken while they were under control of a different person. Even over-eating and gambling are more frequently defined as illnesses these days.

There are certain unfortunate consequences associated with the labeling of too many varieties of undesirable conduct as illness. Society in general and those who are closest to them may cease to demand better conduct from individuals who are defined as patients.

Physicians who are insensitively committed to a medical model are also unlikely to insist that patients assume maximum responsibility for their behavior. Many individuals who grasp onto the illness role and who become inured to accepting excuses for their behavior are at risk of becoming refractory to psychotherapeutic change. They become comfortable with the reinforcements of the illness role but, at the same time, they pay a high price for remaining there (Fordyce, 1976). In order to remain sick, these patients must retain their symptoms and whether they do this consciously or not, they continue to suffer. All of this could be avoided. Ultimately, it is the failure of physicians or society to appreciate the importance of the concept of responsibility in medical practice that puts many patients at unnecessary risk.

I have tried to show that the concept of responsibility is as important in psychiatric practice as it is in assessing criminal responsibility. There was a time about two or three decades ago when scholars in both psychiatry and law agreed that the two professions had a great deal to learn from one another. This was largely based on the belief that psychiatry would soon develop sufficient scientific knowledge of human behavior to help the law understand and deal with all varieties of deviant conduct. As the erroneousness of this view became apparent and as it became clear that the legal system had some need to impose limits in its use of scientific knowledge, there was great disenchantment between the two disciplines and less communication.

If one looks at the nature of psychiatric practice, it becomes apparent that psychiatrists deal with the same kinds of issues which the law must resolve in assessing liability. Physicians have considerable experience in assessing responsibility which, if conceptualized, can be useful to the law. At the same time, the law can serve as a stimulus to psychiatrists to begin to conceptualize the problem. Legal scholars have for centuries struggled with the issues of ascribing responsibility. Their painstaking efforts should be studied and emulated by psychiatrists. I have relied on my interest in legal issues and particularly in the insanity defense as a stimulus for reconsidering and conceptualizing the process of psychiatric treatment. The concepts presented here are only a crude beginning. Hopefully, others will be stimulated to produce more useful models.

References

American Law Institute. *Model penal code* (proposed official draft). Philadelphia: Author, 1962.

Ayllon, P., & Azrin, N.H. *The token economy.* New York: Appleton-Century-Crofts, 1968.

Bazelon, D.L. The morality of the criminal law. *Southern California Law Review*, 1976, *49*, 385–403.

Beck, A.T. *Depression: Clinical, experimental, and theoretical aspects.* New York: Harper and Row, 1967.

Bentham, J. *An introduction to the principles of morals and legislation.* New York: Hafner Publishing Company, 1948.

Brooks, A. *Law, psychiatry and the mental health system.* Boston: Little, Brown and Company, 1974.

Byrne, Z. Q.B. at 404, 3 AII E.R. at 5 (1968).

Durham v. *United States*, 214, F. 2nd 862, 876 (D.C. Cir. 1954).

Dusky v. *United States*, 362 U.S. 402 (1960).

Eysenck, H.J. *You and neurosis.* London: Temple Smith, 1977.

Fingarette, H., & Hasse, A.F. *Mental disabilities and criminal responsibility.* Berkeley: University of California Press, 1979.

Fordyce, W.F. *Behavioral methods for chronic pain and illness.* St. Louis: Mosby, 1976.

Freud, S. Moral responsibility for the content of dreams. In *Complete psychological works of Sigmund Freud* (Vol. XIX). Stanford: Stanford University Press, 1961.

Freud, S. Some character types met with in psychoanalytic work: The criminal out of a sense of guilt. In *Collected papers* (Vol. 4). London: Hogarth Press, 1974.

Friedman, J.M., Weler, S.J., Lopiccolo, J., & Hogan, D.R. Sexual dysfunctions and their treatment. In A.S. Bellack, M. Hersen, & A.E. Kazdin (Eds.), *International handbook of behavior modification and therapy.* New York: Plenum, 1982.

Fromm, E. *Escape from freedom.* New York: Holt, Rinehart and Winston, 1941.

Gaylin, W. Psychiatry and the law: Partners in crime. *Columbia University Forum*, 1965, *23*, 204–240.

Glaser, D. A review of crime—Causation therapy and its application. In N. Morris & M. Tonry (Eds.), *Crime and Justice* (Vol. 1). Chicago: University of Chicago Press, 1980.

Goldstein, A. *The insanity defense.* New Haven: Yale University Press, 1967.

Groves, J. Taking care of the hateful patient. *New England Journal of Medicine*, 1978, *298*(16), 883–887.

Guidano, V.F., & Liotti, G. *Cognitive processes and emotional disorders.* New York: Guilford Press, 1983.

Guttmacher, M.J. *The mind of the murderer.* New York: Farrar, Straus, and Cudany, 1960.

Hale, M. *The history of pleas of the crown.* London: E.R. Nutt & R. Gosling, 1736.

Hall, J. *General principles of criminal law* (2nd ed.). Indianapolis: Bobbs-Merril Co., Inc., 1947.

Halleck, S.L. *Psychiatry and the dilemmas of crime.* New York: Harper and Row, 1967.

Halleck, S.L. *The treatment of emotional disorders,* New York: Aronson, 1978.

Halmi, K.A. Anorexia nervosa. In H.Z. Kaplan, R.M. Freedman, & B.J. Sadock (Eds.), *Comprehensive textbook of psychiatry.* Baltimore, MD: Williams and Wilkins, 1980.

Heidel, F. *The psychology of interpersonal relations.* New York: Wiley, 1958.

Hermann, D.H.J. *The insanity defense.* Springfield, IL: Charles C. Thomas, 1983.

Justice Burke's opinion in *People* v. *Goedecke*, 65, Cal. 2nd 850, 423 P. 2d 777, 56 Cal. Rptr. 625 (1967).

Judge Weintraub's opinion in *State* v. *Lucas*, 30 N.J. 37, 152, A. 2nd, 50 (1959).

Kadish, S.H., & Paulsen, M.C. *Criminal law and its processes* (3rd ed.). Boston: Little, Brown and Company, 1975.

Kaiser, H. *Effective psychotherapy: The contribution of Hellmuth Kaiser.* New York: Free Press, 1965.

Lafave, W., & Scott, A. *Handbook on criminal law.* St. Paul: West Publishing Co., 1972.

Lazarus, A. *The practice of multi-modal therapy.* New York: McGraw-Hill, 1981.

Lombroso, C. [*Crime: Its causes and remedies*] (H. Horton, trans.). Boston: Little, Brown and Co., 1918. (Originally published, 1899.)

Mednick, S.A., & Volavka, J. Biology and crime. N. Morris & M. Tonry (Eds.), In *Crime and justice* (Vol. 2). Chicago: University of Chicago Press, 1980.

Menninger, K. *Whatever became of sin?* New York: Hawthorn, 1973.

Minuchin, J. *Families and family therapy.* Cambridge, MA: Harvard University Press, 1974.

M'Naghten's Case, 8 Eng. Rep. 718, 722 (1843).

Monroe, R.R. The medical model in psychopathy and dyscontrol syndromes. In W.A. Reid (Ed.), *The psychopath.* New York: Brunner-Mazel, 1978.

Morse, S.J. Diminished capacity: A moral and legal conundrum. *International Journal of Law and Psychiatry*, 1979, *2*, 271–298.

Morse, S.J. The twilight of welfare criminology. *Southern California Law Review*, *49*, 385–403.

Mullaney v. *Wilbur*, 421 U.S. 684, 706 (1975).

Orne, M.T. On the simulating subject as a quasi-control group in hypnosis research: What, why and how? In E. Fromm & R.E. Sher (Eds.), *Hypnosis: Research developments and perspectives.* Chicago: Aldine Atherton, 1972.

Orne, M.T., Dinges, D.F., & Orne, E.C. On the differential diagnosis of multiple personality in the forensic context. *International Journal of Clinical and Experimental Hypnosis*, in press.

Perls, F. *Gestalt therapy verbatim*. New York: Bantam Books, 1969.

Perkins, R.M. *Perkins on criminal law* (2nd ed.). Mineola, NY: Foundation Press, 1969.

Pollock, F., & Mattland, F. *History of English law*, Vol. 1 (2nd ed.). Cambridge, England: Cambridge University Press, 1952.

Rennie, Y. *The search for criminal man*, Lexington, MA: D.C. Heath and Company, 1978.

Robitscher, J. *The powers of psychiatry*. Boston: Houghton Mifflin, 1980.

Shapiro, D., & Surwit, R.S. Biofeedback in behavioral medicine: Theory and practice. In *Handbook of behavioral medicine*, O.F. Pomerleau & J.P. Brady (Eds.). Baltimore: Williams and Wilkins, 1979.

Stone, A. *Mental health and law: A system in transition*, Washington, D.C.: National Institute of Mental Health, 1976.

Strong, S.L. Social psychological approach to psychotherapy research. In S.L. Garfield & A.E. Bergin (Eds.), *Handbook of psychotherapy and behavior change* (2nd ed.). New York: John Wiley, 1978.

Strong, S.R. Causal attribution in counseling and psychotherapy. *Journal of Counseling Psychology*, 1970, *18*, 106–110.

Szasz, T. *Law, liberty and psychiatry*. New York: MacMillan, 1963.

Watkins, J.G. Ego states and the problem of responsibility: A psychological analysis of the Patty Hearst case. *Journal of Psychiatry and the Law*, 1976, *4*, 471–489.

Weiner, B., & Kikla, A. An attributional analysis of achievement motivation. *Journal of Personality and Social Psychology*, 1970, *15*, 1–20.

Wolfgang, M.E., & Ferracuti, F. *The subculture of violence*. New York: Barnes and Noble, 1967.

Author Index

Subject Index

About the Editor
and Contributors

The Editor

David N. Weisstub is Professor of Law at Osgoode Hall Law School of York University, Ontario, professeur titulaire de recherche at the Department of Psychiatry, Université de Montréal, and Senior Forensic Consultant to the Institut Philippe Pinel de Montréal, Québec. Dr. Weisstub has recently been appointed Policy Advisor to the Criminal Law Review Division of the Department of Justice of Canada, and serves as a consultant to the Federal Law Reform Commission. He has served in various government commissions and task forces in Canada and, as a member of the Ontario Advisory Review Board since 1974, has advised the Cabinet on the release of persons found not guilty by reason of insanity. Dr. Weisstub has been consulted by various governments in mental health law reform and has lectured extensively, in Canada and abroad, on the theoretical relationship between law and psychiatry. He is a member of many boards of editors and the author of numerous books and articles, including *Law and Psychiatry in the Canadian Context*, and *The Western Idea of Law*, co-authored with Joseph C. Smith. He is also the author of "Heaven, Take My Hand", a volume of verse. Since 1977 he has been Editor-in-Chief of the International Journal of Law and Psychiatry.

David N. Weisstub est professeur de droit à la faculté de droit Osgoode Hall à l'Université York (Ontario), professeur titulaire de recherche au département de psychiatrie de l'Université de Montréal, et conseiller principal en psychiatrie légale à l'Institut Philippe Pinel de Montréal (Québec). Le professeur Weisstub a récemment été nommé conseiller de la réforme du droit criminel au ministère de la Justice fédéral et expert auprès de la Commission de réforme du droit fédérale. Il a participé à plusieurs commissions et groupes de travail gouvernementaux au Canada et, en qualité de membre de l'Ontario Advisory Review Board depuis 1974, il a conseillé le Cabinet sur la libération des personnes acquittées pour aliénation mentale. Le professeur Weisstub a été consulté par différents gouvernements en matière de réforme du droit de la santé mentale, et il a fait de très nombreuses conférences, tant au Canada qu'à l'étranger, sur les relations théoriques entre le droit et la psychiatrie. Membre de nombreux comités de rédaction, il a publié plusieurs ouvrages et articles, notamment *Law and Psychiatry in the Canadian Context* ainsi que *The Western Idea of Law* écrit en collaboration avec Joseph C. Smith. Par ailleurs, il est l'auteur d'un recueil de poèmes intitulé "Heaven, Take My Hand". Depuis 1977, il est rédacteur en chef de l'International Journal of Law and Psychiatry.

The Contributors

Paul S. Appelbaum is associate professor of psychiatry and adjunct associate professor of law at the University of Pittsburgh and co-director of the Law and Psychiatry Program, Western Psychiatric Institute and Clinic. His interests include empirical and theoretical studies of the effect of legal regulation on mental health care. Dr. Appelbaum was co-winner with Thomas G. Gutheil of the 1983 Manfred S. Guttmacher Award of the American Psychiatric Association for the outstanding contribution to the literature of forensic psychiatry for his *Clinical Handbook of Psychiatry and the Law*. He is currently the recipient of a Research Scientist Development Award from the National Institute of Mental Health for studies in civil commitment.

Paul S. Appelbaum est professeur adjoint de psychiatrie et professeur adjoint de droit à l'Université de Pittsburg et le co-directeur du programme de psychiatrie légale au Western Psychiatric Institute and Clinic. Il s'intéresse notamment aux études empiriques et théoriques de l'effet de la réglementation juridique des soins de santé mentale. Le professeur Appelbaum a reçu, avec Thomas G. Gutheil, le Guttmacher Award de 1983, distinction décernée par l'American Psychiatric Association pour une contribution remarquable à la psychiatrie légale, avec la publication de l'ouvrage *Clinical Handbook of Psychiatry and the Law*. Il est actuellement titulaire du Research Scientist Development Award attribué par le National Institute of Mental Health pour la recherche sur le placement civil.

George E. Dix is the Vinson and Elkins Professor of Law at the University of Texas. He has published widely in numerous law reviews and journals, having specialized in criminal procedure and mental health. He is particularly known for articles dealing with criminal responsibility and mental health expert testimony in capital punishment proceedings. Included among his many published works are *Criminal Justice Administration*, *Criminal Law* and *The Mental Health Process*.

George E. Dix est professeur de droit "Vinson and Elkins" à l'Université du Texas. Il est l'auteur de très nombreux articles de revues de droit et s'est spécialisé dans la procédure pénale et la santé mentale. Le professeur Dix s'est particulièrement distingué par ses articles sur la responsabilité pénale et le témoignage d'expert en santé mentale dans les actions judiciaires où intervient la peine capitale. Parmi ses nombreuses publications, citons *Criminal Justice Administration*, *Criminal Law* et *The Mental Health Process*.

Thomas G. Gutheil is Director of the Program in Psychiatry and the Law at the Massachusetts Mental Health Center; Associate Professor of Psychiatry at the Harvard Medical School; Visiting Lecturer at the Harvard Law School; and President of the Law & Psychiatry Resource Center, P.C. He has written widely in the principal areas of psychiatry and law from the clinical perspective. Dr. Gutheil was the co-recipient with Paul Appelbaum of the 1983 Guttmacher Award from the American Psychiatric Association for his *Clinical Handbook of Psychiatry and the Law*.

Thomas G. Gutheil est le directeur du programme de psychiatrie légale au Massachusetts Health Center, professeur adjoint de psychiatrie à la Harvard Medical School, professeur invité à la Harvard Law School et président du Law & Psychiatry Resource Center, P.C. Il a fait de nombreuses publications dans les principaux domaines de la psychiatrie légale d'un point de vue clinique. Le professeur Gutheil a reçu, avec Paul Appelbaum, le Guttmacher Award de 1983, distinction accordée par l'American Psychiatric Association, pour son livre *Clinical Handbook of Psychiatry and the Law*.

Thomas L. Hafemeister, J.D., is currently completing his Ph.D. in Psychology at the University of Nebraska-Lincoln. Mr. Hafemeister is particularly interested in the application of applied social psychological theory and methods to mental disability law issues.

Thomas L. Hafemeister, J.D., termine actuellement son doctorat en psychologie à l'Université de Nebraska-Lincoln. Il s'est particulièrement intéressé à l'application de la théorie et des méthodes socio-psychologiques au droit de la maladie mentale.

Seymour L. Halleck is a professor of psychiatry and an adjunct professor of law at the University of North Carolina at Chapel Hill. He is the author of many articles and books in the area of law and psychiatry and has served as a member of several professional editorial boards. In addition to maintaining a clinical practice and full-time teaching appointment, he has remained actively involved with the problems of crime and the criminal justice system throughout his career. He has been the recipient of the Isaac Ray Award granted by the American Psychiatric Association for contributions to the fields of psychiatry and law, and the Sutherland Award presented by the American Society of Criminology for theoretical contributions to criminology.

Seymour L. Halleck est professeur de psychiatrie et professeur adjoint de droit à l'Université de Caroline du Nord, à Chapel Hill. Auteur de nombreux articles et ouvrages en droit et psychiatrie, il a déjà fait partie de plusieurs comités de rédaction dans le domaine. En plus de sa carrière de praticien clinique et de celle de professeur à plein temps, il a toujours été très préoccupé par la recherche en criminalité et sur le système de la justice pénale pendant toute sa carrière. Titulaire du Isaac Ray Award décerné par l'American Psychiatrie Association pour sa contribution dans le domaine de la psychiatrie légale, ainsi que du Sutherland Award décerné par la American Society of Criminology pour sa contribution, au niveau théorique, en criminologie.

Vernon Lewis Quinsey is Director of Research at the maximum security division of the Mental Health Center of Penetanguishene, Ontario. He has published over fifty scientific papers in the areas of animal learning, prediction of dangerousness, assessment and treatment of sex offenders, institutional violence, behavior modification and decision-making. Dr. Quinsey has served on the editorial board of several leading periodicals in his field and has acted as a consultant to various foundations and government ministries in Canada.

Vernon Lewis Quinsey est le directeur de la recherche à la division de sécurité maximale du Mental Health Center de Penetanguishene (Ontario). Il est l'auteur de plus d'une cinquantaine d'articles scientifiques sur des questions aussi diverses que l'apprentissage par les animaux, la prédiction de la dangerosité, l'évaluation et le traitement des délinquants sexuels, la violence institutionnelle, la modification du comportement et la prise de décision. Le professeur Quinsey a été membre de comités de rédaction dans des journaux de grande renommée dans son domaine, et il a été consulté comme expert par différentes fondations et de nombreux ministères gouvernementaux au Canada.

Bruce Dennis Sales is Professor of Psychology and Director of the Law-Psychology Program at the University of Arizona. His recent publications include *Disabled Persons and the Law*, *Making Jury Instructions Understandable*, and *The Trial Process*.

Bruce Dennis Sales est professeur de psychologie et directeur du programme de droit et psychologie à l'Université de l'Arizona. Parmi ses publications récentes, citons *Disabled Persons and the Law*, *Making Jury Instructions Understandable* et *The Trial Process*.

David L. Suggs, J.D., Ph.D., is a litigation associate in the law firm of Donovan, Leisure, Newton and Irvine in New York City. He has published regularly on trial practice issues.

David L. Suggs, J.D., Ph.D., est avocat associé au cabinet Donovan, Leisure, Newton et Irvine à New York. Il a publié plusieurs articles sur des problèmes de pratique judiciaire au procès.